O9-BHL-140

RESEARCH IN LITERACY: MERGING PERSPECTIVES

Thirty-sixth Yearbook
of
The National Reading Conference

JOHN E. READENCE
Louisiana State University

R. SCOTT BALDWIN
University of Miami

With the editorial assistance of

JOHN P. KONOPAK
Louisiana State University

HELEN NEWTON
NRC Headquarters

Published by
The National Reading Conference, Inc.

1987

NRC YEARBOOK is published annually by the National Reading Conference, Inc., 1070 Sibley Tower, Rochester, NY 14604, (716) 546-7241.

POSTMASTER: Send address changes to: NRC Yearbook, 1070 Sibley Tower, Rochester, NY 14604.

SUBSCRIPTIONS: Institutions: $40.00 domestic or $50.00 foreign, per year, or, as part of a combination subscription with NRC's *Journal of Reading Behavior* (total price $75.00 domestic or $90.00 foreign). Available to professional individual, family, or student members as part of membership in the National Reading Conference, Inc. Also available for use in university/college courses. Write for information.

 Microfilm editions are available from ERIC Reproduction Service, 3900 Wheeler Avenue, Alexandria, VA 22304. The articles in the *NRC Yearbook* are indexed in *Psychological Abstracts, Index to Social Sciences & Humanities Proceedings, Annual Summary of Investigations Related to Reading,* and *Educational Research Information Clearing House.* Because the *NRC Yearbook* serves as an open forum, readers should not construe the publishing of the contents as implying advocacy or endorsement by the National Reading Conference, its officers, or its members. NRC is a not for profit, membership corporation. All business correspondence, including changes of address (include the old address) and applications for membership, should be sent to: NRC, 1070 Sibley Tower, Rochester, NY 14604.

Manuscripts accepted for publication in the *NRC Yearbook* undergo an impartial review conducted by the Editorial Advisory Board and the Co-Editors. Manuscripts must be original works which have been presented at the Annual Meeting of the National Reading Conference and have not been published elsewhere or submitted simultaneously to other publication outlets.

OFFICERS AND BOARD OF DIRECTORS OF THE NATIONAL READING CONFERENCE, INC.

JEROME C. HARSTE, *President*
Indiana University

M. TRIKA SMITH-BURKE, *President-Elect*
New York University

JAMES HOFFMAN, *Vice President*
University of Texas-Austin

PATRICIA L. ANDERS, *Treasurer*
University of Arizona

JOY N. MONAHAN, *Secretary*
Orange County Public Schools

P. DAVID PEARSON, *Past President*
University of Illinois

DONNA E. ALVERMANN, *Board Member*
University of Georgia

LINDA B. GAMBRELL, *Board Member*
University of Maryland

ROBERT J. TIERNEY, *Board Member*
Ohio State University

KAREN K. WIXSON, *Board Member*
University of Michigan

HARRY SINGER, *Historian*
University of California-Riverside

MICHAEL L. KAMIL, *Publications Chair*
University of Illinois-Chicago

PETER O. ALLEN, *Executive Director*

Thirty-sixth Annual *NRC Yearbook*
EDITORIAL ADVISORY BOARD

TABLE OF CONTENTS

COMPREHENSION

INSTRUCTIONAL EFFECTIVENESS

ADULT LITERACY

WRITING

PREFACE

For the past 35 years the *NRC Yearbook* has served as the prognosticator of future trends in reading research. Take any *Yearbook* down from the shelf, examine its table of contents, and you will see that this is true. In a very real sense, the *Yearbook* has documented the state of our scholarship, the research fads as well as the mini-paradigm shifts that have marked the history of NRC, and our collective progress as a discipline. In this respect, we trust that the *36th Yearbook* will be no different from its predecessors. There have been, however, several other changes.

The most obvious innovation is that the *Yearbook* now has a hard cover. This will guarantee the preservation of NRC manuscripts for future generations of graduate students and reading researchers. We have also attempted to improve the quality of *Yearbook* articles by increasing the maximum length of manuscripts, adding subject and author indices, implementing a double-blind review process, expanding the editorial board, and by exhorting our board members to rigor and precision in their reviews. Hence, the acceptance rate for manuscripts this year was 28 percent. We are convinced that these represent the very best from the 1986 NRC Conference. Our thanks to a superb editorial board.

We would also like to express our appreciation to our vigorous editorial assistant, John Konopak, and to our authors, whose willingness to meet tough deadlines has made it possible for the membership to receive the *Yearbook* far in advance of the 1987 conference.

John E. Readence
R. Scott Baldwin

OSCAR S. CAUSEY AWARD

Virtually nothing I have done professionally has given me greater pleasure than what I am about to do now. Like the rest of us in this room, I am here to honor Dr. Philip Gough, a great teacher and researcher. As a teacher he has influenced the course of reading through his students. In 1964, while I was finishing my degree at UCLA I took his seminar in psycholinguistics. His seminar as well as the advice he gave to me had a significant impact on my own work. Dr. P. David Pearson, President of National Reading Conference, and Dr. Michael Kamil, Member of the Board of Directors of NRC, were both Post-doctoral students of Dr. Gough. We believe that our own research has been shaped and aided through our contact with Philip Gough.

Dr. Gough did his doctoral work at the University of Minnesota under the guidance of James J. Jenkins, a scholar recognized for his work on language and memory at a time when psychology was finding new methods for studying language. Since getting his degree in 1961, Dr. Gough has been engaged in research on learning, language, and reading. He has served as the Chairman of the Psychology Department at the University of Texas and is currently the Director of the Center for Cognitive Sciences there. For 11 years he was a member and Chairman of the Research Grants Advisory Panel of the National Institute of Health.

His research and writings on processes as diverse as language, reading disability, spelling, and beginning reading have increased our understanding of these important and complex topics. *One Second of Reading,* his fascinating description of what happens to information during the course of one second from the time the information from the page strikes the eye to the time when that information is understood has become a classic in the world of reading.

In recognition of his many contributions to education he was awarded Fellow Status by the American Association for the Advancement of Science, by the Division on Experimental Psychology of the American Psychology Association and the International Academy for Research in Learning Disabilities.

To these honors we add one more. As the representative of the National Reading Conference, it is my pleasure to give the Oscar Causey Award for Distinguished Research to Dr. Philip Gough.

Presented by S. Jay Samuels
December 1986

ALBERT J. KINGSTON AWARD

Anyone connected with the National Reading Conference knew that once Dr. Irene Athey was officially off the Board, the membership would acknowledge her many years of dedicated service to the organization by awarding her the Albert J. Kingston Award for Distinguished Service. Few persons have done more for NRC. In many ways she held the organization together through several difficult periods of growth, effectively bridging an old NRC with a new one.

When Dr. Athey came onto the Board, NRC was in financial trouble. Over the course of her time on the Board—first as a Board Member, and later as Vice President, President, Past President, and Field Council Liaison—NRC grew in both size and breadth. Dr. Athey initiated the idea of the Field Council as a grass roots effort in NRC to increase membership and member involvement. Her idea worked as is evident in the vitality and financial health of the organization today.

Dr. Athey is Professor and Past Dean of Education at Rutgers University. I first became acquainted with Dr. Athey through her writings on the affective dimension of reading. It was years later that I connected her with such notable names in literacy education as Jack Holmes, David Russell, and Guy Buswell, all persons with whom she studied and worked at the University of California at Berkeley.

Dr. Athey has been a Board Member for the Jean Piaget Society as well as organizer and past chair of the American Educational Research Association's Special Interest Groups on Education of the Deaf and on Piaget and Education. In addition to the affective factors in reading, Dr. Athey's areas of interest include the development of comprehension with reading, the psychology and education of the deaf, early childhood education (specifically the role of play in language and cognitive development), and, fortunately for us, the vitality of NRC.

It is a personal and professional pleasure for me to present the Albert J. Kingston Award for Distinguished Service to Dr. Irene Athey on behalf of the Awards Committee and membership of NRC.

Congratulations and thank you, Irene.

Presented by Jerome C. Harste
December 1986

ASSESSMENT

EMERGENT LITERACY

COMPREHENSION

INSTRUCTIONAL EFFECTIVENESS

ADULT LITERACY

WRITING

ASSESSMENT, ACCOUNTABILITY, AND PROFESSIONAL PREROGATIVE*

P. David Pearson and Sheila Valencia
University of Illinois

At a time when Americans are placing greater emphasis upon educational assessment and accountability, it is ironic that the nation's reading educators and teachers find themselves on the horns of a dilemma created, at least in part, by their very ability to evaluate how well children are learning to read. The tools which are intended to help the teacher in the classroom have paradoxically become the chains which frustrate individual initiative and innovation and limit professional prerogative. At the root of this problem is a notion of perceived accountability which manifests itself in many, often contradictory, ways. On the one hand, for example, there is the widespread belief among the public, local and state school boards, and many professional educators that educational accountability can be truly and accurately fixed on the basis of test results. For many teachers, on the other hand, such a belief has not contributed to their sense of professional competence and well-being; to the contrary, this belief has eroded significantly their perceptions of their prerogatives as professional educators and their ability to make or influence important decisions about educating the nation's children.

In the following essay we will pursue these points further by taking a personal and professional tour of the issues that have led us, as reading educators, to our current dilemma. We begin with a visit to three hypothetical but typical classrooms during the last three decades. Then we will examine the dangers and discrepancies which arise when the model which underlies reading research, theory, and practice comes into conflict with the model which governs our reading assessment practices, policies, and decision-making procedures. To remedy the dilemma which has arisen, we will propose an alternative way of conceptualizing the relationship between assessment and instruction. Lastly, we will close by calling for action on a research agenda in the belief that if we do not directly address the research and policy issues stemming from this dilemma, teachers' professional prerogatives will be eroded even more seriously than they have been already, with potentially grave consequences for our ability to educate our children successfully.

*Based on the Presidential Address and supported by the National Institute of Education under Contract No. 400-81-0030 and by the Illinois State Board of Education under Contract No. J61.

THREE SCHOOLS

The first of our hypothetical classroom visits takes place in 1964 in southern California. The classroom has 32 fifth-grade students, 15 of whom are bilingual (Spanish and English) and four of whom are monolingual Spanish speakers. The teacher has a complete set of fifth-grade basals — *Trails to Treasure,* six copies of the fourth-grade basal — *Roads to Everywhere,* a few randomly gathered old basals, a weekly supply of *My Weekly Reader,* a workbook for each of the students reading on grade level, but no ditto masters or back-up workbooks. Standardized testing consists of the Iowa Test of Basic Skills, which is given each March; the tests are scored by hand and the results are dutifully reported to the principal, who seems unconcerned about whether or not the results are reported to either students or parents.

This scenario takes place before the advent of what we have come to expect in modern basals — the ubiquitous end-of-unit and end-of-level tests. Once in a while, an occasional workbook page appears which is characterized as a progress check, but basically the teacher's manual does little to encourage the possible use of these tests to screen students for remedial activity. The teacher's decisions about what to cover in reading are guided by the school's program, as defined by the teachers' manuals in the basal program. Overall, however, the emphasis given to specific skill instruction is not, in any real sense, guided by scores on tests of any sort.

The relationship between tests and instruction in our hypothetical classroom, and during this period, was one merely of *interest:* The security of the teacher's and the principal's position and salary, and of any child's promotion was *not* on the line when they gave either standardized tests or those informal basal reader tests. And, probably most important, the reputation of the school in the public's eye was not dependent on test scores published in the local newspaper.

By the time we visit our second hypothetical classroom — a fifth-sixth grade in a suburb of Denver in 1973 — significant changes in the instruction-assessment relationship can be observed. These changes are apparent from the classroom's physical characteristics. As part of an open space school, the classroom is large but has been divided up into lots of nooks and crannies, including a whole bank of library-type carrels along one long wall. On another wall is a massive structure of cubbyholes, not unlike those used for mail distribution at colleges or public schools.

This school had become, just the year before, an *individually guided education* school and had purchased one of the then popular *skills management systems* that emerged from the mastery learning and criterion-referenced movement of the late '60s and early '70s. Every couple of months, all the students in the class take a set of criterion-referenced tests that define the scope and sequence of skills for those grade levels. Three days per week, reading class consists of students going to see their teacher to receive a list of skills that their test results suggest are weak and need to be practiced. The students then go to the big wall of cubbyholes and pick up one worksheet out of every cubbyhole identified on their skill practice list. Once students have completed the required worksheets, they are allowed to retake the tests that sent them to the cubbyhole wall in the first place. Passing one set of tests allows students to enter a new level of skill performance and begin the process again. Failure on any subtests results in remediation in the form of even more worksheets in another row of the seemingly endless cubbyholes. There was a side-benefit, however unintentional, to this system. The other two days a week, the reading program consisted of reading stories in the basal reader and discussing them without the encumbrance of all the skills activities that typically accompany a basal lesson.

In this scenario, criterion-referenced tests of very specific skills are the foundation for individualized instruction. Instruction in a specific area is offered if, and only if, test performance warrants it. Ironically, norm-referenced, standardized tests play only a minor role in this process. Such tests are used only to evaluate whether or not the entire mastery learning, skills-management system is working generally. This system seriously erodes professional prerogative, at least in comparison to what we depicted as being representative of instructional techniques only a decade earlier. This erosion of professional prerogative is inevitable in such a system because the mastery learning mentality which undergirds it specifies the *means* of instruction very precisely, but leaves open the issue of what the ends are. Without a clear definition of these *ends,* the means become the ends of instruction. The result is that teachers and children spend their time working on activities that do little more than help the children pass the tests.

By defining reading instruction as a set of very specific components, each of which is accompanied by an equally specific test of mastery and an equally specific set of workbook or worksheet pages, there is no room or need for teacher judgment in the assessment process, in instructional decision-making, or in the delivery of instruction. Teachers become just managers, the organizers of material to be learned through repeated interactions with worksheets. Indeed, in this second hypothetical classroom, the two teachers in the team do little more than take turns monitoring the administration of tests and control of materials in the cubbyholes or making sure that students behave themselves while they are so busily engaged in so-called individualized instruction.

Our third hypothetical classroom is in a posh suburb in nothern Illinois and represents what is happening in all too many contemporary American schools. The impression one gets from talking to teachers is that of classrooms virtually inundated by tests: standardized tests, basal reader tests, teacher-made tests to give grades, and now the prospect of annually administered statewide tests of reading, language arts, and mathematics.

Due largely to a seductively attractive movement called outcomes-based education or performance-based education (see Popham, Cruse, Rankin, Sandifer, & Williams, 1985, for a clear description of this movement), standardized tests are more popular than ever before. The great selling point for standardized tests, so the outcomes-based education argument goes, is that if you agree to be accountable for broad outcomes, then you can recapture control over the day-to-day decisions about what to teach, when to teach it, and how to teach it.

Such an argument might be compelling if it were not for the continuing popularity in this district, and most other districts, of the end-of-unit and end-of-level tests in basal reader programs. In essence, standardized tests continue to determine the *ends* of instruction and the basal tests determine the *means* of instruction. Additional evidence of this control can be found in the fact that in 1987 the basal companies correlate their tests with the popular standardized measures, making for a tighter and more constraining relationship between ends and means. And, just last summer, one of the leading test publishers undertook a project to make certain that its tests matched basal reader objectives more closely! In short, the knot becomes tighter and tighter.

The net result of this ever tighter control over both outcomes *and* processes is to leave very few decisions for teachers, principals, or central office staff, except perhaps what tests to purchase. Furthermore, unlike earlier eras, the spectre of accountability now hangs heavy in the district. It is not surprising that teachers feel compelled to worry about test performance, now that school-by-school results are published in the local newspaper. No one has been fired for having students whose performance on tests is abnormally low; however, teachers behave as if their jobs, or at least their professional reputations, are on the line. In terms of professional prerogative, the situation could not be more constraining because teachers control neither the ends nor the means of instruction. They have retained the responsibility for student performance without any authority to alter instructional programs on their own.

THE NUB OF THE PROBLEM

These three scenarios raise a number of key issues that, as researchers, teachers, and teacher educators, we need to address. We have reached a point where the threads of instruction, assessment, and decision-making are very tightly interwoven. While most of us would probably agree that this interweaving is, in principle, desirable, reality reveals that it is problematic for two reasons. First, the interplay among these components does not reflect our best understanding of the reading process. More specifically, reading assessment has not kept pace with reading theory, research, or practice. Instead of being mutually supportive, there is often disruptive tension among the instruction, assessment, and decision-making processes. Secondly, in an attempt to objectify and routinize the way data are collected and used to make decisions, the teacher has been forced out of the assessment process. So much for professional prerogative! As a field, we face a dilemma (Valencia & Pearson, 1987) with some devilish characteristics.

The first and most important characteristic of the dilemma is the conflict between our newly emerging views of reading process and reading instruction, on the one hand, and the model of the reading process that underlies our current assessment practices and procedures. Recent research (e.g., Collins, Brown, & Larkin, 1980; Pearson & Spiro, 1981) has emphasized reading as a constructive process. The reader strategically and thoughtfully uses clues from the text, background knowledge, the reading context, and other sources to gain meaning from the text at hand. At the same time, this view de-emphasizes the notion that progress toward expert reading is guided by the aggregation of component reading skills. Instead, it suggests that skilled reading, at all levels, is reflected in the reader's awareness of how, when, and why to use resources for the goal of constructing meaning. Skilled readers can use knowledge flexibly — they can both learn from the immediate reading situation as well as apply what they have learned to new situations (e.g., Campione & Brown, 1985; Spiro & Meyers, 1984).

While this model of the active, strategic reader dominates our current research base, it bears little resemblance to the model which underlies most of our reading assessment schemes. Consider but a few of the discrepancies between what we know from research and how we assess reading:

> Prior knowledge is a major determinant of reading comprehension, yet we mask any relation between knowledge and comprehension on tests by using many short passages about unfamiliar, sometimes obscure, topics.
>
> Real stories and texts have structural and topical integrity which influence reading comprehension, yet we assess reading comprehension using short bits that rarely approximate authentic text.
>
> Inference is an essential skill for comprehending words, sentences, paragraphs, and entire texts, yet many assessments rely primarily on literal level questions.
>
> Prior knowledge and inferential thinking work together to help the reader construct meaning from the text. Because these attributes vary across individuals (and within individuals from one situation to the next) and because texts may invite many plausible interpretations, we would expect many possible inferences to fit a given text or a question. Reading comprehension, however, continues to be assessed using multiple-choice items with only one correct answer.
>
> To accomplish the goals of reading, readers must orchestrate many so-called skills, yet many of our reading assessment schemes fragment the process into discrete skills, as if each was important in its own right.
>
> Flexibility — the ability to monitor and adjust reading strategies to fit the text and the situation — is one hallmark of an expert reader, yet we seldom assess how, when, and why students alter their approaches to reading.
>
> The acid test of learning from text is the ability to restructure and apply knowledge flexibly in new situations, yet our assessment schemes rarely ask students to do so. Instead, we seem to be comfortable with tasks that seldom go beyond restating textual information.

The point is obvious but insidious: Tests continue to assume a prominent place in the assessment, instruction, and decision-making arenas, yet these very tests often represent an alternative and contradictory view of the reading process. The result is tension and confusion among professionals responsible for instructional improvement and for monitoring student progress.

This tension could easily transform itself into a kind of schizophrenia among reading program directors and reading teachers. While anxious to implement instructional practices based upon the latest research, they are plagued by the threat of low test scores. As a result, they are forced to try to integrate two diametrically opposed curricula—one based upon what is measured by the tests for which they are accountable and one based upon what they have learned from recent research. In such conflict, teachers are not likely to exercise their prerogative.

The second characteristic of the dilemma is its penchant for irony. At a time when reading tests are most in conflict with what we know about reading, they are being used more than ever. Beginning with the accountability movement of the 1970s, and moving toward the current deluge of national reports (Education Commission of the States, 1983; Fisher, Berliner, Filby, Marliave, Cahen, Dishaw, & Moore, 1978; Goodlad, 1984), reading achievement has been a major focus of most of these educational improvement efforts. And, in many cases, they have relied on students' standardized test scores as measures of effectiveness or educational quality (recall our earlier reference to outcomes-based education). Such a reliance has led to an increased focus on testing of all sorts and at all levels.

As evidence of the increasing use of tests, we can now document at least 40 statewide competency testing programs. As one might expect, assessment efforts are not restricted to the federal or state level. One only needs to look inside schools and classrooms to find thousands of locally regulated testing programs, criterion-referenced tests accompanying basal reading programs, and the countless school- and teacher-made tests. The brief snapshot of the hypothetical school in suburban Illinois is not much of a caricature. No matter the perspective one takes on this picture, the conclusion is inescapable: The influence of testing is greater now than at any time in the history of schooling.

A third characteristic of the dilemma is its capacity to breed uneasiness in the various research communities. Our discussion in this paper is prima facie evidence of the reading research community's concern about testing. However, it is not clear that either the policy research community or the assessment research community appreciates the new-found popularity of tests. The instruction/assessment link has been vigorously debated by educators. Some sing the praises of instructional programs driven by test results (Haney, 1985; Popham & Rankin, 1981) and cite positive results to support their case (e.g., Popham, Cruse, Rankin, Sandifer, & Williams, 1985). Opponents of such testing schemes argue that tests should follow rather than lead curriculum (Berlak, 1985). They claim that overreliance on test scores leads to a narrowing of the curriculum, a tendency to teach to the test, and an emphasis on lower level, more easily tested skills (Linn, 1985). Still others (e.g., Madaus, 1985) remind us that some of our large-scale tests have become so generic and curriculum insensitive that they are virtually useless for making decisions in a school setting. While the debate continues, the inescapable truth is that assessment is a powerful force that must be reckoned with.

Dangers to the Field

The dilemmas that erode teacher prerogative are bound to create dangers. One danger stems from the impact of assessment on teachers' thinking and classroom instruction. Using results from existing measures, teachers may develop a false sense of security when they observe high scores. A close review of these tests reveals a narrow, restricted view of comprehension. Not only might teachers begin to take pride in performance that does not reflect meaningful comprehension, but they might also be encouraged to shape instruction to produce high scores on these same measures. Conscientious teachers have always wanted their students to perform well on tests; not surprisingly, they look to these tests as guides for instruction. If tests foster an inappropriate model of skilled reading, inappropriate instruction is likely to result. We end up supporting practices that promote high test scores at the expense of effective reading strategies. Furthermore, we encourage little, if any, change in instruction. Worst of all, we provide no incentive to encourage teachers to recapture their professional prerogative.

One can counter this argument by suggesting that tests, as outcome measures, were never meant to define the instructional process leading to the outcome; one can argue further that these outcome measures only sample the vast set of possible outcomes. Such arguments, however, are specious. Educators, with good intentions, tend to teach to the test. The New York Regents exam, the California Subject A writing exam, and the European notion of the tradition of past exams all illustrate the well-entrenched propensity to teach to the test. On the positive side, look at the redirection of instructional efforts in writing, apparently induced by tests in which students actually had to write.

A second danger stems from the potential insensitivity of current assessment strategies to new instructional programs aimed at promoting strategic reading. Teachers and administrators may mistakenly interpret no, or only small, gains as indicative of an ineffective instructional program. The alternative hypothesis—that the assessment strategies are insensitive to the desired outcomes—may never be considered. Tests that are not designed to tap the strategies and thinking that are integral to skilled reading will not be sensitive to changes in these skills brought about by new instructional programs. In such a situation, educators initially motivated to take risks are not likely to continue to do so.

A third danger is that when some assessment tools become officially sanctioned, teachers tend not to rely on their own assessment skills to make important instructional decisions; ironically, of course, the data a teacher collects has the greatest potential for influencing day-to-day student learning. While most tests may be effective at indicating broad increases in reading achievement, they offer the teacher little useful information for refining specific instructional strategies. The lure of objectivity associated with commercially published tests and the corollary taint of subjectivity associated with informal assessment pushes teachers further and further away from instructional decision-making. For some reason, teachers are taught (and apparently learn) that the data from either standardized or end-of-unit basal tests are somehow more trustworthy than the data they collect each day as a part of the normal course of teaching. The price we pay for such a lesson is high since it reduces the likelihood that teachers will use data they collect themselves for decision-making within their classrooms.

If the responsibility for assessment and instructional decision-making is placed with the teacher, we will produce more capable, concerned teachers. Take this away, and we create teachers who are just managers rather than educational professionals for whom professional prerogative is synonymous with teaching. This last point is revealed most dramatically in the work of Clay (1985) and Johnston (in press). In the recently released edition of her book on informal assessment, Clay details a completely individualized and curriculum-embedded approach to assessment (i.e., there is no need for special tests or materials). In a paper in which he argues persuasively for what he calls a more naturalistic (what we will later call a more informal and locally controlled) approach to assessment, Johnston suggests a number of alternative assessment devices that teachers could use for instructional decision-making were they to abandon their reliance upon formal (norm- and criterion-referenced) tests. In both cases, the measures advocated have the virtue of being so related to instruction that assessment and instruction become indistinguishable. All of these measures also rely heavily upon individual judgment (one type of prerogative); hence, they are remedies for the kind of situations that lead to our third danger.

A FRAMEWORK FOR A COMPLETE ASSESSMENT SYSTEM

What we must do, then, is to help educators and policy-makers reconceptualize assessment. New and better tests, in and of themselves, will not solve the problem. We need to reconceptualize assessment as a framework for making decisions. Basic to this framework, we propose these assumptions:

1. Reading assessment strategies need to be based upon our best and most current models of the reading process.
2. Assessment should not drive instruction, as is currently true in American schools; instead, assessment and instruction should be so interwoven as to be indistinguishable from one another.
3. Assessment schemes which fail to capitalize upon the expertise and contextual advantage of classroom teachers ignore what may be the richest source of data for making instructional decisions.
4. There are different levels of decision-making, each with its own unique demands and, possibly, unique assessment tools. However, whatever is worthy of assessment ought to be assessable in different context levels for different purposes using different strategies.

The framework we propose for developing a complete assessment system is depicted in Table 1. The attributes of skilled reading listed in the first column represent several current working hypotheses about what it means to be a good reader—those outcomes for which students and teachers might want to be held accountable. Columns 2, 3, and 4 indicate contexts of impact at which various types of decisions are made.

It is likely that states and even large school districts will continue, at least for the foreseeable future, to collect data on large numbers of students. Hence, we will continue to need assessment strategies that use efficient and employable tools. Such tools may be useful for determining trends, but they are never likely to guide instruction at the classroom level very well unless the results are amplified by other assessment devices under the control of the school and the teacher.

To better understand what we would like to propose as an ideal for what should occur in columns 3 and 4 (especially column 4), let us consider a completely different relation between reading theory, reading instruction, and reading assessment. What would happen if we took seriously the admonition to base assessment upon a strategic model of reading? What would happen if we redefined the relationship between instruction and assessment so that it was a supportive interaction among assessment, instruction, and teacher prerogative? Readers would read to construct meaning. Every act of reading, and, therefore, every act of assessment, would be identical regardless of who was performing it. What would vary across readers, situations, and levels of sophistication is exactly how readers orchestrate available resources.

Given such a view, optimal assessment and learning would occur when teachers observe and interact with students as they read authentic texts for genuine purposes. As teachers interact with students, they would evaluate the way in which the students orchestrate resources to construct meaning, intervening to provide support or suggestions when the students appear on the verge of faltering in their attempt to build a reasonable model of the meaning of the text. This model, referred to as dynamic assessment (Campione & Brown, 1985), emanates from Vygotsky's notion of the "zone of proximal development," that region of development just far enough—but not

Table 1

The Relationship Between Goals, Decision-making Units, and Methods of Assessment

Hallmarks of a Good Reader	State or District	School or Classroom	Classroom or Individual
Good Readers . . . use prior knowledge to help them construct meaning from text.			
draw inferences at the word, sentence, paragraph and text levels.			
provide many plausible responses to questions about a text.			
vary reading strategies to fit the text and the reading situation.			
synthesize information within and across texts.			
ask good questions about text.			
exhibit positive attitudes toward reading.			
integrate many skills to produce an understanding of text.			
are fluent.			
use knowledge flexibly.			

too far—beyond the students' current level of competence such that sensitive teachers, using scaffolding tools such as modeling, hints, leading questions, and cooperative task completion, can assist learners in moving to their next level of sophistication. Instruction consists, in such a model, not of remediating deficient skills, but of using assessment strategies and observation to determine which of the potentially useful resources students have trouble using to their best advantage and then providing the scaffolding necessary to support its use. The measure of students' ability is not a score; instead, it is an index of the type and amount of support required to advance learning to a higher level of sophistication.

This scenario, in which there is no difference between reading instruction and assessment, and in which both teacher and student provide input, is an ideal. While this model is one that may never be fully integrated into large-scale tests of reading, it should be the goal of classroom and individual student assessment and instruction.

To illustrate how a single goal might be assessed across levels of decision-making, consider the domain of metacognition. Students' sensitivity to the demands of the task, audience, and situation, and their ability to vary reading strategies to meet these demands might best be assessed by observing and interacting with students while they are actually applying these strategies in real reading situations (Palincsar & Brown, 1984, 1986). We can and should attempt to measure these skills in formats amenable to large-scale assessment. But there will always be some limitations to data gathered from group tests of metacognitive activities. These limitations are based on our observations while interviewing and testing students in a variety of situations: (a) what students say may differ from what they do, (b) strategic readers are too flexible and adaptive to allow us to capture their skill in a small sample of situations and options, and (c) for many readers, these strategies operate at an unconscious, automatic level inaccessible to verbalization or even reflection. In short, here is a case in which large-scale assessment may prove moderately useful for some very limited purposes and decisions; however, the assessment strategies that really count are likely to occur at the classroom or individual level.

What we are really saying is that our 80-year history of assessment in America has focussed only upon column 2 in Table 1 (large-scale assessment). The only serious attempt to deal with decision-making needs in columns 3 and 4 was the mastery-based criterion-referenced systems that arose during the 1970s. The problem is that these systems applied the principles and assessment techniques associated with large-scale assessment and decision-making to a situation that demanded fewer constraints and much greater flexibility. The problem with both the norm- and the criterion-referenced versions of commercially available tests is that they have assumed that teacher judgment is unnecessary in making decisions. To achieve our goal of a balanced system of assessment, educators must commit themselves to at least two tasks: (a) they must assume that any data from commercial tests is information that they have to interpret in concert with other information they possess about schools and students, and (b) they must begin to collect data in their own situations so that they can build portfolios of information about students, classrooms, or schools.

One could argue that an opportunity to achieve this goal has always existed and that teachers could, if they desired, avail themselves of a wide range of assessment strategies, including strategies that emphasize rich data bases gathered in interview-like situations. However, this argument fades rather quickly in light of the low status accorded to informal assessment and teacher judgment.

A CALL FOR ACTION

As surely as we see the need for more natural assessment opportunities, we must not forget that standardized, norm-referenced tests are still the most prevalent type of testing in our schools. They deserve our immediate attention. We need research to develop and evaluate new assessment techniques that are both consistent with our understanding of reading and reading instruction *and* amenable to large-scale testing. Unless we can influence the shape of large-scale assessment, we may not be able to refocus assessment at all, thereby losing our opportunity to expand the framework of assessment to include more naturalistic and instructionally valid approaches.

New Research Efforts

The development of new techniques is only one part of this process. And that has been the focus of our work in Illinois (see Valencia & Pearson, 1986) and four colleagues in Michigan (Wixson, Peters, Weber, & Roeber, 1987). There is also a great deal of research still to be done on these issues. If we are ever to develop anything like the assessment system we have argued for in this paper, critical research efforts need to be made in several areas.

Validity efforts. We need different sorts of validity indices for paper and pencil measures. First and foremost, we should recognize that we will develop the best assessment devices, be they formal or informal, as a result of attempts to establish the validity of the theoretical constructs that underlie the tests we create. Such efforts must constantly bear in mind the old truism that reading is a complex process. It is unlikely that a simple test of reading will ever stand the scrutiny of construct validation.

Second, we should outlaw the practices of concurrent validation that permit Test 1 (usually an experimental form) to be validated by suggesting that it correlates highly with Test 2 (usually a widely used standardized test). Such practices only perpetuate the conventional wisdom responsible for where we find ourselves today. If we permit any form of concurrent validation, the criterion against which a candidate test is compared should be a measure of reading which has a high degree of ecological and construct validity.

Third, we need to take the whole issue of instructional validity seriously. We certainly do not want to permit the legal definition of instructional validity, as in the Debra P. case. The issue in that case was whether or not the test tested what was taught in the schools (much like what we have traditionally referred to as face or curricular validity). We need to define instructional validity in terms of instructional sensitivity; that is, a test will be regarded as instructionally valid to the degree that it is sensitive to the growth that we know will occur when we engage students in certain instructional activities. In essence, what we need to do is to turn our usual experimental approach on its ear. Usually we assume the validity of some outcome measure and then evaluate the efficacy of competing instructional approaches in terms of how well students perform on that common measure. In the approach we are suggesting, we would assume the validity of the instruction and evaluate the validity of competing measures of the process being learned.

System exploration. If we are ever to infuse informal (what Johnston wants to call more naturalistic) measures with the degree of credibility necessary to encourage teachers to use them, we need to conduct some very convincing research demonstrating the usefulness of approaches to assessment that are so informal as to be indistinguishable from instruction.

Literacy experiences. For nearly 70 years, we have assumed that the ability to perform some cognitive task was the ultimate in reading assessment. And given the individual differences milieu in which reading tests arose at the time of the First World War, it is not surprising that a cognitive bias prevailed. However, other, less direct and less obtrusive measures, particularly related to programs rather than to individuals, have been overlooked. For example, if you ask yourself, how do you know when your reading program is working?, you might come up with indices like these:

When subscriptions to the local newspaper rise.
When the checkout rates at the local library rise.

When book sales at the local book stores, particularly children's book sales, rise.
When surveys indicate that the amount of time children read voluntarily at home (or in school for that matter), increases.
When attitudes toward reading become more positive.
When students indicate they understand what their teachers are trying to do.
When businesses stop complaining that they have to teach literacy skills to our graduates.
When teachers demand and regain their professional prerogative.

It is only an historical accident that reading tests became established during a period in which educators sought to measure individual differences scientifically and objectively; in another era we might have developed a very different set of measures of reading effectiveness.

Understanding the present. Much of what we have claimed about the current uses of tests is based upon what even the most ardent ethnographers would refer to as informal evidence. We need to understand more fully both the dynamics and the consequences of the public's demand for accountability and assessment. To this end we need good ethnographies of the real and perceived uses of assessment devices conducted at the classroom, school, and district levels. Secondly, we need some intervention work on the assessment-instruction link. For the past several years we have too easily resigned ourselves to the supposed truth that assessment does indeed drive instruction. If such an assertion is true, an assessment system built on a different model of reading should result in categorically different kinds of reading instruction. If this hypothesis is untrue, we need to see if things can be turned around.

Reporting information. We would probably all concede that, as researchers, we are sometimes poor communicators. But if we think our communication about research is inadequate, our communication about assessment (what scores really mean) is abysmal. We need research, most likely done by experts in communication and information dissemination, that will ultimately improve the way in which we report assessment data to various audiences. One of the biggest problems we will have to address is how to get the general public to understand the limitations of test scores (and assessment data generally); at present, the American public is unfortunately all too credulous about standardized test scores.

Creative efforts. Above all, we need for researchers and educators at all levels to think creatively about formats and systems for assessment at all levels of decision-making, be it at the level of the state, district, school, classroom, or individual. This is a time to give rein to our imaginations and our problem-solving capacities.

Development Efforts

While researchers begin to explore the theoretical and psychometric aspects of new large group formats and techniques, we must also all work to develop the disposition and specific assessment techniques needed to answer the varied questions posed by people charged with decisions at different levels. Our goal, as reading educators, should be to develop valid, reliable, and usable strategies to be used at all levels of decision-making. Only if we are able to fill *all* the cells of the chart in Table 1 with conceptually sound assessment strategies will we approach our goal of equipping educators with a portfolio of assessment strategies that they can use to make and then implement, sound decisions.

Finally, there is the issue of what stance we shall take toward improving or reforming the current system of assessment. There are those among us who will say that the current system is so corrupt and compromised that it doesn't deserve any attempt to reform it. Toss it out, they will say, and let's start over from scratch. Then there are those among us who will choose, at least for the moment, to try to reform the system from within. Both positions, it seems to us, have their merits at this point in the history of assessment, and either course of action is preferable to clinging to a moribund status quo.

We close with a telling quotation from a student of medicine. In 1979, Stanley Joel Reiser observed:

> If physicians in general come to accept a fundamentally mechanical view of human beings, in a world that is more and more enamored of technology, the prospect for the future is extremely disquieting.... Machines inexorably direct the attention of both doctor and patient to the measurable aspects of illness, but away from the "human factors" that are at least equally important.... Technologies that improve accuracy, and centralized organizations that enhance efficiency and improve security, are essential factors in modern medicine. Yet accuracy, efficiency and security are purchased at a high price when that price is impersonal medical care and undermining the physician's belief in his own medical powers. To be free to develop his medical skills to their highest point, to increase what is, despite these problems, a positive balance of benefits over harms, today's physician must rebel. He can use his strongest weapon—a refusal to accept bondage to any one technique, no matter how useful it may be in a particular instance. He must regard them all with detachment as mere tools, to be chosen as necessary for a particular task. He must accept the patient as human being and regain and reassert his faith in his own medical judgment. (pp. 229–231)

The analogy between medicine and teaching, while potentially misleading in some cases, is appropriate here. What Reiser has to say about doctors reserving a certain degree of professional prerogative is equally true of teachers. Both are professionals who must, by definition and of necessity, make decisions on the basis of incomplete or ambiguous evidence. Reiser's observation that doctors cannot hide behind the cloak of technology to explain their errors in judgment is a good message for teachers and testing technocrats to remember. With these thoughts in mind, let us redirect our conceptual and technological efforts regarding assessment to activities that acknowledge rather than ignore teachers' professional prerogative. To do less is to insure a system of assessment and instruction that, while tolerated by most, will be admired by few, least of all ourselves.

REFERENCES

Berlak, H. (1985). Testing in a democracy. *Educational Leadership, 43,* 16–17.

Campione, J. C., & Brown, A. L. (1985). *Dynamic assessment: One approach and some initial data* (Tech. Rep. No. 361). Urbana: University of Illinois, Center for the Study of Reading.

Clay, M. M. (1985). *The early detection of reading difficulties: A diagnostic survey with recovery procedures* (3rd ed.). Exeter, NH: Heinemann.

Collins, A., Brown, J. S., & Larkin, K. M. (1980). Inference in text understanding. In R. J. Spiro, B. C. Bruce, & W. F. Brewer (Eds.), *Theoretical issues in reading comprehension* (pp. 385–407). Hillsdale, NJ: Erlbaum.

Education Commission of the States (1983). *Calls for educational reform: A summary of major reports.* Denver, CO: ECS.

Fisher, W., Berliner, D., Filby, N., Marliave, R., Cahen, L., Dishaw, M., & Moore, J. (1978). *Teaching and learning in elementary schools: A summary of the beginning teacher evaluation study.* San Francisco, CA: Far West Regional Laboratory for Educational Research and Development.

Goodlad, J. I. (1984). *A place called school: Prospects for the future.* New York: McGraw-Hill.

Haney, W. (1985). Making testing more educational. *Educational Leadership, 43,* 4–13.

Johnston, P. (in press). Steps toward a more naturalistic approach to the assessment of the reading process. In J. Algina (Ed.), *Advances in content based educational assessment.* Norwood, NJ: Ablex.

Linn, R. (1985). Standards and expectations: The role of testing (summary). *Proceedings of a National Forum on Educational Reform* (pp. 88–95). New York: The College Board.

Madaus, G. F. (1985). Test scores as administrative mechanisms in educational policy. *Phi Delta Kappan, 66,* 611–617.

Palincsar, A. S., & Brown, A. L. (1984). Reciprocal teaching of comprehension-fostering and comprehension-monitoring activities. *Cognition and Instruction, 2,* 117–175.

Palincsar, A. S., & Brown, A. L. (1986). Interactive teaching to promote independent learning from text. *The Reading Teacher, 39,* 771–777.

Pearson, P. D., & Spiro, R. J., (1981). Toward a theory of reading comprehension. *Topics in Language Disorders, 1,* 71–88.

Popham, W. J., Cruse, K. L., Rankin, S. C., Sandifer, P. D., & Williams, P. L. (1985). Measurement driven instruction: It's on the road. *Phi Delta Kappan, 55,* 628–634.

Popham, W. J., & Rankin, S. C. (1981). Minimum competency tests spur instructional improvement. *Phi Delta Kappan, 62,* 637–639.

Reiser, S. J. (1979). *Medicine and the reign of technology.* New York: Cambridge University Press.

Spiro, R. J., & Meyers, A. (1984). Individual differences and underlying cognitive processes. In P. D. Pearson (Ed.), *Handbook of reading research* (pp. 471–504). New York: Longman.

Valencia, S. W., & Pearson, P. D. (1986). *Reading assessment initiatives in the state of Illinois.* Springfield, IL: Illinois State Board of Education.

Valencia, S. W., & Pearson, P. D. (1987). Reading assessment: Time for a change. *The Reading Teacher, 40,* 726–732.

Wixson, K. K., Peters, C. W., Weber, E. M., & Roeber, E. D. (1987). New directions in statewide reading assessment. *The Reading Teacher, 40,* 749–755.

CLOZE PROCEDURE AND THE SEQUENCE OF TEXT

April Ginther Gamarra
Dallas Independent School District

Jon Jonz
East Texas State University

The project to be reported in this paper was designed to determine the sensitivity of standard fixed-ratio cloze procedure to variation in textual sequence. In the study we assume that texts vary in the degree to which their comprehensibility depends upon processing their component parts in sequence. Comprehending some texts, recipes, for example, depends to a great extent upon processing elements of the text in their given sequence. Comprehending other texts, loose collections of descriptive characteristics, for example, is far less constrained by the order in which sentences appear. By demonstrating that standard fixed-ratio cloze test scores vary as a function of the sequentiality of text, we provide evidence that cloze is a sensitive measure of this intersentential quality of written language and, by extension, of the higher-order verbal comprehension processes that operate on text.

At issue in this project are the conclusions drawn on the one hand by Shanahan and his colleagues (i.e., Shanahan & Kamil, 1982, 1983; Shanahan, Kamil, & Tobin, 1982) as well as others whose *scrambled-text* research has led to similar findings (e.g., Kibby, 1980; Leys, Fielding, Herman, & Pearson, 1983) and on the other hand by Oller and his colleagues (e.g., Chavez-Oller, Chihara, Weaver, & Oller, 1985; Chihara, Oller, Weaver, & Chavez-Oller, 1977) and Bachman (1982, 1985), Cziko (1978), and many others. The views of these two opposing camps are as straightforward as they are contradictory. Shanahan and his colleagues are convinced that ". . . the cloze test is insensitive to the integration of information across sentence boundaries" (Shanahan & Kamil, 1982, p. 207). However, Oller and his collaborators are equally clear in their contention that ". . . there remains no evidence against the proposition that cloze items *are* indeed sensitive to long-range constraints" (Chavez-Oller et al., 1985, p. 189).

In addition to providing clarification of the obviously contradictory results of these related research efforts, this study also challenges the central assumption underlying the experimental manipulation (i.e., sentence-scrambling) common to many of the studies cited. The assumption to which we refer has been most succinctly expressed by Halliday and Hasan (1976): ". . . it is characteristic of a text that the sequence of the sentences cannot be disturbed without destroying or radically altering the meaning'' (p. 28). The present study demonstrates that this is not an invariable characteristic of text; some texts, in fact, can be quite dramatically rearranged without causing noticeable interruption of comprehension.

In scrambled-text studies such as those cited above, it is apparently assumed that all texts are equal with respect to the constraint on comprehension attributable to the sequence of their sentences (see, for example, the assumption in Shanahan, Kamil, & Tobin, 1982, that a constraint on time will prevent subjects from *mentally unscrambling* scrambled text, *any* scrambled text, without regard to its comprehensibility). Our project challenges the assumption that sequentiality is equally distributed across texts. In point of fact, texts vary in the extent to which their component elements must be presented (and processed) in some naturally or rhetorically defined sequence. Rearranging the sequence of sentences in a text may indeed have a dramatic effect on that text's comprehensibility; for example:

> *Rearranged*: The experimenters then told the teachers that certain children had tested well and could be expected to make good academic progress. First, a number of selected children were given a test by the experimenters. The experiment began in 1964 in a California elementary school.
>
> *Desirable order*: The experiment began in 1964 in a California elementary school. First, a number of selected children were given a test by the experimenters. The experimenters then told the teachers that certain children had tested well and could be expected to make good academic progress.

With other texts, however, random rearrangement would appear to have little or no effect:

> *Rearranged:* The woodpeckers known as flickers are often seen on lawns and in gardens, diligently searching for ants and grasshoppers. Woodpeckers dwell not only in forests and woods but also in city parks and rural areas. Members of the woodpecker family are found in almost all places where there are trees.
>
> *Original order:* Members of the woodpecker family are found in almost all places where there are trees. Woodpeckers dwell not only in forests and woods but also in city parks and rural areas. The woodpeckers known as flickers are often seen on lawns and in gardens, diligently searching for ants and grasshoppers.

The first set of sentences was taken from the third paragraph of one of the experimental texts (Gregg, 1985) used in the present study (see Appendix for copies of the texts used); the second set is drawn from the other experimental text (Grolier, 1956). Given that the rearrangement causes far more interruption in the continuity of the first set, it would seem obvious that comprehensibility is not equally dependent upon sequence from one text to the next, nor even from one part of the same text to another.

Furthermore, once we call into question the assumption that comprehension is equally dependent upon sequence across texts, the results of many scrambled-text studies become interpretable not only in terms of the validity and utility of cloze procedure but also as indicators of the degree to which textual sequence constrains comprehension. Additionally, the issue of textual sequentiality that is raised in the current study underscores the potential for drawing erroneous conclusions from negative research results (e.g., Shanahan & Kamil, 1982, 1983). The failure of a research design to detect a relationship among variables should never be accepted as a demonstration that no relationship exists, particularly if that relationship has been well and replicably documented elsewhere, as it has indeed been in the current case (see, for example, Bachman, 1982, 1985; Chavez-Oller et al. 1985; Chihara et al., 1977; Cziko, 1978).

METHOD

Subjects

Subjects in the study were equivalent numbers of undergraduate and graduate students at East Texas State University. All undergraduate students were first-semester freshmen enrolled in introductory composition courses. Graduate students were enrolled in professional teacher education courses in counseling/guidance, elementary education, linguistics, and secondary/higher education. All subjects were tested in class-size groups at the beginning of a recent academic term.

A total of 252 subjects (124 graduate, 128 undergraduate) were randomly partitioned into control (naturally sequenced text) and experimental (scrambled text) groups. Each of these groups was further randomly partitioned into two groups by virtue of the topic of the passage (i.e., woodpecker vs. Pygmalion), yielding a total of four randomly created groups of approximately equal sizes (see Table 1).

Measures of reading ability and topic familiarity were not available; however, the random assignment of passages to subjects should have distributed the effects of such variables equally across the passages.

Materials

Two naturally occurring texts (see Appendix) of approximately equivalent length and difficulty level were selected, each representing opposite tendencies on a continuum of inherent structuredness (cf. Meyer, 1985). One passage is a loosely organized collection of descriptive facts about woodpeckers; the other is a condensed version of the formal report of Rosenthal and Jacobson's well-known study of the Pygmalion effect. The woodpecker passage has little discernible inherent structure; the Pygmalion passage, on the other hand, is quite tightly structured.

From each passage, standard cloze tests were created in which every seventh word was removed, for a total of 50 deletions per passage. Deleted words were replaced by underscored blanks of equal lengths. Deletions began in the first sentence of each passage, and every sentence, including the last, contained at least one deletion. The sentences of the passages were not rewritten in any way. This deletion procedure is consistent with others found throughout the cloze-test literature (e.g., Chihara et al., 1977; Jonz, 1976; Oller, 1972), and it follows the guidelines expressed in major works on language testing such as Oller (1979):

> The standard test construction technique, known as the *fixed ratio method,* involves deleting every *n*th word (where *n* usually varies from 5 to 10) and replacing each one with a standardized blank (usually about 15 typed spaces).
>
> The standard length of the cloze test is 50 items—thus the passage length must be approximately 50 times *n*. (p. 375)

Each passage was then reordered, creating *four* test passages: two in their original order exactly as they occurred in their published sources, and two in a scrambled order that was purposefully designed to cause maximum interruption of the sequentiality inherent in each text. To accomplish this reordering, the organization and sequence of each passage was examined, and various randomly generated scrambled versions of each were considered before the scrambled versions that were thought to be most disruptive were chosen (see Ginther, 1986, for details). Our prediction was that the scrambling process would have a significantly larger impact on responses to the well-structured Pygmalion passage than on responses to the loosely structured woodpecker passage, and our goal in creating the scrambled versions was to insure that the textual integrity of each passage was disrupted to the maximum extent possible while still respecting the phrase-structure of individual sentences. We assumed that the sensitivity of cloze to top-level structural constraints would be most convincingly tried under these most disruptive conditions.

Procedure

Subjects were tested during regularly scheduled class meetings. They were instructed to read carefully the directions that appeared on the first page of the cloze exercises and to ask for clarification when necessary. All questions that students asked required nothing more than a restatement of the written directions in response.

No time limit was set for the completion of the cloze exercises, but none of the subjects required more that 30 minutes to complete the entire procedure.

Cloze scores were derived by counting as correct any contextually appropriate response. In this scoring method (see Oller, 1972, p. 157, for a careful comparison of scoring methods), a small number of syntactically, thematically, and stylistically acceptable variant responses to each item is accepted as correct. Allowing such latitude insures that no indication of the operation of text-level constraint on comprehension escapes detection. Exact-word scoring rubrics obviously run the risk of failing to detect this source of variation in test performance by disallowing closely related lexical substitutes generated by the normal operation of comprehension processes.

On the other hand, acceptable-criterion scoring runs the risk of being subjective and not replicable. Therefore, we used the pooled judgment of several experienced readers to determine which words were to be acceptable as contextually appropriate. First, we compiled a list of all the answers for each cloze item on sequentially ordered passages. Then four readers, working independently, were asked to judge how well each word on the list fit into the cloze blank for which it had been intended. Any word that did not violate the syntax of its sentence, that fit the immediately surrounding context, and that was consistent with all preceding and subsequent text was deemed an equivalent replacement and was scored as an acceptable alternative, as long as it drew a positive response from three of the four judges. The number of acceptable alternate answers was approximately the same for both topics: 138 for the woodpecker passage, 134 for the Pygmalion passage.

The list of acceptable responses thus generated for sequential passages was also applied to judging contextual appropriateness in scrambled passages, on the assumption that one would want to apply the same scoring criteria across all responses.

Responses to the scrambled formats that did not occur in the sequential formats were very few in number. These few were judged by the same criteria as were variant responses to the sequential formats, with the obvious difficulty of applying a broad textual criterion. These three or four responses out of a total of more than 12,600 were not considered a significant number; for all intents and purposes, the responses to the scrambled passages were equivalent to the responses to the sequential passages along this dimension of variation.

RESULTS

Results (see Table 1) clearly conform to the predictions that would be made by a sequentiality hypothesis such as the one briefly outlined earlier.

Table 1

Mean Acceptable-criterion Cloze Scores

		Passage		
Cloze-test Format	***n***	**Woodpecker**	***n***	**Pygmalion**
Sequential	66		59	
M		40.76		37.63
SD		4.59		7.46
Scrambled	65		62	
M		39.25		32.66
SD		5.66		5.69

Each cloze test was scored by awarding one point for each contextually acceptable response. A perfect score, therefore, would be 50 on any one of the four tests. Test data thus derived were subjected to a completely randomized 2 × 2 ANOVA comparing two levels of test format (sequential and scrambled) and two levels of passage (woodpecker and Pygmalion). Both main effects were significant, as was the interaction.

Scores on the woodpecker passage were generally higher than scores on the Pygmalion passage, $F(1, 250) = 42.95, p < .001$. This is consistent with the fact that the Pygmalion passage is somewhat more difficult (11th- vs. 9th-grade level on the 1968 Fry graph).

Scores on sequentially ordered text, that is, scores on text ordered as it occurred in its original published source, were substantially higher than scores on scrambled text, $F(1, 250) = 18.20, p < .001$. In isolation, this result contradicts the anti-cloze research findings cited earlier and might be used to argue, generally, for the sensitivity of cloze procedure to higher-order constraints on verbal comprehension.

However, the hypothesis of this study was that the *extent* of disruption to comprehension occasioned by scrambling the components of text would be a function of the *extent* to which sequentiality was a characteristic of the texts under consideration. This hypothesis is supported in the ordinal interaction between test format and passage, $F(1, 250) = 5.39$, $p < .02$. Scrambling the Pygmalion passage had a significantly greater effect on comprehension than did scrambling the woodpecker passage.

DISCUSSION

By demonstrating that top-level structure can affect comprehension as measured by cloze procedure, this study calls into question the negative conclusions drawn by some researchers regarding the sensitivity of the cloze procedure to higher-order constraints on comprehension. Our argument is that experimental studies using a scrambled-sentence paradigm have generally assumed a level effect of scrambling across texts; such an assumption is demonstrably untenable. The present study clearly shows that textual sequentiality is a factor to be considered in scrambled-text studies, even though no simple, objective metric — except perhaps cloze procedure itself — can be proposed for measuring the constraint on comprehension that derives directly from the sequencing of text-level elements.

Many scrambled-text studies (e.g., Shanahan, Kamil, & Tobin, 1982) also depend on a comparison of cloze-test scores with scores on various measures of recall, demonstrating that whereas cloze-test scores do not vary as a function of sentence scrambling, recall scores do. Our study addresses the obvious failure of these studies to consider variation in textual sequentiality; however, another pertinent issue needs also to be raised: to what extent might cloze-test scores be reasonably assumed comparable to recall scores? Clearly, different aspects of comprehension (see Mandler, 1985, p. 37ff) are being measured by these two methods, and it should remain an open question, for the time being, how each of the two reflects the processes and products of reading (see Rankin & Thomas, 1980, p. 54) as well as how each measure might reflect the expenditure of cognitive resource as a function of task requirements. These three variables (sequence, specific aspect of comprehension, and expenditure of resource) need to be considered simultaneously.

Conclusions drawn in scrambled-text cloze studies must be considered as comments on the nature of the texts used as much as they are a reflection of individual human comprehension processes or the psychometric characteristics of cloze procedure itself. However, given this study's consideration of textual variation, it is not an overextension to claim that cloze is quite clearly sensitive to reader/text interaction of the higher orders.

REFERENCES

Bachman, L. F. (1982). The trait structure of cloze test scores. *TESOL Quarterly, 16*, 61–70.

Bachman, L. F. (1985). Performance on cloze tests with fixed-ratio and rational deletions. *TESOL Quarterly, 19*, 535–556.

Chavez-Oller, M. A., Chihara, T., Weaver, K. A., & Oller, J. W., Jr. (1985). When are cloze items sensitive to constraints across sentences? *Language Learning, 35*, 181–206.

Chihara, T., Oller, J., Weaver, K., & Chavez-Oller, M. A. (1977). Are cloze items sensitive to constraints across sentences? *Language Learning, 27*, 63–73.

Cziko, G. (1978). Differences in first- and second-language reading: The use of syntactic, semantic and discourse constraints. *Canadian Modern Language Review, 34*, 473-489.

Fry, E. (1968). A readability formula that saves time. *Journal of Reading, 11*, 513-516.

Ginther, A. (1986). *Textual sequence and cloze procedure.* Unpublished master's thesis, East Texas State University, Commerce, TX.

Gregg, J. Y. (1985). *Communication and culture.* Belmont, CA: Wadsworth.

Grolier Society. (1956). Our common birds V: Woodpeckers, humming-birds, swifts, whippoorwills and nighthawks. In *The Book of Popular Science* (Vol. 8, p. 3,343). New York: Author.

Halliday, M. A. K., & Hasan, R. (1976). *Cohesion in English.* London: Longman.

Jonz, J. (1976). Improving on the basic egg: The M-C Cloze. *Language Learning, 26*, 255–265.

Kibby, M. W. (1980). Intersentential processes in reading comprehension. *Journal of Reading Behavior, 12*, 299–312.

Leys, M., Fielding, L., Herman, P., & Pearson, P. D. (1983). Does cloze measure intersentential comprehension? A modified replication of Shanahan, Kamil, and Tobin. In J. A. Niles & L. A. Harris (Eds.), *Searches for meaning in reading/language processing and instruction* (pp. 111–114). Thirty-second Yearbook of the National Reading Conference. Rochester, NY: National Reading Conference.

Mandler, G. (1985). *Cognitive psychology: An essay in cognitive science.* Hillsdale, NJ: Erlbaum.

Meyer, B. J. F. (1985). Prose analysis: Purposes, procedures, and problems. In B. K. Britton & J. B. Black (Eds.), *Understanding expository text* (pp. 11–64). Hillsdale, NJ: Erlbaum.

Oller, J. W., Jr. (1972). Scoring methods and difficulty levels for cloze tests of proficiency in English as a second language. *Modern Language Journal, 56*, 151–157.

Oller, J. W., Jr. (1979). *Language tests at school.* London: Longman.

Rankin, E. F., & Thomas, S. (1980). Contextual constraints and the construct validity of the cloze procedure. In M. L. Kamil & A. J. Moe (Eds.), *Perspectives on reading: Research and instruction* (pp. 47–55). Twenty-ninth Yearbook of the National Reading Conference. Washington, DC: National Reading Conference.

Shanahan, T., & Kamil, M. (1982). The sensitivity of cloze to passage organization. In J. A. Niles & L. A. Harris (Eds.), *New inquiries in reading research and instruction* (pp. 204–208). Thirty-first Yearbook of the National Reading Conference. Rochester, NY: National Reading Conference.

Shanahan, T., & Kamil, M. (1983). A further comparison of the sensitivity of cloze and recall to passage organization. In J. A. Niles & L. A. Harris (Eds.), *Searches for meaning in reading/language processing and instruction* (pp. 123–128). Thirty-second Yearbook of the National Reading Conference. Rochester, NY: National Reading Conference.

Shanahan, T., Kamil, M., & Tobin, A. (1982). Cloze as a measure of intersentential comprehension. *Reading Research Quarterly, 17*, 229–255.

APPENDIX

The Woodpecker Text (Grolier, 1956)

A bird watcher, in the course of a day's rambling, almost always finds several species of woodpeckers. Sometimes they reveal their whereabouts by piercing call notes, sometimes by their steady hammering on tree trunks. When the watcher finally catches sight of a woodpecker, it is generally spiraling its way up a tree trunk or along a branch. Every so often the bird braces itself and digs for a grub beneath the bark. When it reaches the end of its ascent, it flies off to another tree. In flying, it makes several quick wing beats, pauses, makes several more beats, pauses again and so on. This results in a characteristic undulating, or wavy, flight pattern.

Members of the woodpecker family (Picidae) are found in almost all places where there are trees. They dwell not only in forests and woods but also in city parks and rural areas. The woodpeckers known as flickers are often seen on lawns and in gardens, diligently searching for ants and grasshoppers. As a rule, woodpeckers are solitary birds; family groups break up after the young are able to care for themselves. The Picidae do not migrate great distances as do many other kinds of birds. Certain species live year round in the north temperate areas of the world. Downy and hairy woodpeckers are often seen on the coldest days of the winter accompanying groups of nuthatches and chickadees in their search for food.

There are something like forty-five different species and subspecies of woodpeckers in North America. Many other species of the family are scattered throughout the temperate and tropical parts of the globe. There are no woodpeckers, however, on the island of Madagascar and the continent of Australia.

Woodpeckers are highly specialized for their tree-climbing and grub-hunting activities. Their feet are equipped with sharp, curved claws. Two toes on each foot are directed forward, while the other two point to the rear, thus making an effective pincer for grasping the bark of trees. (Three-toed woodpeckers have only one hind toe on each foot.) The feathers of the tail are stiff and end in sharp spines.

The Pygmalion Text (Gregg, 1985)

Psychologists Robert Rosenthal and Leonore Jacobson performed their initial experiments testing the validity of the self-fulfilling prophecy with laboratory rats. They found that expectation really influences achievement. The rats believed to be bright did, in fact, run their mazes better than the rats labeled dull, even though there was initially no difference in ability between the sets of rats.

The psychologists hypothesized that the self-fulfilling prophecy would operate in the classroom as well as in the laboratory. They believed that the teachers' expectations about their students would affect the students' achievement. It was their hypothesis, for instance, that if teachers were told that certain children were "bright," the teachers would form higher expectations about them. These higher expectations would be communicated to the students in various ways and the students would, in fact, do better work. To validate the hypothesis, it was essential that the teachers' expectations be formed solely by what they were told about the students.

The psychologists devised an experiment to test their prediction about the impact of self-fulfilling prophecy. The experiment began in 1964 in a California elementary school. First, a number of selected children were given a test by the experimenters. The experimenters then told the teachers that certain children had tested well and could be expected to make good academic progress. In fact, these "bright" children had not done better on the tests; all the children had done about the same. Thus higher expectations for these children existed only in the teachers' minds.

Later in the year the teachers were asked to describe the personalities and potential success of their students. They described the children who had been labeled "bright" in very positive ways and rated their chances for future success very good. All the children were tested four different times during the next two years. The children who had been labeled bright and rated highly by their teachers did, in fact, show greater intellectual gains than the others. First- and second-grade children made the most significant intellectual gains. Perhaps this means that younger children are more easily influenced by teacher expectations than older ones.

FACTORS AFFECTING SUMMARY WRITING AND THEIR IMPACT ON READING COMPREHENSION ASSESSMENT

Martha H. Head
Southeastern Louisiana University

Ray R. Buss
Louisiana State University

This study was prompted by a recent trend in research studies in which subjects have been asked to read and then summarize a target passage. Such studies have been conducted with subjects at various age levels from grade two (e.g., N. Johnson, 1983) to graduate school (e.g., Smith, 1985) and have employed both good and poor readers (e.g., Winograd, 1984). Sometimes a summary has been the sole measure of comprehension (e.g., Hidi, 1984) and at other times has been one of several comprehension measures (e.g., Freebody & Anderson, 1983a, 1983b). In all cases, however, researchers seem to have concurred with Kintsch and van Dijk (1978) that readers, when comprehending a text, form a gist in their minds which represents their overall comprehension of the passage. Subsequently, this gist, or summary, is assumed to represent what readers have understood about the text and is regarded as a valid measure of the subjects' text comprehension (Taylor, 1984).

Another line of research has developed which appears to be in conflict with these assumptions. Several researchers, such as Garner (1982, 1985) and N. Johnson (1983) have found that immature readers are universally nonexpert summarizers. Not surprisingly, a strong developmental effect is evident; that is, the subjects do get better as they get older (Brown & Day, 1983). Some possible reasons offered to explain their poor performances are a lack of sensitivity to importance (Winograd, 1984), a lack of awareness of what it means to summarize (Garner, 1982), or deficits in production ability (Garner, 1982). Consequently, these researchers and others have made a strong case for summary instruction in schools so that students may acquire summarizing skills at an earlier age.

Trying to reconcile these two groups of studies raises two questions. First, what factors might affect the quality of summaries produced by young writers and thus influence the use of these summaries for comprehension assessment? Second, can young writers summarize well enough so that their written summaries are a valid measure of their text comprehension? The researchers in the present study sought answers to these questions.

To address the first question, three factors were considered that might be related to the quality of summary writing. The first of these was prior knowledge, which has been investigated previously in relation to other comprehension measures (e.g., Johnston, 1984). It was felt that it might be a particularly important factor in summary writing because of the nature of the summary production task. For example, if subjects possess a low level of prior knowledge about the target passage topic, they would have little schematic framework with which to relate new information. The lack of background knowledge from which to draw might cause the subjects to write a very short summary and to include little information from the target passage, thus giving the appearance of inadequate comprehension. The subjects might, for instance, perform better on a recognition task where cues were provided to prompt their recall, and their text comprehension might not be as inadequate as the summary sample would lead us to believe.

A second factor investigated was the level of interest in the topic of the target passage. Topic interest has been shown to have a singular effect on reading comprehension, independent of prior knowledge (Baldwin, Peleg-Bruckner, & McClintock, 1985). Where recall is prompted, as in the case of multiple-choice questions, low topic interest may not present much of a problem. But in a production task, such as a summary, subjects may be so disinterested in the topic that they lack sufficient motivation to write a summary about it.

A third factor postulated to affect summary writing was the general writing ability of the subjects. Numerous studies have shown that adolescent writers are immature writers in that they lack a sense of purpose, importance, and audience (Vacca & Vacca, 1986). For such subjects, the writing task itself may be so difficult that a summarizing task is almost out of the question. Certainly, young subjects would vary in the degree to which writing ability would affect summarizing quality, but it seems logical that it would be a factor to be considered when written summaries are used.

The second question, concerning the value of summaries for comprehension assessment by novice summarizers, was investigated by comparing a written summary measure to a written free recall of the same target passage information. Based on previous research, the hypothesis was that seventh-grade subjects would not be sufficiently proficient at summarizing that they could differentiate between the two types of recall tasks. It was expected, therefore, that few differences would exist between the subjects' free recalls and their summaries of the same passage.

In addition, in order to compare summaries for assessment purposes with another well-validated comprehension measure, the subjects' summary scores were compared with their scores on multiple-choice postreading questions for the same target passage. This comparison was made in order to gain evidence concerning the kinds of information that could be tapped using a summary as a comprehension measure. The hypothesis was that a relatively strong relationship would exist between the summary scores and the postreading questions scores, indicating that summaries and multiple-choice questions were measuring similar kinds of information.

METHOD

Subjects

Fifty-three seventh-grade students from a large southern city participated in the study. The subjects were members of three social studies classes held concurrently and were classified as average readers on the basis of their reading comprehension scores on a standardized test, the Comprehensive Assessment Program (Wick & Smith, 1980). Additionally, 68% of the subjects were white and 32% were classified as black or another minority group.

Materials

The target passage was 1,845 words in length and dealt with the development of labor unions in the United States. It was written on a seventh-grade readability level (Fry, 1977) and was selected from a previously unread portion of the subjects' regular social studies textbook.

The prior knowledge and postreading comprehension measures each consisted of 15 multiple-choice questions, none of which appeared on both tests. The questions were based on the critical vocabulary in the target passage and had been determined in pilot studies to be passage-dependent.

An interest inventory was constructed to measure the subjects' level of interest in reading about the topic. It contained a list of 29 topics in American history. Subjects were asked to rate their interest in reading about each topic on a scale of *A* (highest) to *F* (lowest), as in school grades. For purposes of this study, the focus was the two items that corresponded to the target passage: the growth of industry and the development of labor unions in the United States.

General writing ability was assessed by having subjects write a short essay entitled "McKinley Middle School through the Eyes of a Seventh Grader." Essays were about one page in length.

Written recalls took the form of both a free recall and a summarized recall. Directions on the data collection sheets emphasized the differences between the two tasks: that a free recall should include everything that a reader could remember, and a summary should contain only main ideas and the details necessary to support them.

Procedure

Data collection. Data were collected by the first author and two trained doctoral students during the subjects' regular social studies class periods. All directions were scripted to maintain uniformity and were read aloud to ensure that subjects understood the tasks.

On the first day, subjects completed the interest inventory. On the following day, subjects answered the questions on the prior knowledge test and wrote the essay for the writing sample.

The third day of data collection took place during the next week after a five-day buffer. First, subjects read the target passage. Then they completed two recall tasks (free recall and summary) from memory. Task order was counterbalanced so that half the subjects were randomly assigned to write the free recall first and the summary second, and vice versa. On the following day, subjects reread the target passage and answered the postreading comprehension questions from memory.

Scoring. Results for the data collected are shown in Tables 1 and 2. Multiple-choice questions on the prior knowledge and postreading comprehension measures were scored as either correct or incorrect using an answer key. One point was awarded for each correct answer. The interest inventory was scored by converting the *A* through *F* ratings for the two target passage topics to numerical scores ($A = 4$ points and $F = 0$ points), with scores between the two extremes ordered accordingly. The scores for the two items were then summed so that scores could range from 0 to 8. The writing sample was scored independently by two of the investigators using holistic criteria described by Diederich (1974). Diederich's system allows scores to range from 0 to 30, based upon the quality of the writers' ideas, organization, wording, and flavor. Percentage of agreement between the two raters was .82, and differences were resolved in conference.

Written recalls were scored by comparing them with a template of idea units. These idea units were obtained by having graduate students parse the text into pausal units and rate their relative importance, using a technique described by R. Johnson

Table 1

Descriptive Statistics for Predictor Variables and Postreading Multiple-choice Test

Variable	*M*	*SD*
Prior knowledge (PK)	4.93	2.13
Writing ability (WA)	13.55	4.77
Topic interest (TI)	3.45	2.23
Postreading multiple-choice test (MC)	8.26	2.12

Note. $N = 53$.

Table 2

Descriptive Statistics for Written Recalls

	Free Recall		Summary	
	M	*SD*	*M*	*SD*
Idea units	9.49	4.90	7.85	4.46
Important idea units	3.62	2.53	3.59	2.52
Proportion of important idea units	.38	.19	.46	.22

Note. $N = 53$.

(1970). Thus, each idea unit in the recalls that could be matched with the text template was assigned a relative importance rating from 1 (least important) to 4 (most important). Measures obtained in this way were (a) number of idea units, (b) number of important idea units, and (c) proportion of important idea units, defined as the ratio of important idea units to total idea units.

RESULTS

Three sets of analyses were undertaken with the data. First, standard regression analyses were used to determine the predictive effects of the independent variables on the three summary criterion measures. Second, a multivariate repeated measures analysis of variance was conducted in order to examine differences between the means for the free recalls and summaries. Finally, correlations between the summary scores and the multiple-choice postreading questions were calculated.

Regression Analyses

There were three predictor variables for the analyses. These variables and the measures from which they were obtained were as follows: (a) prior knowledge (PK), from the prereading multiple-choice questions; (b) topic interest (TI), from the interest inventory; and (c) writing ability (WA), from the essay collected from each subject. The three criterion variables were the scores obtained for each subject's summary: (a) number of idea units, (b) number of important idea units, and (c) proportion of important idea units. Effect sizes for the regression analyses were also calculated. The effect size statistic f^2 refers to the proportion of variance explained to the unexplained variance (Cohen, 1977).

For the number of idea units, only 9% of the variance was explained by the model, and no predictors were statistically significant. For the number of important idea units, the model explained 16% of the variance, $F(3, 49) = 3.21, p < .03$. Two predictors were statistically significant. TI alone explained 8% of the variance, $F(1, 51) = 4.53$, $p < .05$. WA explained an additional 7% of the variance after TI was accounted for, $F(1, 51) = 4.35, p < .05$. Effect sizes for both predictors were relatively small, $f^2 =$ .08. For the proportion of important idea units, no statistically significant predictors were found. Only 8% of the variance was explained, and only WA even approached statistical significance, $F(1, 51) = 1.14, p < .08$.

MANOVA

There were two repeated measures: Task (free recalls and summaries obtained for each subject) and Order (first or second). The dependent variables were the three scores on the free recalls and summaries. For each of the effects, an effect size statistic f was calculated, based on the eta-squared coefficient and according to procedures outlined by Cohen (1977).

The main effect for Order was not statistically significant, multivariate $F(3, 49) =$ $0.87, p < .52$. On the other hand, both the effects for Task, multivariate $F(3, 49) =$

2.81, $p < .02$, and Task × Order interaction, multivariate $F(3, 49) = 4.56$, $p < .001$, were statistically significant. Individual univariate repeated measures ANOVAs indicated statistically significant differences in several cases. Specifically, the effect for Task was statistically significant for two of the dependent variables: number of idea units, $F(1, 51) = 5.25$, $p < .03$, and proportion of important idea units, $F(1, 51) = 4.03$, $p < .05$. Effect sizes were in the small to moderate range, $f = .20$ and $f = .18$, respectively.

Task × Order interactions were statistically significant for the number of idea units, $F(1, 51) = 11.84$, $p < .001$, and the number of important idea units, $F(1, 51) = 8.87$, $p < .004$. Effect sizes were again small to moderate, $f = .25$ and $f = .20$, respectively.

Correlational Analysis

Pearson product-moment correlation coefficients were computed for each of the three dependent measures for summaries with the postreading multiple-choice questions score (MC). The number of idea units attained a statistically significant correlation with MC, $r = .44$, $p < .0009$. The number of important idea units again achieved statistical significance when correlated with MC, $r = .51$, $p < .0001$. Conversely, correlations for the proportion of important idea units with MC were very small and statistically nonsignificant.

DISCUSSION

The examination of factors which could influence summary production revealed that only one of the three dependent measures, number of important idea units, could be reliably predicted by the predictor variables. For this measure, writing ability was found to be a statistically significant predictor. This result was not unexpected, given Johnston's (1983) observations that young writers have difficulty deciding what is important to include in a composition. It would appear that writing proficiency was indeed related to the attempts by these seventh-grade subjects to summarize important information.

Additionally, topic interest was found to explain a statistically significant proportion of the variance in the number of important idea units in the summaries. As in the study by Baldwin, Peleg-Bruckner, and McClintock (1985), readers' interest in the topic may have influenced their comprehension of the passage and the important information that they had available for inclusion in their summaries.

The fact that prior knowledge was not a statistically significant predictor of any of the dependent measures may be an artifact of the target passage chosen. The level of prior knowledge for this topic was really quite low ($M = 4.93$ out of a possible 15), and the variability was also relatively limited ($SD = 2.13$). Despite findings from pilot studies to the contrary, it is possible that this uniformly low level of prior knowledge contributed to a low overall performance in summary writing. It would be desirable in future studies to choose a target passage in which greater variability in prior knowledge levels could be obtained.

Comparisons of the means for the free recalls and summaries revealed statistically significant differences on two of the three dependent measures. The first of these was in number of idea units: free recalls contained more idea units than the summaries did. This measure is primarily an indicator of quantity, that is, the length of the recall. Given the nature of the directions that subjects were given, such a result is not unexpected. Free recalls were to include all information that could be recalled, and summaries were to consist of main ideas only. It seems apparent that some idea units would be deleted in an attempt to keep only that which was important.

The second difference between the summaries and the free recalls is related to the first. Subjects included a proportionally larger quantity of important information in their summaries than they did in their free recalls. This result indicates that the subjects, again, were making an attempt to summarize by including only the most important information.

Both these results would seem to be encouraging for those who advocate using summaries in comprehension assessment. The bad news, however, is that the subjects recalled an appallingly small amount of information from the passage. The mean number of idea units in the somewhat longer free recalls, 9.49, represents only 5% of the 195 idea units that the passage contained. Results for the number of important idea units included in the summaries were not much better, with only 7% of the 49 possible being recalled. Even though a summary is, by definition, a condensation, adults in a pilot study on the same passage outperformed the seventh graders by a three-to-one margin. Therefore, it would appear that neither the free recalls nor summaries were telling us much about what these seventh-grade subjects understood about the passage; they were, in fact, telling us that they had difficulty remembering much about what they read. What was remembered and what was understood are not necessarily one and the same, so it would seem that some additional comprehension measures are necessary.

Hence, the comparison of the summaries with the multiple-choice questions seems to be all the more critical. It was found that the correlations for MC with both the number of idea units and number of important idea units was statistically significant. The fact that multiple-choice questions in this study were passage-dependent implies that an understanding of the target passage is related to the ability to write a summary. The magnitude of the correlations, however, was rather modest, suggesting that there are other aspects of comprehension being measured by summaries that are unrelated to passage comprehension. At best, it can be concluded that multiple-choice questions and written summaries are measuring some of the same aspects of text comprehension.

Based on these results, the following conclusions may be stated. First, the use of summaries, at least for seventh graders, seems to tell us little more than can be found out using a free recall measure. Second, summarizing appears to be a task for which seventh graders are not fully prepared. Third, some factors, other than reading comprehension, may also play a role in the ability to summarize. Finally, summaries appear to measure some, but not all, aspects of reading comprehension.

Several suggestions for future research can be made. First, it is clear that additional investigation is needed into the factors which influence summary quality. This study suggests that topic interest and writing ability may play at least some role, and prior knowledge may also have an effect when variability is wide-ranging. Thus, a refinement of research techniques, including the use of other passages, would be helpful.

Second, since it appears that students at this grade level have some difficulty in summarizing, we would join the ranks of those who have recommended summarizing instruction. It would also be advisable to study what effects a well-designed summary instruction might have. It is possible that trained summary writers would be able to overcome deficits due to lack of prior knowledge, writing ability, or topic interest, and might thus be able to produce a summary more indicative of their actual text comprehension.

In conclusion, summary writing is an area which we have only begun to explore. The findings of this study have indicated that written summaries have a place in the assessment of reading comprehension. Clearly, however, more research is needed to determine just what that place is.

REFERENCES

Baldwin, R. S., Peleg-Bruckner, Z., & McClintock, A. H. (1985). Effects of topic interest and prior knowledge on reading comprehension. *Reading Research Quarterly, 20,* 497–504.

Brown, A. L., & Day, J. D. (1983). Macrorules for summarizing texts: The development of expertise. *Journal of Verbal Learning and Verbal Behavior, 22,* 1–14.

Cohen, J. (1977). *Statistical power analysis for the behavioral sciences* (rev. ed.). New York: Academic Press.

Diederich, P. B. (1974). *Measuring growth in English.* Urbana, IL: National Council of Teachers of English.

Freebody, P., & Anderson, R. C. (1983a). Effects of vocabulary difficulty, text cohesion, and schema availability on reading comprehension. *Reading Research Quarterly, 18,* 277–294.

Freebody, P., & Anderson, R. C. (1983b). Effects on text comprehension of differing proportions and locations of difficult vocabulary. *Journal of Reading Behavior, 15,* 19–39.

Fry, E. B. (1977). Fry's readability graph: Clarification, validity, and extension to level 17. *Journal of Reading, 21,* 242–252.

Garner, R. (1982). Efficient text summarization: Costs and benefits. *Journal of Educational Research, 75,* 275–279.

Garner, R. (1985). Text summarization deficiencies among older students: Awareness or production ability? *American Educational Research Journal, 22,* 549–560.

Hidi, S. (1984). *Summarization of complete texts* (Occasional Paper No. 4). Toronto: Ontario Institute for Studies in Education, Center for Applied Cognitive Science.

Johnson, N. S. (1983). What do you do if you can't tell the whole story? The development of summarization skills. In K. E. Nelson (Ed.), *Children's language: Vol. 4* (pp. 315–383). Hillsdale, NJ: Erlbaum.

Johnson, R. E. (1970). Recall of prose as a function of the structural importance of the linguistic units. *Journal of Verbal Learning and Verbal Behavior, 9,* 12–20.

Johnston, P. H. (1983). *Reading comprehension assessment: A cognitive basis.* Newark, DE: International Reading Association.

Johnston, P. H. (1984). Prior knowledge and reading comprehension test bias. *Reading Research Quarterly, 19,* 220–239.

Kintsch, W., & van Dijk, T. A. (1978). Toward a model of text comprehension and production. *Psychological Review, 85,* 363–394.

Smith, S. P. (1985). Comprehension and comprehension monitoring by experienced readers. *Journal of Reading, 28,* 292–300.

Taylor, B. M. (1984). The search for a meaningful approach to assessing comprehension of expository text. In J. A. Niles & L. A. Harris (Eds.), *Changing perspectives in research in reading/language processing and instruction* (pp. 257–263). Thirty-third Yearbook of the National Reading Conference. Rochester, NY: National Reading Conference.

Vacca, R., & Vacca, J. (1986). *Content area reading* (2nd ed.). Boston: Little, Brown.

Wick, J. W., & Smith, J. K. (1980). *Comprehensive assessment program.* Iowa City, IA: American Testronics.

Winograd, P. N. (1984). Strategic difficulties in summarizing texts. *Reading Research Quarterly, 19,* 404–425.

A SURVEY OF STUDENT LITERACY EXPERIENCES IN A LARGE-SCALE STATE ASSESSMENT

Timothy Shanahan
University of Illinois at Chicago

The states of Illinois and Michigan are attempting to develop new state assessments of reading comprehension. These tests promise to be quite different from traditional standardized reading comprehension tests now in wide use. These new tests will require students to read long, coherent prose passages—entire stories or expositions on science or social studies. The questions for these tests will be based upon constructive notions of reading comprehension, and there will be measures of students' prior knowledge and of their metacognitive awareness. The Illinois Inventory of Educational Progress in Reading also will attempt to assess manipulable features of the literacy context. This paper will explain the need for this type of contextual assessment, describe its design, and suggest how it will be developed to insure the provision of a reliable and valid body of information about literacy experiences. Some preliminary results from a pilot analysis of eighth-grade data will be used to illustrate various points.

Traditionally, state assessments have described reading achievement with no regard for the educational contexts that produced that achievement. This oversight is surprising, given that state assessments are usually conducted to inform policy-makers and educators as to what future courses of action might be advisable. Assessments that provide information about manipulable features of school practice offer educators better grounds for decision-making than are often available.

Surprisingly, some national assessments have provided a better model of the assessment of productive influences of school achievement. The recent reading assessment of the National Assessment of Educational Progress (NAEP, 1985), for example, asked students about their amount and uses of reading. An earlier NAEP writing assessment (1981) focused on instruction even more directly by questioning students about classroom writing and revision activities, although this information was not subsequently linked to achievement.

State assessments, especially those that attempt to reconceptualize reading and to measure achievement in new, more instructionally relevant ways, *need* to provide information on instructional practices in order to test the validity of the reading measure itself, and to satisfy concerns about fair treatment across districts. If these new measures cannot be influenced by instruction to any greater extent than traditional standardized comprehension tests can be, then these measures might only have a superficial, rather than a substantive, impact upon teaching. Of course, if different educational experiences lead to advantaged performances on the tests, then it is important that such information be made available to communities so that schools can either change their practices or challenge the validity of the tests.

MEASURES

The survey items in the Illinois test consider four separate issues: (a) literacy instruction, (b) functional uses of literacy, (c) home academic experiences, and (d) reading strategies.

Instructional Questions

Questions about literacy instruction make up the greatest number of items in the survey. These items assess the incidence of certain reading, writing, and content area reading practices and ask students questions about their attitudes toward such practices.

Students are questioned about the reading instruction that they receive. They are asked about the frequency of occurrence of such prescribed instructional practices as the preteaching of new vocabulary, discussion of background information prior to reading, establishment of purposes for reading, use of oral and silent reading, provision of postreading questions, summarization of text, and comparisons of multiple texts. These questions emphasize some issues that have been considered in instructional studies, such as amount of classroom reading (Rosenshine & Stephens, 1984), but they also consider several variables that have been ignored in large-scale studies although their relevance to comprehension, especially as measured here, is clear (Tierney & Cunningham, 1984).

The reading instruction questions consider students' understanding of the goals of instruction. Students are asked about the reading strategies that are being taught. They are asked whether they are being taught how to figure out unknown words, to predict what comes next in a selection, to remember what they have read, to use author's organization to understand a text's content, or to write summaries. Instruction is most effective when students understand teacher's goals (Duffy, Roehler, & Wesselman, 1985), and it seems reasonable to consider the relationship between such knowledge and the strategic processes that children claim to use in other parts of the assessment.

Second, instructional questions ask about the reading emphasis in content subjects such as science and social studies. Educators have long called for a reading emphasis in content area subjects (Harris & Sipay, 1985), and evidence indicates that such instruction can have a positive impact on reading achievement (Wolf & Greenwald, 1980). The questions that focused on content area reading were similar to the instructional questions already described, but they were directed specifically toward understanding the use of comprehension instruction in content area materials.

Third, instructional questions asked about classroom writing experiences. School districts have been increasing the amount of writing instruction. Because reading and writing achievement are related (Langer, 1986; Shanahan, 1984) and because the effectiveness of various writing practices is still in question with regard to both reading (Stotsky, 1983) and writing achievement (Hillocks, 1985), it seems reasonable to attempt to estimate the impact various writing practices might have on reading achievement. Students are asked about preparation for writing, amount and type of revision, source of subject matter for writing, attention to audience, use of reading material as a source of information to be used in writing, and amount of in-class sharing of compositions.

Functions of Reading Questions

The second set of context questions focuses on uses of literacy. These items assess students' uses of literacy in their daily lives. School achievement tests are not a complete indicator of performance levels on actual literacy tasks such as the reading of documents or the completion of applications (Kirsch & Guthrie, 1984; Kirsch & Jungeblut, 1986). The uses of literacy have a greater impact on human thinking than does literacy itself (Scribner & Cole, 1981). These items should provide insight as to the relationship between school acheivement and more diverse literacy experiences in which children participate.

The uses questions ask about literacy-related activities such as amount of book sharing with friends, use of libraries, keeping of diaries, and reading of multiple books by the same author. These questions estimate the significance of reading and writing in the lives of these children. These questions consider amount of reading, types of materials read, and the purposes towards which literacy is directed. Students are queried about their use of these in and away from school to allow the comparison of relative diversity of reading alternatives available and to examine the relative impact such experiences have on achievement, strategic processing, and motivation.

Purpose questions focus on the goals toward which reading and writing activity is directed. Students are asked about the role of reading and writing in their learning, entertainment, religious practice, social relationships, aesthetic appreciations, as well as the more mundane uses of these to follow directions or as an adjunct to memory. Such questions can be used both to help to explain reading achievement and as an outcome variable of similar value to achievement.

Home Environment Questions

A third set of questions focuses on the home literacy environment. There are fewer of these because many aspects of the home environment are beyond school control and because the functional uses domain overlaps with the home literacy environment domain. Nevertheless, there is little doubt as to the importance of the home environment in school achievement (Walberg, 1985), and though schools do not directly manipulate home environment, they can influence it (Walberg & Shanahan, 1983).

The home environment questions ask about the availability of literacy materials (i.e., dictionaries, books, newspapers). They also ask about a number of less tangible home features that have been found to be significantly related to school achievement and which conceivably could be influenced by educators. Students are asked about the amount of parent-student discussion of schooling (Shanahan & Walberg, 1985), such as amount of parental monitoring of homework completion, or discussion or encouragement of reading. Students are asked about amount of homework and televison viewing, too (Walberg, 1985).

Reading Strategies Questions

The fourth set of questions asks about the specific reading strategies that students use. For example, students are asked how often they consider what they already know about a topic during reading, or whether they ask themselves questions about what they read, or whether they stop and reread if it does not make sense.

There have been many calls for the specific teaching of reading strategies to increase children's comprehension (Durkin, 1978–1979; Tierney & Cunningham, 1984), and it appears that students benefit from knowing why they are being taught strategies so that they can make conditional use of them on the basis of their purposes and text demands (Paris, Lipson, & Wixson, 1983). Strategy questions provide an estimation of the frequency of use of some specific reading strategies, and they will permit the use of these to be linked with comprehension, metacognition, and instructional experiences.

ANALYSIS AND RESULTS

The first pilot of the Illinois test is now being analyzed. To demonstrate the importance of this type of a contextual assessment, I will describe some very preliminary results from a random sample of 1,069 eighth-grade students, and I will explain the type of analysis that will be used to validate it. (The pilot sample included 5,000 subjects at each of four grade levels: third, sixth, eighth, and tenth.) Because of the preliminary nature of the data, these findings will be more provocative than substantive. The information provided is an example of the types of information that a state assessment might provide.

Survey data can help to reveal the current status of literacy instruction. For example, researchers have stressed the importance of teaching students to consider audience when they write (Faigley, Cherry, Jolliffe, & Skinner, 1986). However, only about 40% of these eighth graders indicated that they usually considered what their readers know, and only about 30% said that they usually wrote differently for different audiences. This type of information suggests that teachers are not stressing audience in writing, or that such instruction is not having much influence on what students actually do. Given that 24% of these subjects indicated that they *never* share their writing with others in class, and that 48% of them said they did so only occasionally, it seems likely that sense of audience currently is not receiving much instructional emphasis.

Nor, evidently are other social aspects of literacy: 32% of these students said they never considered during reading why an author has written a particular text, 42% said they never tell their friends about books they read, and 62% said they only occasionally write to share their ideas. These students do not view literacy as a social semiotic; one of the major social values of literacy is not apparent to a large segment of this population.

This survey also provided information that might help school personnel to influence community practices. The results indicated, as has been reported in previous studies, that eighth graders do a great deal of television viewing. More important, however, is the fact that a majority of these students (54%) indicated that their parents placed no controls on the amount of their viewing. This is not to suggest that these parents are not concerned about their children's education, only that they have not adequately addressed the issue of amount of television viewing. (In fact, these parents appear to be very involved in their children's schooling; about 70% of them regularly check to make certain that their children have done their homework correctly.)

These types of data also can reveal relationships between various contextual variables and reading achievement. Many questions that asked about students' strategic thinking during literacy activities were significantly related to reading comprehension. For example, students who reported that they stopped and reread text when they were confused or that they thought about what they wanted to say before writing did best on the comprehension test.

The relationship between different uses of literacy and reading achievement is not quite as clear, however. It might be expected that students who use literacy for the greatest number of purposes would be the best readers. This was not the case because some of the uses measures were negatively related to school achievement. Writing to share ideas and to complete schoolwork are positively correlated with reading achievement. Reading to satisfy parents and reading television listings are negatively related to achievement, probably because they index significant background variables such as amount of television viewing. Reading for the purposes of religion, enjoyment, or escape are not significantly related to achievement, despite sufficient amounts of variance associated with each of these items. Kirsch and Jungeblut (1986) have reported that success in school literacy does not guarantee successful use of literacy. These data seem to indicate that the successful use of nonacademic literacy does not necessarily guarantee success in school reading.

Examples such as these demonstrate the potential this type of assessment has for raising and, ultimately, answering important instructional questions. Rather than simply running through a number of provocative frequencies or correlations of individual measures, it would be more productive to describe the types of analyses that are in progress in order to show how such measures must be validated. First, there are far too many items currently being used and the set will be reduced on the basis of an examination of the intercorrelations among these items, and between these items and the achievement variables. For example, it appears that four specific items would be sufficient to provide all the information currently asked for in one set of twelve functional uses questions.

Second, confirmatory factor analysis is being used to determine whether the four sets of questions hang together as sets. There is no reason to believe that these four sets of questions will be uncorrelated with each other; in fact, it is expected that they will be, so the analysis that is used will simply attempt to indicate whether the sets of items are more closely related within sets than across sets. Preliminary results suggest that there are, in fact, four separate factors represented by these questions.

Third, although there might be some very interesting bivariate correlations between these items and achievement, the more interesting policy questions will focus on how entire sets of questions combine to explain the outcomes of interest. Such combinations provide more reliable estimates of outcomes and allow us to invest greater confidence in the findings. Future work with these data will provide an evaluation of more complex models of instructional effects by using path analyses of the influence of literacy environment on students' strategy use and motivation and, subsequently, on reading comprehension.

Fourth, it must be remembered that this is self-report data drawn from students. How accurately students can provide such information is not known, so we are evaluating the reliability and validity of the survey information. Some students were interviewed about two months after the testing in order to estimate the test-retest reliability of the survey. Testing took place over two days. Questions were divided across the days to permit a test of the consistency with which children answer alternative forms of the same questions. Soon we will begin to collect data from classroom observations of teaching practices and we will attempt to link these observations with students' responses on the assessment survey. This procedure will provide a check of the validity of the information provided by students.

CONCLUSIONS

State assessments, if they are to be informative, useful, and fair, need to provide information about the instructional contexts within which achievement is obtained. One reasonable way to provide such information is through the type of survey questionnaire used here or in recent national assessments. The information about classroom instruction, functional uses, home environment, and strategy use that is collected needs to be directly relevant to the model of comprehension that is being tested and must represent features of the environment the manipulation of which could influence eventual achievement. It is important that these data have more than face validity. There must be reasonable statistical evidence that such information can be collected reliably and that it is a valid representation of student experiences.

REFERENCES

Duffy, G., Roehler, L., & Wesselman, R. (1985). Disentangling the complexities of instructional effectiveness: A line of research on classroom reading instruction. In J. Niles & R. Lalik (Eds.), *Issues in literacy: A research perspective* (pp. 244–250). Thirty-fourth Yearbook of the National Reading Conference. Rochester, NY: National Reading Conference.

Durkin, D. (1978–1979). What classroom observations reveal about reading comprehension instruction. *Reading Research Quarterly, 14,* 481–533.

Faigley, L., Cherry, R., Jolliffe, D., & Skinner, A. (1986). *Assessing writer's knowledge and processes of composing.* Norwood, NJ: Ablex.

Harris, A., & Sipay, E. (1985). *How to increase reading ability* (8th ed.). New York: Longman.

Hillocks, G. (1985). *Research on written composition.* Urbana, IL: National Council of Teachers of English.

Kirsch, I., & Guthrie, J. (1984). Prose comprehension and text search as a function of reading volume. *Reading Research Quarterly, 19,* 331–342.

Kirsch, I., & Jungeblut, A. (1986). *Literacy: Profiles of America's young adults.* Princeton, NJ: Educational Testing Service.

Langer, J. (1986). *Children reading and writing.* Norwood, NJ: Ablex.

National Assessment of Educational Progress. (1981). *Reading, thinking and writing.* Denver, CO: Education Commission of the States.

National Assessment of Educational Progress. (1985). *The reading report card: Progress towards excellence in our schools.* Princeton: Educational Testing Service.

Paris, S., Lipson, M., & Wixson, K. (1983). Becoming a strategic reader. *Contemporary Educational Psychology, 3,* 293–316.

Rosenshine, B., & Stevens, R. (1984). Classroom instruction in reading. In P. D. Pearson (Ed.), *Handbook of reading research* (pp. 745–798). New York: Longman.

Scribner, S., & Cole, M. (1981). *The psychology of literacy.* Cambridge, MA: Harvard University Press.

Shanahan, T. (1984). The nature of reading-writing relation: An exploratory multivariate analysis. *Journal of Educational Psychology, 76,* 466–477.

Shanahan, T., & Walberg, H. (1985). Productive influences on high school student achievement. *Journal of Educational Research, 78,* 357–363.

Stotsky, S. (1983). Research on reading/writing relationships: A synthesis and suggested directions. *Language Arts, 60,* 627–642.

Tierney, R., & Cunningham, J. (1984). Research on teaching reading comprehension. In P. D. Pearson (Ed.), *Handbook of reading research* (pp. 609–656). New York: Longman.

Walberg, H. (1985). Synthesis of research on teaching. In M. C. Wittrock (Ed.), *Handbook of research on teaching* (pp. 214–229). Washington, DC: American Educational Research Association.

Walberg, H., & Shanahan, T. (1983). High school effects on individual students. *Educational Researcher, 7*(7), 4–9.

Wolf, A., & Greenwald, J. (1980, December). *Frequency of reading in secondary content areas: A follow-up observation study.* Paper presented at the National Reading Conference, San Diego, CA.

ASSESSMENT

EMERGENT LITERACY

COMPREHENSION

INSTRUCTIONAL EFFECTIVENESS

ADULT LITERACY

WRITING

EMERGENT LITERACY: READING AND WRITING DEVELOPMENT IN EARLY CHILDHOOD*

William H. Teale
University of Texas at San Antonio

The concept of emergent literacy has, in recent years, been adopted more and more widely by reading researchers and educators. For example, an emergent literacy strand appeared in 1984 as part of the National Reading Conference, one chapter of *Becoming a Nation of Readers* was entitled Emerging Literacy, and numerous journal articles over the last year or so have contained the phrase. Publishers of instructional materials are even showing interest in the concept. Though the term is being used increasingly, it, like other nascent concepts, is subject to differing interpretations. Therefore, it seems appropriate to begin this review of emergent literacy research by defining the area itself.

A DEFINITION OF EMERGENT LITERACY

Emergent literacy centers on young children and their reading and writing. More specifically, the period of emergent literacy can be defined as that between birth and the time when children write and read in conventional ways, ways that adults generally would identify as actually being reading and writing. Thus, emergent literacy represents the beginnings of reading and writing for the child.

But emergent literacy is not to be confused with the term *beginning reading* which has a history of its own closely associated with formal reading instruction in school. Emergent literacy should be thought of as literacy development and learning prior to formal school instruction.

In this respect it may seem to be the same as the first stage of Chall's developmental scheme (Chall, 1983), the stage she called "Prereading." However, important theoretical and practical differences exist between Chall's and others' descriptions of prereading or reading readiness and the concept of emergent literacy. It is not insignificant, for instance, that Chall called this stage Prereading Stage 0 (zero); in her stages of reading development there is a clear break between Initial Reading, or

*Annual Review of Research.

Decoding, and all that preceded it. Likewise, reading readiness is generally seen as a precursor to reading.

Emergent literacy, on the other hand, treats young children's reading and writing conceptions and behaviors as legitimate aspects of the ontogeny of literacy. The emergent literacy perspective has clear roots in some child development research and literacy research extending back to the beginning of this century. However, it is only recently that various social, educational, and research factors coalesced to lead to a widespread effort at studying young children's literacy development and to a significant shift in conceptualizing young children's literacy development.

Of course, numerous studies of literacy development in one type of young child, the early reader, have a history extending back some 40 years or more (Teale, 1980). But such children were always thought to be exceptional. Emergent literacy research treats literacy learning as much more nearly universal. By looking not merely at conventional manifestations of reading or writing, but considering also such manifestations such as children's rereadings of familiar books before they are fully literate, three-year-olds' uses of environmental print, or writing with scribbles or random-appearing letters, and by examining literacy not merely from adult perspectives but also from the children's viewpoints, we can see that legitimate literacy learning occurs in virtually every young child in a literate society like ours.

In the introduction to *Emergent Literacy: Writing and Reading,* Elizabeth Sulzby and I provided an account of the forces that shaped the emergent literacy perspective (Teale & Sulzby, 1986a). That account will not be reiterated here, except to remark that the notion of emergent literacy appears first to have been used by Marie Clay in her doctoral dissertation from 1966, *Emergent Reading Behavior*. However, it would be useful to consider once again the significance of the two words used in naming this new perspective. Let us begin with *literacy.*

The word *literacy* is of extreme importance, for it emphasizes that writing and reading should be considered in conjunction with each other, rather than, as has traditionally been the case, settle for a focus merely on reading development or reading readiness. It is clear from Read's pioneering research on young children's phonology (Read, 1970) and from subsequent work on a variety of research questions that writing does not wait on reading. Considerable attention has recently been devoted to the reading-writing connection in older children (Tierney & Pearson, 1985). The connection is equally important in early childhood. In fact, there is now (as we shall see in examining the research more closely) substantial evidence of a dynamic relation between the two, indicating that each influences the other in the course of development.

The word *emergent* completes the term. *Emergent* has considerable history in a variety of fields—philosophy, sociology, biology, and developmental psychology, for example. Though having somewhat different connotations in each of these disciplines, *emergent* describes something in the process of becoming. Such an idea is elegantly suited to describing literacy development in the young child for four reasons:

1. It emphasizes the notion that at whatever point in development we look, we see children *in the process of becoming* literate. As researchers have increasingly focused on literacy learning in very young children, it has become apparent that it

is not reasonable to point to *a* time in a child's life when literacy begins. Rather, the literacy behaviors and knowledges of one-, two-, three-, four-, or five-year-olds are legitimate parts of the literacy learning process.

2. *Emergent* emphasizes the continuity in literacy development. Reading or writing conventionally is not a process different in kind from emergent literacy. Many of the motives, functions, and uses associated with reading and writing, knowledges about reading and writing, and the psycholinguistic processes employed in reading and writing by children not yet literate in the conventional sense are identical to those of adults or older children (Harste, Woodward, & Burke, 1984b; Heath, 1980, 1983; Sulzby 1985a, 1985b, 1986b; Taylor, 1983; Teale, 1986).
3. At the same time *emergent* suggests *discontinuity.* Development is taking place. As we freeze the action at points in this process of becoming, we can identify new things—new conceptions, new psycholinguistic processes—that had not been there before. Children do become literate (whereas they had not always been literate), and it is in this sense that development is a discontinuity.
4. Finally, *emergent* suggests that growth in this period of development occurs without the necessity for an overrriding emphasis on formal teaching. Instead, the young child develops literacy in the everyday contexts of home and community.

Emergent is a forward-looking term. It suggests that children are continuously learning to read and write, that there is a general direction in which children are progressing. In short, it suggests development. It is hoped that this discussion of terms has helped set parameters for this review. Even so, it can legitimately be argued that a review of emergent literacy touches on a wide range of research literature (e.g., oral language acquisition work, knowledge of story structure). In many respects it is, therefore, difficult to specify what should and should not be included. Nevertheless, this discussion will be restricted as much as possible to children's developing knowledges about written language.

It should be kept in mind that the field of emergent literacy is itself emerging. Only relatively recently has there been a widespread effort by researchers to investigate the reading and writing of very young children. Another point can be noted about the overall body of emergent literacy research; it is characteristically descriptive in nature. Likely, this descriptive character of much of the research stems from a combination of factors. First, the area of investigation is developing in an era when descriptive and ethnographic research efforts have credibility in the wider research community. Futhermore, description is a sensible activity to engage in at this point in the development of the area itself. In many respects, emergent literacy researchers are still defining the nature of the area of inquiry, a useful beginning step in researching anything. Finally, the intellectual traditions of the researchers themselves have led to a heavy emphasis on description. Influenced by descriptive language acquisition research and by anthropological methods, many researchers have, in turn, attempted to describe the nature of literacy learning in early childhood.

Thus, *emergent literacy* draws upon both recent and well-established findings about young children and literacy development. Overall, however, research on literacy, language acquisition, and child development has been synthesized to arrive at a new perspective for understanding the nature and importance of children's reading and writing development during the early years. Research that has contributed to this new perspective is reviewed in the remainder of the paper.

A FRAMEWORK FOR THE REVIEW

How does one organize a review of emergent literacy research? One possibility is to build a *model* of emergent literacy, theoretically based and supported by research findings. But I do not believe we are yet anywhere close to having a model, *per se*, of emergent literacy. Too many studies remain to be done. A second possibility is to tell a *story* about emergent literacy research. In the end, the purpose of a review of research is to tell a story, and there will be a story to tell about emergent literacy. But I do not believe there is enough of a structure yet to tell a well-formed story either. Instead, I have attempted to paint a picture of emergent literacy. Perhaps because I am not an artist, I do not notice the constrictions of the form. Significantly, the choice is fitting for describing the current state of the art in emergent literacy research—a picture in its beginning stages. The best-defined part of the picture of emergent literacy is the general outline, the frame. We understand a great deal about the general context of literacy in early childhood—that is, the functions and uses of reading and writing for young children—and that is where the review begins. Subsequently, the following research areas are discussed: Early Reader Studies, Environmental Print Studies, Acquisition of Reading and Writing Concepts, Storybook Reading, and Classroom Applications of Emergent Literacy Research.

The Functions and Uses of Reading and Writing

Historical evidence (Goody, 1977; Schmandt-Besserat, 1978) and recent anthropological and psychological research (Reder & Green, 1983; Scollon & Scollon, 1980; Scribner & Cole, 1981) suggest that it is useful to view literacy in terms of its contribution to the ongoing struggles of people to understand and deal with their world. A number of ethnographic studies of young children's home literacy environments lead to a similar conclusion. Heath's ethnography of communication in two working-class communities (one white, one black) and one mainstream community (black and white mixed) in the Piedmont, Carolinas, showed reading and writing to be intimately connected with the histories and day-to-day lives of the members of each community (Heath, 1983). Her catalogues of the Types of Uses of Reading and Writing in each of the communities showed that literacy served a variety of functions and uses, such as instrumental, social interactional, recreational, and critical/educational.

Taylor (1983) studied the family literacy of six white middle-class families repeatedly in suburban towns around New York City. Though she produced no listing, she stated that the families used reading and writing to solve practical problems and to maintain social relations.

Taylor and Dorsey-Gaines (1987) also studied six families, in this case urban black families living in poverty. They concluded that literacy was part of the social world in which these children lived, just as it was in the white middle-class families of Taylor's initial study. All of the types and uses of literacy identified by Heath were in evidence in the families Taylor and Dorsey-Gaines studied. Observations even revealed new understandings of the types and uses of reading and writing that occur in home settings.

Research that I and colleagues at the Laboratory of Comparative Human Cognition conducted focused on the literacy occurring in the lives of 24 low-income Anglo, black, and Mexican American children in the San Diego, CA area (Teale, 1986). Findings on the functions and uses of literacy in the families reflected the results of Heath and Taylor. Literacy in the households mediated nine domains of activity including Daily Living Activities, Entertainment, School-Related, Work, Religion, Interpersonal Communication, Participating in Information Networks, Storybook Time, and Literacy for the Sake of Teaching/Learning Literacy. The vast majority of the time, literacy mediated an activity for which the goal went beyond reading or writing itself (e.g., to pay bills, be entertained, transmit information). Only in Literacy for the Sake of Teaching/Learning Literacy was the focus of the activity literacy itself, and this context constituted but 19.8% of the events observed and accounted for only 11.6% of the time that families were engaged in literacy-related events.

These studies, as well as other case studies of individual children (e.g., Baghban, 1984; Hoffman, 1982; Miller, Nemoianu, & DeJong, 1986), indicate that literacy is deeply embedded in the culture of the family and community, functioning primarily as an aspect of human activity (rather than a set of isolated skills). Such findings are important to emergent literacy research for a number of reasons. First, they clearly show that studying literacy development is basically an investigation of the acquisition of culture. The task for researchers is not merely to study in isolation the cognitive operations of children, but rather to understand cognition in terms of the social systems for utilizing literacy. In other words, motives, goals, and conditions are intrinsic parts of the processes of reading and writing (and of becoming readers and writers), and they cannot be abstracted away without losing characteristics essential to the attempts to analyze literacy and literacy development.

The theory of activity, developed by Soviet psychologists (especially by Leont'ev, 1981) provides a framework for this conceptualization. Leont'ev viewed activity as "the molar unit of life" for the individual. Activity orients the individual in the world. Neither the external, objective world, on the one hand, nor the person, on the other hand, is solely responsible for the person's developing knowledge of the world (Wertsch, 1981). Rather, the individual develops knowledge by the processes through which he or she enters into practical contact with the objective world. By conceptualizing literacy development as learning how to participate in a socially organized set of practices involving the use of written materials, we are better able to understand what is involved in young children's literacy learning. Bruner (1986) has stated that both the child's cognitive system for becoming literate and social systems for teaching literacy must be understood. Thus, what has traditionally been thought of as the psychological must come together with what has traditionally been thought of as the social (or anthropological) in order to understand emergent literacy.

Ethnographic studies help to provide the frame or background to our emergent literacy picture. They suggest that in becoming literate young children are, in a complex and simultaneous way, learning about (a) functions and uses of literacy, (b) attitudes toward literacy, (c) conventions of written language, (d) decoding and encoding strategies, and (e) comprehending and composing strategies.

Having established the frame of our picture, let us examine more specifically the knowledge and strategies young children are developing in the process of becoming literate. Findings from these studies enable us to paint many important details in our picture.

Early Reader Studies

Studies of early readers, children who learn to read before attending formal school, are of interest to our review of emergent literacy because they provide some insight into factors that promote literacy in early childhood. Early reader research goes back a number of years. Much of the research consists of case studies of one or two children (e.g., Krippner, 1963; Söderbergh, 1971; Torrey, 1969; Witty & Blumenthal, 1957; Witty & Coomer, 1955); several seek to identify distinguishing characteristics of small samples of early readers (Briggs & Elkind, 1973, 1977; Ellis, 1975; Harty, 1975; King & Friesen, 1972; Plessas & Oakes, 1964; Thomas, 1981); and there are a few relatively large-scale projects on early readers—i.e., Durkin's (1966) research from the late 1950s and early 1960s in California and New York, Clark's (1976) longitudinal study of 32 Scottish children, and Tobin's (1981) studies comparing early readers, non-early readers, and preschool readers (children who attended a preschool offering a formal program of reading instruction).

Investigators have sought to determine factors related to the development of early readers or factors distinguishing early readers from non-early readers. These factors were of two general types, with several subcategories under each type:

Characteristics of the child	*Characteristics of the environment*
Developmental	Demographic
Perceptual	Socioeconomic
Cognitive	Materials
Language	Parental Factors
Personality	Interactions
Habits	Attitudes

Discrepancies among the studies are considerable. As an example, let us examine two relatively recent studies. Thomas (1981) matched 15 early reader/non-early reader pairs of nursery and kindergarten children. To investigate similarities and differences among the pairs, she examined six major areas: auditory perception, visual perception, cognitive readiness factors, conservation, personal attributes, and home/family factors. She reported significant differences in favor of the early readers on auditory perception, visual perception, two of the three cognitive readiness factors (letter naming and language facility), conservation, and home/family factors.

Tobin (1981), on the other hand, as part of a comparatively more comprehensive study, examined 85 predictor variables grouped under 13 general aspects. Using a multiple discriminant cross-validation analysis, she found that early reading achievement was "associated with a relatively small set of circumstances" (p. 186). These circumstances revolved around parental assistance (which she found to have a greater impact than a formal preschool program of reading instruction). Specifically, she found that the types of parental assistance most conducive to the development of precocious reading achievement were (a) strategies that direct a child's attention to the relationship between spoken word and its graphic representation, and (b) informal games and similar activities that emphasize letter-sound correspondence and rhyming. Tobin added that a synergistic relationship between certain child personality traits (curiosity; being observant) and the parents' interest in promoting the child's academic potential may also have motivated early reading achievement.

Thus, in the one study we have two significant variables; in the other, many more. These studies illustrate the discrepancies not uncommon among early reader research. However, consistencies have also been identified. These are very important because they are strongly suggestive of positive influences on emergent literacy development. Repeatedly, findings of the early reader studies pointed to the importance of the adults in providing assistance. Parents made the task of learning to read enjoyable, and they assisted their children by listening to them and answering their questions about reading and writing. They also read to their children. (The only exception I can find to this in all reports on early readers is the child in Torrey's [1969] case study.) There is relatively little information, however, on what parents actually did with their children in interactions or on the actual nature of children's learning in learning to read. Even Tobin's characterizations of type of parental assistance are relatively vague (and they are reliability somewhat suspect) because of the fact that data on home/family factors were collected retrospectively, relying on parent interview or questionnaire. It should also be kept in mind that these children are special, in the sense that less than 5% of the children in the U.S. are early readers and that the subjects of these studies are largely Anglo children.

It might be said, then, that the early reader studies are important to emergent literacy research because they are a significant historical building block and they give strong indications of the significance of reading to children and providing a literacy-rich environment in which materials and adults are available to the child to assist literacy development. But again, the early reader studies provide only brush strokes in our picture.

Environmental Print Studies

A number of studies that have come to be termed environmental print studies have added other parts to the emergent literacy picture. Buildings on Ylisto's 1967 study of four-, five-, and six-year-olds' abilities to identify (in a series of six steps progressing from highly contextualized to more symbolic) 25 print items common in children's environments, Yetta Goodman and her colleagues (Goodman, 1986; Goodman & Altweger, 1981; Goodman & Goodman, 1979; Romero, 1983), Harste, Burke, and Woodward (1981, 1983), Hiebert (1978, 1981), and Mason (1980) all conducted series of studies aimed at describing what children know about print in their environment in various stages of contextualization.

Goodman's results indicated that children as young as age three exhibited print awareness (Goodman & Goodman, 1979). Goodman and Altweger (1981) and Romero (1983) conducted more extensive studies of the print awareness of three- to five-year-old Anglo, black, Mexican American, and Papago children, finding that 60% of all three-year-old subjects and 80% of all four- and five-year-olds could read environmental print. Goodman (1986) concluded that "the development of print awareness in environmental contexts is the root of literacy most common to all learners and the most well developed in the preschool years." From environmental print, she goes on to say, the child develops "a model . . . which includes rules about the features of written language in situational contexts" (p. 7).

Harste, Burke, and Woodward (1981, 1983) also found that three-, four-, and five-year-olds could identify words in environmental contexts correctly or produce responses that were pragmatically or semantically appropriate. Hiebert (1978, 1981) was specifically interested in young children's incorrect responses to environmental print. The vast majority of errors she found in the highly contextualized condition were of a meaningful sort. In the context-independent setting, though, children made more errors, almost all of which fit in the no response or don't know category.

In a recent study of print awareness, Kastler, Roser, and Hoffman (1986) investigated preschool children's developing notions of the forms and functions of written language. Using a branched-question framework to get 47 two- through five-year-old children to talk about a wide variety of environmental print items, they found that preschoolers exhibited knowledge of written language forms and functions growing steadily from age two to age five. At all ages, knowledge of forms outpaced knowledge of written language functions.

The environmental print studies suggest that children do develop concepts about the functions and uses of written language through contact with print in the everyday environment. They also suggest that knowledge of environmental print provides the foundation which enables children to begin learning about the graphic system.

The relation between knowledge of environmental print and subsequent reading achievement remains unclear, however. Mason (1980) has proposed that children are reading the entire context rather than the print when they interact with environmental print. Thus, although recognizing words on signs or cereal boxes is part of the young child's emerging literacy abilities, it is actually reading the environment, not the print.

Research by Dickinson and Snow (in press) found that ability to read contextualized print showed a weak relation to other measures of early reading and writing (e.g., phonemic awareness, print decoding, print production), suggesting that it would be a poor predictor of later reading achievement in school. Huba and Kontos and their colleagues (e.g., Huba & Kontos, 1985; Huba, Robinson, & Kontos, 1986; Kontos & Mackley, 1985) have conducted several studies of the relation between children's explicit understanding of the purposes of print and their subsequent reading achievement. Results have been varied, with some studies showing knowledge of reading and reading ability unrelated to knowledge of purposes and others giving at least indirect support to the notion that knowledge of purposes of print facilitates reading achievement.

Masonheimer, Drum, and Ehri (1984) studied directly the question of whether context-free word reading evolves out of extensive experience with environmental print. They found three- to five-year-olds who could read environmental print in context. The children's ability to read environmental print items declined somewhat when the full contexts were removed (no logo), but declined substantially when the item was depicted in conventional orthography. Futhermore, few children could detect graphic alterations in items (OcDonald's for McDonald's). The authors concluded that environmental print experience by itself does not lead children into word reading. Instead, they contended, some other types of learning experiences, for example, familiarity with the alphabet and alphabet letter patterns within words, are necessary for word learning.

Thus, studies of environmental print knowledge remain equivocal. On the one hand, they suggest that certain general literacy knowledge does develop out of children's interactions with print in their everyday environments. However, the relation between such knowledge and more conventional reading skills like context-free word reading has not been established. Our current state of understanding might best be characterized by saying that environmental print knowledge clearly plays a role in the beginnings of literacy. The nature of that role remains unclear, however.

Acquisition of Reading and Writing Concepts and Strategies

Let us turn now to studies that focus more specifically on the acquisition of reading and writing concepts in young children to see what other parts of the emergent literacy picture they fill in for us. How do children come to learn features of the writing system itself, and how do these features relate to what they know about oral language?

Distinctions between oral and written language serve as a backdrop for understanding a great deal about this aspect of early childhood literacy development. Clearly, there are differences between oral and written language. Some of these differences, for example, modality, are readily apparent, and though certainly significant to the issue of emergent literacy, are handled directly and rather easily by most young children. Others are at once more subtle, and more conceptual and (psycho)linguistic. These differences provide young children with interesting cognitive problems to solve. For example, there are structural differences between oral and written language (Chafe, 1985), as well as differences in what oral and written language are suited to do. Olson has long argued that oral language is more contextualized while written language is more decontextualized (Olson, 1977, 1985). That is to say, a central issue in oral language is what one means by a word or sentence; a central issue in written language is what a word or sentence means. Tannen (1985), too, discusses differences between oral and written language, arguing that oral language focuses on involvement whereas written language focuses on information. However, she also stresses that there is no dichotomy between the oral and the written. A continuum more suitably described the relationship.

Thus, in becoming literate, children must learn to deal with the distinctive characteristics of written language. Some scholars have, in fact, described the acquisition of literacy as a transition from oral to written language (Cook-Gumperz & Gumperz, 1981). It seems, however, that this description is too linear, too suggestive that there is some sort of abrupt shift from one to the other. As Sulzby (1985a) has suggested, some children grow up speaking in both oral and written languages. In any case, written language is another register with which children must learn to deal.

Different aspects of this very broad issue have received attention in research. One aspect of learning about written language relates to the conventions of print, such as directionality, or the fact that one reads the print, not the picture. Most of the research conducted in this area stems from some of Clay's early work in the reading behaviors of five-year-olds (Clay, 1967). Subsequent to the early research, Clay (1979) developed the *Concepts about Print Test,* several items of which tap children's knowledge of the conventions of reading written language. Other tests have items which measure these same aspects, for example, *The Linguistic Awareness in Reading Readiness* (Downing, Ayers, & Schaefer, 1986) and *The Written Language Awareness Test* (Taylor & Blum, 1980). Tests such as these have been used in various studies seeking to describe children's development and compare children on their aspects of knowledge of certain concepts of print. These studies will not be reported in detail except to say that they are aspects of emergent literacy and that children learn these conventions through interacting with print, not by teaching them in isolation or by *waiting* until the child is mature enough to learn them. Futhermore, they are not precursors to learning to read but are integral aspects of the process.

More central to the issues of this review is how children learn to use the print system to produce and comprehend written language. Ferreiro (1984) has identified two distinct ways of considering a child's written production: the figurative and the constructive. The figurative aspects (often considered the most relevant issues in early childhood curricula) are those related to the quality of graphic shapes, that is, handwriting, spacing on the page, and so forth. The constructive aspects are much more interesting. Instead of examining young children's writing merely to see how well formed the letters are, we should ask ourselves questions like these:

1. What is the connection among the elements used to write?
2. Are there systematic rules of production explored by the children?
3. What are the letters supposed to represent, from the children's point-of-view?

Such questions take us squarely into a very interesting area of young children's learning about written language—the conceptions which underlie their early attempts to produce or comprehend written language. This research focuses on many different aspects of the oral-written connection and virtually defies categorization. Thus, rather than pretend to offer some taxonomy of these aspects, it seems best simply to plunge into the work. Let us examine research related more to reading concepts and then address the writing research.

In attempting to gain insight into young children's conceptions of what is written in a written sentence, Ferreiro (1978) wrote four- or five-word sentences (e.g., Papá patea la pelota [Daddy kicks the ball]) in manuscript and in cursive, with and without spacing between the words, in front of four-, five- and six-year-olds from working-class and middle-class families. The sentences were then read to the children while pointing to the text in a continuous sweeping motion. Finally, the children were asked about the words they thought made up the sentence, for example, "Where did I write *papá*?," "Where did I write *pelota*?," "Where did I write *patea*?," "Where did I write *la*?" Based on the children's responses, Ferreiro proposed the following *psychogenetic progression* in the successive levels of development of children's conceptualizations:

1. Only nouns are represented in the text.
2. The whole sentence is attributed to one written segment.
3. The utterance cannot be separated in parts.
4. Both nouns appear independently; the verb is linked to whole sentence or predicate.
5. Everything is written except articles.
6. Everything is written.

Ferreiro emphasized that responses like these were widespread. Her results gave insights into the very beginnings of literacy, showing that children's attempts to understand the writing system start very early and proceed not according to adult logic. Initially written language is a way of representing objects or, as Ferreiro put it, is a particular way of drawing. Only objects and persons, that is, the referential content, are represented, but not the message itself as a linguistic form. The names of referents (rather than their figural characteristics) are what is drawn. Eventually children believe that the verb is also represented in writing. Children come to suppose that the text is a representation of the words of the utterance. At this point what is believed to be written is the words that are pronounced in the order of their emission (perhaps a representation of the logical structure of the sentence). In other words, the link between oral and written language is established. Finally, children can locate all the words. They assume that even function words are represented in writing and that there is a phonological representation of the utterance in the written text.

I have presented this one aspect of Ferreiro's work in some detail because it emphasizes two principles extremely important to understanding literacy development in early childhood. First, much of the conceptualization about oral-written language relations described in this scheme occurs prior to conventional assumptions about the correspondence between the parts of an utterance and the parts of a text. Yet, we clearly see that knowledge is involved in these early efforts to understand the writing system and that children are logically working through solutions to the cognitive problems they face in seeking to understand the relations. *Knowledge* and *cognitive* are key words in understanding what is taking place. Children are applying *logic* to understand the written language system of representation. We as adults need to understand the learning taking place. Second, Ferreiro conceptualizes this learning as a process of *construction*. Children, she states, "assimilate in order to understand," but they "create in order to assimilate" (Ferreiro, 1984, p. 155).

One other point about this work of Ferreiro needs to be made. Ferreiro refers to the six response types just described as successive levels of conceptualization. Though this research was not longitudinal, she argued that the data strongly suggested a developmental line, where the sequence of understandings is developmentally ordered. Ferreiro's work emanates from a Piagetian tradition, and like Piaget she has sought to describe stages of understanding about written language through which children go. The issue of developmental sequence is a central one for the area of emergent literacy, one to which we return later in the review.

At this point, however, let us focus on writing. The early conceptions of reading just described—that written language is initially a way of representing static objects, not a way of representing a linguistic message—resonates well with results reported by Dyson (1982, 1983, 1986) in her participant observation study of kindergarten children's writing. Dyson found interesting links among oral language, drawing, and writing in children's early writing development. In fact, as several researchers have pointed out, one of the primary distinctions children must make in learning to write conventionally is the distinction between writing and drawing. At first, writing is approached as first-order symbolism, just like drawing. Dyson found that often children were not trying to encode speech in writing but were making meaningful graphics they could talk about, much as they talked about their drawings. What the children must do, concluded Dyson, is discover that they cannot only draw things but draw speech. Writing as a symbol system, she argued, begins as a form of drawing.

Evidence of using graphic symbols to represent static objects can also be seen in the writing research interviews of Ferreiro and her colleagues. A child, for example, might make three graphs when asked to prepare a sign to label three peppers in a pretend market. However, the work of Ferreiro and Teberosky (1982) also described development in children's hypotheses about how the writing system works once they discover that writing is a way of representing speech.

Ferreiro and Teberosky described a number of principles, or hypotheses, children employed in learning about the writing system: the principle of minimum quantity, the principle of internal variation, the syllabic hypothesis. There is not space here to go through each of these principles in detail. A key point, however, is that children operate according to certain assumptions about the nature of the writing enterprise. Furthermore, these assumptions come to act as anticipatory schema in planning (and then conducting) writing. The assumptions the children develop are logical, yet they are wrong in the conventional sense. The assumptions are constructed by the child on the basis of interactions with the environment. Once again Ferreiro and Teberosky presented a developmental framework for interpreting the various stages children go through in these preconventional hypotheses about how writing works.

Sulzby and her colleagues (Barnhart & Sulzby, 1986; Sulzby, 1981, 1983a, 1985a, 1986a, 1986b) have also researched the writing of young children. In particular, Sulzby has investigated longitudinally the children's use of different forms of writing and how they reread these forms. Major questions guiding her research have been the following:

What are the forms of writing and rereading used by kindergarten children?

What are the developmental patterns of writing and rereading?

Do these patterns shift consistently as they are observed in the classroom setting and in individual interview settings?

Sulzby's work clearly shares many questions with the research of Ferreiro and Dyson. At the same time it takes a slightly different tack; it pays greater attention to children's *rereading* of their own writing, and it investigates both classroom and interview settings. It also brings together the writing and reading issues.

Sulzby has found that children used different writing forms for different tasks. They tended to use conventional or invented spelling to write short, familiar words, and employed less mature-appearing forms when asked to write sentences, and even less mature-appearing forms when asked to write stories or other pieces of connected discourse. In addition, Barnhart (1986) reported similar findings when using tasks designed to replicate Ferreiro's methodology. Furthermore, she found that children may produce invented conventional spelling, yet give explanations of the relationship between graphs, speech, and meaning that fit Ferreiro's lower level categories.

In two studies of kindergarten children, Sulzby (1981, 1982) analyzed children's rereading from dictated and handwritten stories. She found that seven categories of description could capture all of the relation of rereadings to these two forms of writing. Although this system furnished useful rankings of children and correlations with other measures, it lacked the precision needed to understand the relationship between writing and rereading.

A two-year longitudinal study of nine children (Sulzby, 1983a) reinforced the conclusion that the forms of writing and their relationship to rereading were critically important. Furthermore, it led to the hypothesis that developmental patterns in young children's writing were complex but understandable. In a subsequent analysis of the data from her 1981 study, Sulzby (1985a) reported that a group of 24 kindergarten children used the following not-yet-conventional forms when asked to write stories in one-to-one interviews: drawing, scribbling, letter-like forms, well-learned elements, and invented spelling. In another study (Sulzby, 1983a), Sulzby found that the same children would use different forms of writing when asked to write stories, if the setting were varied from in-classroom writing to out-of-classroom individual interviews. She has also reported that the use of a less mature-appearing writing form might be paired with a quite complex form of rereading. Children would often use a less-mature form of writing to accomplish a more-mature compositional task, and their subsequent rereading would also be high level (Sulzby, Barnhart, & Hieshima, in press; Sulzby & Teale, 1985).

Sulzby's most recent analyses were performed on story writing and rereading samples gathered from 123 kindergartners in October of the school year (Sulzby, Barnhart, & Hieshima, in press). Although children used a variety of forms of writing and rereading, interesting patterns appeared. Drawing, scribbling, and random or patterned letter strings were the most frequently occurring forms of writing. Very little invented spelling was seen in this October collection, a finding consistent with data from her other classroom studies. Scribbling was a widespread and tenacious form of writing. Patterns in scribble were found that previously had been reported in invented spelling; for example, children used hyphens, vertical lines, and dots to explore spacing between words. Furthermore, children clearly showed an intent to compose with scribble and subsequently reread the same scribble with the same speech over time. In these cases, children actually tracked the scribble with their fingers while rereading. Similar data collections were conducted at four other points during the academic year; therefore, longitudinal information on developmental patterns will be available.

As was mentioned previously, Sulzby has reported on patterns of development in young children's writing. Her conclusions, however, differ from Ferreiro's in a significant way. She found evidence of patterns of development emerging toward conventional performance. As has already been stated, though, children also maintained a repertoire of writing systems, sometimes relying on a less sophisticated form depending on the task. Also, she noted individual variation within any of these patterns of development. Thus, it might best be concluded from Sulzby's work that children differ in how they develop, yet these differences are not random but understandable when looked at from the children's viewpoints.

The issue of individual differences in young children's writing development is central to Dyson's work also. Dyson (1985) described the writing behaviors of three kindergartners. Her descriptions illuminated the complex and variable nature of the beginnings of writing. Similarities were certainly there, but so were differences. There was Tracy, the constructor; Rachel, the pragmatist and dramatist; and Vivi, the eager investigator. Dyson's work reinforces the notion that we must look carefully at individual children as well as at results from large groups of children in attempting to understand the nature of development in early childhood writing.

These studies are but a sampling of the significant work being done on the acquisition of reading and writing concepts and strategies in early childhood. Much has been omitted from this section that relates directly to what and how young children learn in regard to these concepts and strategies. The whole body of work on metalinguistic awareness and the young child's developing concept of word, as well as the research on phonemic awareness, for example, has only been mentioned. I have chosen not to detail these studies because extensive reviews have been published recently (e.g., Yaden, 1984; Yaden & Templeton, 1986). Suffice to say that work in these areas is intimately connected with emergent literacy and related directly to issues raised in this section. Also, the considerable and informative body of research on invented spelling has received but passing mention. These studies, too, have contributed greatly to the development of an emergent literacy perspective on reading and writing in early childhood. Again, however, it was felt that this area is reasonably familiar to readers and, owing to space limitations, has not been discussed in any detail.

Some general conclusions emerge from research on the development of reading and writing concepts and strategies in early childhood to help sketch in our picture. First is the characterization of the child as active constructor of knowledge and strategies. To understand children's thinking about how written language works, we must try to understand the systems they create and thereby see things from their perspectives. Clearly, children do not always employ adult-like thinking or strategies; just as clearly, however, their attempts are not wild guesses or imperfect imitations. They represent the working hypotheses that give critical insight into the nature of emergent literacy.

The nature of development is another significant issue in emergent literacy research. It was initially raised in research reviewed in this section but will be considered again in the following section. Hand-in-hand with any discussion of development should be consideration of individual differences in growth. To date, we have insufficient research information to describe a progression of what is learned when it comes to emergent literacy. The research just reviewed from Sulzby and Dyson, however, suggests that the Piagetian concept of developmental stages will not be adequate for describing the literacy learning that takes place. Even Ferreiro has retreated somewhat from the strong developmental stage interpretation taken in her earlier research (cf. Ferreiro & Gomez Palacio, 1982). This issue remains a critically important one for future research.

Finally, as one examines the research reviewed in this section, it may be easy to get the feeling that the young child is rather alone out there, being confronted with the world of print and trying to figure out how it works by her- or himself. Perhaps it is because of the nature of the studies done in this area. How young children learn what they learn about written language is also an extremely significant issue. Before attempting to draw conclusions about the process, however, it would be useful to examine storybook reading research, thereby focusing more on adult-child interaction in literacy and providing a more complete picture of how this all happens.

Storybook Reading in Early Childhood

Of all aspects of young children's literacy experience, storybook reading has received perhaps more attention than any other. The research in this area is largely of two types: *correlational studies* and *case studies*. In addition, an experimental study of the effects of storybook reading was recently conducted (Feitelson, Kita, & Goldstein, 1986).

The correlational studies can be traced back over three decades at least, and many have indicated significant, positive relations between early childhood experience in being read to and vocabulary development (Burroughs, 1972; Fodor, 1966; Templin, 1957), level of language development in prereaders (Burroughs, 1972; Chomsky, 1972; Fodor, 1966; Irwin, 1960; MacKinnon, 1959), children's eagerness to read (Mason & Blanton, 1971), and success in beginning reading in school (Durkin, 1974–1975; Feitelson & Goldstein, 1986; Moon & Wells, 1979; Walker & Kuerbitz, 1979; Wells & Raban, 1978). In fact, Wells (1982, 1985) showed that, for children in the Bristol Language Development Project, of the most frequently occurring preschool literacy activities, only listening to stories was significantly associated with reading achievement in school. In addition, correlational data are available from some early reader studies. Results consistently showed that experience in being read to was associated with becoming literate before formal schooling (e.g., Clark, 1976; Tobin, 1981).

The only experimental study on the effects of storybook reading is one recently conducted by Feitelson, Kita, and Goldstein (1986). They found that regular classroom storybook reading directly promoted children's literacy learning. Twenty-minute, daily storybook readings were implemented for a period of six months in three first-grade classrooms in a disadvantaged suburb of Haifa. Children in these experimental classes outscored children in control classes on measures of decoding, reading comprehension, and active use of language.

Case study research on storybook reading can, in turn, also be divided into two types: (a) what might be called anecdotal reports, and (b) descriptive studies. Anecdotal reports come from more general case studies of individual children's literacy development like those conducted by Baghban (1984), Haussler (1977), Hoffman (1982), or Rhodes (1979), from certain early reader studies (Durkin, 1966; Sutton, 1964), or from classroom studies like that of Putnam (1981) on the effects of a *literate environment* curriculum on kindergarten children's reading-related behaviors. These studies include many rich anecdotes about the role that storybook reading played in children's literacy development or, in the case of early reader studies, indicate from retrospective interviews that experience in being read to featured prominently in the histories of early readers. However, the focus of the studies was not on storybook reading *per se* and thus no attempt was made to systematically isolate and document the nature or effects of storybook reading.

Descriptive studies of storybook reading grew out of a dissatisfaction with the limitations of a quantitative, or correlational, approach to storybook reading research and from a desire to be more systematic than case study research up to that point had been about describing what actually occurs in storybook reading. This research has largely been conducted over the past decade or so.

Recent research has made it apparent that two complementary aspects of descriptive storybook reading studies can profitably be identified: (a) descriptions of the interaction that takes place during storybook reading (both parent-child interaction in home settings and teacher-student interaction in school settings), and (b) descriptions of young children's independent functioning with storybooks. Let us examine the interactional research first.

Storybook reading interactions. Descriptions of parent-child storybook reading generated by Bloome (1985), DeLoache (1984), Heath (1982), Ninio and Bruner (1978), Snow and her colleagues (Snow, 1983; Snow & Goldfield, 1982, 1983), Taylor (1986), and Teale and Sulzby (in press) and classroom storybook reading studies by Cochran-Smith (1984), Green and Harker (1982), Teale and Martinez (1986a), and Teale, Martinez, and Glass (in press) convincingly demonstrate that both in the home and in the classroom, storybook reading is characteristically a socially created activity. Children almost never encounter simply an oral rendering of a text in a storybook reading situation. Instead, the words of the author are surrounded by the language and social interaction of the adult reader and the child(ren). In this interaction the participants cooperatively seek to negotiate meaning. Viewing storybook reading as social interaction has revealed that reading books aloud to children is fundamentally an act of construction.

Examinations of the interaction have drawn our attention to several major conclusions. One is the description of interactional patterns and how they change over time. A study by Ninio and Bruner (1978) has become a widely cited piece of research in this area. Ninio and Bruner examined the readings of picture books by a mother and her very young (eight mo.–1½ yr. old) child and found that the events consisted of dialogue cycles and a standard action format. Snow (1983) also emphasized the routinized nature of storybook reading in her analyses of a parent-child in storybook reading. In addition, Sulzby and Teale (1986) and Heath (1982) reported that picture book or alphabet book reading episodes with young children are most often played out similarly to the pattern described by Ninio and Bruner (1978).

However, Heath also found that for older children the nature of the storybook reading interaction was different. In the two communities she studied where children were read to, when children were about three years of age, adults discouraged highly interactive, dialogic readings and had children listen and wait as an audience. Few interruptions, either by adult or child, occurred during the reading of the text. After the text was completed, however, parents often asked questions about the book or engaged children in prolonged discussions.

In studies of eight families in the San Antonio area that Sulzby and I have been conducting, we have also noticed such shifts in interactional patterns (Sulzby & Teale, 1987). But important to these patterns also is the nature of the texts being used. The Ninio and Bruner (1978) study involved picture/label books, which lend themselves to the action format they describe. When that type of text or an alphabet book is read, even to a four-year-old, the interaction pattern is often the same. The reading of stories is not conducted with the dialogic pattern. Thus, patterns of interaction evolve from the way in which the participants in the storybook reading—the parent, the child or children, and the text—come together. We must consider all these participants in describing changes in storybook reading interaction patterns.

Another interesting facet of changes over time involves repeated readings of the same text. Repeated readings of the same text provide opportunities to see the development of two sorts: (a) dealing with a wider variety of aspects of the text or with the text in greater depth, and (b) internalization by the child of the reading activity itself. Snow (1983; Snow & Goldfield, 1982) has described this first phenomenon in her case study of Nathaniel. In repeated readings of Richard Scarry's *Storybook Dictionary* over a period of approximately 11 months, she reported a move from discussion concentrating on items, item elaborations, events, and event elaborations in the early and middle phases of the study to a much greater focus on motive/cause issues at the end.

Case study data from repeated readings of *Cinderella* with one child from a study conducted by Teale (1984) show a similar change. Initially the discussion surrounding the text focused on identifying characters. In a subsequent reading, the focus shifted increasingly to what the characters were doing.

Martinez and Roser (1985) have also examined the effects of repeated readings, in this case, the effects on young children's responses to literature. Looking both at parent-child storybook reading and teacher storybook reading in a day care setting with four-year-olds, they found that (a) children talked more when the story was familiar, (b) as with studies just described, forms of talk shifted when the story was familiar, and (c) the responses to story indicated an increased depth of processing in repeated readings.

Teale and Sulzby (in press) were especially interested in the language and social interactional changes in storybook reading because their work is heavily influenced by Vygotsky's notion of cognition as internalized social interaction (Vygotsky, 1978, 1981). They described the changes in the language and social interaction that took place over a 14-month period in a mother-child dyad's readings of a counting book. In this case, not only did the level of discussion change from beginning to end (a shift from counting/naming to elaborating on the color of or sounds made by items), but also an important shift in responsibility for *accomplishing* the reading took place; the child gradually took over more and more of the reading. In fact, eight months after the first reading took place, the mother was able to capture a spontaneous reading on tape. She recorded the child reading the *Counting Book* to her doll Judy. The language and social interaction of the previous parent-child readings had become internalized to the point where the child was able to conduct the activity independently. (She even supplied both parts of the dialogue since the doll couldn't talk.) The way in which the mother mediated the *Counting Book* for the child serves as an example of Vygotsky's notion that teaching should always be advance of development (Vygotsky, 1978). Mother and child engaged a mutually constitutive process, reading the *Counting Book*, but as the child demonstrated that she was gaining more and more control over the task, the mother led her on to more sophisticated and elaborated readings. What mother and child did in interaction strongly affected the child's subsequent strategies for and attitudes toward dealing with the *Counting Book* in particular, and books in general.

Such studies emphasize several things about storybook reading and young children's literacy development. First, note that repeated storybook readings are both repetitive and innovative. Considerable language acquisition research shows the importance of routines to oral language development. The same can be said of storybook reading for literacy development. It provides a facilitative framework within which the child can operate. Repetition *is* important to language and literacy learning. Note also, however, that repetition does *not* mean repetitious. Subsequent readings are not mere repetition, but repetition with variation. Thus, the child has a generalized framework but freedom exists within that framework. Construction on the part of the child is a critical element in learning. Also, though, the essential role of adult mediation in literacy interactions should not be overlooked. Storybook reading is perhaps the best activity for making the dual construction of both the child and adult visible.

Independent functioning with storybooks. It may have been Holdaway (1979) who first drew concerted attention to the importance of independent reenactments of books for young children's literacy development. Subsequent research has shown that these behaviors play an integral part in the process of learning to read. Sulzby (1983b, 1985b) found that when children at ages two to six years old were asked to read a favorite storybook, they produced speech that could be categorized first as being an act of reading; that is, the speech was clearly differentiated prosodically, syntactically, and topically from the child's conversation surrounding the reading event. Second, these reading attempts could be placed into 11 subcategories in a classification scheme for emergent reading of favorite storybooks.

This scheme appeared to have developmental properties. There was a cross-sectional progression from younger to older children, with no two-year-old attending to print as the source to be read from and many five- and most six-year-olds treating the print as the source of the story. The intermediate levels on the scale demonstrated the children's growing ability to distinguish between oral and written language. As data from these independent reenactments were analyzed longitudinally, developmental trends were evidenced, with individual children moving from (a) strategies of labeling and commenting on items in discrete pictures, to (b) weaving an oral recount over the pictures in order, to (c) creating a story with the prosody and wording of written language, to (d) beginning to attend to the actual printed story, and finally to (e) decoding the story.

Sulzby's research and Pappas' recent work (Pappas, in press; Pappas & Brown, in press) on what she described as *protoreading* provide important insights into how children learn the registers of written language during the preschool years. As Pappas (in press) concluded, "the approximation observed in reading-like behavior cannot be explained simply in terms of rote memory. The ontogenesis of the register of written language, instead, appears to be just as much a constructive process as we have seen in other areas of children's cognitive/linguistic development."

Thus, the research indicates that a child's independent reenactments of books play a significant role in the ontogeny of literacy. They provide opportunities for the child to practice what was experienced in interactive storybook reading events. Also important, however, is that independent reenactments provide opportunities for the child to develop new understandings about reading in general and about the individual book in particular. The significance of young children's independent activities with books certainly has important implications for early childhood classroom practices.

Variability in storybook reading. It has already been mentioned that the language and social interaction of storybook readings differs over repeated readings. Another type of variation in storybook reading that has received considerable attention recently is that of differences among readers (either parent or teacher) of the same text. Variability in parent-child storybook reading is now well documented. Heath and her colleagues (Heath 1982, 1983; Heath & Branscombe, 1986), Ninio (1980) and Teale (1984), among others, have described variations among different parents reading the same book to their children.

The Ninio (1980) and Heath (1982) research suggests, furthermore, that some ways of reading have more positive effects on children's vocabulary development and school achievement than do others. Examining vocabulary acquisition in the context of joint picture book reading for high-SES versus low-SES mother-infant dyads in Israel, Ninio (1980) found relationships between dyadic interaction styles and language development. During the readings, low-SES mothers were less skilled in eliciting words from their children. The eliciting style of reading (mother asks what questions; new information is provided in form of feedback utterances) used predominately by high-SES mothers was positively associated with the development of productive vocabulary.

Both Roadville and Maintown parents in Heath's ethnography did read to their children. However, while mainstream Maintown parents immersed their children in book reading routines that helped the children learn the basic concepts of reading *and* linked book knowledge and experiences to other contexts in the children's lives, Roadville parents tended *not* to extend the information or skills of book reading beyond its original context. Heath concluded that this pattern of literacy socialization was linked to the children's future school achievement. Children from Roadville and Maintown both tended to do well in the early stages of reading in school. But once children reached the upper elementary school and the curriculum proceeded beyond the basics of decoding and sight word recognition to higher level comprehension skills, the achievement levels of Roadville children fell significantly behind those from mainstream families.

Heath's work suggests that it is not merely the presence or absence of storybook reading that affects the child's literacy development; both the Maintown and Roadville families read to their children. The ways in which Maintown parents actually mediated the book for their children—the language and social interaction surrounding the text—had a significant impact on the children's ultimate attainment of literacy.

Studies of group storybook reading in early childhood classrooms are also showing variability in the way in which adults read to children. Dunning and Mason (1984) analyzed four teachers' readings of a story and found the readings differed greatly. They compared each teacher's style of reading with comprehension patterns exhibited in her classroom. The characterizations of teacher style were global in nature, focusing more on the quantity and the timing (before, during or after the reading of the text) of teacher talk than on the content of the talk in relation to story information, but this research and a follow-up study using similar analyses (Peterman, Dunning, & Mason, 1985) reported that teacher reading style was related to children's comprehension and to their subsequent attempts to read text taken directly from a book that had been read to them.

Teale and Martinez (1986b) and Teale, Martinez, and Glass (in press) have examined two kindergarten teachers' readings of four different books. Developing an analytic system which took into account the language and social interaction of the teacher and children in class vis-à-vis the content of the story, they found that there were describable differences in the ways in which the two teachers read *Strega Nona* to their students. Furthermore, preliminary analyses on the other three books indicated that the teachers demonstrated their characteristic reading styles consistently across stories, not just on one occasion. Analyses of the relations between teacher reading style and children's story comprehension are currently under way.

The parent and teacher storybook reading style differences also have significant implications for early childhood literacy research and instruction. A key factor in the effect of storybook reading is how the adult mediates the reading, because of the important link between social interaction and cognition, in this case manifested as the relation between the adult's mediation of the book and the child's learning. The adult mediator has a definite effect on what the child takes from the reading situation.

The body of research on storybook reading has given us important insights into young children's emergent literacy. Perhaps because the activity itself is a characteristic routine and because of the fact that studying storybook reading overlaps with oral language acquisition research, this area of study has received more attention than any other by researchers. A great deal of work remains to be done, however. Longitudinal studies and studies with diverse social and cultural groups are greatly needed. Much remains to be learned about how storybook reading experience actually affects literacy learning. The surface has been scratched in the area of classroom storybook reading studies as well. We know that being read to correlates with reading achievement. But, for children who come to school not having been read to, can classroom storybook reading experience substitute for the more intimate one-to-one (or one-to-two or -three) interactions typical of the home? These and other challenging issues await future study in the storybook reading aspect of emergent literacy research.

Classroom Applications of Emergent Literacy Research

Let us put the final brush strokes on our emergent literacy picture by taking a brief look at classroom instructional applications of knowledge stemming from emergent literacy research. As with the rest of the review, the focus will be on the period from birth to the start of formal teaching, the emphasis being on literacy instruction in preschool and kindergarten classrooms. For the sake of organization, this last section of the review is divided into two general parts: (a) descriptions of programs that employ insights from emergent literacy research, and (b) a description of some techniques that relate closely to an emergent literacy perspective on reading and writing instruction for young children. In various places across the United States and other countries, individuals have attempted to translate what we know about emergent literacy into classroom practices. Five programs are discussed here.

Instructional programs. The first program considered is a preschool program implemented in a classroom of mixed three-, four-, and five-year-olds at the Boston University Lab School. Its characteristics are alluded to in the final chapter of Judith Schickedanz's *More than the ABCs* (1986). Briefly, the attempt is to use print to organize the daily activities in the classroom and also to make written language an integral aspect of the various dramatic play and other types of play activities in which the children engage. The emphasis is on integrating informal print experiences into the everyday classroom activities of the children. To date, only anecdotal information is available on the effects of the program on young children's literacy learning. However, this would seem a fruitful setting for evaluation studies.

In a recent acticle, Crowell, Kawakami, and Wong (1986) described an experimental kindergarten project being conducted as part of the Kamehameha Early Education Program. The goal of the project is to bridge between the child-centered experiences of the home and the more academic demands of the elementary school in organizing literacy activities for children. The authors described teacher-directed activities like the Morning Message and Story Reading as well as child-centered esperiences like writing, sharing, and independent reading. In another paper, Kawakami-Arakaki, Oshiro, and Farran (1986) have reported on research into the process of implementing the project with the teachers. Research on the effectiveness of the program is under way, but as yet no results have been reported.

A third program is a Kindergarten Emergent Literacy Program, developed and implemented by Teale and Martinez in classrooms in the metropolitan San Antonio, Texas, area. In the course of translating emergent literacy research into a variety of classroom practices, three particular concerns were the special focus of implementation efforts. One was writing. Means were devised for having children participate in the writing process daily (Martinez, Montgomery, Cates, Bercher, & Teale, 1985; Martinez & Teale, 1987; Teale & Martinez, 1986b). The second major focus was teacher storybook reading. Daily storybook readings and response-to-literature activities became prominent classroom activities. Third was development of classroom libraries according to design characteristics shown by Morrow (1982) to be associated with voluntary reading. Research has been conducted on the nature of teacher storybook reading (reported earlier) and on children's reading behaviors in the classroom library (Martinez & Teale, 1987). To date, however, no studies of the overall effects of the program have been conducted.

Working with 164 children, the majority of whom were black, in three Title I classrooms in Philadelphia, Putnam (1981) attempted to duplicate the kind of literacy environment common to the homes of early readers. She described the learning environment and the children's literacy-related responses in this program and in a traditional subskill-oriented reading readiness program which was used as a comparison group. The *literate environment* approach included activities like booksharing, writing, story reading, sustained silent reading, lap reading, and various response-to-literature activities. Putnam's conclusions indicated that children in the literate environment approach spent much more time engaged in holistic reading and writing activities. The teacher in the literate environment approach also had much more positive attitudes toward viewing children's emergent literacy behaviors as valuable learning experiences. Apparently these attitudes were adopted by the children as well, for they were eager to try to read and write.

A final program has undergone considerable research. Mason and her colleagues have evaluated the effects of a home intervention program on low-income, preschool children's early reading skills (Mason, 1977; Mason & McCormick, 1981; Mason,

McCormick, & Bhavnagri, 1986; McCormick & Mason, 1986). The intervention consisted of providing what Mason called *little books* to young children in their homes. Results from a training study in school (the little books were sent home with the children) and from the use of stories in a home intervention program showed positive results for children in the treatment group at the end of kindergarten and first grade. McCormick and Mason (1986) reported that the treatment made the greatest differences to those children who entered kindergarten with low vocabulary test scores. In their most recent studies, Mason and her colleagues studied, over a two-year-period, the impact of the little books on Headstart children's word reading, spelling, and story reading. They found that children in the experimental group outperformed children in the control group at the end of the Headstart year and by an even wider margin at the end of kindergarten.

Instructional practices. The foregoing were implementations of overall literacy programs for young children. In addition to these innovations, many researchers have investigated the effects of promising instructional practices compatible with an emergent literacy perspective. Let us close this review by looking at three of these.

One practice is the work of Morrow and Weinstein (1982) on encouraging voluntary reading through the use of library centers. They studied the effects of library design changes, a program that emphasized literature activities, and a design/program combination on the use of literature during free play in 13 kindergarten classrooms. Results showed that the change in literature use was significantly greater in all three experimental conditions, with the design and program conditions being as effective as the design/program condition. Literature use increased dramatically when teachers incorporated enjoyable literature activities into the curriculum and when they created library centers with appropriate design characteristics.

The second practice is McNamee and her colleagues' work on the effects of having preschool children tell, and subsequently dramatize, stories. Inspired by Paley's (1981) descriptions of her classroom, McNamee, McLane, Cooper, and Kerwin (1985) gave 195 three-, four-, and five-year-old children from 10 preschool, kindergarten, and day care center classrooms a chance to dictate stories to a teacher over a 12-week period. In five experimental classrooms the children's stories were dramatized in teacher-directed group activities. Stories from the experimental classrooms showed greater complexity and coherence. As McNamee and colleagues put it, basic skills need to be taught in the context of basic activities.

Finally, the research of Pellegrini and Galda on the use of dramatic play to increase children's appreciation for, and understanding of, literature has special relevance to early childhood literacy education. Pellegrini and Galda (1982) found that thematic-fantasy play was an effective facilitator of comprehension, especially for kindergarten children. Furthermore, Pellegrini (1985) has shown that structural similarities existed between young children's social symbolic play and literate behavior. In current studies, Pellegrini is examining longitudinally the development of specific aspects of play and aspects of literate behavior in children from age three to age six.

The programs and practices mentioned in this section should be heartening to early childhood educators. They show that insights from emergent literacy research can and are being applied to teaching young children. Additionally, the instructional applications are being researched. In an age when early childhood educators are under increasing pressure to adopt formal reading curricula, it is heartening to see that developmentally appropriate methods of instruction from a sound research base are being implemented.

CONCLUSIONS

It should be apparent that the field of early childhood research and education in general and the field of early childhood literacy development in particular is today invigorated and invigorating. We are in the midst of rethinking notions about young children's reading and writing; much as the studies of Brown (1973) and other researchers in the 1960s and 1970s changed the prevailing conception of oral language acquisition, the evidence gathered over the past decade has caused theoreticians and researchers to change their ways of conceptualizing literacy development in early childhood. The first few years of life are now seen as a time when important knowledge and skills are developed. Furthermore, we have come to understand better the process by which young children's literacy learning takes place.

Literacy is, above all, a cultural practice. Children use and thereby learn literacy in specific cultural and social contexts. Based upon my reading of the literature, I conceive of the process as something like this: Literacy is accomplished through the child's active construction, construction that internalizes social interaction and construction based on independent exploration of written language. The learning takes place through the child's active engagement with the world, particularly through language interactions with adults. Rather than being the product of lessons in literacy, this literacy learning takes place in real life settings for real life activities. Young children's literacy development, like their oral language development, can profitably be described as a process of guided reinvention (Lock, 1980).

Many issues critical to our endeavors to understand early childhood literacy development and many unresolved questions remain. Seven of the main issues and questions follow:

1. There is an interesting phenomenon of performance before competence in many aspects of young children's reading and writing. It seems that learning proceeds from whole to part to whole in development. We need to understand this better.
2. We have the question of how to deal with the compatible, yet conflicting, theories of Vygotsky and Piaget when it comes to literacy development.
3. In a related point, the notion of *scaffolding* in early childhood literacy development has also received considerable attention (e.g., Harste, Woodward, & Burke, 1984a). We must strive to understand better how environment affects young children's literacy learning. A traditional behavioral model of learning is dead. Vygotsky, however, is not behaviorism in a new cloak. Adults *do* play a critical role in young children's literacy learning. Things do not simply happen naturally in the realm of language and literacy; they happen culturally. It is in this sense that we need to see that the concept of scaffolding can be a useful one if it incorporates the notions that the interactions which lie at the heart of becoming literate are truly two-way streets.
4. A key issue is that of developmental patterns. I do not find the developmental stage theory (a la Piaget) adequate for describing the literacy learning we see in young children. But this does not imply that we should abandon the notion of development altogether. Clearly, as children learn, there is something there that was not there

before. The research by Dyson, Sulzby, and Harste, Woodward and Burke, however, also shows that the nature of literacy development is by no means straightforward. I find promising Sulzby's notion of there being developmental patterns in children's learning patterns that, though complex, are nonetheless describable. Her idea of a repertoire of strategies is certainly compatible with the individual differences so many researchers are reporting.

5. Phonemic awareness, print decoding, knowing the alphabet: what role do these play in emergent literacy? These are not issues that emergent literacy researchers should simply sweep under the rug out of fear that attention to them will only increase the tendency toward isolated skills and drills on sounds, letters, and words in early childhood literacy programs. Children do have to learn about letters, sounds, and words. I do not like many of the trends I see in early childhood education either, but only theoretically grounded research in these areas will help us see how these issues can be treated sensibly in the classroom.
6. Decontextualized language ability is a very fruitful issue for research. In some respects Olson's research (e.g., Olson, 1977, 1984) on this issue seems too dichotomized and does not resonate well with what ethnographic studies and the storybook reading literature tell us about how language works in real life settings. But recent research by Snow and her colleagues (e.g., Dickinson & Snow, in press) showing limited correlations between skill on tasks requiring decontextualized abilities and those requiring contextualized abilities while at the same time showing strong correlations between oral decontextualized skills and school achievement but no prediction from conversational skills to school achievement, reinforces the notion that there is something to this that we need to know more about. In some homes children do seem to grow up speaking oral and written language. Certainly there are important implications for the school to consider, that is, in regard to expectations and assumptions it makes about children's language, how it meets the language uses children bring with them from home, and how children's abilities to deal with language that is more decontextualized can be enhanced.
7. In regard to literacy instruction for young children, *developmentally appropriate* is a phrase that will be heard more and more in the coming years. Like *emergent literacy,* I hope it does not become a mere buzz word. Early childhood programs should not be built around skills or activities; they should be built around children and teachers. Insights from emergent literacy research to date and those of the future will help us better understand how to implement developmentally appropriate literacy instruction for young children.

The picture of emergent literacy is as complete as I can make it at this time. Many gray, and even blank, areas remain. But we should take heart at what we have learned about young children's literacy learning over the past decade or so. I can only hope that the enthusiasm and intellectual curiosity of researchers will remain as high over the next decade. I know that young children's enthusiasm and curiosity about reading and writing will.

REFERENCES

Baghban, M. J. M. (1984). *Our daughter learns to read and write: A case study from birth to three.* Newark, DE: International Reading Association.

Barnhart, J. E. (1986). *Written language concepts and cognitive development in kindergarten children.* Unpublished doctoral dissertation, Northwestern University, Evanston, IL.

Barnhart, J. E., & Sulzby, E. (1986, April). *How Johnny can write: Children's uses of emergent writing systems.* Paper presented at the annual meeting of the American Educational Research Association, San Francisco.

Bloome, D. (1985). Bedtime story reading as a social process. In J. A. Niles and R. V. Lalik (Eds.), *Issues in literacy: A research perspective* (pp. 287–294). Thirty-fourth Yearbook of the National Reading Conference. Rochester, NY: National Reading Conference.

Briggs, C., & Elkind, D. (1973). Cognitive development in early readers. *Developmental Psychology, 9,* 279–280.

Briggs, C., & Elkind, D. (1977). Characteristics of early readers. *Perceptual and Motor Skills, 44,* 1,231–1,237.

Brown, R. (1973). *A first language: The early stages.* Cambridge, MA: Harvard University Press.

Bruner, J. (1986). *Actual minds, possible worlds.* Cambridge, MA: Harvard University Press.

Burroughs, M. (1972). *The stimulation of verbal behavior in culturally disadvantaged three-year-olds.* Unpublished doctoral dissertation, Michigan State University, East Lansing.

Chafe, W. (1985). Linguistic differences produced by differences between speaking and writing. In D. Olson, N. Torrance, & A. Hildyard (Eds.), *Literacy, language and learning* (pp. 105–123). Cambridge: Cambridge University Press.

Chall, J. S. (1983). *Stages of reading development.* New York: McGraw-Hill.

Chomsky, C. (1972). Stages in language development and reading exposure. *Harvard Educational Review, 42,* 1–33.

Clark, M. M. (1976). *Young fluent readers.* London: Heinemann.

Clay, M. M. (1967). The reading behavior of five-year-old children: A research report. *New Zealand Journal of Educational Studies, 2,* 11–31.

Clay, M. M. (1979). *The early detection of reading difficulties.* Auckland: Heinemann.

Cochran-Smith, M. (1984). *The making of a reader.* Norwood, NJ: Ablex.

Cook-Gumperz, J. & Gumperz, J. (1981). From oral to written culture: The transition to literacy. In M. Whiteman (Ed.), *Writing: The nature, development, and teaching of written communication, Volume 1* (pp. 89–109). Hillsdale, NJ: Erlbaum.

Crowell, D. C., Kawakami, A., & Wong, J. (1986). Emerging literacy: Reading-writing experiences in a kindergarten classroom. *The Reading Teacher, 40,* 144–151.

De Loache, J. S. (1984). What's this? Maternal questions in joint picture book reading with toddlers. *The Quarterly Newsletter of the Laboratory of Comparative Human Cognition, 6,* 87–95.

Dickinson, D., & Snow, C. (in press). Interrelationships among prereading and oral language skills in kindergartners from two social classes. *Early Childhood Research Quarterly.*

Downing, J., Ayers, D., & Schaefer, B. (1986). *Linguistic awareness in reading readiness test.* Slough, England: NFER-Nelson.

Dunning, D., & Mason, J. (1984, November). *An investigation of kindergarten children's expressions of story characters' intentions.* Paper presented at the annual meeting of the National Reading Conference, St. Petersburg, FL.

Durkin, D. (1966). *Children who read early.* New York: Teachers College Press.

Durkin, D. (1974–1975). A six year study of children who learned to read in school at the age of four. *Reading Research Quarterly, 10,* 9–61.

Dyson, A. H. (1982). The emergence of visible language: Interrelationships between drawing and early writing. *Visible Language, 16,* 360–381.

Dyson, A. H. (1983). The role of oral language in early writing. *Research in the Teaching of English, 17,* 1–30.

Dyson, A. H. (1985). Individual differences in emerging writing. In M. Farr (Ed.), *Advances in writing research, Vol. 1: Children's early writing development* (pp. 59–126). Norwood, NJ: Ablex.

Dyson, A. (1986). Children's early interpretations of writing: Expanding research perspectives. In D. B. Yaden and S. Templeton (Eds.), *Metalinguistic awareness and beginning literacy* (pp. 201–218). Portsmouth, NH: Heinemann.

Ellis, D. J. W. (1975). *The cognitive development of early readers.* Unpublished doctoral dissertation, Northern Illinois University, DeKalb.

Feitelson, D., & Goldstein, Z. (1986). Patterns of book ownership and reading to young children in Israeli school-oriented and nonschool-oriented families. *The Reading Teacher, 39,* 924–933.

Feitelson, D., Kita, B., & Goldstein, Z. (1986). Effects of listening to series stories on first graders' comprehension and use of language. *Research in the Teaching of English, 20,* 339–356.

Ferreiro, E. (1978). What is written in a written sentence? A developmental answer. *Journal of Education, 160,* 25–39.

Ferreiro, E. (1984). The underlying logic of literacy development. In H. Goelman, A. Oberg, & F. Smith (Eds.), *Awakening to literacy* (pp. 154–173). Exeter, NH: Heinemann.

Ferreiro, E., & Gomez Palacio, M. (1982). *Analisis de las perturbaciories en el proceso aprendizaje de la lecto-estitura, Vols. 1–5.* Mexico City: Office of the Director General of Special Education.

Ferreiro, E., & Teberosky, A. (1982). *Literacy before schooling.* Exeter, NH: Heinemann.

Fodor, M. (1966). *The effect of systematic reading of stories on the language development of culturally deprived children.* Unpublished doctoral dissertation, Cornell University, Ithaca, NY.

Goodman, Y. M. (1986). Children coming to know literacy. In W. H. Teale & E. Sulzby (Eds.), *Emergent literacy: Writing and reading* (pp. 1–14). Norwood, NJ: Ablex.

Goodman, Y. M., & Altwerger, B. (1981). *Print awareness in pre-school children: A study of the development of literacy in preschool children* (Occasional Paper No. 4). Tucson: University of Arizona, Program in Language and Literacy, Arizona Center for Research and Development.

Goodman, K. S., & Goodman, Y. M. (1979). Learning to read is natural. In L. B. Resnick & P. Weaver (Eds.), *Theory and practice of early reading* (pp. 137–154). Hillsdale, NJ: Erlbaum.

Goody, J. (1977). *The domestication of the savage mind.* Cambridge: Cambridge University Press.

Green, J. L., & Harker, J. O. (1982). Reading to children: A communicative process. In J. A. Langer & M. T. Smith-Burke (Eds.), *Reader meets author/Bridging the gap: A psycholinguistic and sociolinguistic perspective* (pp. 196–221). Newark, DE: International Reading Association.

Harste, J. C., Burke, C., & Woodward, V. (1981). *Children, their language and world: Initial encounters with print* (Final Rep., N.I.E. Grant 79-0132). Bloomington: Indiana University.

Harste, J. C., Burke, C. L., & Woodward, V. A. (1983). *The young child as writer-reader and informant* (Final Rep., N.I.E. Grant 80-0121). Bloomington: Indiana University.

Harste, J. C., Woodward, V. A., & Burke, C. L. (1984a). Examining our assumptions: A transactional view of literacy and learning. *Research in the Teaching of English, 18,* 84–108.

Harste, J. C., Woodward, V. A., & Burke, C. L. (1984b). *Language stories and literacy lessons.* Portsmouth, NH: Heinemann.

Harty, K. F. (1975). *A comparative analysis of children who enter kindergarten reading and children of the same age who require additional readiness for reading.* Unpublished doctoral dissertation, University of Wisconsin, Madison.

Haussler, M. (1977). *A young child interacting with language in a print-oriented society.* Unpublished master's thesis, University of Arizona, Tucson.

Heath, S. B. (1980). The functions and uses of literacy. *Journal of Communication, 30,* 123–133.

Heath, S. B. (1982). What no bedtime story means: Narrative skills at home and school. *Language in Society, 11,* 49–76.

Heath, S. B. (1983). *Ways with words: Language, life and work in communities and classrooms.* Cambridge: Cambridge University Press.

Heath, S. B., & Branscombe, A. (1986). The book as narrative prop in language acquisition. In B. B. Schieffelin & P. Gilmore (Eds.), *The acquisition of literacy: Ethnographic perspectives* (pp. 16–34). Norwood, NJ: Ablex.

Hiebert, E. H. (1978). Preschool children's understandings of written language. *Child Development, 49,* 1,231–1,234.

Hiebert, E. H. (1981). Developmental patterns and interrelationships of preschool children's print awareness. *Reading Research Quarterly, 16,* 236–260.

Hoffman, S. J. (1982). *Preschool reading related behaviors: A parent diary.* Unpublished doctoral dissertation, University of Pennsylvania, Philadelphia.

Holdaway, D. (1979). *The foundations of literacy.* Sydney: Ashton Scholastic.

Huba, M. E., & Kontos, S. (1985). Measuring print awareness in young children. *Journal of Educational Research, 78,* 272–279.

Huba, M., Robinson, S., & Kontos, S. (1986, December). *Print awareness in prereaders and subsequent reading achievement.* Paper presented at the annual meeting of the National Reading Conference, Austin, TX.

Irwin, O. (1960). Infant speech: Effect of systematic reading of stories. *Journal of Speech and Hearing Research, 3,* 187–190.

Kastler, L., Roser N., & Hoffman, J. (1986, December). *Developing notions of the functions of written language among preschool siblings of successful first grade readers.* Paper presented at the annual meeting of the National Reading Conference, Austin, TX.

Kawakami-Arakaki, A. J., Oshiro, M. I., & Farran, D. C. (1986, October). *Research into practice: Integrating reading and writing in a kindergarten curriculum.* Paper presented at the Reading/Writing Acquisition Conference, University of Illinois, Champaign-Urbana.

King, E. M., & Friesen, D. T. (1972). Children who read in kindergarten. *The Alberta Journal of Educational Research, 18,* 147–161.

Kontos, S., & Mackley, H. (1985, April). *Development and interrelationships of reading knowledge and skills during kindergarten and first grade.* Paper presented at the annual meeting of the American Educational Research Association, Chicago, IL.

Krippner, S. (1963). The boy who read at eighteen months. *Exceptional Child, 30,* 105–109.

Leont'ev, A. N. (1981). The problem of activity in psychology. In J. V. Wertsch (Ed.), *The concept of activity in Soviet psychology* (pp. 37–71). White Plains, NY: M. E. Sharpe.

Lock, A. (1980). *The guided reinvention of language.* London: Academic Press.

MacKinnon, P. (1959). *How do children learn to read?* Montreal: Copp Publishing.

Martinez, M., Montgomery, K., Cates, C., Bercher, J., & Teale, W. H. (1985). Children's writing in a kindergarten emergent literacy program. *Reading Education in Texas, 1,* 7–15.

Martinez, M., & Roser, N. (1985). Read it again: The value of repeated readings during storytime. *The Reading Teacher, 38,* 782–786.

Martinez, M., & Teale, W. H. (1987). The ins and outs of a kindergarten writing program. *The Reading Teacher, 40,* 444–451.

Mason, G., & Blanton, W. (1971). Story content for beginning reading instruction. *Elementary English, 48,* 793–796.

Mason, J. M. (1977). Suggested relationships between the acquisition of beginning reading skills and cognitive development. *Journal of Educational Research, 70,* 195–199.

Mason, J. (1980). When do children begin to read: An exploration of four year old children's letter and word reading competencies. *Reading Research Quarterly, 15,* 203–227.

Mason, J., & McCormick, C. (1981). *An investigation of prereading instruction: A developmental perspective* (Tech. Rep. No. 224). Urbana: Center for the Study of Reading, University of Illinois.

Mason, J., McCormick, C., & Bhavnagri, N. (1986). How are you going to help me learn? Lesson negotiations between a teacher and preschool children. In D. B. Yaden & S. Templeton (Eds.), *Metalinguistic awareness and beginning literacy* (pp. 159–172). Portsmouth NH: Heinemann.

Masonheimer, P. E., Drum, P. A., & Ehri, L. C. (1984). Does environmental print identification lead children into word reading? *Journal of Reading Behavior, 14,* 257–271.

McCormick, C. E., & Mason, J. M. (1986). Intervention procedures for increasing preschool children's interest in knowledge about reading. In W. H. Teale & E. Sulzby (Eds.), *Emergent literacy: Writing and reading* (pp. 90–115). Norwood, NJ: Ablex.

McNamee, G. D., McLane, J. B., Cooper, P. M., & Kerwin, S. M. (1985). *Early Child Development and Care, 20,* 229–244.

Miller, P., Nemoianu, A., & DeJong, J. (1986). Early reading at home: Its practice and meanings in a working class community. In B. Schieffelin & P. Gilmore (Eds.), *The acquisition of literacy: Ethnographic perspectives* (pp. 3–15). Norwood, NJ: Ablex.

Moon, C., & Wells, C. G. (1979). The influence of the home on learning to read. *Journal of Research in Reading, 2,* 53–62.

Morrow, L. (1982). Relationships between literature programs, library corner designs and children's use of literature. *Journal of Educational Research, 75,* 339–344.

Morrow, L. M., & Weinstein, C. S. (1982). Increasing the children's use of literature through program and physical design changes. *Elementary School Journal, 83,* 131–137.

Ninio, A. (1980). Picture-book reading in mother-infant dyads, belonging to two subgroups in Israel. *Child Development, 51,* 587–590.

Ninio, A., & Bruner, J. S. (1978). The achievement and antecedents of labelling. *Journal of Child Language, 5,* 5–15.

Olson, D. R. (1977). From utterance to text: The bias of language in speech and writing. *Harvard Educational Review, 47,* 257–281.

Olson, D. R. (1984). "See! Jumping!" Some oral language antecedents of literacy. In H. Goelman, A. Oberg, & F. Smith (Eds.), *Awakening to literacy* (pp. 185–192). Exeter, NH: Heinemann.

Olson, D. R. (1985). Introduction. In D. Olson, N. Torrance, & A. Hildyard (Eds.), *Literacy, language and learning* (pp. 1–15). Cambridge: Cambridge University Press.

Paley, V. (1981). *Wally's stories.* Cambridge, MA: Harvard University Press.

Pappas, C. (in press). Exploring the textual properties of "protoreading." In R. Steele (Ed.), *Language topics.* Amsterdam: John Benjamins.

Pappas, C. C., & Brown, E. (in press). Learning to read by reading: Learning how to extend the functional potential of language. *Research in the Teaching of English.*

Pellegrini, A. D. (1985). Relations between preschool children's symbolic play and literate behavior. In L. Galda and A. D. Pellegrini (Eds.), *Play, language, and stories: The development of children's literate behavior* (pp. 79–98). Norwood, NJ: Ablex.

Pellegrini, A., & Galda, L. (1982). The effect of thematic-fantasy play training on the development of children's story comprehension. *American Educational Research Journal, 19,* 443–452.

Peterman, C. L., Dunning, D., & Mason, J. (1985, December). *A storybook reading event: How a teacher's presentation affects kindergarten children's subsequent attempts to read from the text.* Paper presented at the annual meeting of the National Reading Conference, San Diego, CA.

Plessas, G. P., & Oakes, C. R. (1964). Prereading experiences of selected early readers. *The Reading Teacher, 17,* 241–245.

Putnam, L. (1981). *A descriptive study of two philosophically different approaches to reading readiness, as they were used in six inner city kindergartens* (Final Rep. to the National Institute of Education, Project No. 0-0202). Philadelphia: University of Pennsylvania.

Read, C. (1970). *Children's perceptions of the sounds of English: Phonology from three to six.* Unpublished doctoral dissertation, Harvard University, Cambridge, MA.

Reder, S., & Green, K. (1983). Contrasting patterns of literacy in an Alaska fishing village. *International Journal of the Sociology of Language, Number 42,* pp. 9–39.

Rhodes, L. K. (1979, May). *Visible language acquisition: A case study.* Paper presented at the annual convention of the International Reading Association, Atlanta, GA.

Romero, G. G. (1983). *Print awareness of the preschool bilingual Spanish-English speaking child.* Unpublished doctoral dissertation, University of Arizona, Tucson.

Schickedanz, J. A. (1986). *More than the ABCs: The early stages of reading and writing.* Washington, DC: National Association for the Education of Young Children.

Schmandt-Besserat, D. (1978). The earliest precursor of writing. *Scientific American, 238,* 50–59.

Scollon, R., & Scollon, S. B. K. (1981). *Narrative, literacy, and face in interethnic communication.* Norwood, NJ: Ablex.

Scribner, S., & Cole, M. (1981). *The psychology of literacy.* Cambridge, MA: Harvard University Press.

Snow, C. E. (1983). Literacy and language: Relationships during the preschool years. *Harvard Educational Review, 53,* 165–189.

Snow, C. E., & Goldfield, B. A. (1982). Building stories: The emergence of information structures from conversation. In D. Tannen (Ed.), *Analyzing discourse: Text and talk* (pp. 127–141). Georgetown University Round Table on Languages and Linguistics. Washington, DC: Georgetown University Press.

Snow, C. E., & Goldfield, B. A. (1983). Turn the page, please: Situation-specific language acquisition. *Journal of Child Language, 10,* 535–549.

Söderbergh, R. (1971). *Reading in early childhood.* Stockholm: Almqvist & Wiksell.

Sulzby, E. (1981). *Kindergartners begin to read their own compositions: Beginning readers' developing knowledge about written language project* (Final Rep. to the Research Committee of the National Council of Teachers of English). Evanston, IL: Northwestern University.

Sulzby, E. (1982). Oral and written mode adaptations in stories by kindergarten children. *Journal of Reading Behavior, 14,* 51–59.

Sulzby, E. (1983a). *Beginning readers' developing knowledges about written language* (Final Rep. to The National Institute of Education, N.I.E.-80-0176). Evanston, IL: Northwestern University.

Sulzby, E. (1983b). *Children's emergent abilities to read a favorite storybook* (Final Rep. to the Spencer Foundation). Evanston, IL: Northwestern University.

Sulzby, E. (1985a). Children's emergent reading of favorite storybooks: A developmental study. *Reading Research Quarterly, 20,* 458–481.

Sulzby, E. (1985b). Kindergartners as writers and readers. In M. Farr (Ed.), *Advances in writing research, Vol. 1: Children's early writing development* (pp. 127–199). Norwood, NJ: Ablex.

Sulzby, E. (1986a). Young children's concepts for oral and written text. In K. Durkin (Ed.), *Language development during the school years* (pp. 95–116). London: Croom Helm.

Sulzby, E., (1986b). Writing and reading: Signs of oral and written language organization in the young child. In W. H. Teale & E. Sulzby (Eds.), *Emergent literacy: Writing and reading* (pp. 50–89). Norwood, NJ: Ablex.

Sulzby, E., Barnhart, J., & Hieshima, J. (in press). Forms of writing and re-reading from writing: A preliminary report. In J. Mason (Ed.), *Reading/writing connections.* Boston: Allyn and Bacon.

Sulzby, E., & Teale, W. H. (1985). Writing development in early childhood. *Educational Horizons, 64,* 8–12.

Sulzby, E., & Teale, W. H. (1987). *Young children's storybook reading: Hispanic and Anglo families and children* (Final Rep. to the Spencer Foundation). Ann Arbor: University of Michigan.

Sutton, M. H. (1964). Readiness for reading at the kindergarten level. *The Reading Teacher, 17,* 234–240.

Tannen, D. (1985). Relative focus on involvement in oral and written discourse. In D. Olson, N. Torrance, & A. Hildyard (Eds.), *Literacy, language and learning* (pp. 124–147). Cambridge: Cambridge University Press.

Taylor, D. (1983). *Family literacy: Young children learning to read and write.* Exeter, NH: Heinemann.

Taylor, D. (1986). Creating family story: "Matthew! We're going to have a ride!" In W. H. Teale & E. Sulzby (Eds.), *Emergent literacy: Writing and reading* (pp. 139–155). Norwood, NJ: Ablex.

Taylor, D., & Dorsey-Gaines, C. (1987). *Growing up literate: Learning from inner city families.* Portsmouth, NH: Heinemann.

Taylor, N. E., & Blum, I. H. (1981, April). *The effects of written language awareness on first grade reading achievement.* Paper presented at the annual meeting of the American Educational Research Association, Los Angeles, CA.

Teale, W. H. (1980). *Early reading: An annotated bibliography.* Newark, DE: International Reading Association.

Teale, W. H. (1984, November). *Learning to comprehend written language.* Paper presented at the annual convention of the National Council of Teachers of English, Detroit, MI. (ERIC Document Reproduction No. ED 255 871)

Teale, W. H. (1986). Home background and young children's literacy development. In W. H. Teale & E. Sulzby (Eds.), *Emergent literacy: Writing and reading* (pp. 173–206). Norwood, NJ: Ablex.

Teale, W. H., & Martinez, M. (1986a). Teachers' storybook reading styles: Evidence and implications. *Reading Education in Texas, 2,* 7–16.

Teale, W. H., & Martinez, M. (1986b, October). *Connecting writing: Fostering emergent literacy in kindergarten children.* Paper presented at the Reading/Writing Acquisition Conference, University of Illinois, Champaign-Urbana.

Teale, W. H., Martinez, M. G., & Glass, W. L. (in press). Describing classroom storybook reading. In D. Bloome (Ed.), *Learning to use literacy in educational settings.* Norwood, NJ: Ablex.

Teale, W. H., & Sulzby, E. (1986a). Emergent literacy as a perspective for examining how young children become writers and readers. In W. H. Teale & E. Sulzby (Eds.), *Emergent literacy: Writing and reading* (pp. vii–xxv). Norwood, NJ: Ablex.

Teale, W. H., & Sulzby, E. (Eds.). (1986b). *Emergent literacy: Writing and reading.* Norwood, NJ: Ablex.

Teale, W. H., & Sulzby, E. (in press). Literacy acquisition in early childhood: The roles of access and meditation in storybook reading. In D. A. Wagner (Ed.), *The future of literacy in a changing world.* New York, NY: Pergamon Press.

Templin, M. (1957). *Certain language skills in children.* Minneapolis: University of Minnesota Press.

Thomas, K. F. (1981). *Early readers: A comparative analysis of matched pairs and their performance on selected cognitive and effective variables.* Unpublished doctoral dissertation, University of Pittsburgh.

Tierney, R., & Pearson, P. D. (1985). Toward a composing model of reading: Writing, reading and learning. In C. Hedley & A. Baratta (Eds.), *Contexts of reading* (pp. 63–78). Norwood, NJ: Ablex.

Tobin, A. W. (1981). *A multiple discriminant cross-validation of the factors associated with the development of precocious reading achievement.* Unpublished doctoral dissertation, University of Delaware, Newark.

Torrey, J. W. (1969). Learning to read without a teacher: A case study. *Elementary English, 46,* 550–556, 658.

Vygotsky, L. S. (1978). *Mind in society.* Cambridge, MA: Harvard University Press.

Vygotsky, L. S. (1981). The genesis of higher mental functions. In J. V. Wertsch (Ed.), *The concept of activity in Soviet psychology* (pp. 144–188). White Plains, NY: M. E. Sharpe.

Walker, G. H., & Kuerbitz, I. E. (1979). Reading to preschoolers as an aid to successful beginning reading. *Reading Improvement, 16,* 149–154.

Wells, G. (1982). Story reading and the development of symbolic skills. *Australian Journal of Reading, 5,* 142–152.

Wells, G. (1985). Preschool literacy-related activities and success in school. In D. R. Olson, N. Torrance, & A. Hildyard (Eds.), *Literacy, language, and learning: The nature and consequences of reading and writing* (pp. 229–255). Cambridge: Cambridge University Press.

Wells, C. G., & Raban, B. (1978). *Children learning to read* (Final Rep. to the Social Science Research Council). University of Bristol, Bristol, England.

Wertsch, J. V. (Ed.). (1981). *The concept of activity in Soviet psychology.* White Plains, NY: M. E. Sharpe.

Witty, P., & Blumenthal, R. (1957). The language development of an exceptionally gifted pupil. *Elementary English, 34,* 214–217.

Witty, P., & Coomer, A. (1955). A case study of gifted twin boys. *Exceptional Children, 22,* 104–108, 124–125.

Yaden, Jr., D. B. (1984). Research in metalinguistic awareness: Findings, problems, and classroom applications. *Visible Language, 18,* 5–47.

Yaden, D., & Templeton, S. (Eds.). (1986). *Metalinguistic awareness and beginning literacy: Conceptualizing what it means to read and write.* Portsmouth, NH: Heinemann.

Ylisto, I. P. (1967). *An empirical investigation of early reading responses of young children.* Unpublished doctoral dissertation, University of Michigan, Ann Arbor.

THE EFFECT OF ONE-TO-ONE STORY READINGS ON CHILDREN'S QUESTIONS AND RESPONSES

Lesley Mandel Morrow
Rutgers University

Reading to a class of children in a school setting is valuable in developing literacy skills (Huck, 1976). It increases children's interest in books and in learning to read (Cullinan, 1977). It enhances background information, familiarity with book language, and sense of story structure (Cohen, 1968; Chomsky, 1972; Morrow, 1985). Those factors, in turn, aid comprehension when children themselves read. The vocabulary and syntactic structures found in books are often assimilated and become part of the child's vocabulary and syntax. Futhermore, reading to children is most always a pleasant event and helps children to associate reading with pleasure (Clark, 1984; Hiebert, 1981; Schickedanz, 1978; Teale, 1984; Tovey & Kerber, 1986).

The practice of parents' reading to children on a one-to-one basis is also beneficial to the development of early literacy skills. Home story reading stimulates language development and relates positively to beginning reading achievement (Chomsky, 1972; Durkin, 1966; Holdaway, 1979). Being read to at home also helps children develop print awareness, directionality in a book, sense of authorship, and book handling skills as well as metacognition about how to approach reading tasks and interact with adults (Clay, 1979; Mason, 1983; Tovey & Kerber, 1986). Recent studies have made it quite clear that the type and amount of verbal interaction between parent and child during story reading is a major contributing factor in literacy development (Cochran-Smith, 1984; Flood, 1977; Ninio, 1980; Teale, 1981). A primary goal of reading aloud is the construction of meaning that results from the interactive process between adult and child. During story reading, the adult helps the child to understand and make sense of the text in a meaningful way through personal interpretation of the written language based on the readers' experiences, background, beliefs, and purposes for listening (Altwerger, Diehl-Faxon, & Dockstader-Anderson, 1985).

Investigators have described interactions during story reading events that seem to enhance literacy development in young children. A pattern emerged. Flood (1977) found four variables that combined to predict success on readiness scores: (a) number of words spoken by the child, (b) number of preparatory questions asked by the parents, (c) number of evaluative questions asked by the parents, and (d) positive reinforcement by parents. Ninio and Bruner (1978) identified a four-step dialogue routine: attention-getting, questions, labeling, feedback. Scaffolding, in which the adult models responses until the child learns what is expected, has been reported by Applebee and Langer (1983) and Tovey and Kerber (1986). Cochran-Smith (1984) noted that story readings are based on cooperative negotiations of textual meanings (''life to text'' and ''text to life'') by both readers and listeners. Shanahan and Hogan (1983) found that minutes of book reading per week, answering children's questions during readings, and making references to children's own experiences were valuable. Roser and Martinez (1985) described parents as co-responders, initiating discussion, recounting parts of a story, sharing personal reactions, and inviting children to share responses in the same way. Heath (1980) reported that interactive behaviors during story reading change in time, the child taking on some of the roles played earlier by the parent, who then steps back from total direction.

For the most part, these studies took place in middle-class homes. Ninio and Bruner (1978) found that children in lower socioeconomic communities tended to be read to less than in middle-class homes or were not read to at all. In middle-class homes, ''why'' questions and affective comments were frequent; in low SES settings, when children were read to, ''when'' and ''what'' questions prevailed, putting children at a disadvantage when addressing higher level thought questions at school (Heath, 1980) and somewhat restricting vocabulary development (Ninio & Bruner, 1978).

The review of literature concerning interactive behaviors during storybook readings suggests that the process is crucial. Children's questioning and commenting responses throughout any story reading activity are a critical aspect in the interactive process. Torrey (1969) suggests that becoming literate must be done through learning, not just teaching. Children's questions aid their literacy development. Answers to children's questions provide a direct channel of information for them (Yaden, 1985). Yet, schools rarely provide one-to-one story readings. In fact, one survey of early childhood classrooms found that even when teachers read to whole classes it was on only half the days observed in a 10-week period (Morrow, 1982).

Most of the literature presented concerning the interactive behavior between adults and children during story readings and children's responses to these readings have taken place in middle-class homes with the parent as the responding adult. The present research focused on the effects of one-to-one story readings in a classroom setting with children from lower socioeconomic homes who in many cases had not been read to at home. One purpose of the investigation was to learn about children's knowledge of and interests concerning story meaning, print awareness, and sense of story structure from the questions and comments they made during one-to-one story readings. An effort was made to replicate at school the interactive behaviors that occur in home settings during story readings. The following specific questions were asked: (a) Do frequent one-to-one story readings at school increase the number of questions and comments children make about stories? and (b) Do such readings increase the type and complexity of questions and comments children make about stories?

METHOD

Subjects

The study took place in two day care centers located in the same county. The children in these day care centers were eligible to attend based on financial need; the maximum income for a family was $10,000 a year. Seventy-five percent of the children were from single parent homes, and 40% of the population consisted of minorities. Twenty percent of the children were referred by the Department of Youth and Family Services because the children had been abused or neglected. From a total population of 88 four-year-olds in the two centers, 30 were randomly selected for the experimental group and 30 for the control group. At the end of the study, completed data were available for 54 children: 27 in the experimental group and 27 in the control group.

Materials

Based on the following criteria, 10 different picture storybooks were selected for readings during the study. They were similar in length according to numbers of pages and words per book. They had well-developed story structures with delineated characters, definite settings, clear themes represented in characters faced with problems or goals, plot episodes that led to the attainment of the main character's goal, and a resolution. All stories involved characters and concepts familiar to preschoolers.

Procedure

Research assistants who were to work with the experimental group attended two training sessions. At session one, they reviewed guidesheets describing the procedure for reading stories to children and for prompting responses to the literature and then simulated the treatment with each other. The second session involved practicing the treatment with children and was monitored by tape for correct administration of the treatment. Research assistants who were to work with the control group attended a separate training session devoted to procedures for working with the children in that group.

During treatment, research assistants met with children individually once a week for 10 weeks. To prompt responses from children in the experimental group, research assistants were instructed to utilize three types of interactive behaviors based on positive interactive behaviors between parents and children identified earlier in the review of literature. They were to (a) act as *manager* by introducing a story with its title and some background information to provide some prior knowledge of the story; (b) *prompt responses* by inviting children to comment and ask questions, and scaffolding or modeling responses for children to imitate when no responses were made; and (c) *support* and *inform* by positively reinforcing children's responses, answering questions asked by children, reacting to their comments, and relating these reactions to the story and to real-life experiences. After each story was read, the research assistant asked the student to go back to the beginning of the book, turn through each page, and share comments or questions.

Children in the experimental group were read a different story at each meeting. At a particular story session, the same story was read to each child individually. All story reading sessions were tape-recorded. Children in the control group also met with research assistants once a week for 10 weeks. During these sessions, they worked on reading readiness tasks, such as color and letter identification. Meetings with all children lasted for 15 minutes each.

The first meeting with each child in both groups was used to allow research assistants and children to get acquainted and feel comfortable with each other. A story was read during this first session and conversation was encouraged about the child's family, friends, favorite television show, and play activities. The sessions were tape-recorded to get the children used to the equipment.

Administration of pre- and posttests. Pre- and posttests consisted of reading a story to the children similar to the regular story sessions. Research assistants administered pre- and posttests to the experimental and control groups during the second (pretest) and 10th (posttest) sessions. During the testing, stories were introduced. Children were encouraged to ask questions or comment during the story. Adults' responses to children were to be limited to brief answers if questions were asked.

Scoring procedure. Children's questions and comments were counted and categorized into types: (a) focus on story structure (setting, characters, theme, plot episodes, resolution), (b) focus on meaning (labeling, detail, interpretation, prediction, drawing from one's experience, word definitions, narrational behavior), and (c) focus on print (letters, sounds, reading words, reading sentences, book management).

If comments and questions were related to illustrations, they were coded first in their appropriate focus category, then counted again as a comment or question related to illustration. If a comment or question could fit into two coding categories simultaneously—which seldom occurred—it was coded in both. It was counted only once, however, in calculating total number of comments or questions. Total numbers of comments and questions were tallied separately as well as by overall total of combined comments and questions. The coding system was devised from the work of individuals who have studied young children's responses to literature in one-to-one story readings (Cochran-Smith, 1984; Heath, 1984; Morrow, 1985; Ninio & Bruner, 1978; Roser & Martinez, 1985; Sulzby, 1985; Yaden, 1985; Yaden & McGee, 1984). The coding system provided information concerning types and complexity of responses made by children and their interest in print material, with implications for instruction.

Coding practice sessions were held for all scorers. A reliability check among eight coders for four different subjects yielded the following percentages of agreement: focus on print, 100%; focus on meaning, 87%; focus on story structure, 87%; total questions, 88%; and total responses, 88%.

RESULTS

To determine if differences existed between the experimental and control groups, a one-way analysis of covariance was conducted for each of the major categories in the posttest measures: total questions and comments, focus on meaning, focus on structure, and focus on print. In addition, the analysis was run for the subcategories under the focus areas. The score on the corresponding pretest served as the covariate. The statistical model included the two different groups treated as one independent variable with two levels, experimental group and control group. A separate analysis was carried out for each of the dependent variables. Tests for homogeneity of within-class regressions, an assumption of the analysis of covariance (Winer, 1971, p. 758) were statistically nonsignificant.

Total Questions and Comments

Table 1 presents the mean scores for the pretests ($N = 54$) and adjusted means for the posttests ($N = 54$) for the children's total number of question and comment responses.

Table 1

Mean Scores for Comment and Question Responses

	Experimental				Control			
	Pretest	*SD*	Posttest	*SD*	Pretest	*SD*	Posttest	*SD*
Questions	4.28	(2.25)	9.88[a]	(4.56)	2.40	(2.97)	2.94[b]	(2.18)
Comments	5.42	(4.34)	14.42[a]	(8.36)	6.66	(4.94)	9.66[b]	(6.95)
Combination	9.70	(4.24)	24.30[a]	(14.68)	9.06	(6.41)	12.60[b]	(6.21)

[a] Posttest entries are adjusted for pretest scores.
[b] Posttest scores in any row are significantly different, $p < .05$, if they do not share the same subscript.

There was a statistically significant difference between groups on the total questions score on the posttest, $F(2, 73) = 9.54$, $p < .001$, with the experimental group mean showing more questions asked than the control group. Also, there was a statistically significant difference between groups on the total comments score on the posttest, $F(2, 73) = 20.63$, $p < .001$, with the experimental group mean indicating more comments made than the control group. Finally, there was a statistically significant difference between groups on the total questions and comments, $F(2, 73) = 30.62$, $p < .001$, with the experimental group asking more questions and making more comments than the control group.

Focus on Meaning

Table 2 presents the mean scores for the pretests ($N = 54$) and adjusted means for the posttest ($N = 54$) for the children's total number of responses dealing with meaning. The subcategories in the area of meaning are also shown.

There was a statistically significant difference between the experimental and the control group in the number of responses made in the meaning category, with higher scores for the experimental group, $F(2, 73) = 20.45$, $p < .001$. In subcategories, there were statistically significant differences between groups in the area of detail, $F(2, 73) = 15.01$, $p < .001$, in intrepreting, $F(2, 73) = 6.68$, $p < .001$, and in drawing from one's experience, $F(2, 73) = 8.05$, $p < .001$. In each case, the experimental group scored higher than the control. There were no statistically significant

Table 2

Mean Scores for Focus on Meaning

	Experimental				Control			
	Pretest	*SD*	Posttest	*SD*	Pretest	*SD*	Posttest	*SD*
Focus on Meaning	8.91	(5.78)	20.61[a]	(10.7)	9.23	(5.10)	10.63[b]	(4.90)
Detail	2.28	(3.55)	6.60[a]	(5.79)	2.23	(2.63)	2.58[b]	(2.32)
Interpretation, (elaborating, associating, judging)	1.50	(.70)	3.50[a]	(2.1)	1.10	(.85)	1.50[b]	(.75)
Prediction	1.50	(.60)	1.66[a]	(.77)	1.00	(.20)	1.50[a]	(.75)
Word Definition	0		0		0		0	
Drawing on Experience	1.20	(1.01)	3.20[a]	(1.42)	1.10	(1.2)	1.33[b]	(1.5)
Labeling	1.10	(1.04)	2.84[a]	(1.46)	1.20	(.75)	1.22[b]	(.70)
Narrational	1.33	(.98)	2.80[a]	(2.1)	2.60	(1.6)	2.50[a]	(1.5)

[a] Posttest entries are adjusted for pretest scores.
[b] Posttest scores in any row are significantly different, $p < .05$, if they do not share the same subscript.

differences between the experimental and control groups on predictive, $F(2, 73) = 1.20$, n.s., and narrational responses, $F(2, 73) = 1.01$, n.s.

Focus on Structure, Print, and Illustrations

Table 3 presents the mean scores for the pretests ($N = 54$) and adjusted means for the posttests ($N = 54$) for the total number of responses dealing with story structure, print, and illustration-related responses.

Table 3

Mean Scores for Focus on Structure, Print, and Illustrations

	Experimental				Control			
	Pretest	*SD*	Posttest	*SD*	Pretest	*SD*	Posttest	*SD*
Focus on Story Structure	1.08	(.75)	2.28[a]	(2.4)	1.82	(1.2)	1.08[b]	(.75)
Focus on Print	2.12	(1.0)	2.60[a]	(1.2)	1.40	(1.3)	1.5[a]	(.75)
Illustration Related Responses	3.53	(2.40)	9.64[a]	(3.50)	3.22	(2.2)	3.45[b]	(2.0)

[a] Posttest entries are adjusted for pretest scores.
[b] Posttest scores in any row are significantly different, $p < .05$, if they do not share the same subscript.

In focus on story structure, there was a statistically significant difference, $F(2, 73) = 6.26$, $p < .001$, with the experimental group making more responses than the control. Generally, there were few responses in this area and most subcategories were not used at all. Because of the limited response, only total focus on story structure was analyzed statistically.

There were very few responses in the category dealing with focus on print (book management, sounds, letters, reading words, reading sentences), therefore, only total focus on print was analyzed statistically. There were no statistically significant differences between the groups, $F(2, 73) = 1.20$, n.s.

For the number of responses related to illustrations, there was a statistically significant difference between the groups, $F(2, 73) = 16.35$, $p < .001$, with the experimental group having more responses in this area than the control.

DISCUSSION

It is apparent that reading stories to children with their active participation is valuable for building literacy skills. Reading to the entire class provides one type of positive experience and one-to-one story reading another. While one-to-one readings are not likely to take place in school because they are deemed impractical in time and staffing, it is important to determine if their benefits are such that they should indeed become an instructional mandate. The experimental group asked more questions and made more comments than the control. Since all sessions were analyzed and plotted, it was observed that by the fourth session, children began to respond to the treatment, then progressed steadily. Their increased responsiveness seemed to result from a combination of the repeated experience of one-to-one readings plus interactive behavior with adults. It should be noted that these children for the most part were not initially responsive to one-to-one readings. In addition, it had been an earlier policy in their preschools to insist that children NOT interrupt stories being read to the class.

The progress of the experimental group during the investigation reflected the stages of children whose parents had read to them at home from their early years (Cochran-Smith, 1984; Heath, 1982; Teale, 1984). Initially, they responded minimally, then began questioning and commenting, and finally responded at natural points in a story. The number, type, and complexity of their questions and comment increased with story readings.

Overall, the results substantiate other data indicating that adaptation to school programs of the literacy experiences some children have at home can make a difference in their performance in the school setting (Durkin, 1966; Morrow, 1983; Teale, 1981). One-to-one story readings in a school setting are able to increase lower SES children's question and comment responses to literature in number and complexity, providing a rich source of information for the child and the teacher.

Children were more interested in the meaning of stories than issues about print (sound symbol relationships, names of letters, etc.). As reading progressed, some interest for specifics about print began to appear.

The children also demonstrated that they were capable of more interpretive responses than one might expect in early childhood, such as associating and elaborating. We need to accommodate that capability by providing discussions on an interpretive level, a departure from typical early reading activities with literal thinking and the mechanics of reading emphasized more than its meaning.

Because many children are not offered the opportunity of one-to-one reading at home and are thus at a disadvantage in their literacy development, it seems necessary to carry out strategies in school that make up for what is not provided at home. Whole class readings alone cannot accomplish the vital interactive responses between adult and child that are so important in literacy development. While it is difficult for a teacher to provide one-to-one readings, aides, volunteers, and older children can read to youngsters one-to-one to help solve the problem. In addition, many school districts have federal funding to work with early childhood youngsters identified as possible learning problems. In these situations the teacher–child ratio can be as low as five children with one teacher. Certainly, one-to-one readings can take place in this setting as part of their literacy development program. We also need to include instruction in interactive story reading behavior in our preservice and inservice teacher education and to continuously inform parents about the importance of reading to their children.

REFERENCES

Altwerger, A., Diehl-Faxon, J., & Dockstader-Anderson, K. (1985). Read-aloud events as meaning construction. *Language Arts, 62,* 476–484.

Applebee, A. N., & Langer, J. A. (1983). Instructional scaffolding: Reading and writing as natural language activities. *Language Arts, 60,* 168–175.

Chomsky, C. (1972). Stages in language development and reading exposure. *Harvard Educational Review, 42,* 1–33.

Clark, M. M. (1984). Literacy at home and at school: Insights from a study of young fluent readers. In J. Goelman, A. A. Oberg, & F. Smith (Eds.), *Awakening to literacy.* London: Heinemann.

Clay, M. M. (1979). *Reading: The patterning of complex behavior.* Auckland: Heinemann.

Cochran-Smith, M. (1984). *The making of a reader.* Norwood, NJ: Ablex.

Cohen, D. (1968). The effect of literature on vocabulary and reading achievement. *Elementary English, 45,* 209–213, 217.

Cullinan, B. (1977). Books in the life of the young child. In B. Cullinan & C. Carmichael (Eds.), *Literature and young children.* Urbana, IL: National Council of Teachers of English.

Durkin, D. (1966). *Children who read early.* New York: Teachers College Press.

Flood, J. (1977). Parental styles in reading episodes with young children. *The Reading Teacher, 30,* 864–867.

Heath, S. B. (1980). The functions and uses of literacy. *Journal of Communication, 30,* 123–133.

Heath, S. B. (1982). What no bedtime story means. *Language in Society, 11,* 49–76.

Heath, S. B. (1984). The achievement of preschool literacy for mother and child. In H. Goelman, A. A. Oberg, & F. Smith (Eds.), *Awakening to literacy.* London: Heinemann.

Hiebert, E. H. (1981). Developmental patterns and interrelationships of preschool children's print awareness. *Reading Research Quarterly, 16,* 236–260.

Holdaway, D. (1979). *The foundations of literacy.* Sydney: Ashton Scholastic.

Huck, C. (1976). *Children's literature in the elementary school* (3rd ed.). New York: Holt, Rinehart & Winston.

Mason, J. M. (1983, March). *Acquisition of knowledge about reading in the preschool period: An update and extension.* Paper presented at the Society for Research in Child Development Convention, Detroit.

Morrow, L. M. (1982). Relationships between literature programs, library corner designs and children's use of literature. *Journal of Educational Research, 75,* 339–344.

Morrow, L. M. (1983). Home and school correlates of early interest in literature. *Journal of Educational Research, 76,* 24–30.

Morrow, L. M. (1985). Retelling stories: A strategy for improving children's comprehension, concept of story structure and oral language complexity. *Elementary School Journal, 85,* 647–661.

Ninio, A. (1980). Picture-book reading in mother-infant dyads belonging to two subgroups in Israel. *Child Development, 51,* 587–590.

Ninio, A., & Bruner, J. (1978). The achievement and antecedents of labelling. *Journal of Child Language, 5,* 1–15.

Roser, N., & Martinez, M. (1985). Roles adults play in preschoolers' response to literature. *Language Arts, 62,* 485–490.

Schickedanz, J. A. (1978). Please read that story again: Exploring relationships between story reading and learning to read. *Young Children, 33,* 48–55.

Shanahan, T., & Hogan, V. (1983). Parent reading style and children's print awareness. In J. A. Niles & L. A. Harris (Eds.), *Searches for meaning in reading/language processing and instruction* (pp. 212–217). Thirty-second Yearbook of the National Reading Conference. Rochester, NY: National Reading Conference.

Sulzby, E. (1985). Children's emergent reading of favorite books: A developmental study. *Reading Research Quarterly, 20,* 458–481.

Teale, W. H. (1981). Parents reading to their children: What we know and need to know. *Language Arts, 58,* 902–911.

Teale, W. H. (1984). Reading to young children: Its significance for literacy development. In H. Goelman, A. A. Oberg, & F. Smith (Eds.), *Awakening to literacy.* London: Heinemann.

Torrey, J. (1969). Learning to read without a teacher. *Elementary English, 46,* 550–556, 658.

Tovey, D. R., & Kerber, J. E. (Eds.). (1986). *Roles in literacy learning—A new perspective.* Newark, DE: International Reading Association.

Winer, B. J. (1971). *Statistical principles in experimental design.* New York: McGraw-Hill.

Yaden, D. (1985, December). *Preschooler's spontaneous inquiries about print and books.* Paper presented at the annual meeting of the National Reading Conference, San Diego, CA.

Yaden, D. B., Jr., & McGee, L. M. (1984). Reading as a meaning-seeking activity: What children's questions reveal. In J. A. Niles & L. A. Harris (Eds.), *Changing perspectives on research in reading/language processing and instruction* (pp. 101–109). Thirty-third Yearbook of the National Reading Conference. Rochester, NY: National Reading Conference.

UNDERSTANDINGS OF THE FORMS AND FUNCTIONS OF WRITTEN LANGUAGE: INSIGHTS FROM CHILDREN AND PARENTS

Lesa A. Kastler,
Nancy L. Roser, and
James V. Hoffman
University of Texas-Austin

During the past 15 years there has been a marked increase in research attention directed toward what young children know about written language, especially prior to their entering formal school programs. Documentation of this accruing knowledge comes from longitudinal studies of early readers (e.g., Clark, 1976; Durkin, 1966), case studies of individual children's reading acquisition (e.g., Baghban, 1984; Soderbergh, 1971; Torrey, 1973), investigations of children's developing concepts about reading (e.g., Downing, 1969, 1970; Ferreiro & Teberosky, 1982; Mason, 1980, 1982, 1984; Reid, 1966), and investigations of children's knowledge about environmental print (e.g., Goodall, 1984; Goodman & Altwerger, 1981; Harste, Burke, & Woodward, 1982; Hiebert, 1978, 1981; Ylisto, 1967). What is clear is that children do in fact have a considerable amount of knowledge about literacy before they come in contact with formal school programs. What is less clear is the kind of knowledge they have about the forms and, especially, functions of written language. Goodman and Goodman (1979), Mason (1980, 1982, 1984), Smith (1976), and Teale (1978), among others, argue that children often understand the functional nature of print before they recognize the print they encounter. With respect to function, for example, it has been demonstrated that children expect print to be meaningful (Harste, Burke, & Woodward, 1982) and that children exhibit a better understanding of the function of writing than of reading (Goodman & Altwerger, 1981). However, there exists to date no systematic description of children's perceptions of the functions of written language. In an attempt to address this need, we investigated children's knowledge about written language—before they became readers—by listening to their language of explanation for the forms and functions of selected written language examples. In particular, we were interested in learning what children growing up in homes in which an older child had already achieved success with learning to read know about print, as well as discovering how parents account for their children's success in becoming literate.

METHOD

Subjects

A total sample of 54 younger siblings of successful first-grade readers was identified. Officials in the Austin Independent School District selected 15 elementary schools to assist in the identification of participants. At the end of the school year, first-grade teachers nominated children in their classes whom they considered to be successful readers. These children may or may not have been reading upon entrance to first grade because teachers were instructed to identify children whom they felt profited from the year's instruction. End of the year Iowa Test of Basic Skills (ITBS) scores offered some validation for the teachers' nominations of successful readers. Reading grade level equivalent scores for nominees ranged from 1.5 to 4.9, with 84% of these children receiving percentile ranks of 75 or above. Parents of nominees received letters describing our project and requesting volunteer participation if there was a younger sibling between the ages of two and five in the family. Of the 54 families who agreed to participate, 47 usable interviews were obtained from six two-year-olds, 13 three-year-olds, 20 four-year-olds, and eight five-year-olds.

Materials

To provide a context for discussion, we created a set of seventy-seven 2″×2″ color slides representing a comprehensive sampling of written language. This set was reviewed by graduate students in reading education. Using their suggestions, a revised list served as the guide for creating a final set of slides picturing the actual print examples in their natural contexts. Slides rather than the actual items were chosen as the means of presentation to allow for a broader representation of print forms (e.g., a STOP sign) in contextualized settings. Pilot testing of the slide set was accomplished with seven preschool and 20 first-grade children and confirmed the efficacy of these materials as stimuli for discussion.

Parent interviews were organized around a set of guiding questions designed to elicit talk in four literacy-related areas: (a) the home literacy environment, (b) the child's patterns of literacy acquisition, (c) the parents' attributions for success in reading, and (d) the parents' expectations for the children in reading.

Procedure

We held an interview/conversation with each child about the set of slides either in the home or, if more convenient for the parent, at the university. A parent interview followed. All the data were audio-recorded in one setting, with each visit taking between one to two hours. The slide interview attempted to tap (a) the child's categorization of the example with respect to its *form*, (b) the child's notion of the material's *function* (purposes of the specific print), and (c) the child's notion of the material's user (typically, adult, child, self, reader, nonreader, or inclusive). None of the questions required a *reading* response. For each print item, the first question was "What is this?". If a general response was given, the child was asked to be more specific; for example, "What KIND of *book, magazine, etc.*?". Using the child's label, the next question was typically, for example, "What makes you think it's a *storybook*?''. At this point, we attempted to focus attention on the print by asking ''What's on it?''. A print-related response led us to questions of function (''What is ____________ for?'') and user (''Who would use ____________?''). If a print-related response did not emerge, we framed the print with our hands and asked ''What is this?''. This questioning framework provided guidance for exploring the children's concepts about the print items using child labels and language rather than a fixed, unalterable script based on adult assumptions about the particular print examples. At least one parent of each of the preschoolers observed their young child's responses to the slides and, following the slides, provided their insights about their child's responses as well as about both of their children's literacy development.

Analysis. Documentation of the knowledge we found represented in the responses of these children comes from two ways we inspected these data. For the initial analysis of children's form/function responses we chose to apply a judgment criterion that mirrors a reader's knowledge. For each slide, the research team established criteria representing the essential literacy-related information contained in the example. We asked whether the form response *reflected* rather than reproduced a label which would be easily understood by a literate person. We inspected the function response for a literate person's understanding of the way print functions in a particular instance. Under this system, scoring produced a 0 or 1 for form and a 0 or 1 for function for each slide.

To illustrate, we will apply this scoring system to the slide picturing Humpty Dumpty and verse. To receive credit for form, the child must have shown some awareness of this example as a unique form of print: a poem, a rhyme, a nursery rhyme, or the particular nursery rhyme, Humpty Dumpty. For function credit, the child must have indicated that the print was for reading. Responses receiving credit for form included ''Humpty Dumpty fell off the wall and had a great fall,'' and ''a Dumpy sat on the wall and he's have a great fall.'' Responses such as the following did not receive form credit: ''a man,'' and ''a picture.'' The next set of responses exemplifies those responses that earned function credit: ''[indicating the print] To tell how you say, how you say the Humpty Dumpty song.'' and ''[again indicating the print] to tell you the story.'' Not receiving function credit were responses such as, ''for see,'' and ''B H J.''

By adopting somewhat strict criteria in what was an initial phase of analysis, we were able to describe the children's knowledge at a fairly sophisticated conceptual level. While we would never expect a young user of language to supply the exact label or to articulate the function as a literate individual might, we wished to capture a sense of the most complete information held by the children. Tallying the responses scored in the manner described enabled us to report the amount of form-function information held by children of each age group.

Our second analysis was an attempt to devise a categorization system which would enable us to preserve the children's responses so that we could inspect *their* language of explanation for form (what the print is) and function (what the print is for) across age by slide and by child; that is, we wanted to let the children's language guide the analysis rather than adult-imposed criteria of correctness. For each slide, then, we grouped the children's responses that communicated similar messages, preserving the essence of their labeling/explanatory language. In addition to the categories generated by the agreement among children's responses, we included categories for nonresponse and other, where the less frequent responses were placed. These language groupings, in turn, enabled us to construct a form-function matrix for each slide to graphically represent the range of responses offered by these children overall, as well as across age groups. These matrices provided the means for inspecting their increasingly successful approximations of the forms and functions of print.

Again, we will use the Humpty Dumpty slide to illustrate. Categories of responses for form were placed along the vertical axis and included "Humpty Dumpty," "Man/Guy," "Letter," "No Response," and "Other." Function response categories, then, were placed along the horizontal axis and included "Tells story," "Reading," "Counting," "No Response," and "Other." To complete the matrix we placed a tally mark in the box where the categories for an individual's form and function responses intersected.

Parent interview tapes were analyzed in the following manner. Each research associate independently listened to the interview tapes, collected notes in the form of verbatim quotes from the parents, and met to compare notes. Working together, we identified dominant themes which reflected the areas receiving the most elaboration in the parents' comments. Where there were discrepancies in the original notes, we returned to the tapes for clarification. Having identified major themes, we again returned to the original tapes and notes to reanalyze the interviews for specific support or exceptions to the identified themes.

RESULTS

These children have guided our learning by providing insights into the characteristics of early knowledge about written language. In particular, they hold surprisingly well-developed notions of the forms and functions of print and they are sensitive to how print is useful in a variety of contexts. We chose to illustrate these insights in two ways: (a) by demonstrating changes in children's ability across age groups to identify the forms and functions of print when adult criteria are used to judge their responses and (b) by characterizing the qualitative differences in children's language as they talked about an example of environmental print.

Children's Form-Function Knowledge in Relation to Adult Judgment Criteria

As one would expect, our results show that older children supply more correct labels and more precise explanations of print use than do younger children. Even with the somewhat strict scoring standards of our first analysis, children as young as two years of age indicated some ability to articulate form and function of certain slide samples. Further, children appeared to continue to grow in form-function knowledge across the preschool years. At each age level, children identified more of the form or formats of print than print functions. Even so, the gap between form and function knowledge narrowed with age. (See Figure 1.)

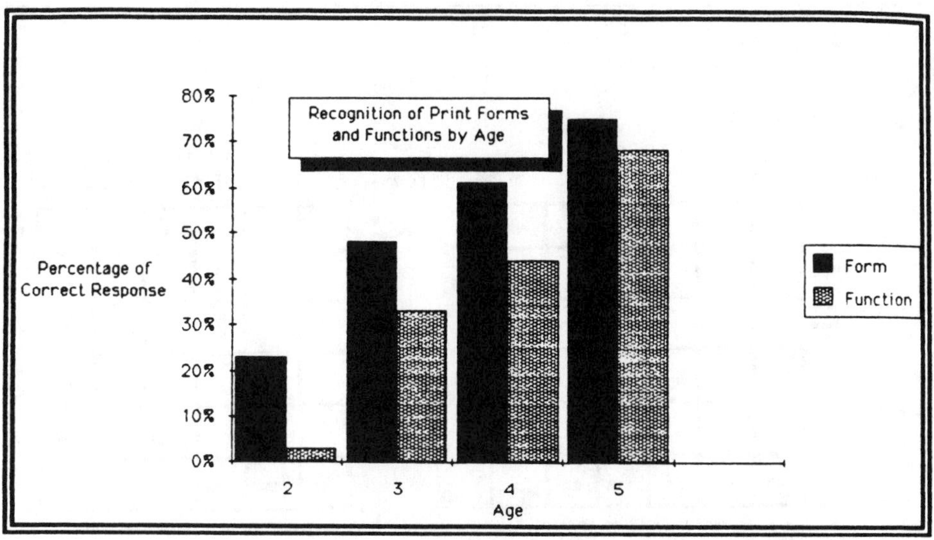

FIGURE 1

Children's Growth in Ability to Articulate Form-Function Knowledge

The responses children provided for the slide picturing a STOP-sign document not only the kind of information children had about an environmental example of written language but also the growth of this knowledge. The STOP-sign slide prompted form responses which ranged from identifying the example as a STOP sign, to calling it a sign, to labeling the sign components as numbers or letter. With respect to function, some of the children said the print was "to say stop" while others described the function of the sign as "to stop." With respect to the message interpretation category, some of the children explained the function of the print by suggesting that the sign offered a different message; for example, "[the print is for] don't pass that street" or "it says outside."

Interestingly, what one might expect to be able to document in regard to children's form-function knowledge growth is in fact evident. That is, the responses of two-year-olds tended to cluster in the lower right corner of the matrix indicating that their labels and explanations were less appropriate or not available. By contrast, the responses of the five-year-olds tended to cluster in the upper left corner where the most complete explanations of form and function intersected. Grids for the three- and four-year-olds enable one to see the progression from the lower right to upper left section of the matrix reflecting the children's increasing ability to explain what the print is as well as what it is for. (See Figure 2.)

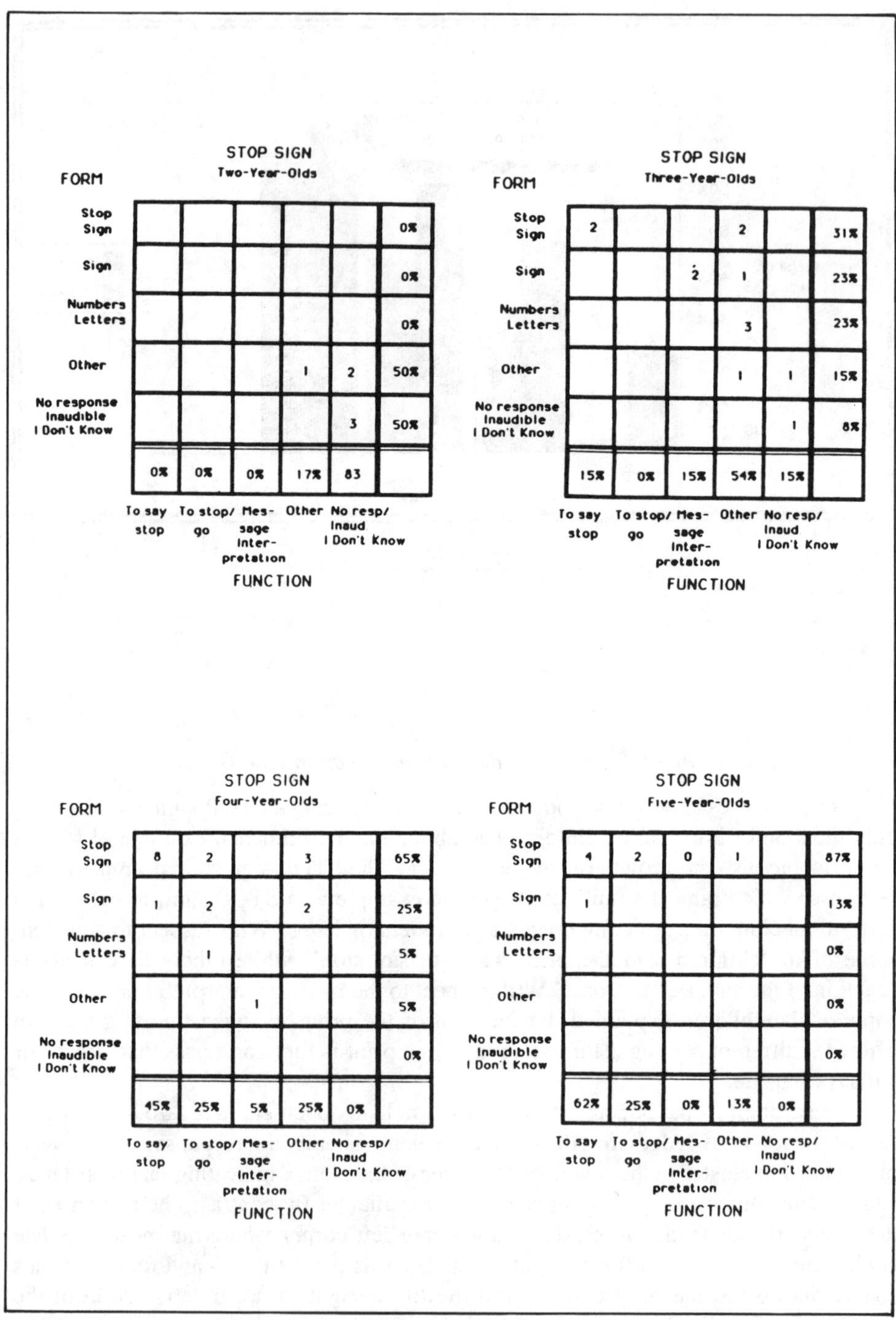

STOP SIGN
Two-Year-Olds

FORM	To say stop	To stop/go	Message interpretation	Other	No resp/ Inaud I Don't Know	
Stop Sign						0%
Sign						0%
Numbers Letters						0%
Other				1	2	50%
No response Inaudible I Don't Know					3	50%
	0%	0%	0%	17%	83	

FUNCTION

STOP SIGN
Three-Year-Olds

FORM	To say stop	To stop/go	Message interpretation	Other	No resp/ Inaud I Don't Know	
Stop Sign	2			2		31%
Sign			2	1		23%
Numbers Letters				3		23%
Other				1	1	15%
No response Inaudible I Don't Know					1	8%
	15%	0%	15%	54%	15%	

FUNCTION

STOP SIGN
Four-Year-Olds

FORM	To say stop	To stop/go	Message interpretation	Other	No resp/ Inaud I Don't Know	
Stop Sign	8	2		3		65%
Sign	1	2		2		25%
Numbers Letters		1				5%
Other			1			5%
No response Inaudible I Don't Know						0%
	45%	25%	5%	25%	0%	

FUNCTION

STOP SIGN
Five-Year-Olds

FORM	To say stop	To stop/go	Message interpretation	Other	No resp/ Inaud I Don't Know	
Stop Sign	4	2	0	1		87%
Sign	1					13%
Numbers Letters						0%
Other						0%
No response Inaudible I Don't Know						0%
	62%	25%	0%	13%	0%	

FUNCTION

FIGURE 2
Form-Function Matrices for Stop Sign

What Parents of Successful Readers Told Us About Emergent Literacy

Analysis of the parent interview tapes yielded dominant themes related to the home literacy context, literacy events, and the parent attributions for success.

Within the literacy context we identified three major themes that parents used to describe the setting in which a successful reader developed:

1. Parents valued reading themselves. (''My dad read to me . . . I can remember as a tiny child he would read big books and I've always loved to read.'')
2. Parents made text available to their children. (''We have lots of books . . . trillions.'')
3. Parents made writing materials available to their children. (''We have an art table they do writing on.'')

The six literacy events these parents described most frequently as being part of the home experience were:

1. Parents read aloud to their children. (''Just after one he was having a book a day.'')
2. Parents took their children to the library. (''We get 22 books from the library every two weeks.'')
3. Parents reported an early interest in writing. (''So as far as wanting to write it's because of his brother . . . it's been going on forever.'')
4. Parents reported the prevalence of playing school behavior. (''His sister teaches him all day.'')
5. Parents reported putting their children to bed with books. (''They take them to bed and pile them all around.'')
6. Parents reported supporting their children's efforts to learn to read. (''I try to get them as much books as I can.'')

Parent attributions for their children's success collapsed into five themes:

1. Parents modeled an interest/value for reading.
2. Parents believed that reading to children was important.
3. Parents commented on their role in helping and encouraging children to read.
4. Parents attributed success in learning to read to the efforts of older brothers and sisters teaching the younger ones.
5. Parents attributed children's success to characteristics of the children themselves. Labels they provided included ''smart,'' ''verbal,'' ''good memory,'' ''interested,'' ''quiet,'' ''achiever/competitive,'' and ''curious.''

DISCUSSION

The insights afforded us through our conversations with these preschool siblings of successful first-grade readers enable us to provide more detailed information about the knowledge young children have about written language before they are readers themselves. In particular, they have demonstrated that the accuracy of labeling the forms of written language runs somewhat ahead of the ability to explain the corresponding functions of written language. Such an insight must be qualified by saying that this picture emerges when these data are considered across all slide examples. There are cases in which the explanations of function exceed the ability to correctly supply the form labels. Furthermore, the notion that print functions for reading develop at very young ages evidences itself time and again as one inspects the language of explanation for the variety of written language examples discussed. Children demonstrated a concept of function much more well developed than a unidimensional perception that print is for reading.

Parents indicated that they held specific notions about their children's success that are grounded both in their own childhood experiences and in their experiences raising children. In this sense, each of the parents interviewed had an implicit theory (i.e., a set of assumptions and beliefs) about reading development that served to guide their nurturing actions.

REFERENCES

Baghban, M. (1984). *Our daughter learns to read and write: A case study from birth to three.* Newark, DE: International Reading Association.

Clark, M. (1976). *Young fluent readers.* London, England: Heinemann.

Downing, J. (1969). How children think about reading. *The Reading Teacher, 23,* 217–230.

Downing, J. (1970). Children's concepts of language in learning to read. *Educational Researcher, 12,* 106–112.

Durkin, D. (1966). *Children who read early.* New York: Teachers College Press.

Ferreiro, E., & Teberosky, A. (1982). *Literacy before schooling* (K. G. Castro, Trans.). Exeter, NH: Heinemann. (Original work published 1979)

Goodall, M. (1984). Can four year olds "read" words in the environment? *The Reading Teacher, 37,* 478–482.

Goodman, K. S., & Goodman, Y. M. (1979). Learning to read is natural. In L. B. Resnick & P. A. Weaver (Eds.), *Theory and practice of early reading* (Vol. 1, pp. 137–154). Hillsdale, NJ: Erlbaum.

Goodman, Y. M. & Altwerger, B. (1981). *Print awareness in young children: A working paper, a study of the development of literacy in preschool children* (Occasional Paper No. 4). Tucson: University of Arizona, Program in Language and Literacy, Arizona Center for Research and Development.

Harste, J. C., Burke, C. L., & Woodward, V. A. (1982). Children's language and world: Initial encounters with print. In J. A. Langer & M. T. Smith-Burke (Eds.), *Reader meets author/Bridging the gap* (pp. 105–131). Newark, DE: International Reading Association.

Hiebert, E. H. (1978). Preschool children's understanding of written language. *Child Development, 49,* 1,231–1,234.

Hiebert, E. H. (1981). Developmental patterns and interrelationships of preschool children's print awareness. *Reading Research Quarterly, 16,* 236–260.

Mason, J. (1980). When *do* children begin to read: An exploration of four-year-old children's letter and word reading competencies. *Reading Research Quarterly, 15,* 203–227.

Mason, J. (1982, March). *Acquisition of knowledge about reading.* Paper presented at the meeting of the American Educational Research Association, New York.

Mason, J. (1984). Early reading from a developmental perspective. In P. D. Pearson (Ed.), *Handbook of reading research* (pp. 505–543). New York: Longman.

Reid, J. F. (1966). Learning to think about reading. *Educational Researcher, 9,* 56–62.

Smith, F. (1976). Learning to read by reading. *Language Arts, 53,* 297–299, 322.

Soderbergh, R. (1971). *Reading in early childhood: An inquistic study of a Swedish preschool child's gradual acquisition of reading ability.* Stockholm: Almqvist and Wiksell.

Teale, W. H. (1978). Positive environments for learning to read: What studies of early readers tell us. *Language Arts, 55,* 922–932.

Torrey, J. (1973). Learning to read without a teacher: A case study. In F. Smith (Ed.), *Psycholinguistics and reading* (pp. 147–157). New York: Holt, Rinehart & Winston.

Ylisto, I. P. (1967). *An empirical investigation of early reading responses of young children.* Unpublished doctoral dissertation, University of Michigan, Ann Arbor.

KINDERGARTEN SPELLING: EXPLAINING ITS RELATIONSHIP TO FIRST-GRADE READING

Lou Ferroli and Timothy Shanahan
University of Illinois at Chicago

This investigation is concerned with the nature of the relationship between reading and spelling at the time of emergent literacy. Research that began with Read's (1971) description of the linguistic basis of preschoolers' "invented spellings" has articulated a view of young children's spelling ability as a series of developmental stages (Beers, Beers, & Grant, 1977; Beers & Henderson, 1977, 1980; Gentry, 1978, 1982; Henderson, 1981; Zutell, 1979) in which children employ a sequence of strategies in their early attempts at spelling. At first, writing is represented by using letter-like squiggles or virtually any symbols. At this *Prephonetic Stage* there is no relationship between sounds in words and letters used. Later, children produce abbreviated spellings of words by matching their knowledge of letter names to at least some sounds in words *(Semiphonetic Stage)*. Eventually they show greater sophistication in segmenting and representing the sounds that comprise spoken words until spelling at the *Phonetic Stage* is best characterized as phonetic mapping. Finally, at the *Transitional Stage,* children progress from simple sound mapping to learning conventional alternatives for spelling different sounds.

Frequently this research has used a developmental spelling test (DST). Words in a DST are chosen to include spelling features which have been shown to be sensitive to developmental changes. Morris (Morris & Perney, 1984) has refined a scoring system for a DST that is more sensitive at the beginning stages. He showed that a DST administered in September of first-grade was a good predictor of later first-grade reading achievement.

Research Questions

The first research question concerned the practicality of using a DST with average students as early as the spring of kindergarten. This question is important because if kindergartners are able to complete such a task in an informal manner, a DST might be useful to teachers and other educators concerned with measuring emergent literacy and predicting later reading achievement. More important, if a DST is sensitive to spelling at this level, the test results could provide teachers with a structure, or frame of reference, for examining test protocols and children's writings.

The second research question asked how well a DST predicts subsequent reading achievement relative to other popular measures of emergent literacy. A DST could be especially useful to practitioners if it reduces formal readiness testing yet provides worthwhile information about how those children are progressing.

The third question attempted to decompose the stages of spelling and to identify the component knowledge characteristic of these stages. In other words, what does a child need to know to spell at the Semiphonetic Stage? What additional knowledge is required in order to progress to the Phonetic or the Transitional stages? Although it seems evident that developmental spelling ability is related to other aspects of emergent literacy, it is not entirely clear just how the various prereading abilities are interrelated and what related knowledge they share.

Ehri, from a broader perspective, offers a coherent explanation of the interrelationships of early language abilities in her Amalgamation Theory (Ehri, 1978, 1980; Ehri & Wilce, 1979). She argues that words have several identities, or images: acoustic, articulatory, morphemic, syntactic, semantic, and orthographic. These separate identities are amalgamated, or blended, in memory. Measuring separate word identities, such as letter production, phonemic segmentation, or concept of word, in conjunction with developmental spelling ability, should provide a picture of which abilities are being focused upon by spellers at different stages of development; such information has value to explanations of early reading, writing, and spelling development.

The study reported here attempts to explain the developmental knowledge that characterizes different stages of beginning reading and spelling ability. It considers the relative role of various forms of knowledge found to be important to early reading and spelling development, including concept of word (Blum, Taylor, & Blum, 1979; Morris, 1983), phoneme segmentation (Liberman, Shankweiler, Fischer, & Carter, 1974), and letter production (Durrell, 1980).

METHOD

Subjects

Children (n = 47) from two of the four kindergarten sections of a suburban elementary school in the Midwest participated in the study. Because the investigation focused on literacy acquisition in English, those children assigned by the school to the bilingual classes, where instruction was in Spanish, were excluded from the study. Hispanic students, who were assigned by the school on the basis of English proficiency, and all other students in the English-only kindergarten were included. Twelve of the children moved away during the 15 months of the study. Scores reported are for those subjects who were enrolled at the school throughout the project (n = 35; 12 boys, 23 girls).

Materials

Six tests were used to examine the reading and spelling knowledge of the children.

Letter production. A subtest of a commercial reading readiness program called

Sound Start (Murphy & Durrell, 1982) was used as a measure of letter production. In a whole class setting, children were directed to locate a space on their papers, told a letter name, and asked to write the designated letter in that space.

Concept of word. Another subtest, Syntax Matching, from the same commercial program was used to determine a child's concept of word. This group-administered test asks children to echo read a printed sentence. ("This sentence says, 'You can't scare me.' Now you read it. 'You can't scare me.' ") The children then "read" it a second time before they are directed to circle one target word within the entire sentence. ("Read it again . . . Circle the word 'scare.' ") The sentences ranged from two to five words in length. An additional set of 10 similar items was developed.

Phoneme awareness. A non-writing measure of phoneme awareness was developed specifically for this project. It began with the easiest of three types of segmentation tasks—isolation of an initial phoneme.

The isolation task used five training items and 10 scored items. The examiner demonstrated the isolation task ("When we say the word *father* the first sound we make is /f/.") and then asked the child to do the same. If a child was unable to successfully isolate the initial sound for at least one of the training items, his or her score was reported as zero.

The two- and three-phoneme word segmentation tasks used the same procedures of modeling correct segmentation followed by repeated demonstrations if the child responded incorrectly. In addition, blocks were used as counters for these segmentation tasks. The children were instructed to move a block each time a phoneme was pronounced. This aided the children in their keeping tally of sounds reported. Only the child's verbal utterance and not the moving of the blocks was considered in scoring the items. The exact items for this test are presented in Appendix A.

Reading achievement. Two reading measures were used. The Reading Comprehension subtest of the Metropolitan Achievement Tests, Primary 1, Form JS (Psychological Corporation, 1978) was used as a criterion measure at the end of first grade. However, in attempting to measure emergent reading ability, a simpler reading instrument was needed. Thirty-three words taken from the "readiness" and "first preprimer" levels of the basal reading series used at the school were presented. Children were asked if "there are any words here that you can read."

Developmental spelling. A DST was the independent variable of interest in this investigation. The kindergarten children were led through a demonstration of spelling in which they were encouraged to listen for letter names within words. They were prompted to spell the words "as best you can" and praised for whatever spellings they produced the first time they produced them. When the children were in first-grade, a traditional spelling test format was used. The words were scored based upon the following spelling stages: Preliterate = 0, Semiphonetic1 = 1, Semiphonetic2 = 2, Phonetic = 3, Transitional = 4, Correct = 5. Appendix B provides the words used in the spelling test as well as illustrative spellings at each stage. See Morris and Perney (1984) for a more complete description of the scoring system.

Procedure

Tests were administered on three occasions, twice in kindergarten (March and May) and once at the end of first grade (May). The reading achievement test was administered only at the end of first grade. The concept of word measure was not given at the end of first grade as the particular task used was very easy for all the children.

RESULTS

The first question asked whether kindergartners could successfully complete a DST in a manner that had a possibility of providing important information about children's early spelling knowledge. The answer to this is yes. Even children who showed some initial reluctance readily warmed to the task as first efforts met with praise. The children who were unable to correctly represent any sounds in their spellings were at least able to participate by writing random letter strings and, in fact, seemed to find the task enjoyable. In March of kindergarten, there was just one subject who was unable to participate.

The results reported in Table 1 indicate that the students in this study had little difficulty in taking part in the DST experience. The average score was equivalent to a Semiphonetic1 Stage rating in March of kindergarten. Almost two thirds of the children scored seven points or more. Even the Preliterate Stage spellers (0—7 points) were able to correctly represent the beginning sounds of words at least occasionally.

Table 1

Mean Scores and Standard Deviations for Predictor Variables at Each Administration

Variable	Possible Score	March Kdg	May Kdg	May Gr. 1
Concept of Word	20	13.3	16.7	—
		(5.1)	(3.6)	—
Letter Production	26	19.4	20.8	25.8
		(6.5)	(5.7)	(0.7)
Phoneme Awareness	30	9.5	14.2	26.2
		(5.7)	(6.7)	(4.7)
Word List Reading	33	1.2	2.0	31.0
		(5.1)	(5.7)	(1.4)
DST	60	10.2	12.2	39.6
		(6.6)	(9.6)	(5.5)

The second research question sought to compare how well each of the measures predict reading achievement at the end of first grade. Table 2 shows that while the single highest correlation with reading achievement was shown by the Concept of Word test completed in March of kindergarten, the DST score is the overall best predictor of reading with correlations that range from .59 to .67. The predictive ability of the other measures drops off severely as children reach ceiling levels by the end of first grade. The spelling test, however, seems to continue to be sensitive to differences in children's abilities.

Table 2

Correlations Between the Reading Achievement Test and Each of the Predictor Variables

	Administrations		
Measures	**March Kdg**	**May Kdg**	**May 1st**
Concept of Word	.72**	.38	—
Letter Production	.54**	.50	.33
Phoneme Awareness	.41	.50*	.33
Preprimer Word List	.20	.34	.26
Developmental Spelling Test	.59**	.67**	.63**

*$p < .01$.
**$p < .001$.

A DST offers reading prediction that is comparable to that of standardized reading readiness tests which most often report correlations with end of first-grade reading achievement of between .50 to .70 (Harris & Sipay, 1975). At the same time, it is an informal measure that can be used frequently to monitor progress.

The third research question asked how the knowledge children seem to use in producing spellings at different developmental stages changes. To determine this, a backwards regression procedure was used to decompose the spelling score in terms of the other measures. The spelling test was regressed against each of the other measures given at that time to identify which variables or combination of variables explained a statistically significant proportion of the variance in the spelling score. The results showed that in March of kindergarten 53% of the variance in the spelling score is explained by Letter Knowledge (beta weight = .44) and Concept of Word (beta weight = .38). By May of kindergarten, 44% of the variance in the spelling score is explained by the Phoneme Awareness (beta weight = .66) measure while Letter Knowledge and Concept of Word have dropped out of the equation. One year later, the Reading Achievement variable enters the equation (beta weight = .52) while Phoneme Awareness plays a reduced role but still contributes (beta weight = .32) toward explaining 50% of the variance in the spelling measure.

DISCUSSION

Teachers and other educators concerned with evaluating emergent literacy might consider using a DST. As a measurement instrument, it is a task that young children can do early on, even before they can do much reading. The DST is easily administered and scored, and, most importantly, it continues to be sensitive for a longer period of time than other kinds of informal measures.

The regression analyses of DST scores indicate that early spelling ability (Preliterate and Semiphonetic Stages) is most dependent on letter knowledge and concept of word. Later, at the Semiphonetic and Phonetic Stages, the spelling task still certainly uses letter knowledge and word awareness, but phonemic segmentation appears to be the most important component ability. Finally, at the end of first grade (Phonetic and Transitional Stages), phonemic knowledge is still used in spelling but by this time reading and spelling become highly interrelated so that the spelling ability contributes to reading ability and reading ability contributes to spelling ability.

These results indicate that a DST could be used informally to identify what early reading and spelling knowledge children have. As the nature of this knowledge develops, instructional emphasis can be changed in the classroom. Preliterate and early Semiphonetic Stage spellers who are first coming to terms with word boundaries, letter names, and other conventions of print might profit from activities that allow them to manipulate printed language while encountering it in connected and meaningful discourse. Big Book activities and the Shared Book Experience (Holdaway, 1979), the dictations of the Language Experience Approach, and activities in which words are physically manipulated in sentence building (Clay, 1979) would all fit into this category. As children's use of this knowledge becomes evident, the teaching of letter-sound relationships should increase in emphasis in accordance with the late Semiphonetic and Phonetic Stage spellers' greater use of phonemic knowledge. Future research needs to test the relative effectiveness of varied programs of instruction at various stages of DST performance.

REFERENCES

Beers, J., Beers, C., & Grant, K. (1977). The logic behind children's spelling. *Elementary School Journal, 77,* 238-242.

Beers, J., & Henderson, E. (1977). A study of developing orthographic concepts among first grade children. *Research in the Teaching of English, 11,* 133-148.

Beers, J., & Henderson, E. (1980). *Developmental and cognitive aspects of learning to spell.* Newark, DE: International Reading Association.

Blum, I., Taylor, N., & Blum, R. (1979). Methodological considerations and developmental trends in children's awareness of word boundaries. In M. L. Kamil & A. J. Moe (Eds.), *Reading research: Studies and applications.* Twenty-eighth Yearbook of the National Reading Conference (pp. 33-37). Clemson, SC: National Reading Conference.

Clay, M. (1979). *The early detection of reading difficulties* (2nd ed.). Exeter, NH: Heinemann.

Durrell, D. (1980). Commentary: Letter-name values in reading and spelling. *Reading Research Quarterly, 16,* 159-163.

Ehri, L. (1978). Beginning reading from a psycholinguistic perspective: Amalgamation of word identities. In F. Murray (Ed.), *The recognition of words* (pp. 1-33). Newark, DE: International Reading Association.

Ehri, L. (1980). The development of orthographic images. In U. Frith (Ed.), *Cognitive processes in spelling* (pp. 311-319). London: Academic Press.

Ehri, L., & Wilce, L. (1979). The mnemonic value of orthography among beginning readers. *Journal of Educational Psychology, 71,* 26-40.

Gentry, J. R. (1978). Early spelling strategies. *Elementary School Journal, 79*(2), 88-92.

Gentry, J. R. (1982). An analysis of developmental spelling in GNYS AT WRK. *The Reading Teacher, 36,* 192-200.

Harris, A., & Sipay, E. (1975). *How to increase reading ability* (6th ed.) New York: David McKay.

Henderson, E. (1981). *Learning to read and spell.* DeKalb, IL: Northern Illinois University Press.

Holdaway, D. (1979). *The foundations of literacy.* Sydney, Australia: Ashton Scholastic.

Liberman, I. Y., Shankweiler, D., Fischer, F., & Carter, B. (1974). Phoneme segmentation in the young child. *Journal of Experimental Psychology, 18,* 201-212.

Morris, D. (1983). Concept of word and phoneme awareness in the beginning reader. *Research in the Teaching of English, 17,* 359-373.

Morris, D., & Perney, J. (1984). Developmental spelling as a predictor of first grade reading achievement. *Elementary School Journal, 84,* 441-457.

Murphy, H., & Durrell, D. (1982). *Sound start, teacher's manual* (2nd ed.) North Billerica, MA: Curriculum Associates.

Psychological Corporation (1978). *Metropolitan achievement tests.* New York: Harcourt Brace Jovanovich.

Read, C. (1971). Preschool children's knowledge of English phonology. *Harvard Educational Review, 41,* 1-34.

Zutell, J. (1979). Spelling strategies of primary school children and their relationship to Piaget's concept of decentration. *Research in the Teaching of English, 13,* 69-80.

APPENDIX A

Phoneme Awareness Test — Directions and Items

Part One: Isolation of Initial Consonant Sound

Directions: "The first sound in (child's name) is /?/. The first sound in ball is /b/. Now you try. What's the first sound in (child's name)? What's the first sound in ball?" Give feedback as needed. Practice items: family, hop, jump, money, number. Test items: father, children, rabbit, window, thumb, cat, voice, lip, dog, sun.

Part Two: Segmentation of Two-Phoneme Words

Directions: "Now let's think about some different words. When we say the word 'it' there are two sounds. Listen. /i/ (Move one block.) . . . /t/ (Move the other block.) Can you try that? I'll say the word. You say one sound at a time and move the blocks." Give feedback as needed. Practice items: ash, all, of, as, ill. Test items: at, is, odd, up, if, edge, add, itch, off, us.

Part Three: Segmentation of Three-Phoneme Words

Directions: "Now let's try some words that have three sounds. Pig. /p/ . . . /i/ . . . /g/. Can you do that? Say one sound at a time and move the blocks." Give feedback as needed. Practice items: sun, chip, good, watch, hug. Test items: tap, neck, fish, should, job, have, pet, zip, book, much.

APPENDIX B

Developmental Spelling Test Items and Illustrative Spellings at Each Stage

Correct 5 Points	Prelit 0 Points	Semi 1 1 Point	Semi 2 2 Points	Phonetic 3 Points	Trans 4 Points
BACK	RE	BET	BC	BAK	[a]
SINK	E	C	SE	SEK	SINCK
MAIL	A	MM	MOL	MAL	MAEL
DRESS	S	DN	JS	GAS	DRES
LAKE	AH	L	LAE	LAK	LACE
PEEKED	TTT	PF	PT	PECT	PEKED
LIGHT	IEIX	LSIE	LAT	LIT	LIET
DRAGON	ATJA	JK	GAN	DAGN	DRAGIN
STICK	F	S	STC	SEK	STIK
SIDE	TC	ST	CI	SID	CIDE
FEET	V	F	FT	FET	[a]
TEST	ABT	TS	TST	TAST	TEEST

[a]No 4-point spellings were produced by the subjects for these words.

LITERACY LEARNING AS AN INTERTEXTUAL PROCESS*

Deborah Wells Rowe
Peabody College, Vanderbilt University

Beaugrande and Dressler (1981) have defined intertextuality as the "ways in which the production and reception of a given text depends upon the participants' knowledge of other texts" (p. 182). When *text* is defined broadly as any unified chunk of meaning, the process of constructing intertextual ties can be seen more generally as a metaphor for learning or cognition. Rosen (1984) has suggested that the creation of a narrative—a text—involves the establishment of arbitrary boundaries in a continuous stream of experience and that it is by constructing a framework for interpreting experience that we are able to give it meaning. Because this interpretive framework is itself made of texts formed on other occasions, text construction is always an *intertextual* process. Learners can make sense of new texts only by making connections to their existing ones. From this perspective, the process of constructing understandable *stories* from the flow of daily events is a primary cognitive act (Hardy, 1978). And this act necessarily involves tying evolving texts to existing ones, as well as making new connections between existing texts. Seen in this way, intertextual tying is an integral part of the interpretation of linguistic texts, and more generally a way of making sense of the world.

But how does this *connection-making* process occur, and what role does it play in the literacy learning of young children? These are questions which emerged as an important focus of the ethnographic study of literacy learning reported in this paper. Generally, the purpose of this study was to explore how young children learned about literacy in the course of their usual classroom activities. More specifically, I proposed two broad research questions which allowed me to take both individual and social perspectives on literacy learning: (a) How are children's understandings and use of written language, music, and graphic/constructive art embedded in the social world of their classroom? (b) How do young children explore the potentials of these communication systems? What socio-psychological strategies do they use? These initial research questions were focused broadly enough to allow me to observe children's attempts to simultaneously learn to communicate using a number of *alternate literacies* (Harste, Woodward, & Burke, 1984)—a research decision based on a semiotic perspective on communication which suggests that literacy involves the use of multiple

*Student Research Award.

sign systems and that a similar process of signification underlies communication regardless of the sign system involved.

As Hymes (1978) has suggested, it is the essence of the ethnographic method that initial research questions are refined and developed through the dialectic which occurs as the ethnographer reflects on the results of ongoing data analysis and plans subsequent phases of data collection. Early in this study, several patterns related to the ways in which my three- and four-year-old informants linked their texts to those of others and to their own cognitive texts emerged as an important focus of the study. My observations of these children over an eight-month period suggested that the construction of intertextual ties had both social and individual features, and that intertextuality was central to their learning. The purposes of this paper are to describe the patterns of intertextual tying I observed as I watched this group of 21 children learning to communicate through writing, art, and music and to present the theoretical hypotheses I generated to describe the role of intertextuality in the literacy learning process.

METHOD

Setting and Participants

The setting for this research was a day care program which served the three- and four-year-old children of faculty and staff at Indiana University. Of the 13 boys and eight girls who participated in the research, 15 children had parents who were faculty or graduate students, and six had parents who were employed in staff positions at the University or elsewhere in the community. In September, 13 of the children were three-year-olds and eight were four-year-olds.

I chose this setting specifically because the director and teachers had developed a curriculum which supported young children's literacy learning by encouraging them to engage in literacy activities for functional purposes, and by valuing their communicative efforts regardless of the conventionality of the resulting product. Each day during two self-selected activity periods, youngsters were allowed to direct their own literacy learning by choosing how, when, and why they would participate in literacy activities. At these times children could choose to work at the writing table, the art table, the book area, the piano, or at other centers such as the block area or housekeeping corner. Teachers provided literacy demonstrations by authoring their own written, artistic, or musical texts at these centers. They also acted as audience for the texts children were producing. In this way, children were encouraged to learn about literacy by using it, and literacy instruction was embedded in informal discussions about in-process authoring activities.

Data Collection Procedures

This study proceeded through four phases in which the focus of data collection, the amount of time spent in the classroom, and the data collection techniques varied. In the first phase of the research, lasting one month, I was present in the classroom four full days per week and focused on becoming familiar with the setting and on negotiating my role with the children and teachers. My major data collection technique during this period was participant/observation. As my participatory role in the classroom developed, the children came to view me as an assistant teacher. I talked and worked with them throughout their day in much the same way as their classroom teachers, with three exceptions: (a) I rarely directed group activities, (b) I spent the majority of my time observing and participating in literacy activities, and (c) I consistently used a variety of techniques to record classroom interactions.

In the second phase of the study, lasting three months, I was present three full days per week and began to use several new techniques to record classroom interactions. These included field notes recorded in the setting, audiotape, photography, and informal interviews with the children about their literacy activities. I also began to provide the classroom teachers with copies of my expanded field notes and the artifacts I had collected. Through informal conversations and indefinite triangulation sessions (Cicourel, 1975; Denzin, 1978), the teachers shared their perspectives on my observations as well as discussed their own observations of children's literacy learning. Though I collected data during all parts of the school day, the most intensive periods of observation involved children's self-selected activities at the writing table, the art table, and the piano. Throughout this phase, I looked for patterns in children's literacy activities and developed tentative hypotheses about their learning.

In the third phase of the study, lasting two months, I continued to participate three days per week and specifically focused on collecting data which would help to refine these hypotheses. Theoretical sampling was used to focus my observations during this period, and videotape was used to record these literacy events. The final phase of data collection occurred during the last two months of the study as I gradually decreased my participation in the classroom to two mornings per week. Though the major focus of my research activity shifted to data analysis during this period, I used my classroom observations to further refine and test my hypotheses about literacy learning.

Data Analysis Procedures

Data analysis was ongoing throughout the research using the constant comparative method (Glaser & Strauss, 1967). I reviewed and coded the data weekly in search of patterns leading to working hypotheses about literacy learning in this setting. In addition, I wrote methodological and theoretical notes to document my research decisions and the hypotheses, so that the steps leading to the theoretical propositions could be retraced. As mentioned above, the field note data and developing hypotheses were discussed frequently with the teachers to add the perspectives of other classroom participants. Regular discussions with a peer debriefer (Lincoln & Guba, 1985) and with other colleagues outside the setting also added new perspectives on methodological and theoretical issues.

During the period of Field Exit, and after withdrawing from the classroom, data analysis continued with transcription and microsociolinguistic analysis of the videotape data, as well as with additional analyses of the field notes and artifacts to refine hypotheses about literacy learning. The videotapes were used to further explore the nature of the interpretive work individual children engaged in during these events. Microanalysis of the social interaction in selected literacy events was aimed at refining hypotheses related to the role of social interaction in literacy learning. In addition, I tracked each child through the data to look for patterns in individual children's literacy learning over the eight months covered by the study. After completing a first draft of the research report, a member check (Lincoln & Guba, 1985) was conducted by asking the classroom teachers to respond to the accounts of events and the interpretations presented in the draft. Their comments were used to extend and clarify some points in final versions of the report.

RESULTS AND DISCUSSION

My observations of this group of young children suggest that the construction of intertextual connections is a central part of the literacy learning process. In this section I will discuss patterns in the data which support this contention and present my hypotheses about the role of intertextuality in literacy learning. Presented first are examples illustrating how children linked their texts to those of their classmates and teachers. This is followed by a discussion of the manner in which children constructed links between their existing cognitive texts to form new literacy knowledge.

Intertextuality as a Social Process

One of the patterns most readily observed in the literacy activities of children and teachers in this classroom was the extent to which they had developed a shared register for literacy events (Halliday, 1975). This shared knowledge included not only the content of their graphic and musical texts, but also the processes or strategies they used, the structural aspects of texts such as genre and conventions, and the purposes for which they used literacy in the classroom. For example, content themes such as spiders, rainbows, and snowflakes were used by many of the children, as were strategies such as mixing colors with markers or using knowledge of classmates' names to help in writing and reading messages. Children also developed a shared repertoire of genre for literacy events including surveys, newspapers, books, notes, signs, musical scores, pictures, hats, and kites, and learned to use the resulting products for purposes such as exploring their newest ideas or initiating positive social interactions with their peers and teachers.

By carefully examining the videotapes of events in which children made obvious connections between their texts and those of other participants, I formed the hypothesis that conversation, observation of the demonstrations of others, and authoring one's own texts played important roles in the construction of these types of intertextual links in this setting. Example 1 demonstrates how this process occurred.

Example 1: Exclamation Points
February 25, 1986 (Videotapes 28, 29)

One of the nap teachers is in the hospital, so we are making a "Get Well" book for her. Kira watches as I write my message, "Dear Carol, We hope you get well SOON!!!" (Figure 1A).

As I write the last word, I read the letters out loud. "S O O N, exclamation point, exclamation point, exclamation point. Because I want her to get well *soon!*" Hana asks me what it says, and I read the message again.

Kira struggles with the word and adds, "And this is extamotion point. How come?"

"Put three cause it's big letters," Hana suggests.

"Because I want her to get well really, really, really soon. I want to emphasize that," I explain.

As we work Kira brings up exclamation points again, and we discuss them. Then Christina who is working at the other side of the table joins the conversation. "I have to put too much exclamation points," she says as she begins to write exclamation points under her name. (Figure 1B) "Look, Debbie, look! I did just like you did!" She adds more exclamation points.

Now Hana begins her picture for Carol. (Figure 1C) When she is finished she shows it to Susie, one of the classroom teachers. "Carol's really gonna like this one," she says. "There's a question mark—"

"Exclamation point," Susie corrects.

"—exclamation point because I really want her to get well quicker!"

FIGURE 1A: Debbie's Message

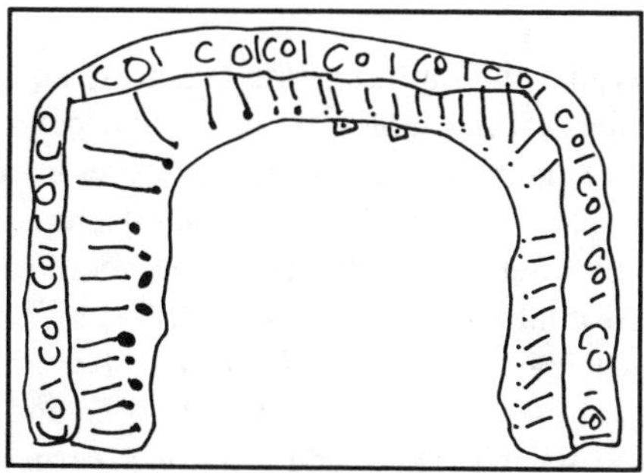

FIGURE 1B: Christina's Message

FIGURE 1C: Hana's Message

In this event as in most events at the piano, writing table, and art table, conversation and demonstrations were linked as integral parts of a literacy event which was familiar and functional for the participants. When an unfamiliar idea was introduced in conversation or in another author's text, the participants had access to many other sources of information about that concept. For example, when I introduced exclamation points as part of my "Get Well" message for Carol, the children were able to explore the meaning of that punctuation mark in relation to our shared feelings for Carol and our shared understanding of the purpose for using literacy in this situation. They were also able to observe how I used exclamation points in my text, to talk about it, to ask questions about it, to try it out in their own texts, and then to share their new ideas about exclamation points in conversation. In addition, as we talked about our texts, the children and I were carefully tracking the meanings formed by our audience and adjusting our conversation so that shared meanings could be reached. Kira demonstrates this type of semantic tracking (Halliday, 1975) when she questions me about "extamotion points."

Literacy events in the classroom frequently provided *interactive demonstrations* of the sort illustrated above. That is, they provided opportunities for children to *observe* another author at work, to *talk* with that person in order to expand and develop their ideas, to *observe* again, and often to *incorporate new ideas* into their own texts. Sometimes children used the demonstrations of others as starting points for developing their own ideas as Christina and Hana did in Example 1. At other times, children chose to use available demonstrations conservatively; that is, they chose to stick as close to the demonstration as possible until they felt they understood it fully. In either case, the construction of intertextual ties appeared to be supported by social interaction in which (a) the activities of other authors were familiar and understandable, (b) the participants worked collaboratively to reach shared meanings through conversation, and (c) conversation and demonstration were linked to form interactive demonstrations. It was by observing the demonstrations of others, by exchanging meanings in conversation, and by authoring their own texts that children formed shared meanings about literacy.

Intertextuality as an Individual Process

Despite the many intertextual connections that the children, the teachers, and I formed as we interacted with one another at the writing table, art table, and piano, there remained differences in our texts and in our interpretations of literacy events, as demonstrated in the Exclamation Points event above. Not only were there differences in the graphic texts produced in this event, but what the children learned about the function of exclamation points also differed. As contradictory as it may seem, differences in the texts or meanings formed by participants can also be explained by the notion of intertextuality. Quite literally, the cognitive texts to which the children and I linked our interpretations of this event affected what we saw and what we learned. Because participants had different stocks of experiences, the meanings they constructed were only partially shared.

Thus, I observed that children were also constructing ties to their existing *cognitive texts* in order to form hypotheses about the meaning of literacy events. The pervasiveness of this second type of intertextual linkage was highlighted by my examination of individual children's learning over time. After tracking each of the 21 children through the data, I observed that in each literacy event their behavior could be seen as connected to previous events in which they had participated. Over time, children seemed to focus their learning around a number of themes related to personally interesting content areas, processes, and social uses for literacy. Then, in order to meet the demands of specific communicative situations, they flexibly connected their existing knowledge in new ways to solve their communicative problems.

To illustrate this, in Figure 2 I have depicted two of the learning themes Gibson pursued early in the study. The first group of events is linked by his exploration of the *conceptual* theme of spiders, and the second by his exploration of the *process* of folding paper and then cutting it. This sequence of events began near the end of September when Gibson drew three pictures of spider webs and spiders and gave them to his teacher. He then dropped this theme for almost two weeks. In the meantime, he began to explore the process of folding/cutting as well as other themes not depicted in Figure 2. On October 2, he observed Hana folding and cutting paper to make intricate

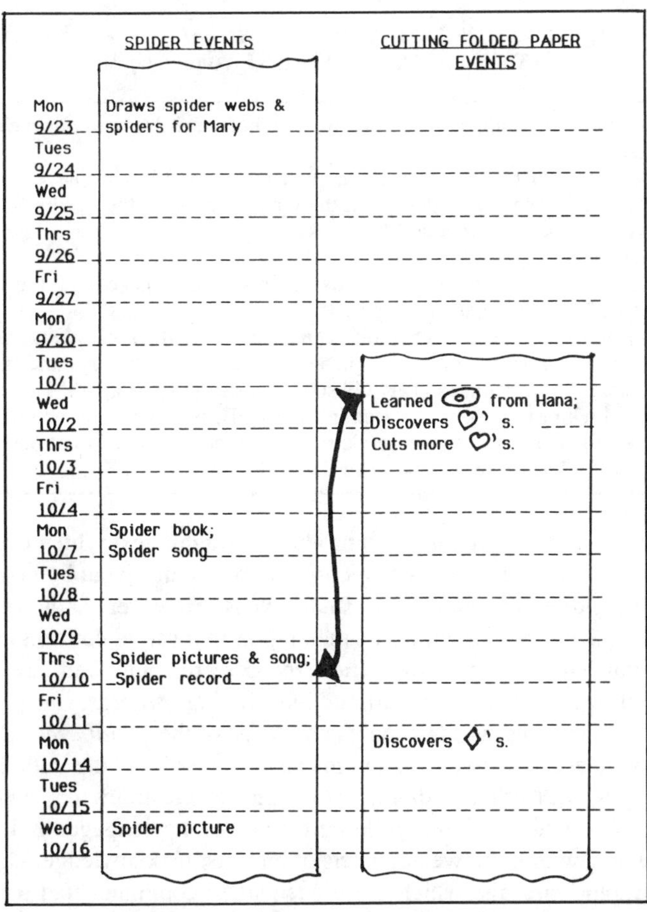

FIGURE 2: Gibson: Two Learning Themes

snowflakes. After realizing that he did not know how to make snowflakes, he watched Hana carefully. His first attempt yielded an oval. After examining it closely, he discarded it and watched Hana again. On his next attempt, he modified his hypothesis to include a second cut from the center of the fold. The result was an oval with a hole in the center, which we later dubbed a "bagel." Later in the day as he was cutting bagels, Gibson accidentally produced a heart. Though he found this occurrence extremely exciting, at first he could not reproduce his discovery. However, the next day he succeeded and cut many more hearts of various sizes and shapes.

The following week brought a return to the spider theme. Gibson drew several spider pictures, stapled them into a book, and read it to me and several of his friends. Later in the afternoon, he composed a spider song to accompany his book. With his teachers, he learned to play the tune on the piano and recorded it on staff paper so that they could play it on another day. It was two days later when Gibson began a literacy event which led him to construct a connection between his conceptual theme of spiders and his procedural knowledge about folding and cutting. This event is described in Example 2 below.

Example 2: Spider Record
Thursday, October 10, 1985 (Audiotape 4)

Gibson has just completed the drawing seen in Figure 3A. He calls me over to the record player.

"You know what?" he says. "This is a record and if you played it, it would go—." He makes a face and puts it on the turn table under the needle.

"It would make spider sounds?" I ask.

He nods.

We talk about the kinds of sounds spiders might make and the difficulties associated with records made of paper.

In the midst of this conversation, Gibson stops and looks at his picture with concentration. "I'm gonna make this picture into a circle," he says and rushes away to the art table. Some minutes later, Gibson comes to find me again. He holds up his spider record with excitement. As seen in Figure 3B, he has folded the picture in half and trimmed the edges to make a semicircle. Then he has cut a small piece from the center of the fold to make it look more like a record.

In this event, Gibson attempted to produce a graphic text which expressed a new concept he had constructed—a spider record. He began the event by using his existing hypotheses about drawing spiders and spider webs. However, as he reflected on the result, he recognized the possibility of making an innovative connection between his *conceptual* knowledge about records (i.e., records are round and have a hole in the middle) and his knowledge of cutting and folding *processes* (i.e., he can cut "bagels"). Also involved was Gibson's knowledge of the *social uses* of literacy (e.g., the creation of an arena for working out his newest ideas, and the initiation of positive social exchanges with other authors). This episode illustrates the *multidimensional* nature of the intertextual linkages children formed as they engaged in literacy events. By constructing new links between aspects of his existing knowledge, Gibson was able to create a graphic message which more adequately communicated the concept of a spider record. By flexibly transferring his previously constructed knowledge to an

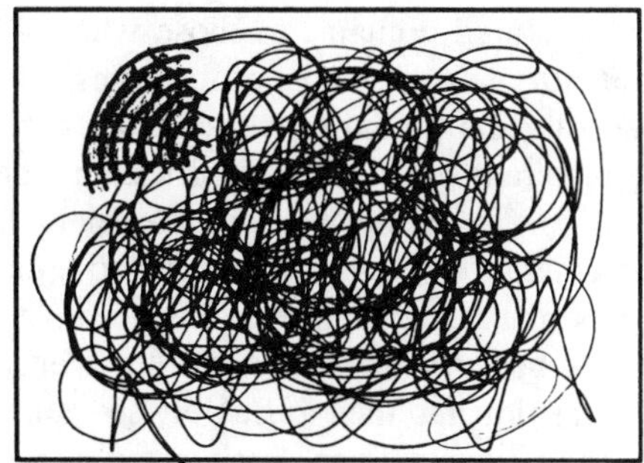

FIGURE 3A: Draft 1: Spider Record

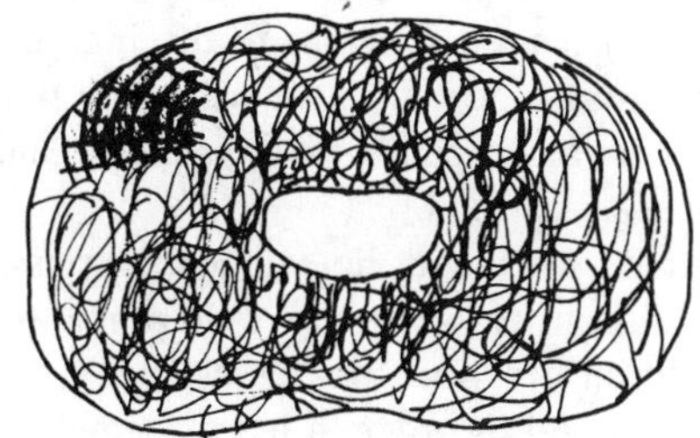

FIGURE 3B: Draft 2: Spider Record

entirely new use in this event, he demonstrated the ability to generate new hypotheses in order to meet the needs of specific communicative situations.

The striking thing about this picture of Gibson's learning is that each event involves intertextual connections between several learning themes, but there is no *single* simplifying structure which predicts how these hypotheses should be combined in the particular situation of use. For example, it is unlikely that Gibson has developed routinized schemata which tell him what processes he should use when he needs to portray a spider record. There seems to be no simple way to describe how existing texts should be combined to fit literacy events of this type; that is, there is no *single* simplifying rule which describes how the content, processes, and purposes of literacy will relate to one another, nor is there one simplifying rule which describes how children should combine knowledge domains, communication systems, or social interactions to achieve their goals as authors. Instead, events are multiple and non-hierarchically interconnected. Though there are commonalities across situations, children must combine parts of several hypotheses to guide their communication in specific literacy events.

Spiro's (Spiro, 1985; Spiro & Myers, 1984; Spiro, Vispoel, Schmitz, Samarapungavan, & Boerger, in press) recent work on learning in ill-structured situations provides some suggestions about the nature of the intertextual connections learners make in complex interactive contexts such as the classroom in which this research was conducted. He defines ill-structured domains as those where "there are no rules or principles of sufficient generality to cover most of the cases; . . . [where] hierarchical relations of dominance and subsumption are inverted from case to case; . . . [where] the same features assume different patterns of significance when placed in different contexts" (Spiro, 1985, p. 6). In such situations, learners have no prepackaged knowledge structures (schemata) already constructed to guide their thought and actions. Instead, they adapt their knowledge flexibly to varying contexts. Spiro theorizes that this is possible because learners are able to encode information from cases in a multiperspectival fashion and then to flexibly see connections between these events to meet the needs of specific situations. Such encoding yields a highly interconnected knowledge base "in which fragments of knowledge are moved about and *assembled* to fit the needs of a given *context* of application. Instead of prepackaged schemas, purpose-sensitive situational schemas are constructed, thus allowing knowledge to be used in different ways on different occasions, for different purposes. The emphasis is shifted from prepackaged schemas to the ingredients for many potential schemas" (Spiro et al., in press, p. 6). It is the assembly of parts of many different cases which allow learners to make sense of the unique and oft-changing contexts where their knowledge must be applied.

Spiro has not commented on whether he extends the possibility of such multifaceted processing to young children. However, I would argue that the natural interactive environment in which children are born possesses many ill-structured features. In order to learn about the world and in order to learn to speak, children must be using flexible intertextual processing of this sort. As research on *oral* language learning has shown (DeVilliers & DeVilliers, 1979; Lindfors, 1980), children are not using an inflexible set of rules learned from adults, instead they are adaptively constructing ways of *meaning* which fit particular situations. Their learning is marked by the ability to make connections and to link their past experiences in new ways. Because speaking is a part of almost every interactive experience, they have many opportunities to build rich networks of connections and to test their hypotheses in different contexts of situation. In a literate society, children have similar opportunities to construct *literacy* knowledge at home before they enter school. In the classroom where this research was conducted, children continued to encounter complex literacy processes in use and had many opportunities to form hypotheses about literacy.

The patterns in children's literacy learning described above have led me to hypothesize that as children formed new communicative goals, they flexibly combined various aspects of their existing knowledge, or linked their existing knowledge to available demonstrations, to construct situation-based hypotheses which met their communicative goals. To accomplish this, they constructed multidimensional intertextual connections among concepts and processes which were related in complex and nonhierarchical ways.

CONCLUSIONS

My observations of the literacy learning of this group of three- and four-year-olds over an eight-month period indicated that there were two general types of intertextual connections which were important in literacy learning in this setting. The first type of connection occurred when children linked their existing knowledge about literacy to the demonstrations provided by other authors. The process of mutual intertextualizing which occurred through conversation and demonstration led to the formation of shared meanings about literacy and allowed members of the same authoring community to use literacy to communicate with others. The second type of intertextual connection reflected the mediation of children's existing texts in their literacy learning. Children interpreted their experiences by flexibly linking their current observations to multiple aspects of their past experiences creating context-specific hypotheses about literacy.

In considering the implications of these observations for educational practice, it must first be noted that ethnographic research generates hypotheses which are grounded in the specific context in which the data is collected. Therefore, the generalizability of the conclusions I have drawn from this study must largely be left to those who wish to apply them in other settings. (For additional details about the context in which this data was collected, see Rowe, 1986.) However, since the children in this classroom have been shown to be flexible and active learners, I would like to point out several characteristics of the curricular environment which appear to be especially supportive of this type of learning. First, children were able to build shared meanings about literacy because they were encouraged to make use of the demonstrations provided by their peers and teachers and because they had many opportunities to talk about these demonstrations in the context of activities which were functional and understandable. Informal interaction among authors played an important role in literacy learning in this classroom. Second, the teachers' expectation and acceptance of varied responses to literacy events supported children's learning. By planning for open-ended literacy activities in which children chose their own focus, teachers encouraged children to pursue those hypotheses that they currently found most interesting and that were most related to their existing knowledge. Since children's existing hypotheses determine, in part, what will be learned, it is vital that children recognize the links between their existing knowledge about the content, processes, and purposes of literacy and classroom literacy events. Third, the teachers' decision not to present preformed generalizations about literacy encouraged children to construct their own complex hypotheses about communicating. And, fourth, the opportunity to pursue these hypotheses in many different types of literacy events over an extended period of time allowed children to form a richly interconnected network of knowledge related to their personal learning themes. Together these curricular characteristics supported children in forming complex intertextual connections as they learned about literacy.

REFERENCES

Beaugrande, R. de, & Dressler, W. (1981). *Introduction to text linguistics.* New York: Longman.

Cicourel, A. (1975). *Theory and method in a study of Argentine fertility.* New York: Wiley.

Denzin, N. K. (1978). *Sociological methods.* New York: McGraw-Hill.

DeVilliers, P. A. & DeVilliers, J. G. (1979). *Early language.* Cambridge, MA: Harvard.

Glaser, B. G., & Strauss, A. L. (1967). *The discovery of grounded theory. Strategies for qualitative research.* New York: Aldine.

Halliday, M. A. K. (1975). *Learning how to mean. Explorations in the development of language.* London: Edward Arnold.

Hardy, B. (1978). Narrative as a primary act of mind. In M. Meek, A. Warlow, & G. Baron (Eds.), *The cool web: The pattern of children's reading.* New York: Atheneum.

Harste, J. C., Woodward, V. A., & Burke, C. L. (1984). *Language stories and literacy lessons.* Portsmouth, NH: Heinemann.

Hymes, D. H. (1978). *What is ethnography?* (Sociolinguistic Working Paper No. 45). Austin, TX: Southwest Educational Development Laboratory.

Lincoln, Y. S., & Guba, E. G. (1985). *Naturalistic inquiry.* Beverly Hills: Sage.

Lindfors, J. W. (1980). *Children's language and learning.* Englewood Cliffs, NJ: Prentice-Hall.

Rosen, H. (1984). *Stories and meanings.* London: National Association for the Teaching of English.

Rowe, D. W. (1986). *Literacy in the child's world: Young children's explorations of alternate communication systems.* Unpublished doctoral dissertation, Indiana University, Bloomington.

Spiro, R. J. (1985). *Knowledge acquisition for application: Cognitive flexibility and transfer of training in ill-structured domains.* Unpublished proposal for funded research, University of Illinois, Center for the Study of Reading, Urbana-Champaign.

Spiro, R. J., & Myers, A. (1984). Individual differences and underlying cognitive processes in reading. In P. D. Pearson (Ed.), *Handbook of reading research* (pp. 471–501). New York: Longman.

Spiro, R. J., Vispoel, W. L., Schmitz, J., Samarapungavan, A., & Boerger, A. (in press). Knowledge acquisition for application: Cognitive flexibility and transfer in complex content domains. In B. C. Britton (Ed.), *Executive control processes.* Hillsdale, NJ: Erlbaum.

ASSESSMENT

EMERGENT LITERACY

COMPREHENSION

INSTRUCTIONAL EFFECTIVENESS

ADULT LITERACY

WRITING

'SHOULD READING COMPREHENSION SKILLS BE TAUGHT?

Ronald P. Carver
University of Missouri-Kansas City

Teachers are now being told to spend more time teaching reading comprehension skills. The research evidence supporting this admonition can be interpreted as exceptionally weak, nonexistent, or even directly counter. This article contains a review of recent admonitions and relevant research along with alternative explanations and admonitions.

RECENT ADMONITIONS

In the recently published *Becoming a Nation of Readers* (1985), we find the following:

> Teachers need to teach comprehension strategies directly. Teachers should devote more time to teaching strategies for understanding not only stories but also social studies and science texts. (p. 81)

The above exhortation comes from an authoritative report published jointly by the National Academy of Education, the National Institute of Education, and the Center for the Study of Reading. It may be expected to have a major effect upon what teachers do in the classroom.

Another recently published article can be expected to have even a bigger influence upon what reading teachers do. In the April 1985 issue of *The Reading Teacher*, P. David Pearson presented a lengthy and persuasive case for ''changing the face of reading comprehension instruction,'' especially by getting teachers involved in the direct instruction of reading comprehension skills. The Pearson article is exemplary in its presentation of exhortations based upon coherent theory and detailed experimental evidence. Before implementing major changes, however, educators may benefit from a closer look at the data that purportedly support these theoretical and practical ideas.

THREE PRINCIPLES

Before looking at the specifics of several recent research studies, it will be helpful to review what we already know about reading comprehension. A concrete example will be given first in order to establish three principles later. Suppose a student at the fourth-grade level of reading ability is presented passages at the first-, fourth-, and seventh-grade levels of difficulty. We say that these passages are at the student's independent, instructional, and frustration levels, respectively. Using the comprehension criteria of Betts (1957), we can estimate that this student will comprehend about 90%, 75%, and 50% of these passages, respectively, when they are read once at a reading rate typical of fourth graders. So, the first principle to remember is that we can increase the degree to which students will comprehend passages simply by using passages easier than those at the frustration level; this will be called the *Easiness Principle*.

The second principle to remember is that students can improve the degree to which they comprehend a passage by spending more time reading the passage. For example, if a passage at the seventh-grade level of difficulty is read twice by this student at the fourth-grade level of ability, the percentage of comprehension can be estimated to increase from 50% to 67%, using prediction equations developed by Carver (1977); this will be called the *Reading Time Principle*.

The third principle is that students ordinarily improve on any reading-related task simply by practicing on that task; this will be called the *Practice Principle*. Reading a passage more than once, the Reading Time Principle, could be considered a form of the Practice Principle, but it will be convenient to separate these two principles.

The three principles described above can be used to explain why an experimental group scores higher than a control group on many of the dependent variables used in reading research studies. If the research results can be explained by one or more of these principles, there is no evidence that individuals have increased their general reading ability. For example, if an experimental group is taught a study skill that involves reading difficult passages two to three times before attempting to answer comprehension questions, any advantage accrued by the experimental group could be explained by the Reading Time Principle. And, there would be no reason to expect that subjects in the experimental group would have increased their general reading ability so that they could comprehend more than subjects in the control group when both groups expended the same amount of reading time. If the general reading ability of the experimental group improves, the subjects should have a higher instructional level or they should score higher on a comprehension test that controlled for reading time.

EVIDENCE REVIEWED BY PEARSON

Introduction

Pearson (1985) contended that researchers have successfully helped students develop strategies for becoming better comprehenders, and he reviewed research in four areas — questions, inference training, question-answer relationships, and reciprocal teaching. The data he presented relevant to these four areas will be reviewed in turn.

Questions

Pearson summarized two studies that investigated the effect of requiring students to answer inferential questions. These two studies will be critiqued in some detail.

The Hansen (1981) study involved eight second graders in each of three groups. One group was given "practice in answering questions which required inferences between text and prior knowledge" (p. 391). Members of another group were asked to use their own experiences to make predictions about events in upcoming stories. These two groups were much better than a control group in answering comprehension questions following instructional stories but were not better in the free recall of test stories. On the comprehension section of the Stanford Achievement Test, the question group scored much higher than the control group. However, the variance of the scores in the control group was nine times larger than the variance of the scores in the question group; this abnormality renders these data suspect. The results suggest that second graders can be taught how to answer certain kinds of questions better given appropriate practice, the Practice Principle. But, there is no compelling evidence that this is a skill that will transfer to reading and comprehending better in general, such as our hypothetical student going from a fourth-grade instructional level to a fifth-grade instructional level. Hansen, herself, notes that "the local results are more impressive than the broad transfer effects in this study" (p. 415).

The above study of Hansen (1981) illustrates the scenario that will be replayed many times in the remainder of the research reviews. A type of study skill is taught and found to be effective. The results can be explained by the Easiness Principle, the Reading Time Principle, or the Practice Principle. But, there is no sound evidence that there is a transfer of this *comprehension strategy* to general reading ability.

The next study, by Hansen and Pearson (1983), involved good and poor fourth-grade readers given experimental and control treatments, 10 students per group. Over a 10-week period, the experimental subjects were given strategy training and a great many inferential postreading questions. The measure used in this research was a 5-point scale applied to answers to open-ended questions on stories, both literal and inferential. It is distressing to note that these subjectively scored measures were administered individually by the experimenters who evidently knew whether the students were in the experimental or the control groups when they were giving the tests; experimenter bias was apparently uncontrolled.

Hansen and Pearson (1983) go on to report that "the results showed that poor readers benefited significantly from the instruction, but good readers did not" (p. 821). It is important to note that the good readers were given materials to read that were two to four grade levels below their measured reading level, presumably at their independent level. Probably, there would have been no effect for the poor readers also if they had been given materials at their independent level. More importantly, however, there appeared to be no control for how long the students spent reading the stories. It seems possible, even likely, that the instructions given the experimentals had the effect of inducing the poor readers to get into the habit of spending more time reading the stories because they could subsequently be more successful in the discussions that involved the inferential questions. There was no apparent control for the

Reading Time Principle, the obvious alternate explanation for these results. There is a great deal of evidence to indicate that the degree to which a passage is comprehended by an individual increases with the amount of time spent reading it (see Carver, 1982), the Reading Time Principle. Unless the experimental group and the control group spent an equal amount of time reading, we do not know whether the experimental subjects have learned a valuable new skill to apply in their reading or whether they have simply been induced to trade off time for better comprehension. In short, these data can alternately be interpreted to mean that when students are given material to read at their instructional or frustration level they can be forced into the habit of slowing down, spending more time, and rereading in order to increase their comprehension. This type of skill is more conventionally known as a study skill, not a *comprehension* skill.

In summary, the two studies above do not present compelling evidence that elementary students can be given a great deal of experience in answering inferential questions which somehow transfers immediately to a higher level of general reading ability. The counter evidence that Hansen (1981) presented, from the comprehension section of the Stanford Achievement Test, was flawed by incredibly large differences in the amount of variance in their treatment groups. At best, these data suggest that elementary students can be taught study skills that help them do better on reading-related tasks that are seldom encountered.

Inference Training

With respect to this second area, which Pearson called "inference training," all the evidence he could muster was contained in an unpublished technical report, released two years earlier in 1983. Evidence presented in referreed journals carries the most weight. Evidence presented in older technical reports that have had time to be published is not exactly in the public domain and does not have to be weighed.

Question-answer Relationships

With respect to this third area, Pearson highlighted two studies that were published in 1985. Raphael and Wonnacott (1985) gave fourth graders training in categorizing questions with respect to whether the answers were textually explicit, called "Right There," textually implicit, called "Think and Search," and scriptually implicit, called "On My Own." After four days of training, the experimental group failed to show any improvement over a control group; this was Experiment 1. Other students were then given one week of training and eight weeks of what was called "maintenance"—Experiment 2. At the end of the training week in this second experiment, these researchers again reported that there was no treatment effect evident. At the end of the nine weeks, one of their two dependent variables "showed no effect of training on response quality" (p. 292). On a second dependent measure, they found a large treatment effect in their low ability group (about 89% correct answers vs. 62% for controls). They found a small treatment effect in their average ability group (about 83% correct answers vs. 77% for controls). And, they found no treatment effect for their high ability group. Unfortunately, Raphael and Wonnacott did not report the readability level of the test passages they used. They also did not report the reading level of their three ability groups even though all three groups had been administered the Iowa Test of Basic Skills (ITBS) achievement tests; the reading comprehension score on the ITBS was used as a covariate. Without having access to this latter information, it is difficult to estimate accurately whether these students were given material at their frustration, instructional, or independent levels. However, it seems reasonable to speculate that the question-answer relationships training had (a) no effect on the comprehension of passages at the independent level for the high group, and (b) little effect at the instructional level for the average group. But, for one of three measures of the treatment effect, the results do suggest that the trained low ability group subjects probably did learn to slow down and study the frustration level passages so that they were able to answer about 80% of the questions. The Reading Time Principle provides a plausible explanation for the shred of positive evidence in this study.

An alternate way of interpreting these data from Raphael and Wonnacott that appears to be more accurate is as follows: The question-answer relationships treatment had no effect when the material was at the instructional and independent levels, but it was partially successful in getting students to study frustration level material until they could answer more than 75% of the questions correctly. Since the treatment had little or no measurable benefit for the average and high readers, and since only one of three comparisons favored the treatment for the low readers, the research of Raphael and Wonnacott can be interpreted as providing evidence *against* teaching these so called comprehension skills.

Raphael and Pearson (1985) conducted a study similar to the one above except it involved sixth graders. Students at high, average, and low ability levels were given tests on passages at the fourth-, sixth-, and eighth-grade levels of difficulty. When reading "level-appropriate materials" (i.e., the low ability group read fourth-grade difficulty material, the average ability group read sixth-grade difficulty materials, and the high ability group read eighth-grade difficulty materials), the experimental groups that received the question-answer relationships training answered 86% of the questions correctly while the control groups answered 80% correctly. This 6% treatment effect probably would be considered small by many researchers, and easily due to one of the following: (a) the treatment group studied the passages a little longer than the control group (the Reading Time Principle), or (b) the treatment group had more practice in answering the questions on the test since the questions were the same type as those used in the treatment (the Practice Principle). Raphael and Pearson completely ignored the Reading Time Principle, but they did present an argument against the Practice Principle. They said that the Raphael and Wonnacott (1985) research, reviewed earlier, found no "significant difference" between one control group that practiced answering the treatment questions and another control group that had no such practice. However, a close inspection of the evidence relevant to their failure to find *statistical* significance reveals that there was no report of the sample size, the mean difference, or the standard deviations involved. It is possible that their nonsignificant difference was as large as the 6% found by Raphael and Pearson, but because of the sample sizes and variances involved, it was not a statistically significant difference. Therefore, it is also possible that their 6% difference was due to a practice effect, in spite of the protestations of Raphael and Pearson. This failure to discriminate between statistical significance and effect size is another example of what Carver (1978) has called the corrupt scientific method.

In summary, this question-answer relationships evidence that Pearson has provided in support of teaching reading comprehension skills is weak at best.

Reciprocal Teaching

With respect to this fourth and last area, Pearson summarized only one publication, but it was described in much more detail than any other research article that he reviewed. This article, by Palincsar and Brown (1984), involved six, seventh-grade students in each of four groups—two groups received instruction and two did not. All 24 students were selected because they were poor readers; the seventh graders read at about the fourth-grade level. The instruction received by the reciprocal teaching group involved 13 passages, each about 1,500 words in length, at the seventh-grade level of difficulty. After reading a segment (paragraph) of a passage, students were taught to both ask and answer questions, to listen to summaries, to do their own summarizing, and to offer predictions or ask for clarifications. This training, called reciprocal teaching, took place over a 20-day period, 30 minutes a day. Pretest to posttest, the reciprocal teaching group improved from about 30% to 80% on the comprehension test scores while the other three groups stayed around 40% comprehension. Furthermore, these six poor readers in this reciprocal teaching group scored higher after treatment, 80%, than 13 average seventh-grade readers who received no treatment, 75%.

Taken at face value, the data collected by Palincsar and Brown seem to suggest that we can administer this reciprocal teaching procedure to seventh-grade children who are reading at the fourth-grade level (with a reported mean IQ of 83) and they will be equal in reading ability to average seventh graders in 20 days (requiring only 30 minutes per day). This finding was described by Pearson as "dramatic"; even that description seems modest. I would describe my first reaction to this treatment effect as breathtaking because of its incredibly large size. After further study, my second reaction was that almost any researcher could get this kind of result by somehow inducing students to spend more time reading and studying passages that are three grade levels higher in difficulty than their ability. Stated differently, I am very confident that if these six students in the reciprocal teaching group had spent the same amount of time reading the passages on the posttest as they did on the pretest, they would have improved from 30% to 40% instead of from 30% to 80%. In this research, there was no control for time spent reading the passages on the assessment tests. Furthermore, this 59-page research report failed to mention the instructions given to the 24 subjects prior to administering these assessment tests. The Reading Time Principle was completely ignored.

It appears that we have a choice in how to interpret these results of Palincsar and Brown. We can view them as indicating that low IQ seventh graders reading at the fourth-grade level can be taught a comprehension skill, in only 10 hours of instruction, that can make them equal in reading ability to average seventh graders. Or, we can alternately interpret these results as indicating that students who are forced to read materials that are very difficult for them can be taught to spend large amounts of time reading them and thereby achieve the same degree of comprehension as average students do when they spend lesser amounts of time reading. The first interpretation implies a breakthrough in reading instruction heretofore unparalleled in efficacy. The second interpretation suggests that we might get the same results in one day instead of 20 days if we simply required the students to read and study the test passages for a long time before we gave them the questions.

Later in the Palincsar and Brown article, we find that they did administer a standardized reading test, pre and post. These data should provide information about whether the instructional level of the treatment group improved, using a test that controls for reading time. Stated differently, this test allows some estimate as to whether reciprocal teaching results in a transfer to general reading ability. The test was administered three months later as a posttest but it was *only* given to the six students in the reciprocal teaching group, that is, none of the students in the other three groups received this test as a control measure. These researchers reported that this test indicated that there was no improvement on the vocabulary measure (mean gain = 1 month), but that the mean gain on the comprehension measure was 15 months, or 1.25 GE units. This was a substantial gain in the comprehension measure. Yet, these researchers neglected to remind the reader that these students had been selected at the outset only if they scored at least 2 years below grade level on the basis of the pretest scores on this same reading comprehension measure. Thus, this entire gain is likely to be due to regression to the mean effects. There was no mention of this possibility, let alone its high probability. Such a cavalier disregard for the fundamental principles of research design, data analysis, and data interpretation is difficult to fathom in a modern research journal.

These data collected by Palincsar and Brown provide the best evidence to date *against* the contention that comprehension skills are being taught. Instead, these data suggest that study skills are being taught and that these study skills will often be helpful when students are forced to read material at the frustration level of difficulty and still comprehend it well. It is misleading to call this a comprehension skill because it suggests that teaching it will somehow help a student better comprehend material at the instructional level or independent level. This instructional strategy probably helps a great deal at the frustration level by trading off time for more comprehension. Yet, it is possible that reciprocal teaching is counterproductive because students might get into the habit of learning to read everything more slowly, even material at the independent level.

Summary

The evidence presented by Pearson (1985) relevant to the case for teaching reading comprehension skills can be alternately interpreted as indicating that elementary students can be taught certain study skills. They can be taught to answer inferential questions better. They can also be taught to comprehend more of materials that are at their frustration level of difficulty as long as they are willing to spend more time studying these materials. There appears to be no compelling evidence that this so-called comprehension instruction transfers to an improvement in a general ability to read as measured by timed comprehension tests. There appears to be no evidence that

students taught by these methods will somehow immediately reach a higher instructional level. There appears to be no evidence that passages presented at the instructional level will somehow be better comprehended without spending more time reading them.

OTHER RESEARCH

At this point some readers may object that there is a great deal more relevant evidence than that reviewed above. In response to this possible objection, I will briefly review six research studies that are often mentioned when a case is made for direct instruction, or explicit instruction, in reading comprehension (e.g., see *Becoming a Nation of Readers*, 1985).

Beck, Omanson, and McKeown (1982) gave 12 skilled readers (GE = 5.1) and 12 less skilled readers (GE = 3.1) stories at the second-grade level; all students were in the third grade. The experimental treatment was to give prior knowledge using pre-story preparation. For the skilled readers, 6% more questions were answered under the experimental treatment. For the less skilled readers, 7% more questions were answered under the experimental treatment. This 6% and 7% treatment effect is smaller than what might be expected to be associated with giving prior knowledge; it is probably due to the fact that the material was not at the frustration level—for the skilled readers it was at the independent level. Nonetheless, this research introduces another principle that must be acknowledged when discussing research on reading comprehension, the *Prior Knowledge Principle*. Students will usually comprehend more of a passage if they have, or are given, more prior knowledge. Giving prior knowledge is often what we do when we engage in instruction, especially when a college professor explains what a student is supposed to comprehend in a college textbook. Yet, it is somewhat misleading to refer to the administration of prior knowledge as direct instruction in reading comprehension. Couching the instruction in these terms suggests that we are teaching a skill that will transfer to reading in general.

Singer and Donlan (1982) reported on a study in which 14 seventh graders were taught to generate questions on short stories. The same teacher taught a control group of 13. Since only one teacher was involved, it is possible that the results cannot be generalized beyond this one teacher, a serious threat to external validity that needs to be considered. The instructional materials were at the sixth-grade level, but no information was given about the reading ability level of the students. Compared to the controls, the experimental subjects answered 5% more questions correctly. Again, this is a small effect for teaching a study skill but there is no evidence that this skill would immediately transfer to other reading comprehension situations.

Tharp (1982) presented a lengthy report on the effect of a teaching program that emphasized comprehension skills throughout the school year, in grades 1–3. Although three studies were reported, only Experiment 3 was a true experiment with students assigned to experimental and control teaching groups. In this experiment, the treatment accounted for only 2% of the variance in a vocabulary measure, only 1% of the variance in a reading comprehension measure, and only 1% of the variance in a reading achievement measure. These effect sizes for teaching comprehension are exceptionally small yet never mentioned by these researchers or their reviewers. Instead of these data supporting a case for teaching reading comprehension, the data may be alternately interpreted as providing counter evidence.

Patching, Kameenui, Carnine, Gersten, and Colvin (1983) gave three, 30-minute instructional sessions to 13 fifth graders in each of three groups. Critical reasoning was taught on an individual basis to one group, and "the major test developed for the study was the critical reading test, a domain-referenced test geared to the three categories taught" (p. 412). Indeed, the group that received the instruction in critical reasoning did much better on the tests that involved critical reasoning—results explained by the Practice Principle. Again, there was no evidence that improvement on this task by practicing it somehow transfers to other reading-related tasks that require comprehension. These data can be interpreted as indicating that fifth graders can be taught certain study skills related to test taking.

Baumann (1984) taught sixth-grade students how to recognize main ideas, using eight lessons of 30 minutes each. Using his techniques for assessing gain in the ability to recognize main ideas, there was credible evidence that this instruction had a large effect—results explained by the Practice Principle. However, on a measure of total ideas recalled, the experimental subjects did worse than the controls in two out of three comparisons. Again, this result indicates that another type of study skill can be taught, but the evidence suggests that the individuals will not comprehend better in general.

Finally, Paris, Cross, and Lipson (1984) gave metacognition training to third and fifth graders and compared the effects to controls. The training lasted four months with two, 30-minute sessions per week. From the data reported, it was possible to calculate Cohen's d as a measure of effect size (see Carver, 1984); Cohen (1977) gives the following criteria for small, medium, and large effects: $d = .2$, $.5$, and $.8$, respectively. On two standardized reading tests (the Gates-MacGinitie and the Test of Reading Comprehension), the comprehension training had small effects in both the third and fifth grades ($d \leq .2$). For the cloze task and the error detection tasks, the effect sizes in both grades were medium to large ($.4 \leq d \leq .7$). Why did this comprehension instruction have little or no effect using standardized reading tests that involved reading passages and answering questions but had a medium to large effect on the cloze task and error detection tasks? These researchers interpreted their results as indicating that something was wrong with the standardized tests. An alternative explanation is that some of the metacognitive skills taught (such as skimming a passage before you read it, reading the same story twice, using the rest of a sentence as a clue to understanding words, and looking back in a story to check what happened) would help a great deal on an untimed cloze task and an untimed error detection task because these are study skills that allow more blanks to be filled in and more errors to be detected. However, these study skills will not help much when there is a time limit or when reading materials are at the instructional level, as was the case with the standardized reading tests. Again, these metacognitive skills seem to be best interpreted as study skills that are helpful when students have to engage in problem-solving to do well, when students are given frustration level passages, or when they are given untimed word skill tasks such as cloze. There is no evidence that the metacognitive skills that were taught have anything to do with improving the normal comprehension processes that occur when reading materials at the instructional or independent levels.

After reviewing all of this recent evidence that purportedly supports the teaching of comprehension skills or strategies, it appears reasonable to summarize these data with two separate statements. First, when students are given material that they cannot comprehend well when they read it as they normally do, they can be taught certain study skills that will increase their accuracy of comprehension. Second, when students are given a specific reading task, such as answering main idea questions, they can be instructed or trained to answer these questions better with guided practice, but there is no evidence that this skill will transfer to more global reading comprehension skills. Therefore, if educators are most concerned with helping students become better comprehenders in general, as is commonly measured by standardized tests of reading comprehension or informal reading inventories, there is no evidence that the currently touted instructional practices are beneficial. In fact, this so-called comprehension instruction is likely to be most effective when students are given materials to read that are at their frustration level of difficulty—a practice that would ordinarily be considered poor teaching.

IMPLICATIONS AND ADMONITIONS

In contrast to the instructional practices that have been reviewed, consider the following alternative: Before students reach the eighth-grade level of reading ability, never ask them to read materials that are above their instructional level. When students reach the eighth-grade level of reading ability, that is, become a reasonably proficient and literate reader, they can be taught various study skills which will help them when they encounter material that they cannot comprehend well. Adoption of the eighth-grade level as a criterion for deciding when to give students relatively difficult material and when to teach them study skills has support from two separate research findings. Carver (1975) randomly sampled newspapers from all states in the United States and found that the lead stories were written at the eighth-grade level on the average. Also, Sticht, Beck, Hauke, Kleiman, and James (1974) found that reading ability catches up to auding ability at about the seventh- or eighth-grade level. Thus, when we have been successful in helping students reach the level at which they can inform themselves about current events by reading newspapers and can also read as well as they can aud, then it seems reasonable to give them relatively difficult materials and teach them strategies for comprehending them better.

Adoption of the above instructional strategy would eliminate almost all of the comprehension instruction reviewed earlier when it was implemented in elementary schools and when it was implemented with poor readers. Adoption of this alternative strategy also would force a focus upon getting children to read more as the best way to improve reading ability (see Carver, 1986). Finally, adoption of this alternative strategy would force schools to adopt textbooks for content area reading that were not written at a difficulty level higher than the ability level of the students. Or, if the given textbooks were indeed at a higher level, teachers would not ask students to read these materials but instead someone would read the books to the students.

It is an empirical question as to whether the greatest yearly gains in reading ability can be achieved by (a) teaching study skills to poor readers so they can eventually comprehend well a particularly difficult passage, or (b) giving poor readers materials at their own level of instructional difficulty and letting them have the same advantages that good readers always have.

At the moment, there appear to be ample reasons to seriously consider this alternative instructional strategy. Why not try getting students to read more materials at their independent level and their instructional level, rather than trying to teach them how to comprehend well materials that are at their frustration level? Why not stop trying to teach students how to answer main idea questions on material that they have trouble understanding in the first place, and simply make sure these students are spending a great deal of time reading materials that they can comprehend well? Why not stop trying to teach specific skills after students reach about the second-grade level of ability, and from then on let the teacher be responsible for inducing students to spend a great deal of time reading?

The above ideas have been presented as a serious challenge to the current generalization that teachers need to devote more time to teaching strategies for understanding, as was noted at the outset. Instead, teachers need to devote more time to getting students to read more because this would increase their vocabulary, increase their prior knowledge, and increase their decoding efficiency, three of the primary ingredients for improving general reading ability.

CONCLUSIONS

The evidence presented to support the case for teachers spending more time teaching reading comprehension skills is frail at best. Too often the Easiness Principle and the Reading Time Principle are not accounted for in research, and there is no solid evidence that gains due to the Practice Principle will transfer to reading ability in general. The most dramatic evidence for teaching comprehension skills was presented by Palincsar and Brown (1984), but few researchers would accept the finding that seventh graders reading at the fourth-grade level can be given 10 hours of reciprocal teaching and then become equal in reading ability to average seventh graders. Instead, the Palincsar and Brown results are more reasonably interpreted as indicating that certain strategies, such as spending more time reading and studying, will result in a higher accuracy of comprehension especially when the materials presented are at the frustration level. Indeed, most of the comprehension skill instruction seems to be more reasonably interpreted as follows: Certain study skills can be taught that are likely to help students comprehend more of the materials at the frustration level, but these skills are not likely to help students comprehend any more of the materials at the instructional level unless they spend more time reading them.

It should not be forgotten that giving students materials at their frustration level of difficulty is commonly considered to be poor teaching. Before we waste more time and effort coercing teachers into teaching these so-called reading comprehension skills, it would seem prudent to acknowledge that the payoff is likely to be small and limited to situations that reading teachers have been taught to avoid. It makes more sense to regard comprehension skills as study skills in disguise, and teaching them to unskilled readers is a questionable practice.

REFERENCES

Baumann, J. F. (1984). The effectiveness of a direct instruction paradigm for teaching main idea comprehension. *Reading Research Quarterly, 20*, 93–115.

Beck, I. L., Omanson, R. C., & McKeown, M. G. (1982). An instructional redesign of reading lessons: Effects on comprehension. *Reading Research Quarterly, 17*, 462–481.

Betts, E. A. (1957). *Foundations of reading instruction.* New York: American Book Company.

Becoming a nation of readers. (1985). Washington, DC: The National Institute of Education.

Carver, R. P. (1975). Measuring prose difficulty using the Rauding Scale. *Reading Research Quarterly, 11*, 660–685.

Carver, R. P. (1977). Toward a theory of reading comprehension and rauding. *Reading Research Quarterly, 13*, 8–63.

Carver, R. P. (1978). The case against statistical significance testing. *Harvard Educational Review, 48*, 378–399.

Carver, R. P. (1982). Optimal rate of reading prose. *Reading Research Quarterly, 18*, 190–215.

Carver, R. P. (1984). *Writing a publishable research report: In education, psychology, and related disciplines.* Springfield, IL: Charles C Thomas.

Carver, R. P. (1986, June). *Improving reading ability: Rauding theory and practice.* Invited Address presented at the University of Wisconsin Symposium on Reading, Milwaukee, WI.

Cohen, J. (1977). *Statistical power analysis for the behavioral sciences* (rev. ed.). New York: Academic Press.

Hansen, J. (1981). The effects of inference training and practice on young children's reading comprehension. *Reading Research Quarterly, 16*, 391–417.

Hansen, J., & Pearson, P. D. (1983). An instructional study: Improving the inferential comprehension of good and poor fourth-grade readers. *Journal of Educational Psychology, 75*, 821–829.

Palincsar, A. S., & Brown, A. L. (1984). Reciprocal teaching of comprehension-fostering and comprehension-monitoring activities. *Cognition and Instruction, 1*, 117–175.

Paris, S. G., Cross, D. R., & Lipson, M. Y. (1984). Informed strategies for learning: A program to improve children's reading awareness and comprehension. *Journal of Educational Psychology, 76*, 1,239–1,252.

Patching, W., Kameenui, E., Carnine, D., Gersten, R., & Colvin, G. (1983). Direct instruction in critical reading skills. *Reading Research Quarterly, 18*, 406–418.

Pearson, P. D. (1985). Changing the face of reading comprehension instruction. *The Reading Teacher, 38*, 724–738.

Raphael, T. E., & Pearson, P. D. (1985). Increasing students' awareness of sources of information for answering questions. *American Educational Research Journal, 22*, 217–235.

Raphael, T. E., & Wonnacott, C. A. (1985). Heightening fourth-grade students' sensitivity to sources of information for answering comprehension questions. *Reading Research Quarterly, 20*, 282–296.

Singer, H., & Donlan, D. (1982). Active comprehension: Problem-solving schema with question generation for comprehension of complex short stories. *Reading Research Quarterly, 17*, 166–186.

Sticht, T. G., Beck, L. J., Hauke, R. N., Kleiman, G. M., & James, J. H. (1974). *Auding and reading.* Alexandria, VA: Human Resources Research Organization.

Tharp, R. G. (1982). The effective instruction of comprehension: Results and description of the Kamehameha Early Education Program. *Reading Research Quarterly, 17*, 503–527.

VARIABLES INFLUENCING IMPORTANCE ASSIGNMENT

Peter Afflerbach
Emory University

Determining important information in text is a crucial, yet little understood, comprehension process (Brown & Day, 1983; van Dijk & Kintsch, 1983; Winograd, 1984). Through the process of importance assignment, the reader allocates memory resources to particular information in the text, depending on the purpose and nature of the reader's interaction with text. van Dijk (1979) has proposed two types of importance assignment: textual and contextual. In general, textual importance is assumed to reflect what the writer considers important. For example, the writer may use text structure (Meyer, 1975) to signal textual importance. In contrast, contextual importance reflects what is important to the reader, which may be influenced by several factors, including purpose for reading (Anderson & Pearson, 1984) and prior knowledge (Afflerbach, 1986). Recent research has explored additional factors which may influence contextual importance assignment, including readers' affective interaction with text (Martins, 1982) and the perceived author of the text (Johnston & Afflerbach, 1985). However, much remains to be learned about importance assignment processes (Roller, 1985; Winograd & Bridge, 1986).

This study investigated competent readers' importance assignment processes on a variety of texts. Subjects gave verbal reports of their importance assignment processes while reading and then performed Likert-scale ratings of the influence of four variables which previous research has shown to influence importance assignment. The four variables were text structure (Meyer, 1975), emotional response to the content of the text (Martins, 1982), prior knowledge (Anderson & Pearson, 1986), and perceived author (Johnston & Afflerbach, 1985).

METHOD

Subjects

Six undergraduate college students from a private, southeastern university participated in this study. Each subject had a GPA $\rangle$ 3.5. All subjects reported that their current courses required frequent reading assignments. Additionally, all subjects reported an interest in reading as a hobby. Thus, the subjects in this study were practiced and competent readers in academic and nonacademic settings.

Materials

To allow for the examination of importance assignment processes used across a variety of text genres, six different texts were selected for the study. The texts included an editorial page essay (''Timid textbook publishers evading responsibility''), a letter about civil rights (''Letter from Birmingham Jail'' by Martin Luther King, Jr.), a *Newsweek* article about pesticide use, and two short poems (''Stopping by Woods on a Snowy Evening'' by Robert Frost, and ''The Red Wheelbarrow'' by William Carlos Williams). In addition, each student read a two-page excerpt from a textbook for a course in which the individual student was enrolled. Topics of the textbook excerpts included organic chemistry, macroeconomics, social psychology, sociology, and religion.

Procedure

All subjects were polled to determine that they had read poems, editorials, letters, news articles, and content area school texts. This was necessary because instructions asked that subjects read each text in a typical manner. The instructions required a tradeoff in terms of control in the study, as purpose-setting was performed by the individual subject. This tradeoff of experimental control for ecological validity allowed for the qualitative analysis of verbal report excerpts which illustrate the variety of importance assignment processes reported. Quantitative analysis of the verbal reports was not appropriate because subjects set their own purposes for reading, and this individual purpose-setting was assumed to have influenced importance assignment processes (Afflerbach, 1986).

The order in which the texts were read was counterbalanced. Subjects read each text aloud and gave concurrent verbal reports of the processes they used to assign importance. After each text was read, subjects performed a Likert-scale rating of the perceived influence of four variables (prior knowledge, text structure, perceived author, and emotional response) on the importance assignment processes used on each text. Following the think-aloud and rating tasks, subjects gave retrospective reports on their purposes for reading.

The think-aloud protocols were analyzed qualitatively for reports of importance assignment. The verbal reports were classified by the primary investigator according to the cues which readers used to assign importance: prior knowledge, text structure, perceived author, and emotional response to text. The fifth category was multiple cue, in which the use of more than one type of cue was reported. A second rater than classified 40 of the importance assignment excerpts using the five categories. Interrater reliability in coding importance assignment processes was .92.

RESULTS

Results of the study will be discussed in the following manner: first, subjects' Likert-scale ratings of the influences on importance assignment will be presented. Next, the results of a series of repeated measures, one-way ANOVAs will be discussed, in which text (letter, magazine article, editorial, poem 1, poem 2, textbook excerpt) was the independent variable and the Likert-scale rating of each of the four variables influencing importance assignment (values of 1–5) was the dependent variable. Concurrently, verbal report excerpts which illustrate the influence of prior knowledge, text structure, perceived author, and emotional response on importance assignment will be presented. It is noted that the verbal report excerpts provide only brief glimpses of some of the many importance assignment processes which occur throughout the reading of a text. However, space limitations require that selected samples be used in lieu of entire think-aloud transcripts. Finally, subjects' retrospective reports of purpose for reading will be considered.

Table 1 presents the mean ratings of the influence of prior knowledge, text structure, perceived author, and emotional response on importance assignment for the six texts.

Table 1

Mean Ratings of Influences on the Assignment of Importance

Text	Prior Knowledge	Text Structure	Perceived Author	Emotional Response
Letter from jail	3.83	2.83	5.00	4.67
Pesticide article	2.83	2.83	2.33	3.00
Textbook excerpt	4.33	3.00	2.00	2.83
Frost poem	3.16	3.16	4.33	3.50
Williams poem	1.16	3.67	3.00	3.00
Censorship editorial	3.00	2.50	2.83	3.83

Note. 1 = relatively small influence; 5 = relatively large influence.

Prior Knowledge

The repeated measures ANOVA for the influence of prior knowledge on importance assignment yielded a univariate $F(5, 25) = 7.85$, $p < .001$. Tukey pair-wise comparisons yielded a critical value of 1.687 ($p < .05$). Prior knowledge was rated as having a statistically significant influence on the importance assignment processes used on each text, when compared with the poem "The Red Wheelbarrow." As indicated by subjects' mean ratings, prior knowledge had the greatest influence on the assignment of importance when subjects were reading current college textbooks.

> . . . that sentence . . what stands out is the "organic compounds have considerably lower densities than water" . . cause I have . I have a hands-on idea of the physical properties of water . . and I understand what "density" is from previous chapters . . . saying these compounds have lower densities . . presents a very real image in my mind . . .

In this excerpt, it appears the subject is using information learned in previous chapters of the chemistry textbook and laboratory work to help determine the importance in text. In a retrospective report, this subject noted that his organic chemistry textbook was in fact the only source of prior knowledge which he applied to subsequent chapters of the textbook:

> . . . it's pretty cut-and-dried . . . I don't think I'll come across anything in a newspaper . . or on TV . . that will help me pick important stuff here . . .

In contrast, prior knowledge was rated as having a significantly smaller influence on the assignment of importance for the poem "The Red Wheelbarrow," compared with all other texts. In the following excerpt, a subject reports a lack of prior knowledge for the poet, the structure of the poem, and the genre of poetry, each of which might be used to inform the process of importance assignment:

> Williams? I'm not familiar with Williams . . don't know his stuff . . and this poem . . is it the whole thing? . . I mean . . . this is pretty strange set-up . . . even for a poem . . I guess these words . . set apart from the others are important . . I don't read that much poetry anyway . . .

Text Structure

The repeated measures ANOVA for the influence of text structure on importance assignment yielded a univariate $F(5, 25) = .86, p < .52$. While there were no statistically significant differences in the perceived influence of text structure on importance assignment, verbal reports allow for consideration of the effects of text structure on subjects' importance assignment processes. For example, one structural feature common to both of the poems used in this study was an economy of language, and subjects noted that they adjusted their importance assignment procedures accordingly. A subject reading the poem "Stopping by Woods on a Snowy Evening" reported the following:

> . . . the "deep" "keep" "sleep" "sleep" is a different rhyme from the rest . . and it has kind of a hypnotic sound . . "dark and deep" . . the repetition of the "miles to go before I sleep" is the same . . . in poetry . . you have to think about the words and how they're put together . . because it's not as long . . so each word has more importance in poetry.

Retrospective reports indicated that subjects did not typically feel accountable for remembering the contents of a poem (as opposed to a textbook or op-ed essay). The retrospective reports indicated that this approach to the task allowed subjects to focus on the structure of the poem, and an emotional response to it:

> y'know . . . I just don't expect to get . . . twen-fifty multiple choice questions about this poem . . I don't know that I'll remember it all but that's OK too . . I can pay more attention to how he set it up . . put it together and the pictures he's made . . and how I feel about them . . .

In the above verbal report, the subject makes reference to the text structure, an emotional response, and the perceived author, all of which can influence the assignment of importance. Thus, this excerpt may indicate the simultaneous use of different cues to assign importance.

Perceived Author

All subjects rated the perceived author of "Letter from Birmingham Jail" as having a relatively large influence on importance assignment. In fact, each subject rated this influence as a "5," the highest possible rating. This resulted in no variance in the dependent variable, subjects' rating of the influence of the perceived author on importance assignment. Thus, "Letter from Birmingham Jail" could not be included in the analysis of the influence of perceived author on importance assignment. With "Letter from Birmingham Jail" excluded from the analysis, the repeated measures ANOVA for the influence of perceived author on importance assignment yielded a univariate *F*(4,

20) = 2.93, $p < .05$. Tukey pair-wise comparisons yielded a critical value of 2.21 ($p < .05$) and indicated that perceived author was rated as a statistically significant influence on importance assignment for the poem "Stopping by Woods on a Snowy Evening," as compared to "The Red Wheelbarrow." Though it was not included in the analysis, it is assumed that the perceived author of "Letter from Birmingham Jail" also had a significantly greater influence on the assignment of importance, when compared with the poem "The Red Wheelbarrow."

The familiarity with the author was used by subjects to help assign importance. For example, all subjects reported familiarity with Martin Luther King, Jr., and his involvement with the civil rights movement. Thus, the perceived author and his goals and intentions could be used in determining importance in the text.

> "we" . . when he says "*we* find it difficult to wait". "we" is important here . . because even though I know he's speaking for others . . on the behalf of others . and for others . . he just asserts it with that sentence.

A second text in which the perceived author had a significant influence on importance assignment was "Stopping by Woods on a Snowy Evening" by Robert Frost:

> from a purely practical viewpoint . . . it seems even silly . . but Frost did not always approach life from a practical viewpoint . . and I need to consider that.

In the above excerpt, the reader encounters a portion of the poem which seems "silly." While under some circumstances a "silly" portion of a text may indicate unimportance, in this instance the reader's perception of the author as one who does not approach life from a practical viewpoint may assist the reader in making an appropriate assignment of importance.

As readers construct meaning from text, they may also construct an author and a set of author intentions (Johnston & Afflerbach, 1985). Ultimately, the perceived author and author intentions may be used to assist in assigning importance. For example, "Letter from Birmingham Jail" received the highest rating for the influence of the perceived author on the assignment of importance. "Stopping by Woods on a Snowy Evening" was rated second highest in terms of perceived author's influence on importance assignment. In the retrospective reports, subjects reported familiarity with only two of the authors: Martin Luther King, Jr., and Robert Frost. Thus, it is noted that the perceived author may be constructed not only through consideration of the text being read but also with the assistance of a reader's prior knowledge of the author.

Emotional Response

The repeated measures ANOVA for the influence of emotional response on importance assignment yielded a univariate $F(5, 25) = 7.85$, $p < .001$. Tukey pair-wise comparisons yielded a critical value of 1.745 ($p < .05$). Emotional response was rated as having a significantly greater influence on importance assignment for "Letter from Birmingham Jail," when compared with the poem "The Red Wheelbarrow." The emotional nature of "Letter from Birmingham Jail" may be inferred from the following report of importance assignment:

> "harried" . . . "living at tiptoe stance" and "inner fears" . . those are all important in . . understanding . . a feeling . . and a kind of anxiety . . the "inner fears and outer resentments" is-is uh the important part of that sentence.

A final example of the influence that emotional response can have on the assignment of importance comes from the protocol of a subject reading the magazine article on pesticide use. The subject had (unknown to the researcher) developed lymphoma while in high school. While the lymphoma had been cured, the subject's encounter with a text which mentioned ''cancer'' prompted the following response and verbal report:

> I've kind of been drawn away from-the-uh what this thing is saying . because I was thinking about the cancer . . and the ''carcinogens'' and . . I've kind of lost track . . of where this-I understand where the paper is going but I haven't been noticing the details . . of what this is saying . . since then.

The reader's emotional response to the mention of a disease which he had personally experienced appears to have had an effect on what was considered important. While this is an extreme example, it is offered to illustrate the potential effect that affect may have on what is considered important in text and on comprehension in general. It is notable that the subject's monitoring of the reading task included keeping track of emotional responses and their potential consequences and that the subject decided to continue in the study.

DISCUSSION

This study examined the influence of four variables on the assignment of importance. Data from concurrent and retrospective verbal reports and the rating task suggest that a variety of textual and contextual variables influence competent readers' importance assignment processes. These variables include readers' prior knowledge, the structure of text, the perceived author, and readers' emotional response to a text.

As indicated by the subjects' ratings, use of a particular type of cue for assigning importance (e.g., perceived author) may vary, depending on the type of text being read and the readers' purpose for reading. Verbal report excerpts were used to illustrate this variety of cue use across texts. For example, there were virtually no reports of use of a perceived author for assigning importance in college course textbooks. In contrast, subjects reported assigning importance in accordance with a perceived author and the author's intentions on all other types of text.

The results also indicate that competent readers are flexible in the standards they set for assigning importance. For example, while reading their course textbooks, readers set relatively stringent criteria for assigning importance. Subjects indicated that they had to account for more of the text being read when reading a textbook for a course. In contrast, readers of the poems reported qualitatively different criteria for importance assignment. As the task was not to memorize the poem, or to be tested on its contents, parts of the poems which elicited emotional responses were considered important. Additionally, the assignment of importance for editorials and news articles indicated an apparent combination of affective and cognitive criteria for assigning importance.

Assigning importance is a crucial academic skill (Williams, 1986), yet explicit instruction in assigning importance is rare (Hare & Milligan, 1984). This is due, in large part, to a lack of understanding of the processes of importance assignment. Thus, there is the need for development of instructional programs which teach developing readers how to assign importance. The results of this study may inform several components of instructional programs, including the different cues which may be used to assign importance, and the relationship of text type and purpose for reading to the flexibility of standards for assigning importance. Excerpts taken from the think-aloud protocols of competent readers may eventually be used in instructional modeling routines for assigning importance to text for the developing reader (Palincsar & Brown, 1984).

There are several limitations to the present study. First, the texts selected for this study should not be considered typical for a genre. Rather, the texts were chosen with the intent of illustrating importance assignment processes on a variety of texts. For example, "Letter from Birmingham Jail" could be classified as a persuasive document, though it is written in letter form. Similarly, poems of different structure, length, and voice may elicit different importance assignment processes.

This study focused on the processes of importance assignment. There are no product measures which might assist in determining the appropriateness of the different importance assignment cues and processes used. Future research might combine product and process measures, to examine the efficacy of use of particular importance assignment processes. Finally, the inclusion of different types of texts in this study was intended to allow for the examination of importance assignment on a variety of texts. As suggested by Rosenblatt's (1980) distinction between efferent and aesthetic reading tasks, assigning importance may not be necessary or desirable for readers to enjoy, and benefit from, their interactions with particular texts.

REFERENCES

Afflerbach, P. (1986). The influence of prior knowledge on expert readers' importance assignment processes. In J. Niles & R. Lalik (Eds.), *Solving problems in literacy: Learners, teachers, and researchers* (pp. 30-40). Thirty-fifth Yearbook of the National Reading Conference. Rochester, NY: National Reading Conference.

Anderson, R., & Pearson, P. (1984). A schema-theoretic view of reading comprehension. In P. D. Pearson (Ed.), *Handbook of reading research* (pp. 255-291). New York: Longman.

Begley, S., Lubenow, G., & Miller, M. (1986, July 14). Silent spring revisited? *Newsweek,* pp. 72-73.

Brown, A., & Day, J. (1983). Macrorules for summarizing texts: The development of expertise. *Journal of Verbal Learning and Verbal Behavior, 22,* 1-14.

Frost, R. (1973). Stopping by woods on a snowy evening. In R. Ellman & R. O'Clair (Eds.), *The Norton anthology of modern poetry* (pp. 204-205). New York: Norton.

Hare, V., & Milligan, B. (1984). Main idea identification: Instructional explanations in four basal reader series. *Journal of Reading Behavior, 16,* 189-204.

Johnston, P., & Afflerbach, P. (1985). The process of constructing main ideas from text. *Cognition and Instruction, 2,* 207-232.

King, M., Jr. (1963). Letter from Birmingham jail. *Why we can't wait* (pp. 4-7). New York: Harper & Row.

McAlister, D. (1986, September 4). Timid textbook publishers evading responsibility. *Atlanta Journal,* p. 19.

Martins, D. (1982). Influence of affect on comprehension of text. *Text, 2,* 141-154.

Meyer, B. (1975). *The organization of prose and its effects on memory.* Amsterdam, Holland: North-Holland.

Palincsar, A., & Brown, A. (1984). Reciprocal teaching of comprehension-fostering and comprehension-monitoring activities. *Cognition and Instruction, 1,* 117-175.

Roller, C. (1985). The influence of normative relative importance on the perceived importance of information. *Journal of Reading Behavior, 17,* 347-367.

Rosenblatt, L. (1980). What facts does this poem teach you? *Language Arts, 57,* 386-394.

van Dijk, T. (1979). Relevance assignment in discourse comprehension. *Discourse Processes, 2,* 113-126.

van Dijk, T., & Kintsch, W. (1983). *Strategies for discourse comprehension.* New York: Academic Press.

Williams, J. (1986). Extracting important information from text. In J. Niles & R. Lalik (Eds.), *Solving problems in literacy: Learners, teachers, and researchers* (pp. 11-29). Thirty-fifth Yearbook of the National Reading Conference. Rochester, NY: National Reading Conference.

Williams, W. (1968). The red wheelbarrow. *Selected poems* (p. 30). New York: New Directions.

Winograd, P. (1984). Strategic difficulties in summarizing text. *Reading Research Quarterly, 19*, 404-425.

Winograd, P., & Bridge, C. (1986). The comprehension of important information in prose. In J. Baumann (Ed.), *Teaching main idea comprehension* (pp. 18-48). Newark, DE: International Reading Association.

EFFECTS OF PRACTICE IN RETELLING UPON THE READING COMPREHENSION OF PROFICIENT AND LESS PROFICIENT READERS

Barbara A. Kapinus
Maryland State Department of Education

Linda B. Gambrell and Patricia S. Koskinen
University of Maryland

Oral language experiences are acknowledged to be a critical dimension of learning to read (Clay, 1972; Downing, 1979; Gibson & Levin, 1975). Observational research, however, suggests that elementary age students rarely have opportunities to talk about what they have read (Durkin, 1978–1979; Gambrell, 1983, 1986; Sirotnik, 1983). One instructional strategy which engages students in the verbal rehearsal of text-acquired information is retelling. Recent research has suggested that retelling enhances reading and listening comprehension for young children (Gambrell, Pfeiffer, & Wilson, 1985; Morrow, 1984, 1985, 1986; Rose, Cundick, & Higbee, 1984). The underlying notion is that retelling requires organization of the text-acquired information and that engaging in retelling focuses the reader's attention on restructuring text in a holistic fashion.

According to the model of generative learning proposed by Wittrock (1974), in order for reading comprehension to occur the reader must engage in constructing relationships with text information. Proficient readers actively engage in building relationships between text information and their own prior knowledge (Anderson, Reynolds, Schallert, & Goetz, 1977), and among the different parts of the text (Linden & Wittrock, 1981). One implication derived from the generative learning model is that teachers can facilitate reading compehension of text-acquired information by providing learning experiences which induce the reader to relate parts of the text to one another and to their background of experience. Retelling is a generative task that requires the reader to construct a personal rendition of the text by making inferences based on the original text and prior knowledge (Morrow, Gambrell, Kapinus, Koskinen, Marshall, & Mitchell, 1986).

Several recent studies suggest that retelling improves story comprehension, sense of story structure, and oral language complexity when used with kindergarten children as a follow-up to listening to stories (Morrow, 1984, 1985, 1986; Pellegrini & Galda, 1982; Zimiles & Kuhns, 1976). Only a few studies have been reported to date which investigate retelling as a postreading instructional strategy. Gambrell, Pfeiffer, and Wilson (1985) reported that fourth graders who engaged in retelling as a postreading activity did better than students producing illustrations on immediate and delayed comprehension tasks. In another study, fourth-grade students who engaged in retelling did as well on comprehension tasks (text-based questions and retelling) as students who answered questions about the text (Gambrell, Koskinen, & Kapinus, 1985). Rose, Cundick, and Higbee (1984) found that retelling significantly increased the reading comprehension performance of elementary age learning-disabled children. Taken together, these findings suggest that engaging in the retelling (verbal rehearsal) of what has been read results in learning with respect to the comprehension and recall of discourse.

Several questions of importance emerge from a review of the research on retelling. First, do children's retellings improve with practice? This is an important question because much of the reading research to date has used retelling as a reading comprehension assessment tool (Johnston, 1983). In the vast majority of the reading research, the retellings are those of novice retellers. There is a substantial body of research which documents that students in elementary classrooms rarely engage in discussing, summarizing, or retelling text-acquired information (Durkin, 1978–1979; Gambrell, 1986; Sirotnik, 1983). The major question of the present study was to investigate how the retelling performance of the novice compares with that of the expert reteller who has had practice engaging in retelling. A second question addressed in this study deals with whether practice in retelling enhances comprehension performance for both proficient and less proficient readers.

METHOD

Subjects

The subjects for this study were fourth-grade students from three elementary schools in Maryland. Criteria for inclusion in the study were as follows: a score at the 20th percentile or above on the Cognitive Abilities Test, for less proficient readers a score at the 41st percentile or below on the reading comprehension section of the California Achievement Test (CAT), and for the proficient readers a score at the 68th percentile or higher on the reading comprehension section of the CAT. The sample for the study consisted of 36 fourth-grade students (20 proficient readers and 16 less proficient readers).

Materials

Eight narrative stories (four at the second-grade level and four at the fourth-grade level) were selected from basals which were not used in the school system curriculum (Ginn, 1982; Macmillan, 1986; Riverside, 1986). The second-grade stories were "Elena Can Do It," "The Collection Club," "The Rabbit's Trick," and "Cook, Little Pot, Cook." The stories ranged in length from 357 to 527 words with an average length of 436 words. Each story was analyzed using the Fry Readability Formula (Fry, 1977) and determined to be written at a second-grade reading level. The fourth-grade stories were "Thanks Anita," "O. D. and the Cyclops," "Jackie Smith, Test Pilot," and "Stella and the Dragon." The stories ranged in length from 740 to 1,038 words with an average length of 812 words. Each story was analyzed using the Fry Readability Formula and was determined to be at the fourth-grade reading level. In all eight stories, the clear presence of basic elements of story structure was a major criterion for selection. Interrater reliability on the presence of basic elements of story structure (setting, theme, plot episodes, and resolution) was 100%.

A cued recall assessment which consisted of four text-explicit and four text-implicit questions was developed for the eight stories used in this study. For the scoring of the retelling task, a text-based outline of the basic story structure elements for each of the eight stories was developed (Thorndyke, 1977). A brief two-item questionnaire was developed to probe children's attitudes and strategy awareness.

Procedure

Subjects were randomly assigned to one of four story conditions. The four stories were counterbalanced across the four practice sessions in order to control for story effects. Across the four sessions, all subjects read all four stories; for example, for session one, the same number of subjects read story A, story B, story C, and story D. Because of the inherent problems involved in having proficient and less proficient readers read the same stories, the investigation was conducted in two phases using stories which were at an appropriate level for the subjects in each group.

The subjects were told that they would meet individually with the researcher for four sessions during the following two weeks. They were informed that during the time together with the researcher they would read stories and get a chance to practice becoming a good storyteller. In order to provide a meaningful context for the retellings, the subjects were told that their retellings would be tape recorded so that young children who have not learned to read would be able to listen to them tell the story. Each story was introduced with a brief motivational statement. Students were then instructed to read the story silently. At the conclusion of the silent reading, subjects were instructed as follows: "Take a minute or two to think about how you will tell the story. Let me know when you are ready to tell the story into the tape recorder." If subjects did not begin retelling within a two-minute period, the reseacher asked, "Are you ready to begin?" and proceeded to begin the retelling by recording the following: "The story for today is (story title) and the storyteller is (subject's name)." The subjects then proceeded to render their retelling of the story. At the conclusion of sessions one and four, subjects responded to eight comprehension questions about the story they had read. Questions were not used during sessions two and three so that the emphasis was solely upon retelling, and there was no anticipation of questioning as a part of the retelling practice. At the conclusion of the final session, the subjects answered a four-item questionnaire which probed their attitudes toward retelling and their strategy awareness.

Procedures identical to those used with the proficient reader group were used throughout phase two of the study which was conducted with the less proficient readers. The only modification was that the fourth-grade, less proficient readers read stories which were at the second-grade level.

Scoring

Interrater reliability was established using 10% of the retellings and cued recall responses. Interrater reliability was 95% for the scoring of the retellings and 92% for the scoring of the cued recall questions. One reseacher scored the remainder of the question responses and both researchers scored one half of the remaining recall protocols.

RESULTS

A repeated measures analysis was employed to test for significant differences between session one and session four performance with respect to the retelling and cued recall tasks for the proficient and less proficient groups. The proficient readers performed better on the fourth session on both the retelling and the cued recall task (Table 1). The proficient readers recalled more elements related to theme, plot episodes, and resolution after four practice sessions.

The less proficient readers also performed better on the fourth session on the cued recall task (Table 2). There were no statistically significant differences for the less proficient readers with respect to the free recall of story structure elements.

Table 1

Means and Standard Deviations for Retelling and Cued Recall Performance for Proficient Readers (N = 20)

	Session 1		Session 2	
	M	*SD*	*M*	*SD*
Retelling Task				
Setting	3.95	(1.43)	4.50	(1.24)
Theme	1.50	(.61)	1.90	(.45)*
Plot episodes	5.25	(2.55)	7.40	(2.83)*
Resolution	.65	(.49)	.80	(.41)
Total story structure	11.30	(4.38)	14.60	(3.56)**
Cued Recall Task	4.70	(1.49)	5.90	(1.74)*

Note. Maximum score possible for the cued recall task was 8.
*$p < .05$.
**$p < .01$.

Table 2

Means and Standard Deviations for Retelling and Cued Recall Performance for Less proficient Readers (N = 16)

	Session 1		Session 2	
	M	*SD*	*M*	*SD*
Retelling Task				
Setting	5.00	(2.03)	5.50	(1.63)
Theme	1.44	(.63)	1.69	(.70)
Plot episodes	3.94	(1.88)	5.00	(1.83)
Resolution	.63	(.50)	.69	(.48)
Total story structure	10.38	(4.22)	12.89	(3.61)
Cued Recall Task	5.18	(1.64)	6.81	(1.28)*

Note. Maximum score possible for the cued recall task was 8.
*$p > .05$.

DISCUSSION

In this study, only four practice sessions in which students engaged in retelling resulted in improved reading comprehension performance for both proficient and less proficient readers. This suggests that the verbal rehearsal of prose in the form of retelling may be an effective instructional strategy for improving the reading comprehension of both proficient and less proficient readers. The results of this study support the hypothesis that, by engaging in the verbal rehearsal of silently read discourse, the reader learns something about the organization and retention of text information.

The fact that there was statistically significant improvement in the cued recall performance of the less proficient readers on the fourth session as compared to the first session suggests that there were beneficial effects for the retelling practice. It may be that less proficient readers need more extensive practice than the four sessions provided in this study in order to improve their free recall performance. It should be noted that, in spite of the small number of subjects in the less proficient reader group ($N = 16$), the means were in the anticipated direction with respect to performance on the retelling task. Future research is warranted which will investigate the effects of retelling across a greater number of practice sessions for less proficient readers.

With respect to the proficient readers in this study, it is clear that practice in retelling resulted in improved free recall and cued recall performance. The findings of this study support previous studies (Gambrell, Pfieffer, & Wilson, 1985; Rose, Cundick, & Higbee, 1984) which have indicated that the verbal rehearsal of what has been read results in increased learning with respect to the comprehension and recall of discourse. The findings of this study, in particular, suggest that practice in retelling enhances story structure awareness for proficient readers.

There are several limitations in this study, and they will need to be amended in future research. First, the design is a simple pre-/post- without controls. This represents a threat to internal validity because, for example, subjects may have performed better in the posttest condition because they became more comfortable and open with us. Control groups are essential. Second, the sample is small. Given the unambiguous trends in Table 2, it is entirely possible that raising the power of the ANOVAs by increasing sample size would result in statistically significant changes for the less proficient readers.

For both the proficient and less proficient readers, text comprehension improved across only four practice sessions. This raises some question about the use of retelling as an assessment tool in reading research. We know that students do not typically have classroom experience with the strategy of retelling. Performance on retelling as an assessment task, therefore, is likely to reflect novice behavior. The validity of using the unfamiliar task of retelling as an assessment of reading comprehension should be pursued in future research.

The debriefing questionnaire provided some insight into students' attitudes and processing strategies. Subjects responded to the question "How do you feel about reading a story and then retelling it?" by indicating one of the following responses: (a) "I really liked it.," (b) "It's O.K.," (c) "I didn't really like it." The majority of both proficient and less proficient readers indicated that they "really liked" retelling the story after reading it. This suggests that retelling is an appealing as well as an effective comprehension strategy.

A second question was "What did you think about when I told you to take a minute to think before you told the story on tape?" Twice as many proficient readers, as compared to less proficient readers, indicated that they rehearsed the story before retelling it. Proficient readers mentioned specifics such as "thought about the beginning, middle, and ending of the story," while less proficient readers reported that they "thought about the words" and "thought about the story." The response of one proficient reader provides some insight into why retelling results in deep processing and, thereby, enhances reading comprehension. The fourth grader said, "Through the whole story I thought about what I was going to say. When you said, 'Think,' I thought about it some more. I always thought I didn't have to pay attention to stories, but now I have to so that I can retell it."

REFERENCES

Anderson, R. C., Reynolds, R. E., Schallert, D. L., & Goetz, E. T. (1977). Frameworks for comprehending discourse. *American Educational Research Journal, 14,* 367-381.

Clay, M. M. (1972). *Reading: The patterning of complex behavior.* New York: Heinemann.

Downing, J. (1979). *Reading and reasoning.* New York: Springer-Verlag.

Durkin, D. (1978-1979). What classroom observations reveal about reading comprehension instruction. *Reading Research Quarterly, 14,* 481-533.

Fry, E. B. (1977). Fry's readability graph: Clarifications, validity, and extension to level 17. *Journal of Reading, 21,* 242-252.

Gambrell, L. B. (1983). The occurrence of think-time during reading comprehension instruction. *Journal of Educational Research, 77,* 77-80.

Gambrell, L. B. (1986, December). *Children's oral language during teacher-directed reading instruction.* Paper presented at the National Reading Conference, Austin, TX.

Gambrell, L. B., Pfeiffer, W., & Wilson, R. (1985). The effects of retelling upon reading comprehension and recall of text information. *Journal of Educational Research, 78,* 216-220.

Gambrell, L. B., Koskinen, P. S., & Kapinus, B. A. (1985, December). *A comparison of retelling and questioning as reading comprehension strategies.* Paper presented at the National Reading Conference, San Diego, CA.

Gibson, E. J., & Levin, H. (1975). *The psychology of reading.* Cambridge, MA: The Massachusetts Institute of Technology.

Ginn Basal Reader Program. (1982). Lexington, MA: Ginn.

Johnston, P. H. (1983). *Reading comprehension assessment: A cognitive basis.* Newark, DE: International Reading Association.

Linden, M., & Wittrock, M. C. (1981). The teaching of reading comprehension according to the model of generative learning. *Reading Research Quarterly, 17,* 44-57.

Macmillan Basal Reader Program. (1986). New York; Macmillan.

Morrow, L. (1984). Effects of story retelling on young children's comprehension and sense of story structure. In J. A. Niles & L. A. Harris (Eds.), *Changing perspectives on research in reading/language processing and instruction* (pp. 95-100). Thirty-third Yearbook of the National Reading Conference. Rochester, NY: National Reading Conference.

Morrow, L. (1985). Retelling stories: A strategy for improving young children's comprehension, concept of story structure, and oral language complexity. *Elementary School Journal, 75,* 647-661.

Morrow, L. (1986). Effects of story retelling on children's dictation of original stories. *Journal of Reading Behavior, 18,* 135-152.

Morrow, L. M., Gambrell, L., Kapinus, B., Koskinen, P. S., Marshall, N., & Mitchell, J. N. (1986). Retelling: A strategy for reading instruction and assessment. In J. A. Niles & R. V. Lalik (Eds.) *Solving problems in literacy: Learners, teachers, and researchers* (pp. 73-80). Thirty-fifth Yearbook of the National Reading Conference. Rochester, NY: National Reading Conference.

Pellegrini, A., & Galda, L. (1982). The effects of thematic-fantasy play training on the development of children's story comprehension. *American Educational Research Journal, 19,* 443-452.

Riverside Reading Program. (1986). Chicago, IL: Riverside.

Rose, M. C., Cundick, B. P., & Higbee, K. L. (1984). Verbal rehearsal and visual imagery: Mnemonic aids for learning disabled children. *Journal of Learning Disabilities, 16,* 353-354.

Sirotnik, K. (1983). What you see is what you get—consistency, persistency and mediocrity in the classroom. *Harvard Educational Review, 53,* 16-31.

Thorndyke, P. W. (1977). Cognitive structures in comprehension and memory of narrative discourse. *Cognitive Psychology, 9,* 77-110.

Wittrock, M. C. (1974). Learning as a generative process. *Educational Psychologist, 11,* 877-895.

Zimiles, H., & Kuhns, M. (1976). *A developmental study in the retention of narrative material, Final Report* (Research Rep. 134), Bank Street College of Education. Washington, DC: National Institute of Education.

IN-PROCESS MEASURES OF AMBIGUOUS TEXT INTERPRETATION: ANOTHER LOOK AT THE INFLUENCE OF PRIOR KNOWLEDGE

William A. Henk
Pennsylvania State University-Harrisburg

John P. Helfeldt
West Virginia University

For several years, researchers have examined the role that prior knowledge plays in the interpretation of written text. To test the hypothesis that readers interpret text in a manner consistent with their background of experience, earlier research efforts utilized passages that were purposely ambiguous but could be given a clear non-dominant interpretation by a specific subgroup of readers (Anderson, Reynolds, Schallert, & Goetz, 1977; Lipson, 1983; Reynolds, Taylor, Steffensen, Shirey, & Anderson, 1982; Steffensen, Joag-Dev, & Anderson, 1979). In a now classic study, for example, Anderson et al. (1977) provided physical education and music majors with two ambiguous passages. One passage could be given either the interpretation of a convict planning an escape or that of a wrestler trying to break a hold during a match. Although the convict interpretation is typically given by most individuals, the physical education majors clearly preferred the non-dominant wrestling interpretation, one assumedly consistent with their background of experience. The same trend emerged for a second passage which could be interpreted as either a night of card playing or the playing of music in a small ensemble. Again, the music majors chose the non-dominant ensemble interpretation in lieu of the more popular card playing interpretation. These same basic trends have been demonstrated in a series of subsequent related investigations although some of the prior knowledge effects have been diminished somewhat by supplying passage titles (Sjogren & Timpson, 1979) and by varying the situational context or setting in which the passages were read (Carey, Harste, & Smith, 1981).

What studies of this type imply is that a reader engages in a form of *selective encoding* of incoming information. Schemata congruent with one's background of experience are naturally activated in lieu of less structured, undifferentiated, and impersonal schemata. Familiar schemata are then used as a framework for assimilating new data as it becomes available. When specific information relative to the topic is not provided, the reader will fill the slots of the active schema with default values, that is, with known concepts that are consistent with the active schema. Interview data presented by Anderson et. al. (1977) indicated that readers' dominant schemata were sufficiently pervasive to obscure the awareness of possible alternative interpretations.

One possible limitation of many previous studies is that dependent measures were obtained *after*, rather than *during*, reading. The basic research paradigms employed (free recall followed by multiple-choice probe statements) made it difficult to determine at what point, if any, prior knowledge may have served as a vehicle for interpretation. What may have happened in these studies is that the postreading measurements unintentionally confused the products of reading with its processes. Specifically, subjects might not have settled on any clear textual interpretation while reading the passages, but instead had become sensitized to a particular interpretation via cues in the multiple-choice probes and distractors. Such an occurrence seems possible since in many prior knowledge studies subjects tend to give the passages an indeterminate interpretation during free recall, yet gravitate to a specific text interpretation while responding to the probes. This is not to say that the probe statements necessarily masked in-process effects for schema engagement, but rather that they might have.

To test this possibility, Henk and Helfeldt (1985) devised a reading task protocol which was intended to tap readers' ongoing mental operations when reacting to ambiguous text. The paradigm was based on the work of Rumelhart (1981) who suggested that readers form hypotheses and continually test the veracity of these interpretations against the nature of incoming information. According to the model, new information influences readers to either confirm, reject, or modify their hypotheses as a function of probability and conceptual congruence. In effect, comprehension processes represent a dynamic, evolving, and cumulative construction of meaning. To reflect this kind of processing, the authors gave physical education majors a packet that probed their confirmation, rejection, and modification strategies. This was done by cumulatively presenting the Anderson et. al (1977) convict/wrestling passage one sentence at a time on separate pages and systematically probing subjects' interpretation up to that point. With each turn of the page, a new sentence was added and readers were asked to check whether the same topic, a somewhat different topic, or an altogether different topic was now implicated. Then they briefly identified the topic and noted why such decisions had been made.

The Henk and Helfeldt study (1985) found considerable evidence for the prior knowledge hypothesis. Physical education majors did tend to impose a wrestling interpretation on the text but to a lesser extent than the physical education majors in the Anderson et al. (1977) study. It was also found that situational context (the setting where the reading was actually done) bore a secondary influence on passage interpretation. Perhaps the most important finding of the study, however, was that both the physical education majors and controls did, in fact, revise their topical interpretations with some regularity during the course of reading. To put it another way, the influence of accommodation processes was more in evidence than previous research had indicated. While assimilation processes were clearly at work, readers vacillated more in their interpretations of ambiguous passages than anticipated. The results portrayed comprehension as a highly personal and dynamic process.

The present study examined the prior knowledge phenomenon using the same research methodology. In this instance, however, the targeted subgroup consisted of music majors and the music/card-playing text was used. As an iterative research effort, it invited comparisons with both the Anderson et al. (1977) and Henk and Helfeldt (1985) studies.

METHOD

Subjects

Subjects were 29 music, 35 physical education, and 28 elementary education majors enrolled at a major northeastern university. All subjects were in their junior or senior year of undergraduate studies. Thus, it was assumed that all subjects possessed sufficient general reading ability to understand the music/card-playing passage. The music majors (14 female, 15 males) were enrolled in a music history class, the physical education majors (17 females, 18 males) were enrolled in a sports exercise/physiology class, and the elementary education majors, all of whom were female, were enrolled in a methods class.

Materials and Procedure

The ambiguous passage used in the present study was adopted from Anderson et al. (1977). It consisted of 14 sentences and approximately 145 words. The content was designed to elicit interpretations centering on an evening of either playing cards or playing music in a small ensemble. The passage read as follows:

> Every Saturday night, four good friends get together. When Jerry, Mike, and Pat arrived, Karen was sitting in her living room writing some notes. She quickly gathered the cards and stood up to greet her friends at the door. They followed her into the living room but as usual they couldn't agree on exactly what to play. Jerry eventually took a stand and set things up. Finally, they began to play. Karen's recorder filled the room with soft and pleasant music. Early in the evening, Mike noticed Pat's hand and the many diamonds. As the night progressed the tempo of play increased. Finally, a lull in the activities occurred. Taking advantage of this, Jerry pondered the arrangement in front of him. Mike interrupted Jerry's reverie and said, "Let's hear the score." They listened carefully and commented on their performance. When the comments were all heard, exhausted but happy, Karen's friends went home.

Subjects were given packets in which the passage was presented one sentence at a time. On subsequent pages, the next sentence was provided along with all preceding sentences of the passage. Each page was formatted so that the passage was centered at the top. Below the passage, the page was divided left-to-right into three distinct columns corresponding to SAME TOPIC, SOMEWHAT DIFFERENT, or ALTOGETHER DIFFERENT.

For each page, following the presentation of the sentence, subjects were asked what they believed the passage was about. They were also encouraged to state why they had chosen a particular interpretation. To quicken the pace, subjects were told to read quickly, to elaborate only at the points where their reasoning changed, and to jot down only very brief explanations. Their alignment with one of the three categories was noted by either a check mark or succinct comment in that column. Subjects were not permitted to return to any previously completed sheet in the booklet. While no explicit time limit was set, all subjects finished within 20 minutes. Research protocols were completed by each respective group of subjects in a music history class, a sports exercise/physiology class, and an elementary education methods class.

RESULTS

To determine the influence of prior knowledge and the degree to which schema accommodation occurred as subjects read the passage, comparisons were made of the initial and final topics indicated on the research protocols. In addition, the number of times that subjects indicated a change of topic was also analyzed.

Based on the topic indicated after reading the first sentence, very few subjects, regardless of group, specified card playing or playing music as the initial topic. Table 1 reveals the similarity among beginning topics identified by music and elementary education majors. That is, 69% of the music majors and 61% of the elementary education majors selected the generic topic of friendship, while 28% of the music majors and 32% of the elementary education subjects specified a particular topic other than cards or music. On the other hand, the physical education majors differed from the other groups, as nearly twice as many (60%) specified other topics while 31% selected the general topic of friendship. Themes such as driving under the influence, drugs, drinking, partying and the portent of a tragic accident were among the other topics specified by subjects. Results of a chi-square test of association indicated that the frequencies with which physical education majors identified the beginning topics of friendship and other differed from the frequencies with which music and elementary majors identified each of these topics ($\chi^2_{(6)} = 12.56, p < .051$).

After completing the passage, nearly all subjects abandoned the nebulous topic of friendship in favor of a more specific topic. From a descriptive or qualitative perspective, it appears that music majors interpreted the passage as a musical performance or rehearsal more often than either of the other two groups. In addition, physical education majors construed the passage as a card playing episode more frequently than the other groups. As Table 1 indicates, music majors concluded the passage with a music interpretation (41%) about as often as physical education majors concluded the passage with a card playing judgment (40%). Table 1 also indicates that approximately one third of the subjects had settled upon an indeterminate topic (something other than cards or music)

Table 1

Percentage of Subjects Selecting Beginning and Ending Topics By Group

	Topic			
Group	Friendship Begin/End %	Music Begin/End %	Cards Begin/End %	Other Begin/End %
Music	69/0	3/41	0/28	28/31
Physical Education	31/0	0/26	9/40	60/34
Elementary Education	61/7	0/36	7/18	32/39

by the end of the passage. In fact, within the elementary education group, 39% of the subjects' responses fell within the *other* category. From a statistical perspective, however, a chi-square test indicated that the frequency with which final topics were identified did not differ among groups ($\chi^2_{(6)} = 9.68, p < .139$).

Table 2 reveals the percentage of subjects within each group that identified different numbers of topics as they read the ambiguous passage. Across all groups, the highest percentage of subjects indicated that a change of topics occurred at least three times during reading. In contrast, the smallest percentage of subjects indicated that they did not consider at least one alternative topical change as they read. A chi-square analysis was computed to compare the groups with regard to the number of times individual subjects identified different topics. This analysis indicated that there were no differences within or between groups with respect to the degree and frequency that topical changes were reported ($\chi^2_{(6)} = 5.71, p > .457$).

Table 2

Percentage of Subjects Making Specified Number of Topical Changes By Group

	Number of Topical Changes			
	0	**1**	**2**	**3 or more**
Group	%	%	%	%
Music	7	21	21	51
Physical Education	0	17	23	60
Elementary Education	11	18	32	39

DISCUSSION

The present study yielded results which differed from those obtained in both the Anderson et al. (1977) and the Henk and Helfeldt (1985) studies. Most notably, the special subgroup of readers, music majors in this case, were not as likely to impose their assumedly dominant music schema on the ambiguous text as other readers had done in earlier investigations. Unlike the Anderson et al. effort, more than 70% of subjects in each group indicated an awareness of alternative textual interpretations during reading. This finding is based on subjects who reported at least two topical changes on their protocols.

The results were not perceived so much as a refutation of previous research but rather as a further refinement of conceptions regarding the impact of prior knowledge on text comprehension. Specifically, the data suggest that accommodation processes play a more significant role in interpreting ambiguous prose than previously believed. Although music majors were expected to be almost immediately predisposed to the music interpretation, they took some time to settle on a text schema, and once they did, it was not consistently music-related. In general, readers withheld or vacillated in imposing a definitive topical interpretation until information could be assimilated into a probable active schema. Further, they attempted to fit incoming information into the existing structure until some cue signaled schema modification or rejection. This premise is reflected in the finding that most readers identified at least three topical changes.

Why didn't music majors demonstrate a stronger predisposition to the music interpretation? Such an effect might be explained by noting that being a music major does not in any way preclude the possibility of both possessing and employing a potent schema for card playing. Music majors may simply have been engaged in unconsciously choosing among available schemata that were not equally probable. In other words, they may have imposed a card playing schema on the basis of background knowledge which stipulates that among the general populace, card playing is more likely to occur than a more specialized and less likely music playing event.

When the results of the present study are compared with those of Anderson et al. (1977), some part of the differential may be explained by virtue of important differences in research methodologies. There is no question that a sentence-by-sentence paradigm requiring written reasoning alters the time course of normal reading. Despite experimental directions that encouraged a brisk reading, conventional reading rates were necessarily altered by the task requirements. Slowing down the reading process in this way may have sensitized readers to alternative interpretations by allowing more time for reflection and deliberation than normal reading permits. Also, probing for topical change information may have predisposed readers to make schema alterations more than they would have under normal reading conditions. Given the current state of measurement technology, however, this is the price one pays in aiming to measure emerging mental operations. At the same time, the fact remains that in an earlier study (Henk & Helfeldt, 1985), this same self-report research methodology yielded findings very similar in nature to those obtained by Anderson et al. (1977) using the more traditional uninterrupted reading/free recall/probe statement approach.

Since the present results depart from a study using identical methodological and statistical procedures, perhaps what we have here is a passage effect. It is possible that the music/card playing passage simply did not initiate sufficiently potent encoding cues to allow for a personal, schema-specific interpretation among the music majors. Or perhaps music majors are not as closely and consistently bonded to their discipline in daily routines as physical education majors. Even if the research methodologies are questioned, the curious fact remains that at the end of this particular passage, when all of the information was fully revealed, approximately one third of the readers chose interpretations other than either music or card playing.

A qualitative examination of subjects' protocols depicted comprehension as a dynamic, personal, and enormously compelling process. This conclusion is perhaps best exemplified by one female subject, an elementary education major. Her interpretation began as four friends going out on the town. By the third sentence, she thought they might be playing cards, and by the seventh sentence she appeared reasonably sure that they were playing musical instruments in a group. Interestingly, by sentence 11, she stated that two people were playing cards, one was playing a recorder, and the fourth was studying. By passage end, she again seemed almost positive that the friends were all playing music.

To conclude, it is likely that the data were influenced by prior knowledge effects at a more specific level. Even among music majors, individual life experiences may have varied to the extent that card playing and other interpretations were sufficiently robust to neutralize a general predisposition to a schema linked only to nominal group membership. Future research must more rigorously monitor specific degrees of prior knowledge and measure in-process mental operations less obtrusively if we are ever to tease out the precise nature of the role background plays in text interpretation.

REFERENCES

Anderson, R. C. (1985). Role of the reader's schema in comprehension, learning, and memory. Reprinted in H. Singer & R. Ruddell (Eds.), *Theoretical models and processes of reading* (3rd Ed.) (pp. 372-384). Newark, DE: International Reading Association.

Anderson, R. C., Reynolds, R. E., Schallert, D. L., & Goetz, E. T. (1977). Frameworks for comprehending discourse. *American Educational Research Journal, 14,* 367-381.

Carey, R. F., Harste, J. C., & Smith, S. L. (1981). Contextual constraints and discourse processes: A replication study. *Reading Research Quarterly, 16,* 201-212.

Henk, W. A., & Helfeldt, J. P. (1985, October). *In-process measures of ambiguous text interpretation: A test of the prior knowledge hypothesis.* Paper presented at the College Reading Association Annual Meeting, Pittsburgh, PA.

Lipson, M. Y. (1983). The influence of religious affiliation on children's memory for text information. *Reading Research Quarterly, 18,* 448-457.

Reynolds, R. E., Taylor, M. A., Steffensen, M. S., Shirey, L. L., & Anderson, R. C. (1982). Cultural schemata and reading comprehension. *Reading Research Quarterly, 17,* 353-366.

Rumelhart, D. E. (1981). Schemata: The building blocks of cognition. In J. T. Guthrie (Ed.), *Comprehension and teaching: Research reviews* (pp. 3-26). Newark, DE: International Reading Association.

Sjogren, D., & Timpson, W. (1979). Frameworks for comprehending discourse: A replication study. *American Educational Research Journal, 16,* 341-346.

Steffensen, M. S., Joag-Dev, C., & Anderson, R. C. (1979). A cross-cultural perspective on reading comprehension. *Reading Research Quarterly, 15,* 10-29.

ASSESSMENT

EMERGENT LITERACY

COMPREHENSION

INSTRUCTIONAL EFFECTIVENESS

ADULT LITERACY

WRITING

LEARNING TO TEACH COMPREHENSION: A COLLABORATIVE APPROACH

Jerome A. Niles and Rosary V. Lalik
Virginia Tech

The cognitive and affective arguments for collaborative learning groups are compelling. Shulman and Carey (1984) have portrayed collaboration as a way to overcome the limitations of human information processing. Similarly, Lortie (1975) asserted that collaboration enables teachers to work together on the difficult problems which reflect the everyday life of teaching because collaboration provides support from colleagues both intellectually and affectively. Moreover, the educational effectiveness of learning in groups in educational settings has been well documented for children (cf. Slavin, 1980; Webb, 1982). Yet, our understanding for the processes and learning outcomes of the collaborative learning group for teachers has remained incomplete. In an earlier study (Lalik & Niles, 1986), we examined the discourse of student teachers as they worked in small collaborative groups to plan a reading lesson. The content of the discussions ranged over a variety of issues but focused heavily on lesson procedures, their own small group behavior, and the reading process. Also, the differences between the content of the target groups' conversation depended on the type of lesson they selected. Finally, each group engaged in a variety of thinking activities which represented reproductive as well as higher level thinking. However, the design of this study did not allow us to examine participants' learning.

This study extended our early work. It examined learning opportunities for students related to the teaching of reading when given a planning task to complete in a collaborative group setting. Specifically, we examined what students said they learned and what opportunities the collaborative setting provided for this learning to occur.

METHOD

Subjects

Twenty-six student teachers participated in this study. Participants were senior elementary education majors engaging in a year-long professional experience which included field placements in elementary and junior high school classrooms and completion of a professional course sequence. Students were asked to self-select themselves into small groups of no more than four members or to work alone. With the exception of one participant, all participants elected to work in a group. Group membership ranged from two to four, with most groups being comprised of three members.

Materials

A workbook page was taken from the *Holt Basic Reading Series*, Level 12 (Weiss, Stever, Sprout, & Cruickshank, 1983). The objective for the page (written in the bottom right-hand corner) was to identify the main idea of the paragraph. Two 100-word paragraphs were presented on the page with three choices of main idea given for each paragraph. The reader was instructed to select the alternative which best represented the main idea of each paragraph. An explicitly stated main idea was represented in the first paragraph and an implied main idea in the second.

Procedure

Session One. Each participant received a copy of a third-grade level workbook page taken from a basal series used in the elementary schools where these student teachers taught. The page was selected because it ostensibly focused on reading comprehension and was typical in format of the basal series. Groups were instructed to improve the existing worksheet by planning a reading comprehension lesson for third graders using the objective stated at the bottom of the workbook page as a guide. They were asked to plan a realistic 30-minute lesson which they would not actually be required to teach but would be expected to present to other student teachers as part of their next scheduled weekly seminar. They were asked to use the available cassette recorders to audiotape the one-hour planning session conducted by their group.

Session Two. The second session was a videotaped feedback session. During this session, a member of each planning group described both the group's lesson and planning process. These presentations were given in two separate rooms with five groups in one room and four groups in another. A question-and-answer period followed each presentation. At the close of this session, each student teacher completed a written evaluation of each experience.

Analysis. Three data sources were used for this study: the participant evaluations, transcriptions of planning sessions, and transcriptions of presentation sessions. Evaluations from all participants were subjected to content analysis. In particular, we coded all statements about student teachers' learning outcomes and affective responses. Next, we selected two planning session transcripts for intensive ethnographic analysis (Spradley, 1979, 1980). These two groups were chosen because their planning had been examined in a previous study (Lalik & Niles, 1986). Since this study extended earlier work, we felt that using the same groups both provided continuity with our previous work and met the validity requirements associated with using participants of similar verbal ability (Erickson, 1979). Finally, relevant segments (those containing reports from focal groups) of transcripts of large group feedback sessions were analyzed using holistic rereading (Griffin, Barnes, Hughes, O'Neal, Defino, Edward, & Heikell, 1983).

Our ethnographic analysis of planning sessions was designed to identify which ideas about teaching emerged during planning to examine how many ideas each group considered and to determine how each group used these ideas. Consequently, we segmented each transcript into individual utterances of the participants, and we examined the utterances to identify prominent planning segments. These segments were represented by clusters of ideas (operationally defined here as a proposition related to instruction) that focused on a specific instructional theme such as evaluation of students. Finally, we classified utterances to reflect the type of information about teaching carried by the ideas the participants shared.

RESULTS

Ideas Related to Instruction

Every participant reported that learning new ideas was the most salient part of the collaborative planning effort. In general, participants expressed satisfaction with the sessions and commented that the group discussion allowed them to share, test, and build their ideas, while hearing and shaping the ideas of others. However, participants were not specific about the nature of their ideas about teaching. Thus, our next step was to analyze the transcripts of the small group planning to identify and describe these ideas and to determine their relationship to the planning task.

The two groups differed in the quantity of ideas produced. Group B produced more ideas than group A, 447 to 314. Group A stayed on their planning task and spent little time talking about unrelated issues. While group B planned about 30% longer than group A, group B also spent about one third of their planning time talking about unrelated issues. Thus, this difference in idea density occurred over approximately equal amounts of time in actual planning work.

Major Planning Segments

During planning sessions, ideas clustered around themes or central issues for the lesson. We labeled these clusters ''lesson segments'' and parsed the planning session according to these segments. Each segment contained at least six related ideas.

Group A

Segment One. Deciding how to *define the planning task* was the first major planning activity pursued by group A. Group members initiated their discussion by reading the statement of the learning objective. Next, they discussed possible answers to the main idea items represented on the worksheet. During the discussion, one group member expressed uncertainty about which of the available alternative statements best represented the main idea of the related paragraph. However, we found no verbal evidence that the group worked to resolve the member's expressed uncertainty.

Segment Two. In the second segment, members *selected a means to evaluate students.* That is, group members decided to use the worksheet to serve as a culminating activity or evaluation for the lesson. This decision was made when the group reached a stumbling block in its analysis of the workbook page. The decision had the effect of closing discussion. Furthermore, group members expressed little apparent uncertainty about what it means to use something as an evaluation. For example, there was no discussion of instructions students would receive or how student answers would be interpreted.

Segment Three. During the third segment of the planning session, the group worked to *select materials to be used for practicing the identification of the main idea.* Members' expressed conceptions of the practice activity focused on the use of pictures, paragraphs, and alternatives. Ideas about the amount and order of use for each practice material were the topics for much of the group's talk. Members raised these issues early in their discussion and returned to them intermittently. However, even at the end of the session, it was not clear how many paragraphs would be used, how many of the selected paragraphs would have accompanying pictures, or whether alternative statements of main idea would be used with each paragraph. Further, it was not clear whether or what the teacher would be telling (or showing) the students about main idea.

Analysis of the group's presentation at the large group session suggested that a second planning session occurred prior to the presentation. As compared to the lesson described during the first planning session, there was more specificity to the presented lesson. For example, the spokesperson identified five specific paragraphs which had been selected from a third-grade basal. Two of these would be presented to students, each with a picture from the basal to illustrate the main idea; two would have accompanying pictures and alternative statements from which students would be asked to select a main idea, and one would have alternatives but no pictures. She explained that the sequence of formats was designed to provide assistance that would be gradually withdrawn. While we have no data from the second planning session for this group, comments made at the presentation session suggest that certain issues were considered during that session. For example, the spokesperson reported considering how the use of pictures might stimulate the students to visualize a representation of the main idea of a paragraph.

Group B

Segment One. Similar to group A, the first step for group B was to *define the task.* Members agreed to use the worksheet as a starting point for planning. However, they decided that they must use it somewhere else in the lesson and that they could incorporate anything else they wanted. The group completed this segment by providing time for members to independently complete the work page.

Segment Two. After defining the task, group B decided to *construct a class collaborative paragraph* to demonstrate the relationship of the parts to the whole (details to the main idea in a paragraph) as the first major activity of the lesson. They generated this thought early in their discussion and then elaborated on it periodically. The intent was to assist students in offering related ideas sparked by a focusing idea, to convert these ideas into sentences, and to tie the sentences together using the focusing or main idea. The primary reasoning for the activity was that it allowed the teacher to control the paragraph building by doing one sentence at a time, while encouraging student participation by using an interesting and familiar topic, "the circus is fun."

The original thought was modified to include a review of main idea, since the group decided that third graders "had main idea previously." The review was mainly a teacher question-and-answer session in which the students were asked to tell what they knew about main ideas and supporting details.

After the review interchange, attention would be returned to the listing of ideas and converted into sentences. An example is "funny clown," "Funny clowns make me laugh." Subsequent to sentence generation, the teacher would tie each of the sentences to the focusing idea—"The circus is fun"—and show the students how they had constructed a paragraph by generating a group of ideas related to a more general or main idea.

As a final step in their planning, Group B raised the importance of introducing the paragraph-building activity with some flair to capture student attention. They decided to incorporate props such as music, circus pictures, and colored chalk to help generate initial enthusiasm for the activity.

Segment Three. The group also decided that it was inportant for students to *practice identifying main ideas* by inferring a main idea from a paragraph of related ideas. The general structure for this segment was that the students would process the paragraph, write a main idea, share their idea with the class, and discuss why they had selected that idea.

The group made several important decisions regarding this segment. First, it was important that the main ideas were implied and that students had to write their main idea rather than select them from a multiple-choice format. The group felt that this would encourage deeper understanding of the concept of main idea rather than just reproducing someone else's suggestion for main idea. Tied to this was the notion that one sentence should express the main idea because a sentence may reflect more of the richness of a main idea than a word or phrase. Further, the group thought that the written format for implicit main ideas would provide opportunity for discussion about main ideas. They wanted students to produce a "million different main ideas" so students could discuss their reasoning.

To control this discussion process, guide the discussion, and maintain student attention, the group decided to do two of these paragraphs in a whole group setting by presenting the paragraphs to the students on an overhead and reading the passages to them. To provide variety, the remaining two passages were distributed to the students for silent reading and a written response. Monitoring of student responses was to occur during both of these settings. Further, they planned a reteaching loop back to the paragraph construction activity if the students encountered difficulty in identifying the main idea. Also, they believed the monitoring would help direct additional feedback opportunities.

Segment Four. Another segment for group B was *evaluation of students.* The group decided that five passages were needed to provide adequate opportunity to demonstrate the understanding of main idea. Since the worksheet provided had only two examples, three more would be added. Further, two passages would require the selection of the main idea from three choices. None of the answers would be either the first sentence or an explicitly stated sentence in the paragraph. Three passages would require writing a main idea sentence similar to segment two responses. They expressed the notion that the two different ways of identification of main idea would provide additional diagnostic information.

Segment Five. Group B considered *accommodating time* as part of their planning process. They were concerned that they would be able to conduct all four of their activities in the half-hour time limit. They decided it would be possible but that they might run over to 45 minutes which would still be appropriate for third graders.

Segment Six. Group B used *recapitulations* of their discussions as important features in their planning. They used recaps for memory aids, informing a tardy group member, testing the cohesiveness of and elaborating on the tentative ideas in their plan.

Comparison and Contrast

The groups showed a marked difference in planning segments (see Table 1). Group B had more identifiable segments than group A (six to three, respectively). Group B included all three of group A's segments but also included a segment on constructing a paragraph which was intended to teach about main idea as well as two other definable segments, accommodating time and period recaps of the planning process.

Table 1

Segmentation of Planning Process by Groups

Group	Segment	Portion of Ideas
Group A	Defining Task	.02
	Evaluation of Students	.06
	Practicing Identifying Main Ideas	.92
Group B	Defining Task	.03
	Constructing a Class Collaboration	.28
	Practicing Identifying Main Ideas	.41
	Evaluation	.18
	Accommodating Time	.02
	Recapitulations	.07

Note. Scores are proportions of ideas in categories to total ideas.

While both groups spent most of their time sharing ideas about how to get students to practice identifying main idea, group B distributed its ideas more evenly over the planning segments. That is, most of the ideas shared by group A were focused on practice. On the other hand, group B shared less on practicing main idea but contributed more ideas on evaluation and more variety through their discussion of constructing a paragraph.

Content of ideas. Four categories of information carried by ideas emerged from the data: (a) learners, (b) the reading process, (c) contextual factors, and (d) activities. Ideas about learners are those that referred to such considerations as abilities, background knowledge, interests, or behaviors of students. The ideas about the reading process considered such things as the thinking processes that go on in reading or features of text. Contextual features were ideas about things that exist in the school environment, such as people, space, or number of students. Activities were student and teacher actions (not thinking) and materials.

Analysis of the content of ideas revealed both similarities and differences in group performance (see Table 2). The groups shared the same number of ideas related to learners and contexts. They differed for ideas about reading and activities. A larger proportion of group B's ideas was related to the reading process. Conversely, group A shared relatively more ideas related to activities than group B.

Table 2

Content of Ideas Present in Planning Segments

	Learners	Reading	Context	Activities
Group A	13	18	01	68
Group B	13	30	02	55

Note. Scores are proportions of ideas shared by each group.

DISCUSSION

Students find collaborative work on planning for a lesson beneficial and satisfying. The participants in this problem-solving activity chose to work with one or more colleagues. They reported that they learned many ideas in the small- and large-group discussion sessions and said that the group provided a safe place for trying out ideas. The evaluative reports of our participants seem to bear out the assertions of Lortie (1975) that collaborative work provides a forum for testing ideas and gaining new ideas. These prospective teachers clearly believed that they learned "many new ideas" and had opportunities to present their own ideas for collective reflection.

The participants generated many ideas about teaching in their group planning discussions. Nemser (1983) and Little (1982), for example, are two researchers who have made the compelling case that when teachers are given opportunities to talk about teaching they broaden their knowledge base on the practice of teaching. The assertion apparently applies for beginning teachers also. Our participants reported that they learned new ideas from collaborative planning. Further, the analysis of the discourse during collaborative planning suggests that numerous opportunities for learning occurred when ideas carrying information about learners, reading, contexts, and activities were shared for the purpose of solving educational problems. Subsequent investigations which include the actual teaching of the lessons and compare individual to group plans may further help to document specific learning outcomes.

There are important differences between groups in the number and nature of ideas shared, as well as the manner by which the groups cluster or focus those ideas during the planning process. Given the scope of this study, it is difficult to explain these differences. However, the finding certainly raises a number of questions about characteristics of certain groups such as individual differences, group dynamics, and intentions. At a general level, we believed our groups were equivalent on a number of common characteristics such as begin successful, thoughtful, and articulate. It is possible that the differences between groups A and B could be attributed to their purpose for planning. Group B planned as if they were going to teach their lesson and, in fact, talked about arranging to teach it, although the task assignment didn't require it. Group A seemed to plan for the purpose of presenting to the large group of peers. Such a difference in purposes could have created the differences in planning ideas and segments that have been noted. A follow-up investigation which considers group characteristics and also holds the purpose of the group constant by adding the teaching of the lesson in an everyday setting would help to answer some of the questions raised by this study.

As teacher educators, this study has shown us that collaborative planning groups can be rich settings for learning to think about the teaching of reading. However, there is much more that we must understand about the content and process of learning in these collaborative groups before we can be confident about when and how such settings ought to be used in preparing teachers to teach reading.

REFERENCES

Erickson, F. (1979). *Reading comprehension of descriptive validity in studies of classroom acitivity* (Occasional Paper No. 16). East Lansing: Institute for Research on Teaching, Michigan State University.

Griffin, G., Barnes, S., Hughes, R., O'Neal, S. Defino, M., Edwards, S., & Heikell, H. (1983). *Clinical preservice teacher education: Final report of a descriptive study.* Austin, TX: Research and Development Center for Teacher Education, The University of Texas at Austin.

Lalik, R. V., & Niles, J. A. (1986, May). *Teacher planning in collaborative groups.* Paper presented at the Thirty-first Annual Convention of the International Reading Association, Philadelphia, PA.

Little, J. W. (1982). Norms of collegiality and experimentation: Workplace conditions for school success. *American Educational Research Journal, 19,* 325-340.

Lortie, D. C. (1975). *Schoolteacher: A socio-logical study.* Chicago: University of Chicago Press.

Nemser, S. (1983). Learning to teach. In L. Shulman & G. Sykes (Eds.), *Handbook of teaching and policy.* New York: Longman.

Niles, J., & Lalik R. (1985, May). *New directions in teacher education.* Paper presented at the Thirtieth Annual Convention of the International Reading Association, New Orleans, LA.

Shulman, L. S., & Carey, N. B. (1984). Psychology and the limitations of individual rationality: Implications for the study of reasoning and civility. *Review of Educational Research, 54,* 501-524.

Slavin, R. (1980). Cooperative learning. *Review of Educational Research, 50,* 315-342.

Spradley, J. (1979). *The ethnographic interview.* New York: Holt, Rinehart and Winston.

Spradley, J. P. (1980). *Participant observation.* New York: Holt, Rinehart and Winston.

Webb, N. M. (1982). Student interaction and learning in small groups. *Review of Educational Research, 52,* 421-445.

Weiss, B., Stever, L., Sprout, J., & Cruickshank, S. (1983). *Special happenings.* New York: Holt, Rinehart and Winston.

MAIN IDEA TREATMENT IN SECONDARY READING SKILL DEVELOPMENT MATERIALS

David W. Moore
University of Northern Iowa

Bonnie-Louise Smith
Waterloo (IA) Public Schools

Much evidence supports the conclusion that reading for important information is an essential comprehension strategy (Williams, 1986; Winograd & Bridge, 1986). Readers who note important concepts assimilate information better than readers who treat each concept equally. One problem with teaching students to read for important information is that they have difficulty transferring main idea strategies from skill development materials to content area textbooks (Taylor, Olson, Prenn, Rybczynski, & Zakaluk, 1985). This difficulty might be due in part to the instructional materials in reading that students receive.

The study reported here is a description of main idea treatment in reading skill development materials produced for upper grade students. Teachers with deep understandings of instructional materials might adjust their instruction according to the strengths and limitations of the materials in order to be most effective.

Two studies (Hare & Milligan, 1984; Winograd & Brennan, 1983) described basal reader series' treatments of getting the main idea. These reports characterized the main idea practices in six elementary school basal reader series. The following summarizes the findings from these two studies (if only one study presented particular information, then that study is cited):

1. Each series provided a reasonably consistent definition of main idea. However, the distinction between topic and main idea occasionally was confused.
2. The series frequently explained how to determine main ideas, but the explanations tended to be repetitious and sparse. For instance, explanations for finding explicit main idea statements in passages centered about looking for topic sentences in the first or last sentences of paragraphs. Explanations for deriving unstated main ideas tended to be vague. For instance, explanations such as "The main idea tells what is most important" frequently were included (Hare & Milligan, 1984).
3. Most main idea practice activities were in answer-recognition multiple-choice formats rather than answer-production composition formats. Despite this tendency, some series did emphasize answer-production tasks.
4. Narrative passages predominated in primary grade materials, but expository passages became more common and eventually predominated in intermediate grade materials.

5. Passages containing explicit main idea statements (i.e., topic sentences) occurred about as frequently as passages not containing such statements. The presence of topic sentences seemed related to text genre, with expository passages containing such sentences more frequently than narrative passages (Winograd & Brennan, 1983).

6. Determining main ideas was said to be valuable because that procedure helped readers understand and remember passages. However, no series explained in depth how students could realize this benefit (Hare & Milligan, 1984).

The findings listed above inform educators concerned with elementary school instruction, but they only suggest what might exist in secondary level materials. No description was located of the main idea treatment in secondary school reading materials. However, materials designed specifically for reading skill development are used frequently during secondary level remedial English and remedial reading instruction (Escoe, 1982). Thus, the purpose of this study was to describe the main idea treatment in secondary level reading skill development materials.

METHOD

Materials

Three series were selected for analysis: (a) Prentice-Hall *Be a Better Reader (BBR)* (Smith, 1984), (b) Scholastic *Project Achievement (Proj Ach)* (Spache & Spache, 1982), and (c) Scott, Foresman *Tactics* (Niles & Memory, 1981). These materials were chosen because they are meant to develop secondary students' reading proficiencies and because they present specific main idea activities. We analyzed the books designated by their publishers for the seventh-, ninth-, and twelfth-grade levels.

Procedure

Main idea exercises first were located in the materials. Exercises consisted of directions, some discourse, and a set of subsequent tasks. Main idea exercises were identified as such if they were listed in the table of contents, index, or a chart under the heading *main idea* or *central focus,* which was the term used by *Tactics.*

A coding system was derived from Hare and Milligan (1984) and Winograd and Brennan (1983). The system comprised four main categories: (a) guidelines for identifying a main idea, (b) main idea tasks, (c) main idea passages, and (d) values of identifying a main idea. Initially, all the main idea exercises of one series were identified. One of the researchers and an assistant, with the four main categories in mind, studied the exercises in order to form subcategories as well as instances of each subcategory. This system then was modified during the study when new instances were encountered.

Four points should be noted about the procedures. The first point is that we used the terms *stated* and *unstated* rather than *explicit* and *implicit* to classify types of main ideas. Stated main ideas consist of single sentences that are included in target passages and that express the main idea; stated main ideas are the same as topic sentences in single-paragraph passages. We used the term *stated* rather than the more common term *explicit* because topic sentences rarely are signaled explicitly (e.g., The main idea of this passage is X). Instead, readers need to infer which sentence, if any, is the topic sentence/explicit main idea. Unstated main ideas also need to be inferred; however, the difference is that no sentence in the passage is appropriate as a main idea statement, so one needs to be produced.

The second point about our procedures is that some exercises called for students to react to each main idea of individual paragraphs and then react to the main idea of the entire passage. In this situation, we coded only the task that related to the entire passage. The third point concerns our definition of exercise. The *BBR* main idea exercises differed from *Proj Ach* and *Tactics*. *BBR* included main idea questions among other types of questions appended to one passage, whereas the latter series contained lessons devoted specifically to main idea that consisted of several exercises. *BBR* lessons that contained only one main idea question were considered one exercise; each component in the *Proj Ach* and *Tactics* lessons that fitted our definition of exercise counted as one, also. Finally, we coded items as particular subcategory instances if the wording differed slightly from the original statements but the intent was the same. This final coding procedure required interpretation by the judges.

Following the procedures listed above, two judges separately tallied each item included in our coding system. The overall interjudge agreement was 93%; discrepancies were resolved in conference.

RESULTS AND DISCUSSION

In this section, the results for each subcategory first are presented. Interpretations of the results for each category then follow immediately.

Guidelines for Identifying a Main Idea

Guidelines show the way to be followed. Guidelines for identifying a main idea consisted of explanations of a stated main idea's characteristics, its probable locations in a passage, and explanations of an unstated main idea's characteristics. The materials we analyzed yielded 76 guidelines.

Characteristics of stated main ideas. Thirty comments were found about the characteristics of stated main ideas. *Tactics* presented twice as many characteristics (n = 18; 60%) as the other series. The two most common characteristics were that stated main ideas *summarize key details* (n = 6; 20%) and *reflect what the details emphasize* (n = 5; 17%).

Locations of stated main ideas. Twenty guidelines about the locations of stated main ideas were found. *Tactics* again contained about twice as many guidelines (n = 11; 55%) as the other series. Stated main ideas most frequently were said to be located *usually in the first or last sentence or the first or last paragraph* (n = 11; 55%).

Characteristics of unstated main ideas. Proj Ach provided more characteristics of unstated main ideas (n = 14; 54%) than either *Tactics* (n = 8; 31%) or *BBR* (n = 4; 15%). *Proj Ach* also was the only series to present a particular characteristic of unstated main ideas more than twice at any grade level. The two most commonly stated characteristics of unstated main ideas were that they *piece together emphasized details* (n = 9; 35%) and they *give an overall view of what the details suggest* (n = 8; 31%).

Discussion. Two points about the guidelines for identifying a main idea deserve comment. First, the explanations of a main idea's characteristics presented in the secondary materials seemed as vague as the explanations presented in the elementary basal reader series. Materials at both levels seem to substitute one imprecise term (*main idea*) for another (e.g., *summary of key details*). The sparseness of these explanations might account for the confusion regarding main ideas reported by Cunningham and Moore (1986). Cunningham and Moore obtained from students and teachers numerous different, yet logical, responses to the inquiry "What is the main idea of this passage?" They concluded that students frequently have difficulty with the main idea task because it is ambiguous. Hare and Milligan (1984) suggested that explanations of main ideas were vague because the knowledge available about them was vague. Researchers have not fully explained the characteristics of main ideas, and instructional materials reflect this limitation.

The second point about the guidelines is that substantial differences were noted among the series. *Tactics* provided more information about stated main ideas, and *Proj Ach* presented more information about unstated main ideas. The materials students receive might affect their understandings of the features of certain types of main ideas.

Main Idea Tasks

Tasks consist of the work students are expected to perform within each exercise. Tasks begin with a question (e.g., What is the main idea of this paragraph?) or directive (e.g., Underline the statement that best expresses that main idea). One task was counted each time a student was expected to respond to a question or directive; 524 tasks were identified. We analyzed each task's response mode (recognition or production) and focus (attention to details or to generalizations).

Response mode. Answer-recognition tasks (n = 330; 63%) substantially outnumbered answer-production tasks (n = 194; 37%). However, the materials varied substantially in their balance of the two modes. One series, *Proj Ach*, contained only answer-recognition tasks, *BBR* contained about 2½ times more answer-recognition tasks than answer-production ones, and *Tactics* contained approximately equal numbers of the two types.

Response focus. Response focus refers to the information contained at various levels in passages' hierarchical structures. Main idea tasks can focus students' attention to superordinate top-level generalizations as well as subordinate bottom-level details. Fifty percent (n = 263) of the tasks studied here involved recognition or production of details that supported particular main ideas, and 50% (n = 261) involved recognition or production of generalizations. Again, the materials varied. *Tactics* presented few main idea tasks that focused on details.

Discussion. Several points about the tasks warrant attention. First, as with the guidelines, the materials presented discrepant tasks. Each secondary level reading skill development series treated main idea distinctively. Another point involves the predominance of answer-recognition tasks in some materials. Researchers generally agree that producing main idea statements leads to better overall comprehension than selecting statements from multiple-choice formats (Bridge, Belmore, Moskow, Cohen, & Matthews, 1984; Doctorow, Wittrock, & Marks, 1978). Secondary teachers, like elementary teachers, who wish to help students compose independent statements of the main idea will need to change many of the tasks found in their skill development materials.

Finally, the finding that many tasks focus students' attention to details indicates that teachers who wish to help students form generalizations will need to be cautious with certain skill development materials. Noting details and forming generalizations are related processes (Kintsch & van Dijk, 1978), but the nature of this relationship and the reciprocal outcomes of instruction in each are unknown at present. Identifying details that support given main idea statements is a process that probably differs from producing generalizations about details. The outcomes of instruction in these two processes is a prime candidate for future research.

Main Idea Passages

The nature of the passages that students react to help determine the treatment of main ideas in instructional materials. In this study, 110 passages were analyzed. The function (demonstration or practice), main idea condition (stated or unstated), and genre of the passages were tallied.

Function. The function of main idea passages was studied in order to determine the proportion of demonstration materials and practice materials. Of the 110 passages analyzed, 14% (n = 15) were for demonstration and 86% (n = 95) were for practice. *Tactics* presented about three times as many demonstration passages as the other two series.

Main idea condition. Main idea condition refers to whether main ideas are stated in a passage or unstated. The studies of elementary materials cited earlier referred to this comparison as between explicit or implicit main ideas. The passages studied here included roughly equal numbers of passages containing stated main ideas (n = 52%; 47%) and unstated ones (n = 58; 53%).

Genre. In descending order of frequency, the genres of the passages were as follows: (a) expository (n = 72; 65%), (b) narrative (n = 17; 15%), (c) descriptive (n = 17; 15%), (d) persuasive (n = 2; 2%), and (e) poetry (n = 2; 2%).

Discussion. The function of the main idea passages was proportionate with regard to demonstration and practice, although *Tactics* contributed substantially to this balance by including many demonstration passages. The inclusion of many demonstration passages is a positive feature because explanations about how to discern main ideas are paltry, as noted earlier. Some instructional materials at least provide examples of what main idea statements should be.

Given the predominance of unstated main ideas in general materials (Baumann & Serra, 1984; Braddock, 1974), the balance of stated and unstated main ideas seems appropriate. If anything, an even greater number of passages with unstated main ideas might be desirable. Finally, the emphasis on exposition deserves attention. Different types of discourse elicit different types of inferencing (Bridge & Tierney, 1981), so teachers who want students to produce main idea statements for genres other than exposition will need to provide appropriate passages. Nevertheless, secondary students encounter much expository writing in classrooms (Stake & Easley, 1978), so emphasizing this genre in reading skill development materials seems appropriate.

Value of Identifying a Main Idea

The benefit to readers of identifying a main idea seems to be an important item for reading skill development materials to include. Knowing why to do something deserves attention along with knowing how to do it (Paris, Lipson, & Wixson, 1982). The materials analyzed in this study reported two essential values: (a) main idea identification helped comprehension of the relationships of ideas and (b) main idea identification aided memory of content. The first value was presented six times across the series, and the second value was noted seven times. As with elementary materials, these values provide only vague reasons for attending to main ideas, and the values are presented rarely. Teachers who want their students to value main idea identification will need to present a convincing case on their own.

CONCLUSIONS

The treatment of main ideas in the elementary materials studied previously and in the secondary materials studied here is quite similar. Each series treats main idea instruction differently. The materials for both age levels provide numerous, albeit vague, explanations of how to determine main ideas. Passages containing roughly equal numbers of stated and unstated main ideas are presented. Answer-recognition tasks predominate in most materials. Expository passages generally are found for older students. The value of determining main ideas is left unclear.

A finding not mentioned in the elementary studies that emerged in this study of secondary materials is the substantial emphasis on details by some series. Determining details that support main ideas and determining main ideas in the first place seem to be two related, yet different, processes. This emphasis on details warrants the attention of practitioners as well as researchers.

Finally, an impression that emerged from our analysis of the elementary studies and the secondary materials is that a systematic program of main idea instruction within and across grade level materials was missing. Reports by Baumann (1984) and Sjostrom and Hare (1984) indicate that a systematic program based on principles of direct instruction can be used successfully to teach students to produce main idea statements. Progressing from simple to complex materials and gradually releasing responsibility to students characterize this instruction. However, we found no evidence that any series presented such a sequence. For instance, answer-recognition tasks did not fade to answer-production ones, and passages containing stated main ideas did not fade to passages containing unstated main ideas.

In closing, the study reported here is descriptive. It characterizes secondary reading skill development materials' treatment of main idea instruction. This description should serve to suggest areas of main idea instruction that teachers and publishers might capitalize on or modify.

REFERENCES

Baumann, J. F. (1984). The effectiveness of a direct instruction paradigm for teaching main idea comprehension. *Reading Research Quarterly, 20,* 93-115.

Baumann, J. F., & Serra, J. K. (1984). The frequency and placement of main ideas in children's social studies textbooks: A modified replication of Braddock's research on topic sentences. *Journal of Reading Behavior, 16,* 27-37.

Braddock, R. (1974). The frequency and placement of topic sentences in expository prose. *Research in the Teaching of English, 8,* 287-302.

Bridge, C. A., Belmore, S. M., Moskow, S. P., Cohen, S. S., & Mathews, P. D. (1984). Topicalization and memory for main ideas in prose. *Journal of Reading Behavior, 16,* 61-80.

Bridge, C. A., & Tierney, R. J. (1981). The inferential operations of children across text with narrative and expository tendencies. *Journal of Reading Behavior, 13,* 201-214.

Cunningham, J. W., & Moore, D. W. (1986). The confused world of main idea. In J. F. Baumann (Ed.), *Teaching main idea comprehension* (pp. 1-17). Newark, DE: International Reading Association.

Doctorow, M., Wittrock, M. C., & Marks, C. (1978). Generative processes in reading comprehension. *Journal of Educational Psychology, 70,* 109-118.

Escoe, A. (1982). *Remedial reading and English instruction for junior high and senior high school students: A description of common practices in teaching and assessment* (Tech. Rep. No. 75). Los Alamitos, CA: SWRL Educational Research and Development.

Hare, V., & Milligan, B. (1984). Main idea identification: Instructional explanations in four reader series. *Journal of Reading Behavior, 16,* 189-204.

Kintsch, W., & van Dijk, T. A. (1978). Toward a model of discourse comprehension and production. *Psychological Review, 85,* 363-394.

Niles, O. S., & Memory, D. (1981). *Tactics in reading.* Glenview, IL: Scott, Foresman.

Paris, S. G., Lipson, M., & Wixson, K. K. (1982). Becoming a strategic reader. *Contemporary Educational Psychology, 8,* 293-316.

Sjostrom, C. L., & Hare, V. C. (1984). Teaching high school students to identify main ideas in expository text. *Journal of Educational Research, 78,* 114-118.

Smith, N. B. (1984). *Be a better reader.* Englewood Cliffs, NJ: Prentice-Hall.

Spache, G. B., & Spache, E. B. (1982). *Project achievement.* New York: Scholastic.

Stake, R. E., & Easley, J. (1978). *Case studies in science education* (vol. 2: Design, overview and general findings). Washington, DC: National Science Foundation.

Taylor, B., Olson, V., Prenn, M., Rybczynski, M., & Zakaluk, B. (1985). A comparison of students' ability to read for main ideas in social studies textbooks and to complete main idea worksheets. *Reading World, 24,* 10-15.

Williams, J. P. (1986). Extracting important information from text. In J. A. Niles & R. V. Lalik (Eds.), *Solving problems in literacy: Learners, teachers, and researchers* (pp. 11-29). Thirty-fifth Yearbook of the National Reading Conference. Rochester, NY: National Reading Conference.

Winograd, P., & Brennan, S. (1983). Main idea instruction in basal readers. In J. A. Niles & L. A. Harris (Eds.), *Searches for meaning in reading/language processing and instruction* (pp. 80-86). Thirty-second Yearbook of the National Reading Conference. Rochester, NY: National Reading Conference.

Winograd, P., & Bridge, C. A. (1986). The comprehension of important information in written prose. In J. F. Baumann (Ed.), *Teaching main idea comprehension* (pp. 18-48). Newark, DE: International Reading Association.

LEARNING FROM DISCUSSION: REQUIREMENTS AND CONSTRAINTS ON CLASSROOM INSTRUCTION IN READING COMPREHENSION STRATEGIES

James H. Mosenthal
Michigan State University

In the second study reported in Palincsar and Brown (1984), based on A. Palincsar's dissertation (1982), classroom teachers and school specialists were trained in the use of the reciprocal teaching strategy. They used the strategy over a period of 20 sessions with groups of four to seven students. In an impressive display of effective comprehension instruction, all groups reached and maintained the 75% criterion set for the daily assessment task. Few interventions have shown as powerful a set of results as the Palincsar and Brown intervention. In the present study, a replication of the second study in Palincsar and Brown (1984) was carried out in a classroom setting. The purpose of the replication was to document how readily and effectively the reciprocal teaching strategy could be implemented in the classroom so as to produce significant improvement in students' comprehension of text.

The reciprocal teaching strategy engages students and teachers in the task of generating questions, summaries, requests for clarification, and predictions of subsequent content based on the content of a short section of an expository text selection, usually one paragraph. The task is carried out by students acting as teachers for a section of text. Students' engagement in the tasks of the strategy is complemented by the teacher's modeling of the use of the strategy and probing of inadequate student responses in order to construct adequate ones.

The effectiveness of the reciprocal teaching strategy is determined by the quality of the interaction between students and teacher over responses meant to tap relevant content. As a result of probing, a final form of the response is reached that satisfies the main substantive requirement of the strategy—that a response tap relevant content. It is from the adequacy of the final form of a response that a student learns correctness in the use of the strategy and internalizes, over time, the cognitive principles underlying that correctness. In the original study and in the replication, internalization is manifested when students perform at or above 75% on 10-item comprehension tasks given immediately after each discussion session. When performance is below 75%, it is concluded that internalization has not taken place and that this is a result of ineffective interaction in the use of the reciprocal teaching method. In other words, it is argued that comprehension performance is a consequence of the internalization of cognitive strategies for comprehending text which are, in turn, learned as a result of the effective use of the reciprocal teaching method. Given this argument, a major focus of this report is to document whether, and how, the strategy was used effectively or ineffectively.

METHOD

Subjects

Eight students were selected from a class of 25 to participate as group members. Criteria for determining group membership were the same as those reported in Palincsar and Brown (1984). The eight students chosen scored below 50% on a 10-item comprehension test administered after reading a short expository passage but decoded the same passage at or above 95% accuracy. Each of the eight students scored at or below 4.9 on the comprehension subtest of the Iowa Test of Basic Skills (ITBS) administered in the Spring of the students' sixth-grade year (6.9 = grade level score). The group had a median score of 4.3 on the ITBS and a range of 4.1 to 4.9 (with one outlier of 2.6). The class as a whole (N = 25) had a median score of 4.9 and a range of 4.1 to 5.8. Baseline measures were taken over seven days prior to training. On each day, the students read an assessment passage and answered a 10-item comprehension test. All eight students averaged below 50% on the tests.

Materials and Procedure

The teacher of the group and five other junior high classroom teachers were instructed in the use of the reciprocal teaching strategy by the experimenter. Instruction took place over six one-hour sessions prior to training. During training, the experimenter sat in on one session per week and discussed the session with the teacher following its completion.

Training took place over 23 days within seven weeks. Only the first six weeks or 21 sessions were tape-recorded. The discussion data reported is based on transcripts of the discussions over those 21 sessions. The group averaged 3.5 sessions per week. Discussion of paragraphs in a training passage (of about 1,500 words) took 20–25 minutes. An assessment passage of approximately 400 words was administered immediately after each discussion, taking 10–15 minutes. Five minutes were spent going over the answers to the assessment questions. The training and assessment passages were identical to the ones used in the original study (Palincsar, 1982). These passages were basal, expository selections written at a seventh-grade readability level according to the Fry Readability Formula.

Coding of responses. What was coded as a response to a strategy component was the final form of a question, summary, clarification, or prediction after discussion and probing. In other words, the final form of a response was one left intact and accepted by the teacher which thereby served as an example of a strategy response. The final form of a response was coded according to which component of the strategy it was a response (question, summary, clarification, or prediction) and according to its locus. The locus of the final form of a response to a strategy component indicates whether it was the initial response given by a student, a response given by a student as a result of probing by the teacher, or whether it was a response modeled by the teacher. (Hereafter, *the final form of a response* will be referred to as *response.*)

In addition, each response was coded as to whether it was adequate or inadequate. The general requirement was held that a final form of a response must tap relevant content. For the questioning component, three requirements were set: (a) questions must be syntactically articulate, (b) they cannot misrepresent information presented in the text section, and (c) they cannot be irrelevant to the content of the text section. For the summary component, one requirement was set, that is, that the summary reflect the main idea of the section. For the clarification component, all requests for clarification were accepted as adequate. For the prediction component, one requirement was set. Reiterations of the prediction ''I predict they will talk more about [topic of the training passage]'' were rated as inadequate after the initial use of this prediction.

All coding of the final form of responses was done by two raters working independently. The raters compared their coding of each session. All disagreements were resolved in discussion.

RESULTS AND DISCUSSION

The daily mean performance of the group on the assessment tests are given in Figure 1. The group's mean performances during baseline, training, and follow-up are 37, 52, and 49, respectively.

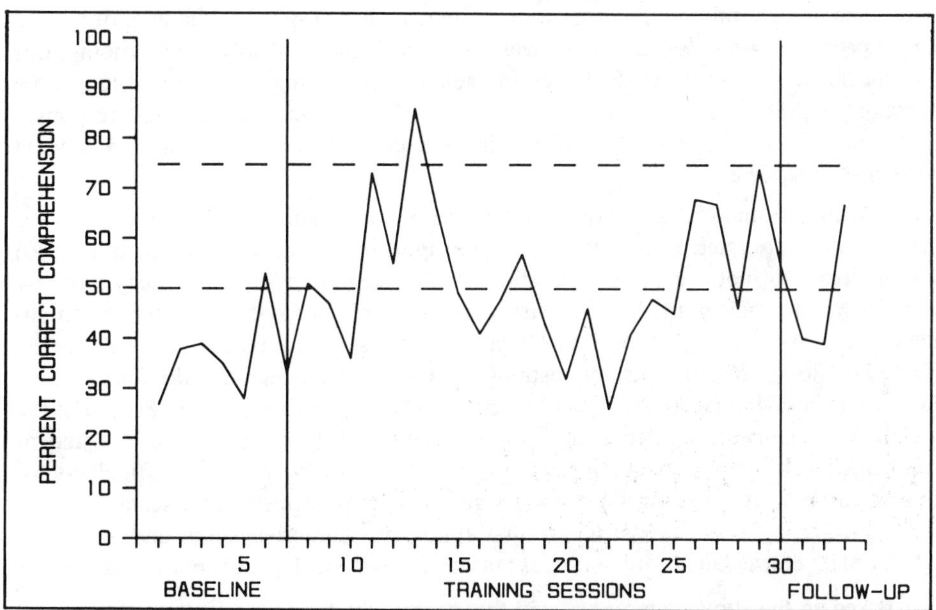

FIGURE 1. Daily Mean Performance of Students During Baseline, Training, and Follow-up

In the results discussed below, the adequacy of the interaction between students and teacher and the adequacy of the teacher's modeling are examined to see how the group discussions prevented internalization, leading to the low performance of the group. Table 1 presents the proportion of students' and teacher's questions and summaries that were rated inadequate.

Table 1

Weekly Proportion of Student's and Teacher's Questions and Summaries Rated Inadequate

Week	1	2	3	4	5	6	Total
				Students			
Questions	.33	.18	.31	.18	.42	.12	.26
Summaries	0	.75	.39	1.00	.67	0	.51
				Teacher			
Questions	.09	0	0	.33	.14	.17	.11
Summaries	0	.44	0	.33	.25	.67	.26

Interaction data. When considering the adequacy of student responses, a negative picture of the discussions emerges. A profile of the adequacy of student responses was calculated by determining the proportion of total student responses (the total of probed and unprobed student responses) that were rated inadequate. Ideally, with probing, this statistic should approach 0% for all components of the strategy. In other words, if the function of probing by the teacher is to make initially inadequate student responses adequate in their final form, the ratio of inadequate student responses to total student responses should be zero.

The above situation is true only in the case of clarifications where all requests for clarification were rated as adequate. A high proportion of inadequate predictions (.40) was the result of not accepting reiterations of the prediction "I predict they will talk more about [the topic of the training passage]." With respect to the questioning component, it appears that students approached acceptable use of this part of the strategy (see Table 1). Though 26% of student questions were rated inadequate, the flip side of a 26% failure rate is a 74% success rate, slightly below an acceptable standard of 80%. For the summary component, performance is almost random. Fifty-one percent of the student summaries were rated inadequate (see Table 1). Summarizing is a more difficult cognitive task to perform. It requires the processing of a macrostructure for the section read. It is the processing of a macrostructure that epitomizes comprehension, and the group displayed no consistent ability to process information at this level of sophistication.

Based on the above data, it appears that not enough probing took place during the summarizing phase of the strategy. It is less clear whether this is so during the questioning and prediction phases of the strategy.

Modeling data. The above discussion considers the interaction between students and teacher when the students give the final form of a response. It is important to ask whether the teacher provided adequate modeling of the effective use of the strategy. Modeling is the other half of the instructional responsibility of the teacher when using the reciprocal teaching strategy. It is necessary that the teacher model adequate use of the strategy so that students may learn what is expected of them when asked to use the strategy.

A profile of the adequacy of the teacher's modeling was calculated by determining the proportion of modeled responses rated inadequate. It is expected that the proportion of modeled responses rated inadequate approach 0%. In other words, as a competent comprehender, the teacher should be able to model the adequate use of basic comprehension strategies.

For the modeled clarifications and predictions, 0% were inadequate. This is one aspect of the teacher's modeling that appears to be satisfactory. Eleven percent of the questions modeled by the teacher and 26% of the summaries modeled by the teacher were rated inadequate (see Table 1). Whether these percentages are acceptable or not is unclear. Practically, the percentage of inadequately modeled questions may be acceptable given the level of success students had generating adequate questions (74%). However, the percentage of inadequately modeled summaries is probably not acceptable given the low level of success students had generating adequate summaries (49%).

Besides the above percentages, what is noteworthy about the teacher's responses is the fact that, during the final three weeks of training, the quality of the modeling of questions and summaries degenerates (see Table 1). The proportion of responses modeled remains consistent with the overall averages (over the final three weeks, 27% of the questions generated were modeled compared to 27% overall, and 36% of the summaries generated were modeled compared to 37% overall). However, over the final three weeks, 21% of the modeled questions were inadequate compared with 11% overall, and 38% of the modeled summaries were inadequate compared with 26% overall.

Intuitively, it does not make sense to say that the teacher became a poor comprehender over the final three weeks of training. The immediate causes of this degeneration in performance are perhaps best understood by comparing discussion during week 2, where there is a high proportion of inadequate summaries given by students and teacher, with week 1 when the opposite is true. It may be the case that the real trouble began during the second week of training when 44% of the modeled summaries were rated inadequate.

Over the first seven days of training, performance follows the pattern reported in Palincsar and Brown (1984; see Figure 1). It can be argued that performance reflected what was learned as a result of a careful beginning. During week 1 of training, no inadequate summaries were generated (see Table 1, week 1). Of the summaries generated, six adequate student summaries were generated. Three were initial responses and three were probed responses. Nine adequate summaries were modeled.

However, during week 2 of training, 75% of the student generated summaries and 44% of the teacher's modeled summaries were inadequate (see Table 1, week 2). Of the summaries generated by the students, nine were inadequate. All were initial responses unprobed by the teacher. Only three adequate student summaries were generated (two were initial responses and one was probed). Four inadequate summaries were modeled during week 2 while five adequate summaries were modeled.

It should be noted that a total of 12 student summaries were generated during week 2 as compared to six during week 1. This represents a 100% increase in the number of summaries for which the students were responsible. This increase was not matched by an increase, as we have seen, in effective probing. Nor is the increase in student responsibility for summarizing matched by an increase in the amount of teacher modeling. Rather, 57% of the summaries generated during week 2 were student summaries, whereas, during week 1, 40% of the summaries generated were student summaries. The average percentage of the summaries generated by students over weeks 2–6 is 67%. It appears that after week 1, the teacher gave over primary responsibility for summarizing to the students when they were not ready for it. There was no gradual release of responsibility to the students for generating summaries. A similar situation exists with questioning. During week 1, 58% of the questions generated were student questions. During week 2, 80% of the questions generated were student questions. Over weeks 2–6, 74% of the questions were generated by the students.

The percentages given above are not unacceptably high, or low, in and of themselves. What is an unacceptably high proportion of student responses depends upon the corresponding percentage of inadequate student responses. What seems unacceptable is the sudden shift in reponsibility given over to the students and the maintenance of the high level of student responsibility with high levels of inadequate responses.

For whatever causes, the above description of the summary responses shows that during week 2 the pace of instruction and the modeling and probing of the teacher became unacceptable. By the end of the second week, the group's comprehension performance had fallen off to an average of 46 over the Thursday and Friday sessions. This represents a decline from an average of 69 over Monday, Tuesday, and Wednesday. It was a decline in comprehension performance anticipated by a decline in the adequate use of the reciprocal teaching strategy and from which the group never recovered.

GENERAL DISCUSSION

In general, the extent of the teacher's probing was inadequate and the quality of the teacher's modeling degenerated over time. It may be concluded, then, that the strategy was not used effectively, that this prevented the internalization of the cognitive principles underlying the reciprocal teaching strategy and caused the poor performance on the assessment tests.

However, it is not clear why this is the case. Based on the instruction in reciprocal teaching given to the junior high teachers, it was the experimenter's evaluation that the teacher of the group understood the effective use of the reciprocal teaching strategy. In the data presented, the teacher did demonstrate the ability to provide adequate probing and modeling. Why was it not done consistently? One answer, contrary to the experimenter's evaluation, is that the teacher had not internalized the principles underlying the use of the strategy. As a result, the teacher may not have been aware of the extent of the inadequacy of the discussions. From a teacher education perspective, it is important to determine what must be understood by a teacher and how that understanding can be cultivated, before the teacher can effectively train students in the use of a discussion strategy.

Another answer is that though the group was appropriately screened, classroom factors prevented the effective use of the strategy. Several examples of such factors can be identified. For instance, the seventh-grade classroom studied had a large number of low ability students. The time allocated for group instruction broke a routine of whole class instruction and created, for the teacher, the problem of keeping the remaining students of the class on task. The small group reciprocal teaching forced students into a mode of social interaction with which they were unfamiliar. The materials proved difficult given the level at which the students were asked to process them. The influence of such factors and their interactions on adequate coverage of material are discussed in Barr (1982). When such conditions are considered, it is not clear whether the teacher could have taken the time to pursue adequate probing and modeling without restricting participation and coverage and, in doing so, denying the dynamic of reciprocal teaching, the vehicle by which comprehension strategies are to be learned.

Some support for this argument comes from remarks made by the teacher. The teacher noted in an interview after the training that the strategy was a powerful one because it made the students think about what they read. The teacher pointed to the summarizing and reciprocal teaching as especially important aspects of the strategy. However, the teacher complained that, at times, the strategy was too difficult to use with the materials, that the students were not used to small group discussions, that they became bored with the strategy, and that grouping within the classroom made it difficult to maintain order among nonparticipating students.

Though the rigor with which the teacher carried out the discussion strategy could have been improved, the complaints point to the difficulty of providing adequate group instruction in a junior high, low ability classroom. Documented improvement in such a setting requires a subtle and complex coordination of grouping, student ability, material difficulty, group size, and instructional time. It is, perhaps, a large contextual leap to expect ready implementation of a discussion strategy and observed improvement on a standard comprehension task.

Such work as Palincsar and Brown's (1984) reveals the potential of discussion strategies to improve students' comprehension of text. Reading practitioners and researchers must work to discover how this potential can be realized in ongoing classroom instruction. To this end, future classroom-based research needs to address several issues: (a) teacher training in the use of discussion strategies in the classroom, (b) the interaction between a teacher's understanding of strategy use and the classroom context in which that understanding is called into action, and (c) appropriate performance expectations for students trained in strategy use as a part of ongoing classroom instruction.

REFERENCES

Barr, R. (1982). Classroom reading instruction from a sociological perspective. *Journal of Reading Behavior, 14,* 375-389.

Palincsar, A. S. (1982). *Improving the reading comprehension of junior high students through the reciprocal teaching of comprehension-monitoring strategies.* Unpublished doctoral dissertation, University of Illinois.

Palincsar, A. S., & Brown, A. L. (1984). Reciprocal teaching of comprehension-fostering and comprehension-monitoring activities. *Cognition and Instruction, 1,* 117-175.

EXPLICITNESS IN SIXTH-GRADE SOCIAL STUDIES TEXTBOOKS

Mariam Jean Dreher
University of Maryland

Harry Singer and Catherine A. Letteer
University of California, Riverside

Teachers and researchers have been concerned with the effect of textbooks on students' reading performance since the pioneering work of Gray and Leary (1935). In recent years, a major topic of research has been the *friendliness* or *considerateness* of texts. Friendly texts contain features that presumably make them easier to comprehend.

Features that a friendly or considerate text should contain have been proposed. For example, Anderson and Armbruster (1981), Langer (1983), and Tierney, Mosenthal, and Kantor (1984) have all offered guidelines for examining textbooks. In addition, Singer (1986) has developed a comprehensive Friendly Text Inventory (FTI). This FTI groups items for evaluating texts into the following seven major categories:

1. *Text organization:* the arrangement of information including such factors as a text's cohesiveness and use of signal words.
2. *Explication:* the direct statement of information so that the reader is not required to infer.
3. *Conceptual density:* the number of new ideas and vocabulary introduced per text sample.
4. *Metadiscourse:* the author's direct comments to the reader about the information in the text.
5. *Readability:* the adequacy of the text with regard to such factors as sentence and word length and use of personal pronouns.
6. *Instructional devices:* features that aid learning from the text such as preposed questions, diagrams, and summaries.
7. *Instructional appropriateness:* the inclusion of such features as up-to-date information and the suitability of the text for the curriculum at a particular grade level.

Critics have written some bleak appraisals of the friendliness of textbooks (Anderson & Armbruster, 1981, 1986; Anderson, Armbruster, & Kantor, 1980; Davison & Kantor, 1982; Kantor, Anderson, & Armbruster, 1983; Langer, 1983; Tierney, Mosenthal, & Kantor, 1984). These appraisals have generally consisted of numerous examples of poorly written textbook passages. Although the examples are striking, Kane (1980) noted that critiques may be misleading when a text segment from the middle of a lesson is presented out of context or when a critic assigns a purpose to a text which was not intended. Moreover, the examples cited in these critiques may or may not be representative of the texts from which they are drawn, since they have not been accompanied by evidence of systematic sampling from particular texts or by evidence of the reliability of the ratings.

In contrast, our purpose was to conduct an empirical study of a sample of sixth-grade social studies textbooks that are or have been widely used in the schools. In this initial phase of our research, we focused on one major aspect of text friendliness, a text's degree of explicitness. We compared both recent and older textbooks since the intensive burst of research on reading in the past 10 to 15 years may have influenced the nature of textbook writing.

Explication of information, one of the major factors hypothesized to contribute to text friendliness (Singer, 1986) and learning (Bransford, 1985), refers to direct statements that do not require the reader to infer, organize, or construct relationships. In a schema-theoretic view, readers comprehend a message when they are able to bring to mind a schema that gives a good account of the objects or events described in a message (Anderson, 1985; Rumelhart & Ortony, 1977). Therefore, well-explicated texts should facilitate comprehension since they should enable readers to locate or construct appropriate schemata and relationships among schemata more easily.

If a text is inexplicit or imprecisely elaborated, students are faced with what is essentially an arbitrary list of facts, the most difficult type of material to learn and retain (Bransford, 1985; Stein & Bransford, 1979; Stein, Morris, & Bransford, 1978). If an inexplicit text deals with familiar concepts, students may be able to locate appropriate existing schemata to make the text meaningful. Indeed, Bransford (1985) has pointed out that experts are not likely to notice when facts are presented in an arbitrary way because they already have schemata that allow them to understand the significance of the information. Since content-area textbooks are designed to teach students *new* information, inexplicitness presents a more challenging problem. Content-area texts require the *construction* of new schemata or the modification of old ones, not just the activation of existing knowledge structures. As a result, content-area texts need to facilitate schema construction by clarifying the significance and relevance of facts and relationships.

In our analysis of social studies texts, we used the Explication Inventory of the FTI, shown in Appendix A. This inventory lists six areas that could be expected to contribute to explicitness. First, since arbitrary lists of facts are harder to learn than related sets of information, textbooks need to explicate relationships such as how properties are related to categories and how function relates to structure. For example, in a biology text, a set of facts about veins and arteries can seem arbitrary and confusing unless the text clarifies such points as the relevance of elasticity and thickness of arteries to the functions they perform (Bransford, 1985). Thus, texts need to directly state core concepts and elaborate relationships so that students can understand the significance of information. In other words, explicit texts provide reasons for functions and events. Second, an explicit text highlights and clearly defines terms as they are introduced since understanding the vocabulary contributes to the understanding of new concepts. Third, explicit texts use vivid examples, analogies, or figurative language to help clarify new ideas. Fourth, explicit texts help activate necessary background knowledge. For example, they show students how new ideas in the text are related to knowledge students already have. Fifth, explicit texts use sentence structure that facilitates comprehension. They may, for example, use relatively short, direct sentences as opposed to unnecessarily complex structure and terminology. Sixth, explicit texts orient readers to the central ideas in a unit, chapter, or text segment. Such an orientation occurs when a text informs readers about the goals and purposes they are to read for or signals the central ideas with such devices as the questions asked and the purposes or introductions given.

METHOD

Materials

The materials used in this study included the Explication Inventory, a rater's manual to accompany the Inventory, and 12 sixth-grade social studies textbooks.

As shown in Appendix A, the Explication Inventory consists of six items. Each item rates a textbook sample on a five-point scale. The Inventory was accompanied by a 12-page manual. The first page of this manual consisted of an overview of the task and general instructions such as advising raters to consider a single criterion at a time. The rest of the manual presented examples to illustrate the rating levels for each of the six items. Each example was accompanied by a comment about why it received that particular rating. The manual was constructed by making an intensive search for appropriate examples in randomly selected passages from four sixth-grade social studies textbooks. An extensive revison process was carried out to assure that the examples and comments would be clear to the raters.

Six recent sixth-grade social studies textbooks were sampled from a list of widely used texts that had been identified independently by two social studies professors. These texts were published in 1980 or later. Six texts, published between 1970 to 1973, were also selected. In all but one case, these older textbooks were selected from the same publishers as the newer textbooks. The texts are listed in Appendix B.

Procedure

Three random samples were selected from each of the 12 textbooks. In most cases, a sample was a complete chapter. However, some 45- to 50-page chapters were subdivided at lesson boundaries. In other cases, segments that were three to four pages long that were labeled chapters in their respective textbooks were combined into samples of two to three chapters. The average sample segment was 13 pages long.

Two raters were instructed on the Explication Inventory and the manual. Their ratings for the three samples from each textbook were averaged to get a total for that text. Differences in the ratings for the two independent raters were resolved in conference. Then, to check for reliability, a third rater rated the three segments for a random sample of half the textbooks. The interrater reliability between the initial ratings and the third rater's scores was $r = .88$. All raters were experienced teachers who were also graduate students.

RESULTS

Total Scores

The Explication Inventory has six items that can each be rated from 1 to 5. Therefore, the total scores on the Inventory can range from to 6 to 30. The closer the score is to 6, the more explicit the text.

The mean total score for the 12 texts was 14.16. As shown in Table 1, the total scores ranged from 10.67 to 20. The mean from the 1980 through 1986 texts was 14.61, while that for the 1970 to 1973 texts was 13.72. A *t* test between the means for the older and newer texts indicated no statistically significant difference ($t = .59$, $df = 10$).

These total scores can be divided by 6 to allow them to be interpreted according to a 5-point scale with 1 being very explicit, 2 explicit, 3 mixed, 4 inexplicit, and 5 very inexplicit. Table 1 indicates that on such a 5-point scale, nine of the texts fall into the explicit category while three texts are mixed with regard to explication.

Table 1

Total Explication Scores for Sixth-Grade Social Studies Textbooks

Text Publication Date	Total Explication Score		Category of Explicitness[a]
1986	13.50		2.25
1983	10.84		1.81
1983	20.00		3.34
1982	12.50		2.08
1980	17.17		2.86
1980	13.67		2.28
1973	15.17		2.53
1972	14.49		2.42
1972	13.65		2.28
1972	14.50		2.42
1970	13.84		2.31
1970	10.67		1.78
	Mean for 1980–86 texts	14.61	
	Standard deviation	3.36	
	Mean for 1970–73 texts	13.72	
	Standard deviation	1.59	
	Mean for all texts	14.16	
	Standard deviation	2.55	

[a]Categories are 1 = very explicit, 2 = explicit, 3 = mixed, 4 = inexplicit, 5 = very inexplicit.

Individual Items

To obtain specific information on particular aspects of explication, older and newer textbooks were also compared on the six individual items of the Explication Inventory. *t*-Test analyses indicated a statistically significant difference between texts only for Item

6. This item deals with whether the central idea of a text segment is explicit ($t = 2.23$, $df = 10$, $p = .050$). Newer texts rated somewhat less explicit than did older texts, as can be seen in Table 2.

As with the total explication scores, mean text ratings for the individual items fell into categories 2 and 3. Table 2 indicates the texts rated most explicit on using direct sentence structure (Item 5) and least explicit on defining new vocabulary and activating prior knowledge (Items 2 and 4).

Table 2

Explication Scores for Sixth-Grade Social Studies Textbooks by Individual Items

Item[a]	Text Publication Date	Mean	Standard Deviation
provides	80–86	2.44	.65
reasons	70–73	2.02	.44
	total	2.24	.57
defines	80–86	2.67	.98
terms	70–73	3.06	.73
	total	2.86	.85
uses	80–86	2.67	.70
examples	70–73	2.17	.30
	total	2.42	.58
reviews	80–86	2.70	.72
prior	70–73	2.83	.62
knowledge	total	2.76	.64
uses	80–86	1.58	.29
direct	70–73	1.61	.33
sentences	total	1.60	.30
explicit	80–86	2.61	.52
central	70–73	2.02	.39
idea	total	2.32	.53

[a]See Appendix A for full items.

DISCUSSION

The results indicated no statistically significant differences on total explication scores between the recent and older textbooks we analyzed. Although there was a statistically significant difference between newer and older texts on one of the individual items (in favor of the older texts), there appears to be little change in degree of explicitness despite considerable research and discussion on reading since the 1970–1973 publication dates of the older texts.

None of the 12 widely used texts which we analyzed rated in the top category of very explicit. Most fell into the second category indicating that they tended to satisfy the six criteria of explication. However, three of the texts rated in the third category which indicates that they were mixed on their degree of explicitness. The mean ratings of the individual items suggests that the 12 texts may be weaker in highlighting new vocabulary and helping students activate appropriate knowledge than in the other areas of explication.

Thus, although our results suggest areas of explication to which a teacher may need to give extra support, they do not indicate as bleak a picture as has been painted in some critiques. Our findings may be less bleak because the length of the passages we examined differed from those used in previous critiques. We used chapter-length segments whereas previous critiques used paragraph segments. The longer sample was necessary because expository text often requires cumulative paragraphs to develop a topic. In addition, our findings may appear to differ from other studies because we have not focused on the same area that others examined. For instance, Crismore (1983), who found differences in friendliness between school texts and nonschool social studies books, looked only at metadiscourse.

Although this study analyzed one major aspect of text friendliness, and although similar research is needed on other text dimensions, it should be noted that text friendliness is also affected by extra-text determinants such as student abilities and curricular and instructional factors (Singer, 1986). Even if a textbook rates well on explication or other text dimensions, the text can still vary in difficulty for differing ability groups. For example, Zack and Osako (1986) found that inconsiderate (unfriendly) text features which disrupted the comprehension of average and poor second-grade readers did not affect better readers' comprehension.

Moreover, text friendliness is also affected by an extra-text instructional variable—the effect the teacher has on all the components in the process of learning from text (Singer, 1985; Yopp & Singer, 1985). Indeed, teachers can make texts friendly for students. For example, Flood, Lapp, Singer, and Mathison (1985), in a study with college students, found that students' reading performance was affected not by friendly or unfriendly text features but rather by the prereading input the instructor provided.

To summarize, critiques of content-area texts imply that there is a prevalence of unfriendly texts including arbitrary, list-dominated, or inexplicit ones. But this generalization was based on anecdotal rather than on empirical research. In contrast, our empirical study revealed that most of the widely used sixth-grade social studies textbooks that we analyzed received an explicit rating. In addition, there was very little difference in ratings of older and more recent textbooks in our sample despite the intervening years of criticism. Therefore, we conclude that the social studies textbooks we examined tend to be friendly on the criterion of explicitness.

REFERENCES

Anderson, R. C. (1985). Role of the reader's schema in comprehension, learning, and memory. In H. Singer & R. B. Ruddell (Eds.), *Theoretical models and processes of reading* (3rd ed.) (pp. 372–384). Newark, DE: International Reading Association.

Anderson, T. H., & Armbruster, B. B. (1981). Content area textbooks. In R. C. Anderson, J. Osborn, & R. J. Tierney (Eds.), *Proceedings of the conference on learning to read in American schools: Basal readers and content text* (pp. 377–441). Champaign, IL: University of Illinois.

Anderson, T. H., & Armbruster, B. B. (1986). Readable textbooks, or, selecting a textbook is not like buying a pair of shoes. In J. Orasanu (Ed.), *Reading comprehension: From research to practice* (pp. 151–164). Hillsdale, NJ: Erlbaum.

Anderson, T. H., Armbruster, B. B., & Kantor, R. N. (1980). *How clearly written are children's textbooks? Or, of bladderworts and alfa.* (Read. Educ. Rep. No. 16). Champaign, IL: University of Illinois.

Bransford, J. D. (1985). Schema activation and schema acquisition: Comments on Richard D. Anderson's remarks. In H. Singer & R. B. Ruddell (Eds.), *Theoretical models and processes of reading* (3rd ed.) (pp. 385-397). Newark, DE: International Reading Association.

Crismore, A. (1983). Interpersonal and ideational metadiscourse in learning from text. In H. Singer & T. Bean (Eds.), *Learning from text: Explanation and strategies* (pp. 15-30). Riverside, CA: University of California, Learning from Text Project.

Davison, A., & Kantor, R. N. (1982). On the failure of readability formulas to define readable texts: A case study from adaptations. *Reading Research Quarterly, 17*, 187-209.

Flood, J., Lapp, D., Singer, H., & Mathison, C. (1985). *Teacher and text feature effects upon students' comprehension.* Unpublished paper, San Diego State University.

Gray, W. S., & Leary, B. (1935). *What makes a book readable?* Chicago, IL: University of Chicago Press.

Kane, M. J. (1980). Response from Ginn and Company. In T. H. Anderson, B. B. Armbruster, & R. N. Kantor (1980). *How clearly written are children's textbooks? Or, of bladderworts and alfa.* (Read. Educ. Rep. No. 16). Champaign, IL: University of Illinois.

Kantor, R. N., Anderson, T. H., & Armbruster, B. B. (1983). How are children's textbooks inconsiderate? Or of flyswatters and alfa. *Journal of Curriculum Studies, 15*(1), 61–72.

Langer, J. A. (1983). Inconsiderate text. In H. Singer & T. Bean (Eds.), *Proceedings of the Lake Arrowhead conference on learning from text: Selection of friendly texts* (pp. 143–149). Riverside, CA: University of California, Learning from Text Project.

Rumelhart, D. E., & Ortony, A. (1977). Representation of knowledge. In R. C. Anderson, R. J. Spiro, & W. E. Montague (Eds.), *Schooling and the acquisition of knowledge* (pp. 99–178). Hillsdale, NJ: Erlbaum.

Singer, H. (1985). Toward an interactive reading instructional model: The role of the instructor in determining task difficulty and reader resources required for success in beginning reading instruction. In J. Niles & R. Lalik (Eds.), *Issues in literacy: A research perspective* (pp. 324–329). Thirty-fourth Yearbook of the National Reading Conference. Rochester, NY: National Reading Conference.

Singer, H. (1986). Friendly texts: Description and criteria. In E. K. Dishner, T. W. Bean, J. E. Readence, & D. W. Moore (Eds.), *Reading in the content areas: Improving classroom instruction* (2nd ed.) (pp. 112–128). Dubuque, IA: Kendall Hunt.

Stein, B. S., & Bransford, J. D. (1979). Constraints on effective elaboration: Effects of precision and subject generation. *Journal of Verbal Learning and Verbal Behavior, 18*, 769-777.

Stein, B. S., Morris, C. D., & Bransford, J. D. (1978). Constraints on effective elaboration. *Journal of Verbal Learning and Verbal Behavior, 17*, 707–714.

Tierney, R. J., Mosenthal, J., & Kantor, R. N. (1984). Some classroom applications of text analysis. Toward improving text selection and use. In J. F. Flood (Ed.), *Understanding reading comprehension* (pp. 139–160). Newark, DE: International Reading Association.

Yopp, H. K., & Singer, H. (1985). Toward an interactive reading instructional model: Explanation of activation of linguistic awareness and metalinguistic ability in learning to read. In H. Singer & R. B. Ruddell (Eds.), *Theoretical models and processes of reading* (3rd ed.) (pp. 135–143). Newark, DE: International Reading Association.

Zack, J. E., & Osako, G. N. (1986). Inconsiderate text and the second-grade reader. In J. Niles & R. Lalik (Eds.), *Solving problems in literacy: Learners, teachers, and researchers* (pp. 339–343). Thirty-fifth Yearbook of the National Reading Conference: Rochester, NY: National Reading Conference.

APPENDIX A

Explication Inventory Adapted from the Friendly Text Evaluation Inventory (Singer, 1986)

Text Publisher ____________________ Pages ____________ Rater ____________________

Friendly Text Evaluation Inventory

Directions: Read each criterion and judge the degree of agreement or disagreement between it and the text. Then circle the number to the right that indicates your judgment.

1 = Strongly agree (SA)	= indicates that the text sample consistently meets the criterion
2 = Agree (A)	= indicates that the text sample meets the criterion for the majority of the sample
3 = Uncertain (U)	= indicates that the criterion is met irregularly, unclearly, or in a mixed fashion
4 = Disagree (D)	= indicates that the criterion does not appear to be met for a majority of the text sample
5 = Strongly Disagree (SD)	= indicates that the criterion does not appear to be met in the text sample at all

Explication	*SA*	*A*	*U*	*D*	*SD*
1. The text provides reasons for functions or events. For example, a social studies text would not just describe the Indian caste system but would also explain the beliefs that perpetuate it.	1	2	3	4	5
2. The text highlights or italicizes and defines new terms as they are introduced at a level that is familiar to the student.	1	2	3	4	5
3. The author clarifies new ideas and makes them vivid by using examples, analogies, metaphors, similes, personifications, or allusions.	1	2	3	4	5
4. The text helps students activate appropriate prior knowledge by reviewing or reminding readers of previously acquired knowledge or concepts.	1	2	3	4	5
5. The author explains ideas in relatively short, direct sentences.	1	2	3	4	5
6. The author makes explicit the central idea(s) of the text segment.	1	2	3	4	5

APPENDIX B

Textbooks Reviewed

Bass, H. J. (1972). *Man and society.* Morristown, NJ: Silver Burdett.

Brandwein, P. F., & Bauer, N. W. (1980). *The world.* NY: Harcourt Brace Jovanovich.

Brandwein, P. F., Bauer, N. W., Daly, D. J., Knutson, J. N., Rubin, L., Scott, W. R., Simpson, E. L., & Wise, A. M. (1970). *The social sciences: Concepts and values: Brown.* NY: Harcourt Brace Jovanovich.

Branson, M. S. (1980). *Around our world.* Boston, MA: Houghton Mifflin.

Buggey, J. (1983). *Our world today.* Chicago, IL: Follett.

Cooper, K. (1982). *The world and its people: Europe, Africa, Asia, and Australia.* Morristown, NJ: Silver Burdett.

Dawson, G. S., Tiegs, E. W., & Adams, F. (1983). *The world.* Lexington, MA: Ginn.

Hane, M., Hantula, J. N., Mysliwiec, N., & Yohe, R. S. (1973). *The world of mankind: Cultures in transition.* Chicago, IL: Follett.

Hanna, P. R., Kohn, C. F., & Ver Steeg, C. L. (1970). *Inter-American studies.* Glenview, IL: Scott, Foresman.

King, F. M., Epperly, H. V., Rudman, H. C., & Cooke, R. J. (1972). *The social studies and our world.* River Forest, IL: Laidlaw.

Schreiber, J., Stepien, W., Patrick, J., Remy, R., Gay, G., & Hoffman, A. J. (1986). *Our world: Lands and cultures.* Glenview, IL: Scott, Foresman.

Shorter, B., Starr, N., & Kenworthy, L. S. (1972). *Eleven nations.* Lexington, MA: Ginn.

AN ANALYSIS OF AMBIGUOUS ORAL DISCOURSE DURING READING INSTRUCTION

Joann J. Sweetland, Dorothy Abel-Carrick, and Charles K. Kinzer
Vanderbilt University

After reviewing selected vocabulary words, a sixth-grade teacher calls on Jerry to begin reading orally the story that was introduced on the previous day. He begins reading and has difficulty pronouncing several words. Other students can be heard whispering answers to him. When he mispronounces *albatross,* one of the lesson's identified vocabulary words . . .

Teacher: What's an albatross, Jerry? We talked about it yesterday. You were supposed to study that last night. What is an *albatross*?
(Five other students raise their hands. Jerry is looking down at his book. He does not answer.)
Teacher: All right, Linda, help him out.
Linda: A large bird.
Teacher: Right. It was a bird of the sea, a sea bird. All right. Continue, Mike.

Jerry was expected to know the pronunciation and meaning of the word *albatross* because it had been talked about the previous day and he was to have studied it. Teachers may wonder why, after presenting information in class, sometimes repeatedly, learning apparently does not take place.

Consider, however, two categories of variables that may have caused Jerry's apparent lack of knowledge: learner variables such as motivation, memory, and study habits, and variables more directly under the teacher's control, such as the difficulty level of content, the ambiguity of initial presentation, and the general quality of teacher/student interactions. One aspect in the second category—teacher-based ambiguity in instructional interactions—is the focus of this paper. Since language is the most frequently used communicative vehicle for accomplishing teachers' instructional strategies, critical attention should be paid to effective teacher discourse, as well as to effective instructional methods and strategies. This paper documents and presents prevalent types of ambiguous instructional discourse in the classroom. The approach taken is grounded in theoretical constructs in sociolinguistics (e.g., Gumperz & Hymes, 1972), ethnography of communication (e.g., Sevigny, 1981), conversational analysis (e.g., Green & Wallat, 1981; Mehan, 1979), and cognition (e.g., Piaget, 1972).

The teacher, or mediator, is in the position to assist and lead students to learning through verbal interaction (Feuerstein, 1980; Vygotsky, 1962). Smith-Burke (1985) agrees, noting that "through interaction, readers may collaboratively create a more integrated interpretation and learn from [both] the text and the discussion" (p. 205). In fact, the best of procedures cannot be effectively used by students if the procedures have not been clearly communicated. The communication cycle of feedforward/feedback, where each participant listens and makes decisions based on what the other participant has said, may break down if ambiguity is present in the teacher's oral discourse (W. von Raffler-Engel, personal communication, April, 1986).

METHOD

Subjects

The teacher and 15 students from the average reading group in a sixth-grade, self-contained classroom participated in this study. This school served a population of lower socioeconomic status students. The teacher had a doctoral degree in education and 11 years of teaching experience. A basal reader approach was used in the reading lessons. Students were on or above grade level according to the Stanford Achievement Test. The group included equal numbers of Asian, Black, and Caucasian students.

Materials and Procedure

Three lessons from this reading group were videotaped using two cameras, one stationary and one roving. Videotaping occurred on three consecutive days for approximately 45 minutes per day. Verbatim transcriptions were made of these tapes.

A framework for classifying the observed and videotaped interactions was developed to categorize patterns and types of ambiguous oral discourse. The classification system categorized similar types of ambiguous discourse observed in the videotapes as determined by two investigators and was independently verified by a linguist. The four categories of ambiguity found in the sample were labelled (a) ambiguity due to inappropriate presuppositions, (b) ambiguity due to ambiguous anaphora, (c) ambiguity due to inadequately signaled topic shifts, and (d) ambiguity due to multiple meanings of signals such as *OK.* Examples and discussion of these four categories are the focus of the following section.

Two investigators independently viewed and analyzed the videotapes and accompanying transcripts. Decisions to categorize discourse as ambiguous were made by examining both verbal and nonverbal behavior. As an initial step, instructional sequence *units* (Green & Wallat, 1981), defined as interactions which are thematically tied, were identified. Interrater reliability on identification of these units was .92. Second, the raters independently categorized ambiguous *segments* (specific words, referents, and phrases) within each unit, with an interrater reliability of .96. This coding system allowed for the identification of more than one instance of ambiguity within one instructional sequence unit. Disagreements between the investigators were resolved by consensus.

Additionally, the teacher and students completed questionnaires and participated in structured interviews exploring conceptions of reading and classroom verbal interaction. The responses to these activities were also considered in the development of the classification system and in making decisions about what constituted ambiguous discourse within the four categories noted above.

RESULTS

There were 113 instructional sequence units identified during the three 45-minute data collection sessions. Of these, 63 (56%) were classified as ambiguous. Within these ambiguous sequence units, 167 specific ambiguous segments were found. Frequencies of occurrence for these segments, across the four categories of ambiguous discourse, are shown in Table 1. Each category noted in Table 1 is discussed below.

Table 1

Frequencies and Percentages of Ambiguous Discourse Types Within Instructional Sequence Units

Ambiguous Discourse Type	Number	Percentage
Inappropriate presuppositions	25	15
Anaphora	107	64
Inadequately signaled topic shifts	20	12
Multiple meanings of signals	15	9
Total	167	100

Ambiguity Due to Inappropriate Presuppositions

Interestingly, ambiguity due to inappropriate presuppositions occurred most often when the teacher deviated from the teacher's manual, on which there was a heavy dependence for lesson format and activities. The teacher generally read information from the teacher's manual to give background information and also used suggested questions verbatim. Ambiguity due to inappropriate presuppositions was detected on departure from the manual's suggestions and/or activities. Ambiguity resulted primarily from assumptions that the students understood story-dependent content *before* reading had occurred, that is, in prediscussions and in prevocabulary lessons. Excerpt 1 demonstrates ambiguity due to inappropriate presupposition of story-event knowledge (lines 6–7). The example occurred during a departure from the manual.

Excerpt 1

[Prior to students' reading, the teacher is using a map to show where the story takes place.]

Teacher: All right. (She holds up a map for the children.)
Here's a view of the Unite . . . of the world.
All right. Now we're in the little islands,
the Polynesian islands . . . in the South
Seas . . . and they are located right there.
All right, you can see the trauma Mafatu had to go
through to get from one island to another and to
see how much . . . how set apart they are from the
other countries of the world. OK?

Ambiguity Due to Ambiguous Anaphora

Ambiguous anaphora occurs when referents are vague or unstated. In our observations, ambiguity resulted when the students were not sure what or to whom the teacher referred. This ambiguity was magnified when the teacher spoke for a long period of time without allowing questions or answers by students, although ambiguous anaphora was also noted within teacher/student interactions, as shown in Excerpt 2. Ambiguity was created through the parallel use of the referent *they* (lines 2–3).

Excerpt 2

[From the vocabulary lesson. Michelle has read three sentences to find the vocabulary word *vengeance*. She mispronounces the main character's name. The teacher spells the word by syllables, writes the sound-spelling on the board, pronounces the word by syllables, and asks the students to do so.]

Students in chorus: Ma- fa- tu
Teacher: All right. Now. They told you in that first
sentence that they sought to seek vengeance. Now,
what is seeking vengeance on someone or something?
Student: Revenge.
Teacher: Right. Sort of like revenge . . . Mark, please stop.
All right, the next [word is] *profound.*

Ambiguity Due to Inadequately Signaled Topic Shifts

In this category, ambiguity resulted when it was not made explicit to the children when a topic or activity was to be discontinued and/or a new concept was upcoming. Inadequately signaled or inserted topic shifts inappropriately assumed that students were following the teacher's train of thought. This led to inappropriate student responses and some frustration on the part of the teacher. Excerpt 3 illustrates ambiguity due to an inadequately signaled topic shift (lines 3–5), leading to an inappropriate, incorrect student response (line 6). Prior to this excerpt, students had been asked only rhetorical questions after reading, followed by a student's being asked to continue reading.

Excerpt 3

[The students have been reading orally, one at a time, while the others were following along.]

Jerry: ". . . the warriors stopped and continued back to
shore . . . (continues reading).
Teacher: OK. They had more powerful canoes than Mafatu had
yet. Mafatu had a little bit of an edge having
what kind of canoe? Jason?
Jason: (He starts to read.)
Teacher: Jason! I'm asking a question.
Jason: Oh.
Teacher: And of course, you're not listening. I asked,
that the cannibals had one type of canoe . . . no
one . . . leave it on the floor (Jason dropped
something on the floor.) They had one type of a
canoe. Mafatu had another type of canoe that may
have helped him. What kind of a canoe did Mafatu
have as compared to the cannibals? Dexter?

Dexter: He had one made out of a tree and it had a sail so the wind . . .
Teacher: Right, and it was a much lighter canoe. All right. Continue, Laura.

Jason expected the prior turn-taking procedures for the oral reading lesson to continue. To this point in the lesson, students were asked only rhetorical questions before being called on to read. The procedure was changed by the asking of a nonrhetorical question about what was read. It appeared that Jason was not listening to the teacher's explanation because of his concern for success in the anticipated reading aloud task. After the teacher reprimanded Jason, Dexter was called on to answer, and Laura was asked to continue reading. It appears that Jason, who was in fact eager to read, was ultimately penalized by not being allowed to either attempt to answer the question or to read orally.

Ambiguity Due to Multiple Meanings of Signals

Unshared meanings, between teacher and students, of signal words also caused ambiguity in our observations. For example, *OK* and *all right* have multiple meanings and the teacher's intended meaning was not always grasped by the students. In one sense, this occurred above in Excerpt 3, where the teacher may have intended *OK* (line 3) to signal movement away from rhetorical to nonrhetorical questioning, while the student may have felt *OK* simply signaled the end of the previous student's turn at reading.

At times, *OK* and *OK, now* serve to hold a speaker's turn in a conversation. In this sense, the signals can be defined as meaning *Stay with me* or *It's still my turn.* However, the signals can be used to signify a change in topic, that is, *Get ready, something is coming* (Green & Harker, 1982) and can also show either acceptance or correctness of an answer. Acceptance connotes that the answer has been heard, but not necessarily evaluated or approved. Our analysis indicated that some students were unsure of the meanings intended by the teacher in interactions when these terms were used.

In Excerpt 4, Tina's answer is apparently accepted with an *OK* (line 4), but the teacher does not seem totally satisfied with the answer. If *OK* meant *right answer,* then students would have to look no further. However, the teacher's *OK* appears to mean *Now it's my turn to talk* and is coupled with a request to search further for the answer (lines 4–7). This may encourage other students to believe that Tina's answer is incorrect and to activate a search for responses that are incorrect in this context (lines 8–9).

Excerpt 4

Teacher: All right, let's move down to the next word. *Daft. D-A-F-T.* Tina?
Tina: Silly and stupid and crazy.
Teacher: OK. Any questions? Look on page 378. The laaaast sentence. It says, "He dashed his hands across his eyes." Had the sun stricken him *daft*? What happens when you're in the sun for a long period of time?
Students: (Individually) You tan. You burn. You get a tan. You turn color.

DISCUSSION

This paper has provided examples of four types of ambiguous, oral instructional discourse found in a three-day observation of reading lessons. Our observations of both verbal and nonverbal behavior around ambiguous discourse segments indicate that ambiguous discourse as identified by inappropriate presuppositions, ambiguous anaphora, inadequately signaled topic shifts, and multiple meanings of signal words, appears to influence negatively students' participation in instructional conversations and also their understanding of information being discussed. The classification of ambiguous instructional discourse, as illustrated through the examples noted above, addresses the call for a more extensive, subjective approach to the study of discourse in classroom settings and contributes an attempt to provide a systematic description for interactions in reading instruction (e.g., Bloome & Green, 1984; Sevigny, 1981).

Consider also that, during the past several years, the reading teacher's role has generally been accepted as that of a guide who is responsible for helping students construct meaning from text. Current literature emphasizes the teaching of strategies or procedures for helping students comprehend text and has included story grammars (Beck & McKeown, 1986; Mandler & Johnson, 1977; Stein & Trabasso, 1982), semantic/conceptual networking (Hanf, 1971; Heimlich & Pittelman, 1986; Novak & Gowan, 1984), increasing background knowledge (Bransford, 1984; Langer & Purcell-Gates, 1985), training of metacognitive abilities (Palincsar & Brown, 1984), and emphasizing inferential comprehension (Smith-Burke & Ringler, 1986).

Implicit in all of the above-noted instructional procedures is that effective strategies for comprehending text be communicated to the learner. That is, understanding teachers' explanations is crucial, and teacher/student discussions and interactions are the means by which success was accomplished in the studies cited above. Clear, unambiguous language is assumed in all of the procedures.

Follow-up work based on the present study has used the four categories of ambiguous discourse in teacher awareness training. Although data analysis is ongoing, preliminary findings indicate that awareness of factors leading to procedural and/or instructional ambiguity result in a lowered incidence of such occurrences (Sweetland & Carrick, in progress). Further research, however, is needed to determine whether teachers differ in the amount of ambiguous language they use with students of differing abilities, and whether or not ambiguous instructional discourse is differentially distributed across reading skill areas. Additional research and replication are also needed before generalizing to reading instruction in other settings the finding that 56% of the instructional sequences in the present sample are ambiguous.

We conclude with a comment on the finding that ambiguous discourse due to inappropriate presuppositions occurred mainly on departure from the teacher's manual. We feel that this observation, though pertinent, should not be used to make general claims that teachers' manuals can solve problems of ambiguous instructional language. Rather, we suspect that the issue is one of preplanning and familiarity with the general direction of a lesson. Teachers who are familiar with a lesson's goals and activities, familiar with the thematic organization of the text, and who have made preliminary plans or outlines for their verbal instructional segments, may be more likely to provide on task, facilitative information. Deviating significantly from anticipated instructional plans, whether or not based on a teachers' manual, may yield similar results to those observed above. This is yet another important area for further investigation.

REFERENCES

Beck, I. L., & McKeown, M. G. (1986). Instructional research in reading: A retrospective. In J. Orasanu (Ed.), *Reading comprehension: From research to practice* (pp. 113-134). Hillsdale, NJ: Lawrence Erlbaum.

Bloome, D., & Green, J. (1984). Direction in the sociolinguistic study of reading. In P. D. Pearson (Ed.), *Handbook of reading research* (pp. 395-421). New York: Longman.

Bransford, J. D. (1984). Schema activation and schema acquisition: Comments on Richard C. Anderson's remarks. In R. C. Anderson, J. Osborn, & R. J. Tierney (Eds.), *Learning to read in American schools* (pp. 259-272). Hillsdale, NJ: Lawrence Erlbaum.

Feuerstein, R. (1980). *Instrumental enrichment: An intervention program for cognitive modifiability.* Baltimore: University Park Press.

Green, J., & Harker, J. (1982). Gaining access to learning: Conversational, social, and cognitive demands of group participation. In L. C. Wilkinson (Ed.), *Communicating in the classroom* (pp. 183-221). New York: Academic Press.

Green, J., & Wallat, C. (1981). Mapping instructional conversations: A sociolinguistic ethnography. In J. Green & C. Wallat (Eds.), *Ethnography and language in educational settings* (pp. 161-208). Norwood, NJ: Ablex.

Gumperz, J., & Hymes, D. (Eds.). (1972). *Directions in sociolinguistics.* New York: Holt, Rinehart & Winston.

Hanf, M. B. (1971). Mapping: A technique for translating reading into thinking. *Journal of Reading, 13,* 225-230.

Heimlich, J. E., & Pittelman, S. D. (1986). *Semantic mapping: Classroom applications.* Newark, DE: International Reading Association.

Langer, J. A., & Purcell-Gates, V. (1985). Knowledge and comprehension: Helping students use what they know. In T. L. Harris & E. J. Cooper (Eds.), *Reading, thinking, and concept development* (pp. 53-70). New York: College Entrance Examination Board.

Mandler, J., & Johnson, N. (1977). Remembrance of things parsed: Story structure and recall. *Cognitive Psychology, 9,* 111-151.

Mehan, H. (1979). *Learning lessons.* Cambridge, MA: Harvard University Press.

Novak, J., & Gowan, D. (1984). *Learning how to learn.* Cambridge: Cambridge University Press.

Palincsar, A. S., & Brown, A. L. (1984). Reciprocal teaching of comprehension-fostering and monitoring activities. *Cognition and Instruction, 12,* 117-175.

Piaget, J. (1972). *Judgment and reasoning in the child.* Totawa, NJ: Littlefield/Adams.

Sevigny, M. J. (1981). Triangulated inquiry: A methodology for the analysis of classroom interaction. In J. Green & C. Wallat (Eds.), *Ethnography and language in educational settings* (pp. 65-85). Norwood, NJ: Ablex.

Smith-Burke, M. T. (1985). Reading and talking: Learning through interaction. In A. Jaggar & M. T. Smith-Burke (Eds.), *Observing the language learner* (pp. 199-211). Newark, DE: International Reading Association.

Smith-Burke, M. T., & Ringler, L. (1986). STAR: Teaching reading and writing. In J. Orasanu (Ed.), *Reading comprehension: From research to practice* (pp. 215-234). Hillsdale, NJ: Lawrence Erlbaum.

Stein, N. L., & Trabasso, T. (1982). What's in a story: An approach to comprehension and instruction. In R. Glaser (Ed.), *Advances in instructional psychology* (pp. 213-267). Hillsdale, NJ: Lawrence Erlbaum.

Sweetland, J. J., & Carrick, D. A. (in progress). *Strengthening teacher discourse: Decreasing ambiguity in instructional conversation.* Unpublished paper, Vanderbilt University.

Vygotsky, L. S. (1962). *Thought and language.* Cambridge: M.I.T. Press.

CHILDREN'S ORAL LANGUAGE DURING TEACHER-DIRECTED READING INSTRUCTION

Linda B. Gambrell
University of Maryland

Research by sociolinguists studying classroom interaction has shown that learning is not a simple transfer of knowledge from the teacher to the student. Learning is mediated through complex interactive and interpretive processes (Cazden, 1982; Gumperz & Herasimchuk, 1975; Michaels, 1984).

It is widely acknowledged that the most important strength that students bring to the task of learning to read is their oral language ability. Oral language experiences help children gain access to meaning as they discuss the stories that they have read. The process of talking about text-acquired information requires collaboration among the teacher and the students as they negotiate meanings, share insights, and seek common understandings.

While the importance of oral language is frequently mentioned in the reading literature (Clay, 1972; Downing, 1979; Gibson & Levin, 1975), the information we have with respect to classroom interaction indicates that children are given few opportunities to actively engage in oral language activities (Sirotnik, 1983). Specifically, with respect to classroom reading instruction, Durkin's (1978–1979) research revealed that student verbalization during teacher-directed reading lessons is typically limited to responding to teacher-posed questions which require a brief, and usually literal level, text-based response.

One important characteristic of classroom communication, and reading lessons in particular, is that teachers play an active role in controlling and sustaining dialogue. Through questions and directives, teachers can determine who talks, how long the child talks, and the specific topic to be addressed. Through questions and comments, teachers also can provide support, encouragement, and assistance to children in expanding and elaborating their oral language responses (Michaels, 1984).

The purpose of the present study was to investigate the oral language experiences that children have during teacher-directed reading lessons and the types of teacher cues which encourage elaboration of oral responses. While there has been a great deal of research which has focused upon children's oral language experiences and competence in the classroom setting, there has been relatively little research which has specifically investigated the oral language patterns of children during teacher-directed reading lessons.

METHOD

Subjects

Teachers of grades 1, 2, and 3 in a Maryland county and in Washington, DC, were asked to volunteer to participate in a research project which would focus upon teacher-directed reading instruction. Fifteen teachers volunteered to participate and 41 teacher-directed reading lessons were observed. The teachers were informed that the researcher was interested in typical lessons and that if an observed lesson was judged to be atypical by the classroom teacher, the observational records would be destroyed. Therefore, the data reported in this study reveal what teachers identified as representative lessons which reflected their best teacher-directed reading instruction.

Materials and Procedure

Observers for the study were trained to establish rapport in the classroom and to record classroom information (teacher, number of children in the group, and instructional materials used for the lesson) on a form. The observers tape-recorded the teacher-directed reading lessons. Copies of all stories used for instruction were duplicated as well as information from accompanying teachers' manuals. The tape recordings of all lessons were transcribed for analysis. Transcripts of the lessons were coded according to the length of children's oral responses, the stimulus for the responses, and type of teacher questions. Teacher questions were coded according to whether the question called for a literal response (text explicit) or a response beyond the literal level (text implicit and scriptal). For the purposes of this study, only student and teacher verbalizations about the story or instructional materials were coded for analysis. Therefore, incidental language such as, "I dropped my pencil" and "Will you pay attention" were not included in the analysis.

RESULTS AND DISCUSSION

As expected, the major function of children's oral language during teacher-directed reading lessons was to respond to teacher-initiated questions. Only one student-posed question was identified across the 41 lessons. Student responses were predominately at the word level. For first grade, only 1% of the student responses were beyond the sentence level and, at second and third grades, only 3% were beyond the sentence level (Table 1).

There were 54 instances across the 41 lessons where children responded beyond the sentence level. An inner analysis of the cues which elicited these responses revealed that teacher questions which asked students to share personal experience, make predictions, and draw conclusions accounted for over 70% of the children's expanded responses (Table 2).

The children in this study verbalized about the stories they read only in direct response to teacher questions. There was a single student-posed question about the content of a story observed across the 41 lessons in this study. It appears that, during

Table 1

Mean Number and Percentage of Teacher Questions and Student Responses by Level (Word, Phrase, Sentence, and Sentence Plus)

	Teacher Questions			Student Responses				
	Total	Text Explicit	Text Implicit and Scriptal	Total	Words	Phrases	Sentences	Sentence Plus
Grade 1 12 lessons 4 teachers	80	38(47%)	42(53%)	84	39(49%)	20(25%)	20(25%)	1(1%)
Grade 2 17 lessons 7 teachers	59	33(56%)	26(44%)	55	23(43%)	14(25%)	16(29%)	2(3%)
Grade 3 12 lessons 4 teachers	58	28(48%)	30(52%)	55	15(27%)	16(30%)	22(40%)	2(3%)

Table 2

Sources of Student's Sentence Plus Responses

Source	Observed	Percentage
Text Explicit Teacher Questions		
Text-based response	8	14
Text Implicit and Scriptal Teacher Questions		
Sharing of personal experience	20	37
Predicting	11	20
Drawing conclusions	9	17
Explaining/elaborating	2	4
Defining	2	4
Summarizing	2	4

teacher-directed reading lessons, students talk only to the teacher in response to the teacher's demand.

The findings of this study suggest that children engage in very limited oral language expression about the stories and information they read during teacher-directed reading lessons. Their responses are primarily at the word level and rarely do they exceed the sentence level. It appears that students do not talk to accomplish personal goals, such as telling about what they thought was the most exciting or interesting part of the story. Their talk about stories is not self-generated, instead it is always dictated by teacher request for specific responses. The findings of this study suggest that the limited oral language opportunities which children are afforded during reading instruction focus on a *piecemeal approach* to comprehension as opposed to verbal responses which reflect a holistic concept of reading comprehension.

As Cazden (1982) has stated, we know what the typical teacher-directed reading lesson looks and sounds like. The teacher controls student verbalization and the teacher talks about two thirds of the total instructional time, primarily asking known-answer questions and evaluating children's answers. Little is known, however, about how children talk about text they have read and how verbalization effects the comprehension process.

One consistent finding across studies investigating classroom interaction is the large portion of time spent on teacher talk and the small portion of time which is available for student verbalization. Only recently has research been conducted which attempts to link children's verbalization about text and reading comprehension (Kapinus, Gambrell, & Koskinen, 1986; Rose, Cundick, & Higbee, 1984). One study in which children silently read stories and then engaged in peer retelling found that retelling resulted in superior inferential comprehension and that these effects transferred to the reading of new stories (Gambrell, Pfeiffer, & Wilson, 1985). In other words, when children had opportunities to read stories and then talk about what they had read, comprehension was improved in subsequent reading.

One problem identified by Cazden (1982) with respect to student verbalization during reading lessons is that verbalization is apt to get out of control for the following reasons: children have a hard time waiting for their turn, the typical reading lesson includes a demand for pupil performance, and there are very limited possibilities for student verbalizations due to time constraints. In discussing the results of the present study with the teachers who were observed, one teacher commented about her reactions to having children share personal experiences related to the story being read by the group. She said, ". . . the sharing of personal experience is easy to elicit but it takes time and patience. I find myself feeling impatient when more than one student wants to share their experience on a topic. I look at my watch and the planbook full of information to cover and after I wait for that student to finish, I say, 'It's time to move on.' "

This teacher's comment brings us back to the reality of the situation. The teacher-directed reading lesson is typically about 30 minutes and pupil talk is very time consuming. If talking about what they have read does indeed help children learn about the reading process, research on time-efficient instructional strategies which incorporate opportunities for student verbalization should be explored.

In many instances (e.g., Slavin, 1980), children learn more when they talk to each other. This is in keeping with Vygotsky's (1978) assertion that "learning awakens a variety of internal developmental processes that are able to operate only when the child is interacting with people in his or her environment and in cooperation with peers" (p. 90).

When children are encouraged to talk with other children during teacher-directed reading lessons, the opportunities for pupil talk are greatly expanded. Children can talk with peers in response to teacher-posed questions such as "Describe your favorite character in this story to your partner," "Tell about what you thought was the most exciting part of the story," and "What was the goal of the main character in this story?."

There is great value in teacher-questioning. Teacher-posed questions facilitate, encourage, and support children's comprehension of text. Helping children learn to read, however, requires that we understand and acknowledge the crucial role that oral language plays in both the formation and sharing of meaning, especially with respect to comprehension of text. The real goal of reading instruction should have as its core the engagement of students in reading, thinking, and talking about text, from both a prior knowledge and text-based perspective. Children should be encouraged to create their own oral renditions of text, to say more than a short answer to teacher questions, and to discuss self-selected aspects of what has been read.

REFERENCES

Cazden, C. B. (1982). Contexts for literacy: In the mind and in the classroom. *Journal of Reading Behavior, 14,* 413-427.

Clay, M. M. (1972). *Reading: The patterning of complex behavior.* New York: Heinemann.

Downing, J. (1979). *Reading and reasoning.* New York: Springer-Verlag.

Durkin, D. (1978-1979). What classroom observations reveal about reading comprehension instruction. *Reading Research Quarterly, 14,* 481-533.

Gambrell, L.B., Pfeiffer, W. R., & Wilson, R. M. (1985). The effects of retelling upon reading comprehension and recall of text information. *Journal of Educational Research, 78,* 216-220.

Gibson, E. J., & Levin, H. (1975). *The psychology of reading.* Cambridge, MA: The Massachusetts Institute of Technology.

Gumperz, J., & Herasimchuk, E. (1975). The conversational analysis of social meaning: A study of classroom interaction. In M. Sanchez & B. Blount (Eds.), *Sociocultural dimensions of language use.* New York: Academic Press.

Kapinus, B., Gambrell, L. B., & Koskinen, P. S. (1986, December). *The effects of retelling upon the reading comprehension of proficient and less proficient readers.* Paper presented at the National Reading Conference, Austin, TX.

Michaels, S. (1984). Listening and responding: Hearing the logic in children's classroom narratives. *Theory Into Practice, 3,* 218-224.

Rose, M. C., Cundick, B. P., & Higbee, K. L. (1984). Verbal rehearsal and visual imagery: Mnemonic aids for learning disabled children. *Journal of Learning Disabilities, 16,* 352-354.

Sirotnik, K. (1983). What you see is what you get—Consistency, persistency and mediocrity in the classroom. *Harvard Educational Review, 53,* 16-31.

Slavin, R. E. (1980). Cooperative learning. *Review of Educational Research, 50,* 315-342.

Vygotsky, L. S. (1978). *Mind in society: The development of higher psychological processes* (M. Cole, V. John-Steiner, S. Scribner, & E. Souberman, Eds. and Trans.). Cambridge, MA: Harvard University Press.

STUDENTS' AND TEACHER'S PERCEPTIONS OF AN INNOVATIVE READING STRATEGY

Nancy D. Padak and Gary M. Padak
Kent State University

Most teachers seek to refine instruction so that student learning is enhanced, a process that may involve the use of new teaching strategies or techniques. In such instances, both students and the teacher may undergo a period of adjustment as they become accustomed to the new strategy. The process by which teachers adjust to instructional innovations has been fairly well documented (e.g., Hall & Loucks, 1978; Wade, 1984–1985). Given the complexity of student-teacher-text interactions, several types of student adjustment may also be necessary. For example, students may need to learn new ways of participating in lessons or to develop new perceptions of their roles within the lessons. Both of these factors may mediate actual performance and subsequent learning (Wittrock, 1986). Understanding students' adjustments to unfamiliar teaching strategies, then, may be as important as understanding the change process from the teacher's perspective.

The unfamiliar teaching strategy employed in this study was the Directed Reading-Thinking Activity (DR-TA; Stauffer, 1980), familiar to many reading educators but unfamiliar to the students we studied. The DR-TA evolves through a cycle of student hypothesis generation and subsequent validation, rejection, or modification of hypotheses. First, students read the selection title and make predictions about text content based upon the title. Students then read silently to predetermined stopping points. Discussions follow, which the teacher facilitates by asking students if their predictions were confirmed and by asking them to support their statements with reference to the text. Next, students refine their original predictions and/or make new ones. The cycle of predicting, reading to confirm, modify, or reject, and providing support from the text continues until the entire selection has been read.

The DR-TA framework encourages cooperative inquiry within an open communication environment. Thus, being a student in a DR-TA is different than being a student in discussions about reading that are organized around a recitation model (Alvermann, 1986; Stodolsky, Ferguson, & Wimpelberg, 1981), for example. This study was designed to explore how students' and the teacher's perceptions of lessons changed as students became more accustomed to participating in DR-TAs.

METHOD

Subjects

Subjects for the study were students and a teacher in an Upward Bound English class. Student eligibility was dependent upon criteria related to socioeconomic and educational disadvantage, as defined by the federal government. Participation in the Upward Bound program and in the English class was voluntary but restricted to students earning at least Cs in their regular high school English classes. Those in academic difficulty were tutored individually rather than attending a class.

Nineteen high school freshmen and sophomores attended the class during the course of the study. The group included five males and 14 females. The teacher was a male.

Materials and Procedure

The class, which met for one hour on Saturday mornings, was designed to provide supplementary reading and writing experiences for students. The teacher established the goals and activities for each session; he was not required to follow a preset curriculum.

The study was conducted over a three-month period. During that time, students and the teacher read and discussed seven different short stories on seven different Saturdays using the DR-TA. No student had participated in a DR-TA prior to the study, but the teacher had extensive experience with the procedure. Stories used in the lessons (e.g., Merchant, 1983; Moore, 1979; Stewart, 1972) were selected by the teacher based on their potential interest for students and on their potential comprehensibility.

Following each DR-TA, students and the teacher recorded their perceptions in learning logs. Both teacher and students wrote in their learning logs during class time. Students' logs were not graded. Directions for the logs were open-ended: Record your thoughts and/or feelings about today's story and lesson. All logs were collected and photocopied.

RESULTS

Preliminary examination of log entries revealed that the teacher and students addressed a variety of issues related to the stories and the lessons in their logs. Since the intent of the study was to explore change in perceptions, an attempt was made to establish categories or domains that could account for log contents and provide a framework for analysis. A two-stage procedure was employed to establish categories. First, two independent raters partitioned all log entries into segments that seemed to express single thoughts or ideas. Interrater agreement was 310/397 (78%); a third rater resolved discrepancies. This partitioning yielded 379 separate thoughts or ideas, 102 generated by the teacher and 277 generated by students. Next, the 379 thoughts were analyzed inductively in order to establish the descriptive categories. One rater grouped the thoughts according to thematic similarity and then analyzed the groups so that general descriptions (e.g., comments about story endings) could be developed. Descriptions were then explained to a second rater, who sorted the thoughts into the categories. Interrater agreement for this stage of the procedure was 359/379 (95%); again, a third rater resolved discrepancies.

The general categories that emerged are provided in Table 1, along with the number of log comments during the first month and the last month within each category. A content analysis of the teacher's and students' perceptions, as reflected in their logs, revealed several aspects of change. These results are described below.

Table 1

Categories and Frequencies of Teacher and Student Comments

Categories	Frequencies First Month*	Third Month**	Total
Teacher			
About story (general)	5	2	8
About lesson (general)	11	5	19
About DR-TA as an instructional strategy	5	4	10
About student participation and on-task behavior	12	8	26
About students' prediction and confirmation	6	20	27
About students' use of prior knowledge	3	8	12
Student			
About stories (general)	32	33	77
About general type of story	6	13	24
About specific information from stories	9	17	26
About story endings	5	23	30
About lessons (general)	22	27	58
About lesson's impact/effect			
a. on learning	13	10	24
b. on interest	11	13	29
About the teacher	1	5	7

*Lessons 1–3.
**Lessons 5–7.

Teacher's Perceptions

Examination of the teacher's log entries revealed several general aspects of similarity among all lessons. He felt that all seven selections used were appropriate and that all lessons were relatively successful. He also felt that students enjoyed and benefited from each of the lessons. The teacher's log entries showed change in his perceptions about two key aspects of the lessons over the course of the study. He perceived changes in some facets of participation within the lessons and in the nature of discussions about the stories.

The participation structure of DR-TAs differs from more traditional reading lessons (Davidson, Padak, & Wilkerson, 1986a, 1986b), and the teacher's log entries provide his perceptions of student adjustment to this difference. For example, in his first log entry, he expressed "a concern—hand-raising to speak and be acknowledged detracted from the 'free' atmosphere." This situation apparently continued through the second lesson, since his third log entry states that he began the lesson by suggesting that students "could speak spontaneously (like getting word in at the dinner table), rather than raising their hands to be acknowledged by the teacher." Despite this suggestion, the fourth log entry notes that students continued to raise their hands. The fifth entry, however, states that "there was a bit more free-flowing dialogue—without hand raising—during this story." Even with explicit explanation from the teacher, then, it took some time for students to adjust to this inherent rule for participation in DR-TAs.

The teacher's log entries also note changes in the number of students participating in the lessons. Discussions during the early lessons appeared to be dominated by a few students: "there were three or four people (out of 12) who spoke freely and regularly" (lesson 3); "the same students . . . would comment/discuss every time" (lesson 4). More students participated in the discussions during the later lessons; several "who [were] usually quiet were quite animated" (lesson 6). The teacher's logs for the sixth and seventh lessons note that all students joined in the discussions. Over the course of the study, then, students seemed to adapt to the inherent rules for gaining access to DR-TA discussions and became more willing to participate verbally.

Though not all students participated verbally in the early lessons, the teacher perceived that all students were involved: "people wanted to read the next section to see what would happen" (lesson 1); "what I did notice was that everyone intently read the story as we progressed" (lesson 4). This tendency was noted in later lessons as well: "again, after stopping at each point in the story . . . all students returned to task with great assiduity. (I know that they do not *all* enjoy reading *that* much!) They were eager to read what happened" (lesson 6).

Cooperation and group problem-solving are also aspects of the participation structure of the DR-TA. The teacher's log notes several instances, spanning all seven lessons, of students adding to one another's comments or clarifying issues for each other during discussions. This indication of participation, like students' eagerness to read, seemed to characterize all lessons from the teacher's perception.

Story discussions during a DR-TA center upon students' predictions, confirmations, and justifications. Each of the teacher's log entries addressed student prediction. In his entry for the first lesson, for example, he suggests that many predictions seemed based on prior knowledge and that students refined predictions as the story was read. Similar comments were made in several other log entries, although he did note that, in later lessons, predictions became "more sophisticated" (lesson 6) and "noticeably better than previous stories" (lesson 7). Logs for later lessons also included more comments about students' use of prior knowledge. His log for lesson 5 mentions that "students are clearly identifying that they are using more of their personal experiences" to understand the story. As students became more comfortable with the DR-TA, the teacher perceived that students began to share prior knowledge more freely and that "this contributed to the discussion in a helpful way" (lesson 7).

During DR-TAs, students are often asked to justify their comments about the text. The teacher's log entries noted that students were generally able to justify their comments with reference to the text when asked to do so. He also noted, however, that their initial responses to requests for proof were often vague: "they say they're guessing" (lesson 2) or that they "feel it" (lesson 6). Overall, the teacher perceived that students were able to justify their comments, but were "hesitant" (lesson 6) or "reluctant" (lesson 7) to provide proof spontaneously.

Over the course of the study, the teacher perceived both similarities and differences among the lessons. He felt that all lessons were successful and that students cooperated and engaged in group problem-solving in all lessons. His perceptions about the manner in which students gained access to conversations, the number of students participating, the sophistication of students' predictions, and students' use of prior knowledge changed over the seven lessons studied. These changes suggest an evolution in students' understanding of their roles during a DR-TA.

Students' Perceptions

Comments in students' logs clustered around the stories read and the DR-TA procedure, which was expected given the general directions for the logs. As with the teacher's perceptions, examination of students' log entries revealed both similarities across all seven lessons and differences among them.

Students' reactions to the stories were mixed within and across lessons. No story was liked or disliked by all; no student consistently liked or disliked all stories. About half of the general comments about stories were positive, about one fourth were neutral, and about one fourth were negative. Many reactions, whether positive, negative, or neutral, seemed related to interest: "I really liked it. It caught my attention" (Cathesia); "it was OK, but nothing to go home and brag about" (Mark); "The story needs more BAM. It just lays there like a rock" (Alicia).

Students also mentioned preference for particular types of stories in their overall evaluations: "I liked it because it could have been true" (Mark); "it was suspenseful because you weren't sure what to think" (Erika); "it keeps you in suspense for a while, then it has a different change in the story" (Alyisha). Students mentioned suspense or mystery in their comments about five of the stories, yet only two were traditional suspense stories. During DR-TAs, students are encouraged to speculate about possibilities, to consider alternatives, and to make predictions about plot development. These discussions may have made stories seem more suspenseful.

Two categories of student comments about the stories were much more prevalent in the later lessons, those that made reference to specific elements within the stories and those about story endings. In both cases, students' comments included evaluations or judgments about these aspects of the stories: "The older people were smarter than I thought they were" (Erika); "I thought the farmer was kind of gullible" (Chris); "the ending was a bit corny" (Matisse); "and all this time they've been leading us up to a wonderful ending and then they end it just like that without any thought behind it'' (Erika). Students' entries for the earlier lessons contained few such evaluative comments. Their log entries for the later lessons contained more judgments about characters' motives and actions and evaluations of story lines.

All but one student responded favorably to the DR-TA procedure. The few comments about the teacher were favorable as well. Neither the positive opinions nor the negative opinion about the DR-TA changed over the three-month period. Students' positive comments centered upon discussion opportunities: ''it's better than reading it all at once'' (Mark); ''I like guessing at what is going to happen next'' (Chris); ''I couldn't figure out what was going to happen and when the best parts of the story came, we had to stop'' (Erika). The student who disliked the strategy wrote that she preferred not to be interrupted while reading: ''I think we should have just read through the whole thing. That's the way I like doing things.''

Students also wrote about the influence or effect of the DR-TA on their reading. These comments, which focused on cognitive impact and affective response, were evenly distributed across all seven lessons. Many students perceived that discussions fostered their understanding of the stories: ''we didn't read too much at one time and get all mixed up'' (Susan). Students also wrote that the procedure helped them think about the stories: ''we thought and talked about it before reading it'' (Lori); it ''lets your mind soar'' (Erika); ''we took time to think about what was going to happen, where on our own we wouldn't'' (Lynette). Finally, students mentioned that the discussions affected their interest in the stories: ''The way we read the stories enticed me and made me like it more'' (Zeneta); ''it's a good way to compel yourself into the drama'' (Vanessa).

Except in one case, students' written comments about the instructional procedure were favorable, even when they were negative or neutral about the stories they had read. Students perceived the lessons to be interesting; many believed that discussions helped them think about the stories. One student log entry described this relationship well: ''I liked reading that way, but you are kept in suspense. Other than that, it's kind of fun and makes you want to learn'' (Krista).

DISCUSSION

The findings from this study must be considered in light of its limitations, most notably reliance on written reports of perceptions of lessons. Our intent was not to provide definitive answers, but rather to raise some questions and to suggest some avenues for further exploration. These issues center upon how students adjust to new instructional situations, how they learn new ways of participating in lessons, and what influence these adjustments may have on the academic context.

The teacher perceived some changes in student participation in the lessons. It apparently took some time for students to participate freely in discussions without first raising their hands to be acknowledged by the teacher, for example. This change coincided with more complete verbal participation by all members of the group. Are these aspects of participation related? Why did it take so long for students to speak without first raising their hands? Could the teacher have encouraged free discussion more effectively or is hand-raising so deeply ingrained in students' perceptions of their roles that it is resistant to change?

Students wrote that the lessons helped them maintain interest and facilitated their thinking about the stories. This finding supports those of Davidson (1985, 1986), who found that students' introspections following DR-TAs center upon text concepts, the predictions generated by the group, and their relevant prior knowledge.

The teacher's log also noted his belief that student predictions and use of prior knowledge became more sophisticated over the course of the study. Students' logs did not make specific reference to these changes; that is, no student wrote about feeling more comfortable making predictions or using prior knowledge. However, students' written comments about the stories may have reflected the change that the teacher noted in another way. Their comments about the characters and plots of the stories were more evaluative and judgmental in logs written about the later lessons, which may reflect a change in their thinking about the stories. Others have found that student participants in DR-TAs evidence greater concept learning (Wilkerson, 1984, 1986) and recall of text concepts (Biskin, Hoskisson, & Modlin, 1976; Hammond, 1979) than students involved in more recitation-type lessons.

It is interesting to note that changes in students' written reactions to stories also coincided with their apparent adjustment to participating in the lessons. Are these issues related? Is there a relationship between text interpretation and the ability to interpret the instructional context and to participate appropriately? Since this was an exploratory investigation, conclusions should be considered tentative and subject to further validation. Nonetheless, our results suggest that the teacher's perceptions about lessons and students' perceptions about text may change as students become adjusted to the socio-communicative demands inherent in an instructional innovation.

REFERENCES

Alvermann, D. E. (1986). Discussion versus recitation in the secondary classroom. In J. A. Niles & R. V. Lalik (Eds.), *Solving problems in literacy: Learners, teachers, and researchers* (pp. 113-119). Thirty-fifth Yearbook of the National Reading Conference. Rochester, NY: National Reading Conference.

Biskin, D. S., Hoskisson, K., & Modlin, M. (1976). Prediction, reflection, and comprehension. *Elementary School Journal, 77,* 131-139.

Davidson, J. L. (1985). What you think is going on, isn't: Eighth grade students' introspections of discussions in science and social studies. In J. A. Niles & R. V. Lalik (Eds.), *Issues in literacy: A research perspective* (pp. 238-243). Thirty-fourth Yearbook of the National Reading Conference. Rochester, NY: National Reading Conference.

Davidson, J. L. (1986). The teacher-student generated lesson: A model for reading instruction. *Theory into Practice, 25,* 84-90.

Davidson, J. L., Padak, N. D., & Wilkerson, B. C. (1986a, April). *Instructional frameworks in junior high science and social studies: How lessons evolve.* Paper presented at the meeting of the American Educational Research Association, San Francisco, CA.

Davidson, J. L., Padak, N. D., & Wilkerson, B. C. (1986b, April). *Instructional frameworks in junior high science and social studies: The hidden curriculum.* Paper presented at the meeting of the American Educational Research Association, San Francisco, CA.

Hall, G. E., & Loucks, S. (1978). Teacher concerns as a basis for facilitating and personalizing staff development. *Teachers College Record, 80,* 36-53.

Hammond, W. D. (1979, May). *The effects of reader predictions on prequestions in the recall of relevant and incidental information found in expository material.* Paper presented at the meeting of the International Reading Association, Atlanta, GA.

Merchant, R. (1983). Abused. *Trust.* New York: Cambridge.

Moore, G. (1979, June). Sister was a scrapper. *Readers Digest,* pp. 23-28.

Stauffer, R. G. (1980). *The language-experience approach to the teaching of reading* (2nd ed.). New York: Harper and Row.

Stewart, D. R. (1972, April). Summer of the broken calf. *Readers Digest,* pp. 108-110.

Stodolsky, S. S., Ferguson, T. L., & Wimpelberg, K. (1981). The recitation persists, but what does it look like? *Curriculum Studies, 13,* 121-130.

Wade, R. K. (1984-1985). What makes a difference in inservice teacher education? A meta-analysis of research. *Educational Leadership, 42,* 48-54.

Wilkerson, B. C. (1984). *A study of students' inferences during and following a group directed reading-thinking activity and a group directed reading activity in social studies.* Unpublished doctoral dissertation, Northern Illinois University, DeKalb, IL.

Wilkerson, B. C. (1986). Inferences: A window to comprehension. In J. A. Niles & R. V. Lalik (Eds.), *Solving problems in literacy: Learners, teachers, and researchers* (pp. 192-198). Thirty-fifth Yearbook of the National Reading Conference. Rochester, NY: National Reading Conference.

Wittrock, M. C. (1986). Students' thought processes. In M. C. Wittrock (Ed.), *Handbook of research on teaching* (3rd ed.). New York: Macmillan.

ASSESSMENT

EMERGENT LITERACY

COMPREHENSION

INSTRUCTIONAL EFFECTIVENESS

ADULT LITERACY

WRITING

THE STATUS OF LITERACY IN OUR SOCIETY*

Larry Mikulecky
Indiana University-Bloomington

During the past few years, the popular press and other media have purveyed a good deal of information and misinformation about the status of adult literacy in our society. Many educated people are unable to keep abreast of current adult literacy research and have sometimes depended upon the popular media for information. This dependence has been upon some accurate information mixed with a muddle of exaggerations and misinformation. This paper will focus upon what is known about literacy levels of adults—giving special attention to changes in literacy demands—and what is currently being done for adults experiencing literacy difficulties. The conclusion will address major recommendations, trends, and problems associated with adult literacy.

WHAT IS LITERACY AND WHO IS LITERATE?

The question of who is literate and who isn't has been inadequately answered by politicians, well-intended social activists, the advertising agency for the National Coalition for Literacy, and nearly every local and national news publication in the nation. The result is confusion on the parts of many intelligent people about who needs what sorts of help with what sorts of reading and writing.

The most often seen misinformation reported in the media suggests that 23 to 26 million people are totally or functionally illiterate with an additional 23 million people functioning at a marginal level. Concrete examples and anecdotes intended to clarify these data often portray individuals barely able to read and write. These figures indicating tens of millions of illiterates are usually attributed to the Adult Performance Level (A.P.L.) study performed in the early 1970s (Northcutt, 1975). Northcutt and his colleagues selected 65 reading- and writing-related tasks which they felt Americans should be able to perform. Inability to satisfactorily perform these tasks classified one into various categories of functional illiteracy. By the late 1970s, the A.P.L. study and its subsequent media abuse had received severe criticism in the research literature to

*Annual Review of Research.

the point that very few researchers were willing to report data in terms of "millions of illiterates." Data were reported in less simplistic formats which indicated the portion of the population able to perform specific tasks. To Northcutt's credit, the A.P.L. data were *also* available in this format. Many reporters, politicians, and agency bureaucrats have ignored more accurate presentations as well as more recent data on literacy and have continued to inaccurately report 23 to 60 million illiterates based on misinterpretation and misuse of data over a decade old.

In many cases, the reporting of this information has been well-intended, creative, and industrious. During 1985–1986, advertising executives for the National Coalition for Literacy attempted to raise national awareness about literacy problems. They creatively extended the figures reported from the A.P.L. study and proclaimed in newspaper advertising throughout the nation that by the year 2,000, two out of three adult Americans may be illiterate. Departments of Education in many states have also performed manipulations of the A.P.L. data. Indiana, for example, has multiplied the number of illiterates reported in the early 1970s by the subsequent increase in population and then estimated the proportion of that expanded illiterate population living in Indiana. The result is an exact-sounding figure which reports the number of illiterates in Indiana. This process has been extended to the point that I have heard a recent radio report of the number of illiterates in my home county based on 15-year-old misinformation gathered in a different part of the nation.

In addition to newspaper stories which often quote each other about the number of illiterates, the nation has been inundated with news documentaries, docu-dramas, and interviews with Jonathan Kozol discussing his most recent book on illiteracy. The result is that school teachers and some university professors requote media-derived information, thus giving it an additional cachet of apparent accuracy and authority.

Definitions of Literacy

Part of the explanation for this muddled situation is that literacy is not easily defined. In a recent paper for the United States Office of Educational Research and Improvement, Valentine (1986) addresses issues central to definitions of literacy. He points out that much of the confusion derives from the fact that there is little agreement upon what skills comprise literacy. For example, which clusters of skills comprising reading and writing are essential? One can side-step the issue of what skills comprise reading and writing and simply look at materials people are able or unable to read and write. This, however, creates another problem of definition: Literacy is being able to read and write which materials? Bormuth (1975) suggested that the list of materials will always differ from person to person and situation to situation and therefore offers the definition of literacy as "the ability to respond competently to real-world reading tasks" (p. 65). Guthrie (1983) expands on this notion by noting that the "reader's literacy depends on the context of the situation, not on a specific achievement level" (p. 669).

Some writers focus on specialized forms of literacy. Sticht (1975) differentiated externally imposed literacy tasks from internally imposed tasks and defines functional literacy as

> the possession of those literacy skills needed to perform some reading task *imposed by an external agent* between the reader and a goal the reader wishes to obtain. (pp. 4–5)

Such definitions rapidly create new problems. Kirsch and Guthrie (1977–1978) pointed out that reading the same material (i.e., a news magazine) is functional for some people and leisure reading for others. Valentine (1986) suggested functional literacy is the area of overlap between print literacy and functional tasks. He leaves it to others to define exactly what comprises print literacy.

Some researchers and government agencies have attempted to define literacy by linking it to a grade level of performance. Harmon (1987) reported that researchers "have variously proposed standards ranging from a fourth- to a twelfth-grade level. This search has almost become a modern-day quest for the Holy Grail"(p. 8). Some government agencies simply use grades completed in school as a measure of literacy. Smith, Balian, Brennan, Gorringe, Jackson, and Thone (1986) indicated the National Health Survey suggests fourth grade is literate, the Census suggests sixth grade is literate, and the Department of Education suggests eighth grade is literate. Rationales are usually not discussed. The unacceptability of this sort of approach is highlighted by Kirsch and Guthrie (1977–1978) who point out that the average grade scores of eighth graders in Chicago range from a 4.4-grade level in the lowest school to a median level of 10.5 in the best school. Darling (1981) made an even stronger case for unacceptability by noting that of students registered for adult basic education in Jefferson County, Kentucky, the median grade completely was 8.6, but the median tested reading grade level of entering students was 2.0.

The problem of establishing a sensible grade level indicator becomes even more problematic when the role of reader background is considered. Diehl and Mikulecky (1980) and Mikulecky (1982) have reported data that indicate workers in a variety of occupations competently read work-related material that averages 1–2 grade levels in measured difficulty above the difficulty levels of general newspaper-like material the workers can successfully comprehend. The authors attribute this *seeming* higher ability to familiarity with topic and format of the job-related material. Sticht, Amijo, Weitzman, Koffman, Roberson, Chang, and Moracco (1986) presented military data which indicate a range of four grade levels of tested reading ability between the reading abilities required for job-related reading of highly experienced workers and workers with no experience on the topic being read. This suggests that background knowledge can account for up to four grade levels of reading ability with a given topic and print format. Grade level definitions of literacy levels are particularly ineffective as background knowledge of readers increases.

The research literature is filled with attempted definitions of literacy and critiques of those definitions. The more focused the definition, the less likely it is to apply for all cases. More general definitions tend to be more accurate but not very useful. William Gray's (1956) omnibus definition seems to be as complete as any. Gray stated that

> A person is functionally literate when he has acquired the knowledge and skills in reading and writing which enable him to engage effectively in all those activities in which literacy is normally assumed in his cultural group (p. 24).

Since literacy appears to be more in the nature of changing relationships than measurable quantities, it is unlikely that anyone will arrive at an acceptable *level* or *criterion* allowing one to accurately and usefully state the number of *illiterates*.

Who Can and Cannot Accomplish Literacy Tasks?

Though it may not be possible to define literacy in a fashion which allows us to usefully and accurately state the number of *illiterates*, it is possible to roughly suggest proportions of the population who can and cannot successfully accomplish particular literacy tasks. This section of the paper will briefly address a few studies performed before 1980 giving special attention to the previously mentioned A.P.L. study. More detailed examination will be made of data from National Assessment of Educational Progress studies released in 1985 and 1986.

When examining the data presented below, it is important to note that few studies report a high degree of basic *can't read a word* illiteracy. This is important from an educator's perspective because teaching approaches and materials required to teach basic reading and writing differ significantly from the approaches required to teach more complex tasks like competently reading equal opportunity announcements, consumer information, and government forms.

Listed below are indicators of areas of adult reading difficulty derived from the findings of the A.P.L. study (Northcutt, 1975). A.P.L. results indicate that, of adults tested,

60% did not accurately calculate from advertisements price differences between new and used appliances;
44% did not successfully match want ad job requirements to personal qualifications;
40% did not accurately determine correct change given a cash register receipt and the denomination of a bill;
36% did not enter the correct number of exemptions on a W4 form;
26% did not determine if their paycheck was correct;
24% did not add their own correct return address to a letter;
22% did not address a letter well enough to ensure it would arrive at its destination;
20% did not comprehend an equal opportunity announcement; and
20% did not write a check that would be accurately processed by a bank.

The general magnitude of the A.P.L. results was supported by other major functional literacy studies of the 1970s. These included the Survival Literacy Study (Louis Harris & Associates, 1970), the Adult Functional Reading Study (Murphy, 1975), the Mini-Assessment of Functional Literacy (Gadway & Wilson, 1975), and military reports from Project REALISTIC (Sticht, Caylor, Fox, Hauke, James, Snyder, & Kern, 1972).

Fisher (1978), in a thorough analysis of major functional literacy studies of the 1970s, concluded that most of these studies tended to be biased in the favor of overestimation. He noted that even a small proportion of college graduates made very basic errors on items they could reasonably be expected to capably master. Fisher reasoned that maybe some subjects grew weary of taking test items and exercised less attention and care than would be employed in real situations. Further, not all subjects who responded to items face real *functional reading tasks* comparable to those with which they were tested. For example, many rural subjects had no need to read urban bus schedules and some subjects had never previously encountered check-writing tasks.

Two recent studies performed by the National Assessment of Educational Progress (N.A.E.P.) provide the most accurate currently available estimation of the literacy abilities of young adults (Applebee, Langer, & Mullis, 1985; Kirsch & Jungeblut, 1986). The first of these studies analyzed reading ability data collected from 251,000 nine- to 17-year-olds between 1970 and 1984. The second study employed some 500 interviewers to assess during 90-minute interviews the functional literacy abilities of 36,000 adults aged 21–25 in the homes of those adults.

The test construction approach in these two studies employed item response theory. In neither study did each subject receive all test items. Item response theory and data manipulation were used to arrive at estimates of item difficulty based on responses of representative portions of the total study samples. As a caveat, the reader should know that a statement like *40% of adults were unable to interpret an appliance warranty* does not literally mean that 40% of all adults taking the test were unable to interpret the warranty. Test items were statistically assigned difficulty levels ranging from 150 to 500 based upon performance of subjects and comparison to performance on other items. Average performance of various demographic groups (i.e., white, black, and Hispanic) is stated in terms of these difficulty levels. Some of the N.A.E.P. test designers caution that it is a somewhat risky inferential leap to assume that if a percentage of a demographic group score below the difficulty level assigned an item (i.e., the appliance warranty), the actual stated percentage of that group will not be able to actually comprehend the item. On the other hand, it is nearly impossible to say what item scores mean without making such inferential leaps. This paper will present test results in terms of percentages of demographic groups scoring below item difficulty levels and request the reader to view such data cautiously.

Among the cautions required in interpreting this data is the recognition that, in the United States, data reported in racial categories are strongly confounded by socioeconomic status. Disproportionate percentages of black and Hispanic Americans have lower incomes and live in conditions nonconducive to literacy development.

In 1985, the National Assessment of Educational Progress released *The Reading Report Card* (Applebee, Langer, & Mullis, 1985). This document reports analyses of the reading performances of over 251,000 randomly selected school children between 1970 and 1984. Examination of the reading performance of 17-year-olds (the oldest group studied) suggests a good deal about the reading abilities of current and future young adults.

The N.A.E.P. study authors report that the reading performance of 17-year-olds improved between 1980 and 1984, but that this may reflect improvements at younger ages rather than an increase in quality of secondary schooling. Further, nearly 100% of this age group was able to read at a *basic* level. According to N.A.E.P. test items, achieving at the basic level implies being able to

follow brief written directions;

select words, phrases, or sentences to describe a simple picture;

interpret simple written clues to identify objects;

locate and identify facts from simple informational paragraphs, stories, and news articles; and

combine ideas and make inferences based on short, uncomplicated passages.

In addition, nearly 84% of 17-year-olds were able to perform at the *intermediate* level. According to N.A.E.P., performance at the *intermediate* level implies being able to do all the tasks described above in addition to being able to

> search for, locate, and organize information found in relatively lengthy passages;
>
> recognize paraphrases of what has been read; and
>
> make inferences and reach generalizations about main ideas and author's purpose from passages dealing with literature, science, and social studies.

To place this *intermediate* level in perspective, it should be noted that this is the level achieved by the average 13-year-old or eighth-grade student. Approximately 40% of 17-year-olds achieve beyond this level and reach the *adept* level. Readers who achieve at the *adept* level are able to

> understand complicated literacy and informational passages; and
>
> analyze and integrate less familiar material and provide reactions to and explanations of the text as a whole.

Less than 5% of 17-year-olds perform beyond the *adept* level and achieve at the *advanced* level. At the *advanced* level, readers are able to

> extend and restructure the ideas presented in specialized and complex texts. Examples include scientific materials, literary essays, historical documents, and professional material;
>
> understand links between ideas even when those links are not explicitly stated; and
>
> make appropriate generalizations even when texts lack clear introductions and explanations.

Though only a tiny minority of 17-year-olds are prepared at the *advanced* level most university professors would prefer for entering freshmen, it seems clear that very few 17-year-olds are illiterate. The N.A.E.P. *basic* level is really a good deal beyond having to struggle to read one's name or a restroom sign.

As heartening as this information is about the reading abilities of the typical 17-year-old, the N.A.E.P. report also sounds a warning. Virtually no minority students (less than 1%) score at the *advanced* level. Indeed, the average reading proficiency of black and hispanic 17-year-olds is only slightly higher than that of white 13-year-olds. Applebee, Langer, and Mullis (1985) compared reading proficiencies of black, Hispanic, and white students from 1971 to 1984. In addition to the large gap between white and minority students, these authors pointed out that reading gains for black nine-year-olds appear to have leveled off, suggesting a future leveling of gains for black young adults.

In 1986 the N.A.E.P. released a major study of the functional literacy abilities of 21- to 25-year-old young adults (Kirsch & Jungeblut, 1986). This carefully designed study selected items from previous N.A.E.P. studies as well as designed items based upon what research indicated were reading tasks encountered by a substantial proportion of adults. Over 3,600 randomly selected adults were tested in their homes by over 500 trained interviewers. The result is a study which is the most accurate available estimation of what young adults can capably read. In addition, selection of items from previous measures allows comparison of the performance of these adults to the performance of other individuals on other tests.

The items and results of this study are categorized and presented in terms of three types of literacy: prose, document, and quantitative. Prose literacy involves understanding and using information from texts (i.e., editorials, news stories, poems, and the like). Document literacy involves locating and using information in documents (i.e., job applications, payroll forms, bus schedules, maps, tables, indexes, and so forth). Quantitative literacy involves applying arithmetic operations to information embedded in printed materials (i.e., balancing a checkbook, figuring a tip, completing an order form, or determining the amount of loan interest from an advertisement).

Not all subjects participated in attempting test items. An extremely simple pretest eliminated from full testing subjects judged to have such limited literacy skills that the literacy simulation tasks in the test would unduly frustrate and embarrass them. Only about 2% of the young adult population was estimated to be at this level. About half or 1% of the total population reported being unable to speak English.

Indicative summary results of this study are found in Tables 1–3 modified from *Literacy: Profiles of America's Young Adults* (Kirsch & Jungeblut, 1986, pp. 16–17, 28–29, 36–37, respectively).

A few observations about the results are in order. When viewing percentages of the total 21- to 25-year-old population, it appears clear that there is not a large degree of basic *illiteracy*. Over 95% of young adults can

sign their names;

locate expiration dates on a driver's license;

locate a time on a meeting form;

enter a caller's number on a phone message form;

write about a job they would like;

locate a movie in a T.V. listing; and

enter personal information on a job application.

As with the N.A.E.P. data on school children, wide racial and ethnic differences appear in the young adult data. The data indicate that it is probable that 98% of whites could fill in a job application while only 82% of blacks and 92% of Hispanics would be able to successfully complete the same task.

Though a vast majority of all ethnic populations can accomplish basic literacy tasks, gaps in populations become even wider as the complexity of tasks increases. For example, it is probable that 22% of whites would have difficulty writing a letter to state that an error was made in billing. On the same item, 60% of blacks and 42% of Hispanics would be likely to have difficulty. Test data indicate that it is probable that 35% of whites would have difficulty following directions to travel from one location to another using a map. On the same item, 80% of blacks and 63% of Hispanics would be likely to have difficulty. Items at slightly higher levels are extremely difficult for all populations. For example, an item on the prose scale asks individuals to orally interpret distinctions between two types of employee benefits. Nearly 90% of whites, 99% of blacks, and 97% of Hispanics would be likely to experience difficulty with this literacy task. Comparable percentages of all populations would be likely to experience difficulty calculating and totaling costs based on item costs from a catalogue.

The young adult literacy data make several points very clear. The vast majority of young adult Americans have mastered basic literacy demands. This vast majority

Table 1

Percentages of People and Selected Tasks At or Above Successive Points on the Prose Scale*

Race/Ethnicity White	Black	Hispanic	Total	Selected Points on the Scale	Selected Tasks at Decreasing Levels of Difficulty**
				— 500 —	
					— 397 Identify appropriate information in lengthy newspaper column
					— 387 Generate unfamiliar theme from short poem
10.8(0.9)	0.7(0.3)	3.3(1.1)	8.8(0.7)	— 375	
					— 371 Orally interpret distinctions between two types of employee benefits
					— 361 Select inappropriate title based on interpretation of new article
24.9(1.3)	3.1(0.6)	12.0(3.2)	21.1(1.1)	— 350	
					— 340 State in writing argument made in lengthy newspaper column
					— 339 Orally interpret a lengthy story in newspaper
42.6(1.7)	10.51(1.6)	23.5(3.4)	37.1(1.6)	— 325	
					— 313 Locate information in a news article
63.2(1.4)	23.7(1.6)	41.1(4.1)	56.4(1.5)	— 300	
					— 281 Located information on a page of text in an almanac (3-feature)
					— 279 Interpret instructions from an appliance warranty
					— 278 Generate familiar theme of poem
					Write letter to state that an error has been made in billing

(Table 1 continued on next page)

Table 1 ***(Continued)***

Percentages of People and Selected Tasks At or Above Successive Points on the Prose Scale*

Race/Ethnicity White	Black	Hispanic	Total	Selected Points on the Scale	Selected Tasks at Decreasing Levels of Difficulty**
78.0(1.3)	39.9(1.9)	57.4(3.2)	71.5(1.4)	— 275	
					— 262 Locate information in sports article (2-feature)
88.0(1.0)	57.5(2.7)	72.1(2.6)	90.8(0.7)	— 250	
94.6(0.6)	73.6(2.3)	80.8(2.3)	90.8(0.7)	— 225	
					— 210 Locate information in sports article (l-feature)
98.0(0.4)	86.2(1.5)	93.8(1.5)	98.5(0.2)	— 200	
					— 198 Write about a job one would like
99.4(0.2)	94.1(0.9)	96.6(1.2)	98.5(0.2)	— 175	
100.0(0.0)	97.7(0.5)	99.8(0.2)	99.7(0.1)	— 150	
				— 0	—

*Numbers in parentheses are estimated standard errors.

**Number indicating difficulty level designates that point on the scale at which individuals with that level of proficiency have an 80% probability of responding correctly.

Table 2

Percentages of People and Selected Tasks At or Above Successive Points on the Document Scale*

Race/Ethnicity White	Black	Hispanic	Total	Selected Points on the Scale	Selected Tasks at Decreasing Levels of Difficulty**
				— 500 —	
10.5(1.0)	0.9(0.4)	3.2(1.6)	8.8(0.8)	— 375	
					— 365 Use bus schedule to select appropriate bus for given departures & arrivals
24.3(1.6)	2.5(0.5)	6.7(2.0)	20.2(1.3)	— 350	
					— 343 Use bus schedule to select appropriate bus for given departures & arrivals
					— 334 Use bus schedule to select appropriate bus for given departures & arrivals
44.0(1.8)	9.0(1.1)	20.8(3.1)	37.6(1.6)	— 325	
					— 320 Use sandpaper chart to locate appropriate grade given specifications
65.4(1.7)	19.8(1.5)	37.0(4.1)	57.2(1.7)	— 300	— 300 Follow directions to travel from one location to another using a map
					— 294 Identify information from graph depicting source of energy and year
					— 278 Use index from an almanac
80.8(1.1)	38.7(2.6)	54.7(3.8)	73.1(1.2)	— 275	
					— 262 Locate eligibility from table of employee benefits
					— 257 Locate gross pay-to-date on pay stub
					— 255 Complete a check given information on a bill
					— 253 Complete an address on order form

(Table 2 continued on next page)

Table 2 *(Continued)*

Percentages of People and Selected Tasks At or Above Successive Points on the Document Scale*

White	Race/Ethnicity Black	Hispanic	Total	Selected Points on the Scale	Selected Tasks at Decreasing Levels of Difficulty**
89.9(0.8)	55.5(2.7)	69.0(3.4)	83.8(1.0)	— 250	
					— 249 Locate intersection on street map
95.0(0.7)	71.0(2.2)	84.4(1.6)	91.0(0.8)	— 225	
					— 221 Enter date on a deposit slip
					— 219 Identify cost of theatre trip from notice
					— 217 Match items on shopping list to coupons
97.9(0.5)	82.3(1.7)	91.5(1.2)	95.5(0.5)	— 200	
					— 196 Enter personal information on job application
					— 192 Locate movie in T.V. listing in newspaper
					— 181 Enter caller's number on phone messages form
99.3(0.3)	93.2(1.2)	96.5(0.7)	98.4(0.3)	— 175	
					— 169 Locate time of meeting on a form
					— 160 Locate expiration date on driver's license
99.9(0.1)	98.6(0.4)	99.1(0.3)	99.7(0.1)	— 150	
					— 110 Sign your name
				— 0	—

*Numbers in parentheses are estimated standard errors.

**Number indicating difficulty level designates that point on the scale at which individuals with that level of proficiency have an 80% probability of responding correctly.

Table 3

Percentages of People and Selected Tasks At or Above Successive Points on the Quantitative Scale*

Race/Ethnicity White	Black	Hispanic	Total	Selected Points on the Scale	Selected Tasks at Decreasing Levels of Difficulty**
				— 500 —	
					— 489 Determine amount of interest charges from loan ad
					— 376 Estimate cost using grocery unit-price labels
11.5(1.0)	0.8(0.4)	3.8(1.7)	9.5(0.9)	— 375	
					— 371 Calculate & total costs based on item costs from catalogue
					— 356 Determine tip given percentage of bill
27.2(1.7)	2.4(0.8)	11.3(2.7)	22.5(1.4)	— 350	
					— 340 Plan travel arrangements for meeting using flight schedule
					— 337 Determine correct change using menu
44.4(1.7)	8.3(1.6)	19.9(3.5)	37.8(1.6)	— 325	
63.3(1.5)	22.0(2.1)	36.9(4.4)	56.0(1.4)	— 300	
					— 293 Enter and calculate checkbook balance
					— 289 "
					— 281 "
78.8(1.1)	39.3(1.9)	57.9(3.8)	72.2(1.1)	— 275	
89.4(0.9)	60.4(2.5)	74.6(3.0)	84.7(1.0)	— 250	
					— 233 Total bank deposit entry
95.5(0.6)	74.4(1.5)	87.3(1.8)	92.4(0.6)	— 225	
98.0(9.4)	87.4(1.5)	93.1(1.3)	96.4(0.4)	— 200	
99.2(0.2)	94.8(0.9)	97.7(0.6)	98.6(0.2)	— 175	
99.8(0.1)	98.3(0.5)	99.6(0.3)	99.6(0.1)	— 150	
				— 0 —	

*Numbers in parentheses are estimated standard errors.

**Number indicating difficulty level designates that point on the scale at which individuals with that level of proficiency have an 80% probability of responding correctly.

drops off rapidly and soon becomes a minority as everyday literacy tasks increase in complexity. Finally, differences in performance between whites, blacks, and Hispanics are extremely wide and distressing, especially at middle and upper levels. Bristow (1986) has observed that older Americans are more likely to experience literacy difficulties at lower levels since the percentage of Americans with less than eight and even less than four years of schooling increases with the age of the population.

The young adults who were tested using N.A.E.P. simulations of functional literacy tasks also responded to items included in the N.A.E.P. school literacy assessment. This allows a comparison between the performances of students in grades four, eight, and eleven and the performances of young adults. Table 4 contains information from Kirsch and Jungeblut (1986, p. 40) which makes this comparison.

Table 4

Percentages of Young Adult Populations At or Above Average Reading Proficiency of Fourth, Eighth, and Eleventh Graders on N.A.E.P. Scale

N.A.E.P. Average Reading Proficiencies at Three Grade Levels		Total (%)	Race/Ethnicity White (%)	Black (%)	Hispanic (%)
	Scale Score				
Grade 11	289.3	61.5	67.6	31.0	52.3
Grade 8	260.7	79.8	85.0	53.0	70.9
Grade 4	217.5	94.0	96.2	82.2	92.4

The data from the above table indicate that only about 6% of the young adult population read below the fourth-grade level, but 20% read below an eighth-grade level, and nearly 40% read below an eleventh-grade level. These totals are somewhat deceptive, however, due to wide racial and ethnic disparities. Nearly 18% of black young adults read below a fourth-grade level, close to half read below an eighth-grade level, and more than two thirds read below an eleventh-grade level. Hispanic young adults perform somewhat better than blacks, but nearly 30% read below an eighth-grade level and close to one half read below an eleventh-grade level. Substantial proportions of our young adult population, and especially our minority population, appear to be ill-equipped for the high and increasing literacy challenges associated with being productive and self-sufficient in our society.

CHANGES IN LITERACY PATTERNS AND DEMANDS

For the same reasons that it is difficult to define literacy, it is difficult to determine changes in patterns of who is literate and difficult to chart literacy demands faced by individuals. Harmon (1986), drawing upon the work of historians Carl F. Kaestle and Lawrence A. Cremin, estimated that

> By counting the number of men who could sign their name to deeds and other public documents as literate (literacy for women was deemed irrelevant in most of the colonies; for slaves dangerous), historians have reckoned that literacy in America rose from about 60 percent among the first white male colonists to about 75 percent by 1800 (p. 118).

It is a bit more difficult to estimate the degree of middle and upper level literacy abilities during this same time period. One method by which it is possible to roughly infer reading abilities is to note what people were reading. Harmon (1986) cited Cremin's observation that Thomas Paine's *Common Sense* "sold 100,000 copies within three months of its appearance in 1776 and possibly as many as a half-million in all" (pp. 118–119). Half a million people was 20% of the colonial population. Cremin estimated that one half or probably 10% "read it or heard it read aloud" (p. 118).

Given the fact that N.A.E.P. young adult data suggest less than 10% of young adults are able to read and distinguish types of employee benefits or generate an unfamiliar theme from a short poem, it appears the nation has not progressed a great deal in terms of higher level literacy. The majority of gains appears to relate to larger percentages of the population mastering lower and middle level literacy abilities.

Another method for analyzing changing literacy patterns is to examine population statistics for changes occurring over the course of a life span. In 1910, the official U.S. Census simply asked individuals if they could read or write in any language. A total of 7.7% of the population answered "No" to that question in 1910. Of that group, 41% were black, 27% were native whites, 30% were foreign-born whites, and 2% were listed as other (Cook, 1977). On a higher literacy level, in 1910, only 8% of 17- to 18-year-olds graduated from high school; 6% of the group went on to enroll in institutions of higher education (*Digest of Educational Statistics*, 1979). The average citizen was probably closer to the 7.7% who said "No" than to the 8.8% who were high school graduates. For example, 25% of World War I enlistees were not able to comprehend extremely simple newspaper passages or compose written communications of any sort (Cook, 1977). Tyler has estimated that 55% of these enlistees were functionally illiterate in terms of being able to put their literacy to any effective military use (Tyler, 1978).

The context for literacy at the turn of the century was a context of elitism. An extremely small percentage of the population received either secondary or higher education. Even the high school graduation figures for 1910 (8.8%) are somewhat deceptive. The percentage of high school graduates in 1870 was 2%. An overwhelming number of adults at the turn of the century had less than a high school education. Of the tiny percentage who did graduate from high school, 75% went on to college. The gap between the tiny percentage of the highly educated, highly literate individuals and everyone else was wide.

Changes in literacy during a single life span have been great. Compulsory schooling and immigration quotas lowered the percentages of totally illiterate individuals. By the original Census Bureau definition, under 1% of adults were totally illiterate in 1970 (Fisher, 1978). This figure coincides with the 1–2% of young adults screened by the N.A.E.P. young adult pretest.

During the time period since 1910, changing social conditions have preceded changes in acceptable levels of literacy. Each major war during this century has brought with it increased literacy demands for military performance. The Second World War was close to a mid-point in this century. During World War II, the U.S. Army found it necessary to set a minimum criterion of a fourth-grade reading level for acceptance into the army. A special 1947 census defined literacy as five years of schooling and found 13.5% of the population illiterate. By the 1960s, the U.S. Office of Education had raised the level of acceptable literacy to eight years of schooling. Even this was considered too low in the 1970s when the Adult Performance Level study was released (Cook, 1977).

During the early 1980s, a survey of citizens in Milwaukee reported the types of materials residents considered essential to normal functioning. These materials provide a reasonable idea of what current functional literacy means to a cross-section of adults. Frequently mentioned materials included relatively simple items like street and traffic signs and medicine bottle directions as well as more complex bank statements, health and safety pamphlets, loan applications, and product warning and antidote directions (Negin & Krugler, 1980).

Current estimates of occupational demands for literacy indicate that over 90% of occupations call for some reading and writing (Diehl & Mikulecky, 1980; Mikulecky, 1982). This is up from not more than 10% in the first decennial census undertaken in 1790 (Tyler, 1978). In addition, there has been a growing demand for literacy in the areas of recreation and self-realization. Newspapers are more varied in content than ever before and reach over 75% of Americans. Magazines and paperback books are experiencing an increase in sales (Dessauer, 1982).

The difficulty levels of occupational reading as well as newspaper and magazine reading are quite high. Mikulecky (1982a) found the difficulty levels of the majority of reading materials on the job ranged from tenth- to twelfth-grade level in difficulty with workers averaging more than two hours of daily job-reading. Even blue collar workers averaged more than 1½ hours of daily job-reading. These findings concur with the findings of Rush, Moe, and Storlie (1986) in other civilian work settings and with Sticht (1982a) for military settings. Though having a wealth of background knowledge on a topic can tend to effectively lower reading difficulty levels, the most heavy job-related reading is performed by new workers least likely to have the wealth of background experience.

The uses to which literacy is put on the job appear to be more complex than typical uses of literacy in schools. The vast majority of school-related reading is reading to learn factual material, while a comparable majority of job-related reading is for problem-solving and making applications (Mikulecky, 1982). In addition, the literacy strategies associated with high job performance ratings are primarily higher level metacognitive strategies involving monitoring, focusing, and managing information (Mikulecky & Ehlinger, 1986; Mikulecky & Winchester, 1983).

The tenth- to twelfth-grade difficulty level of workplace materials is mirrored by similar difficulty levels for other functional reading. Wire service news stories average at the tenth- to eleventh-grade level in difficulty (Wheat, Lindberg, & Nauman, 1977). A recent study done by the College Board (*Reading Today*, Feb/March, 1986, p. 16), using the Degrees of Reading Power assessment of reading difficulty, found newspapers, magazines, and job-related materials to average at comparable difficulty levels (the 63–72 DRP unit range). This range embraces the average ability levels of high school sophomores and juniors. Again, since a wide range of topics and a wide population range are involved, individual reader background knowledge becomes less a factor.

There are a few exceptions to this general trend of higher literacy requirements. Some low-paying jobs can be simplified through fragmentation and automation. West Germany has been cost-effective by breaking down complex tasks to simple tasks done by an individual worker repeatedly. This is not as cost-effective as having a worker who is literate and can adjust flexibly to new tasks when the operation for which he has been trained is temporarily halted. However, fragmentation can be cost-effective if the worker is paid an extremely low wage, as are the immigrant *guest workers* in West German industries. In the United States, where no legal *guest worker* option exists, such fragmented jobs tend to be shipped out of the country leaving Americans with low literacy abilities without employment. Some fast food chains in the United States have eliminated the need for much literacy among employees by using pictures on cash register keys and computerized pricing. A trained manager must be knowledgeable and available in the event of equipment difficulties, but the system works as long as less capable workers can accept extremely low pay for their severely limited performances. Similar approaches are being used in the automating of oil pipeline monitoring gauges and holographic package readers in grocery stores. The grocery store example is useful for examining this low-skill job trend. Fewer mistakes and hold-ups mean faster lines and therefore the need for fewer low-paid check-out personnel and packaging personnel who need to run and check prices. Computerized inventories lower the need for massive warehousing and many of the warehouse jobs associated with such massive operations. Several middle skilled level jobs are created for building, marketing, and servicing the holographic price readers (Harste & Mikulecky, 1984).

The social context for literacy has changed during a single life span to the point where functional literacy means a level of ability achieved by only an extremely small fraction of the population in 1910. Literacy can no longer remain the province of a tiny privileged elite minority. It has become a necessary part of functioning in most aspects of daily life.

ADULT ILLITERACY AND ADULT BASIC EDUCATION

Most literacy problems faced by Americans are not at the rudimentary or basic levels. A small percentage of Americans, however, do experience extreme literacy difficulties and are being left behind by the increased literacy demands of our society.

Demographic Information

According to N.A.E.P. data, from 1-2% of American young adults either are unable to speak English or cannot recognize simple printed words and phrases. Kirsch and Jungeblut (1986) point out that the 1% who could speak English and responded to a set of oral-language tasks performed at a low level suggesting to the authors that this group "may have a language problem that extends beyond processing printed information" (p. 5). If the criterion level for basic literacy is set for performance comparable to a fourth-grade level, approximately 6% of young adults experience problems with basic literacy (3.8% of whites, 17.8% of blacks, and 7.6% of Hispanics).

This section of the paper will examine the limited research information about this bottom percentage of adults experiencing literacy difficulties. Darkenwald (1986), in a research review of effective approaches to teaching basic skills to adults, observed that the "research base in adult basic education is severely deficient, not only in quantity but in quality.'' (p. 2). Still, it is possible to draw upon research in providing a picture of teachers, learners, and programs concerned with basic adult literacy.

Fowler (1986), working through the Center for Survey Research at the University of Massachusetts, performed a survey of adult literacy programs and resources for the Coalition for Literacy. He noted that in the fall of 1985 an estimated 400,000 students were enrolled in classes to teach basic reading and writing (G.E.D. and E.S.L. classes were eliminated). These students were about equally divided between Adult Basic Education (A.B.E.) classes supported by state and federal monies and volunteer programs such as the Laubach affiliates, the Literacy Volunteers of America, and the American Library Association programs. Between fall of 1984 and fall of 1985, there was a 9.3% increase in the number of students and a corresponding 9% increase in literacy program budgets to reach a level of 109 million dollars. Fowler reported a 28.7% increase in the number of volunteer teachers (i.e., from 75,000 to 96,000).

Newman (1986), in an evaluation of the Advertising Council's *Volunteer Against Illiteracy* program during 1985, indicated that 8,000 of the new teachers and 10,000 of the new students came to literacy programs via the special 800 telephone number set up by the advertising campaign. Newman also noted that preliminary data suggest that the 9% increase in students may be occurring more heavily in volunteer programs than it is in A.B.E. programs.

Comprehensive national demographic data is not available on who attends these basic literacy classes. The Literacy Assistance Center, however, has compiled data on the 40,000 learners involved in literacy programs in New York City (Cook, 1986). Data from a large urban center can provide some indication of who attends classes, at least in urban centers.

Of the 40,000 New York students, nearly 52% were enrolled in basic education classes while another 45% were enrolled in classes to teach English as a second or other language. Of the basic education students, 10.7% are reported to read below a third-grade level. When the level is increased to fifth grade, 25.3% are not able to perform adequately. This suggests that of the 40,000 New York students, about 13% or 5,200 would fall within the parameters Fowler (1986) set for estimating the 400,000 students nationally receiving basic reading and writing training. In New York, 41% of students are male and 59% female. The typical learner, at least in New York City basic literacy classes, is likely to be female (59%), a member of a minority group (89%), and between the ages of 25 and 45 (52%). Approximately one third of learners are between the ages of 16 and 24.

Cognitive Competencies and Characteristics

Adults demonstrating low reading levels differ from children with comparably low reading levels. Liebert (1983) compared the oral reading of adult basic education students to elementary-age children of comparable ability levels. He found that, for children, reading accuracy and rate decreased as passages became more difficult. The adult readers demonstrated no comparable variability in accuracy but similar declines in rate. The rates for adults ranged from 23 words per minute to 145 words per minute. Many adult readers in A.B.E. classes read extremely slowly. Bristow and Leslie (in press) found adult reading rate to be a significant diagnostic predictor of comprehension difficulties. Johnston (1985) used case study methodology to monitor the reading abilities and patterns of adult poor readers. He concluded that adult reading disability is influenced by "anxiety, attributions, maladaptive strategies, inaccurate or nonexisting concepts about aspects of reading, and a huge variety of motivational factors." (p. 174). In many cases, Johnston's disabled readers, who were constantly forced by society to confront reading material beyond their abilities, inappropriately overrelied on background knowledge and context in situations where decoding strategies would have been more useful. This finding appears to be in contradiction with the findings of Lytle, Marmor, and Penner (1986) which indicate that 70% of illiterate and low-literate subjects consider reading to be primarily a decoding process. Gambrell and Heathington (1981) found that one third of poor adult readers were unable to provide a strategy for identifying an unknown word other than asking someone for help.

Time Needed to Make Gains

In the late 1970s many adult educators maintained the belief that adults were able to learn to read more rapidly than children because they possessed more *life experience* and background knowledge. To test this belief, Sticht (1982b), investigated the effect of method and rate of presentation of materials on the reading achievement of adults averaging 5.5-grade level in tested reading ability as well as the reading achievement of average third- to fifth-grade students. Sticht found no evidence that adults performed better or learned more quickly than children at comparable grade levels.

Indeed, learning time is high for adults to make a grade level gain in reading ability. Darkenwald (1986) describes the work of Kent (1973) who performed an evaluation of 2,300 A.B.E. students from 200 classes in 90 programs located in 15 states. Reading gains from January to May averaged 0.5-grade level with one third of the population showing no gain or a net loss. Comparable data from Kent's study of Manpower Development Training Act programs indicates that after 54 hours of instruction, the average reading level increase was 0.4. Sticht (1982a), in summarizing dozens of military studies, indicates a grade level gain in reading takes enlisted men from 80 to 120 hours of instruction. The Jefferson County Adult Reading Program provides a sense of the parameters of what is possible. Large-scale evaluation studies suggest 100 hours of instruction per grade level gain in reading is typical. Darkenwald (1986) reports the Jefferson County Adult Reading Program as using a combination of counseling, individualized instruction, functional goals, and group dynamics holds attrition rates to one half to one fourth of comparable programs and achieves reading gains .70 greater than comparable programs (approximately 54 hours of instruction per grade level gain). Pasch's (1985) evaluation of project LEARN indicates that actual practice time is key, with adult reading gains correlating most highly with "lessons completed and . . . not particularly related to number of hours tutored or days in the program" (p. 17).

Achieving the necessary practice and time on task has not been possible for most adult literacy programs, however. Mezirow, Darkenwald, and Knox (1975), in a national survey of urban A.B.E. teachers found that irregular attendance was perceived by 85% as the single most serious impediment to effective learning. Darkenwald and Valentine (1984), in a survey of A.B.E. students, found that more than half reported having trouble attending class. Balmuth (1986) confirms and extends these survey results. After reviewing several studies on attendance, Balmuth noted that

> The high rate of absenteeism in ABE is taken to be a fact of life, although an embarrassing and destructive one . . . A class could have an enrollment of 20 but only 2 or 3 in attendance. (p. 58)

Time on task for a typical A.B.E. student is extremely sparse according to Darkenwald (1986). Learning time is diminished by irregular attendance, the fact that the usual A.B.E. schedule provides only four to six hours of instruction a week, the fact that homework is very rare, and the fact that time-on-task per classroom hour is much lower than is typical for school children.

EFFECTIVE LITERACY PROGRAMS AND THE PROBLEM OF TRANSFER

It is this author's estimate that from 6-10% of adults read below a fourth-grade level and that little more than 2% of adults can be classed as truly illiterate in the sense of not being able to read or write a word. Adults who read at this level have a difficult time learning and attending classes. They face a minimum of several hundred hours of instruction before they can expect to approach meeting what most educated people consider daily functional literacy demands.

Darkenwald (1975), after analyzing a national sample of 478 randomly selected A.B.E. teachers, determined that emphasis on nontraditional subjects like consumer education, health education, and coping skills was associated with substantially lower drop-out rates and substantially higher class attendance. More than a decade later, Darkenwald (1986) analyzed adult literacy programs selected as being the most effective by the U. S. government's Joint Dissemination Review Panel. Darkenwald notes that these most highly selected programs

> almost invariably integrate basic skills focus with instruction in life or "survival" skills needed by students to function effectively in the everyday world. (p. 29)

This observation of Darkenwald's is extremely important. It implies that programs must teach the sort of literacy tasks learners will actually be asked to perform rather than simply teaching the general *school-type* literacy found in traditional materials. A growing body of research supports this observation. For example, Larson (1980) found that a six-week literacy program had no effects on attrition from military job training nor did it affect the time required to complete subsequent job training. Sticht (1982a) reported that military recruits given traditional basic skills training make gains while in class, but tend to revert and lose their skills within eight weeks. In contrast, job-related literacy and computational training does not suffer this reversion. U. S. Army retention studies have indicated that

> personnel retained 80% of their end-of-course gain in job literacy training (but) only 40% of their end-of-course gain in general reading. (p. 40)

Similar indications of nontransfer have been found by Scribner and Cole (1978) in their work with the Vai. They conclude that "the effects of literacy and perhaps of schooling as well, are restricted . . . generalized only to closely related practices'' (p. 457).

Some indication of the degree of transfer one can expect has been provided by the N.A.E.P. study of literacy among young adults. Kirsch and Jungeblut (1986) correlated subject scores on the prose, document, and quantitative literacy scales of the young adult literacy assessment. Correlations ranged from $r = .49$ to $r = .56$. These correlations are surprisingly close and suggest that there is about a 25% overlap in the variance of performance with the different types of literacies measured by the N.A.E.P. Further research is called for, but it may well be that general literacy abilities account for only about one fourth of the performance on a specific type of literacy task. For some literacy tasks, it may account for considerably less of the variance.

These findings about effective programs and lack of transfer are important as educators decide how to allocate their resources. Currently many adult literacy programs and volunteer tutors direct their efforts toward the minority of adults experiencing extreme literacy difficulties. Though some programs teach literacy in functional and occupational contexts, many programs and tutors allocate most time and resources to general literacy training emphasizing decoding, word-attack, and literal level understanding of nonfunctional stories. Research indicates that such approaches are associated with higher attrition, much lower transfer of reading gain, and much higher loss of gain after as little time as six weeks.

Teaching basic general literacy mainly to the bottom 2–6% of the adult population must be questioned as a wise allocation of limited resources. This population, which requires hundreds of hours of training, is generally unable to attend regularly for as many as 50 hours. Those who attend for longer apparently have a difficult time retaining what they have learned or transferring that learning to functional applications of literacy in daily settings.

In addition, major emphasis of attention and resources on this group creates several new problems. The much larger percentage of adults reading above the fourth-grade level but not well enough to easily function in society (14% to 20%) need a different sort of teaching than the basic literacy instructor training being provided by most volunteer tutors. These adults are not likely to get what they need when they attend traditional literacy programs and indeed are likely to be driven off by inappropriate training. This is particularly unfortunate since 50–150 hours of appropriate training for many adults in this group could bring them within reach of being able to function with the new literacy demands of our society.

TRENDS, PROBLEMS, AND RECOMMENDATIONS

One trend is particularly clear in both the N.A.E.P. data and the adult literacy class attendance data. If you are an adult minority group member in the United States, you are considerably more likely to experience literacy difficulties than is a white adult. Hodgkinson's (1985) analysis of demographic data indicates that the baby boomlet which is increasing elementary school enrollments is made of larger percentages of minority group membership than ever before. The birth rate for whites is 1.8, for blacks is 2.3, and for Hispanics is 2.8. The children for whom schools have been least successful are present in increasingly larger percentages.

The racial/educational split can also be observed at other levels. In many urban school districts, drop-out rates range from 50% to 60% and higher. At the same time, in predominantly nonurban states like Minnesota, Wisconsin, Iowa, and North Dakota, statewide averages for high school graduation exceed 80% with approximately two thirds of 18-year-olds enrolling in colleges or universities. Statistically, an urban black or Hispanic has nearly the same likelihood of dropping out of high school as a nonurban white has of enrolling in college.

In *Megatrends,* Naisbitt (1982) observed that information is the currency of the 1980s. To the extent that literacy is access to such information and wealth, in the United States we may be on the verge of becoming a more economically divided society than ever before. This growing social and political problem has literacy and education close to its core.

The political nature of this growing literacy problem is becoming increasingly apparent in the solutions suggested to address the problem. Kozol in *Illiterate America* (1985) called for a massive national mobilization involving mass participation of the people. He offered Cuba and Nicaragua as examples of effective programs with government support, as well as the initial stages of Paulo Freire's work in Brazil. Political/educational responses from the other side of the political spectrum can be observed in the National Advisory Council on Adult Education's (NACAE) recommendations to the President of the United States (Smith et al., 1986). The NACAE suggested 71 solutions to the problem, which address such topic areas as Curriculum and Instruction, the Teaching Profession, Local Administration, Research, the System and Structure of Education, National Attitudes Toward Education, and Illiteracy. Among the suggested solutions for Illiteracy are

> appoint a national task force on teaching reading,
>
> expand the discussion of reading teaching beyond the domain of educators to include the public,
>
> set national definitions for the various levels of literacy and use these definitions to determine eligibility for ABE programs and the "return on the investment" in such programs,
>
> incorporate military research findings into public education programs,
>
> consider requiring illiterate adults on welfare to enter educational programs, and
>
> consider shortening prison sentences for illiterate inmates who successfully complete reading programs.

Another idea which received some political attention during 1985–1986 is the idea of inter-generational transfer of literacy. In 1980, Sticht observed that one of the best ways to improve the reading performance of children is to improve the education level of their parents. Large gains in children's reading improvement followed World War II. A convincing case can be made for these gains being explained by the performance of children whose parents had taken advantage of the G.I. bill to acquire more education.

In 1985, Kozol and others picked up on Sticht's idea of programs to teach literacy to both parents and their children. Two proposed pieces of legislation on this topic were introduced in but not passed by the 99th United States Congress. The concept of improving adult literacy while teaching adults to work with their own children continues to receive a good deal of discussion and may yet offer an avenue for substantial literacy improvement.

Newman (1986) reported increased attention as well as financial and other resources being allocated to literacy improvement by businesses, foundations, and thousands of volunteers. She reports the contribution of more than 24 million dollars in free media advertising time and space toward the goal of focusing national attention on literacy issues. In addition, a two-phased public service campaign has been developed by the media. The Public Broadcasting System has developed Project Literacy U.S. (PLUS) while the American Broadcasting Company has made its own concerted efforts to integrate literacy awareness into its news and information programming. One tangible result of this increased national attention has been the additional 20,000 tutors (for a total of 96,000) who volunteered to work with adult illiterates between November, 1984, and September, 1985. It is highly likely that that number has continued to grow.

In addition to voluntary efforts, corporations and foundations through the leadership of the Business Council for Effective Literacy have made other resources available for literacy program support. Thus far, this support has been primarily in the form of seed resources to initiate or expand literacy programs. An exception to this generalization is the Ford Foundation's support of the production of *Cast-Off Youth* (Sticht, Armstrong, Hickey, & Caylor, 1986). This study compiles the research, policies, and training methods used by the military to teach functional literacy to 100,000 enlisted men during the late 1960s and early 1970s. Its emphasis on integrating literacy training with functional training should prove useful to program developers interested in educating the majority of adults experiencing literacy difficulties in the United States.

CONCLUSION

We have more than one literacy problem in the United States. The problem receiving the most media attention is the painful problem of the small percentage of adults who can barely read or write. A much larger and different problem relates to the millions of adults who can read and write but not well enough to meet the increasing literacy demands for attaining a comfortable living in the United States. Confusion of these two aspects of literacy problems and the fact that these problems need to be addressed using different methods has led to a number of embarrassing misunderstandings including a national advertisement falsely claiming that, by the year 2,000, two out of three Americans may be illiterate.

The line between who has and who has not acquired enough literacy to function and thrive in the United States is, to a great extent, drawn along racial and ethnic lines. This division implies a dangerous potential for future conflict which is exacerbated by the fact that the public schools will soon face even larger percentages of minority youth—sons and daughters, brothers and sisters of the students with whom the schools have already failed.

On the positive side, there is a growing awareness that, to be effective, basic literacy training needs to be integrated with functional uses of literacy. Though the nation is not experiencing the mass literacy mobilization Kozol (1985) calls for, there is a clear increase in awareness as well as in volunteer efforts and resource donations by individuals and businesses. Though there has been no comparable increase in state and federal resources, there are indications that increased public awareness my lead to increased congressional awareness.

REFERENCES

Applebee, A., Langer, J., & Mullis, I. (1985). *The reading report card: Progress toward excellence in our schools.* Princeton, NJ: National Assessment of Educational Progress, Educational Testing Service.

Balmuth, M. (1986). *Essential characteristics of effective adult literacy programs: A review and analysis of research.* New York: Hunter College of the City University of New York.

Bormuth, J. R. (1975). Reading literacy: Its definition and assessment. In J. B. Carroll & J. S. Chall (Eds.), *Toward a literate society* (pp. 61-100). New York: McGraw-Hill.

Bristow, P. G. (1986, December). Personal communication at the National Reading Conference, Austin, TX.

Bristow, P. G., & Leslie, L. (in press). Early indicators of reading difficulty: Discrimination between instructional and frustration range performance of illiterate adults. *Reading Research Quarterly.*

Cook, J. (1986). *Final report: New York City adult literacy initiative.* New York: Literacy Assistance Center.

Cook, W. (1977). *Adult literacy education in the United States.* Newark, DE: International Reading Association.

Darkenwald, G. (1975). Some effects on the obvious variable: Teacher's race and holding power with black adult students. *Adult Education Quarterly, 35,* 220-228.

Darkenwald, G. (1986). *Effective approaches to teaching basic skills to adults: A research synthesis.* Paper prepared for the Office of Higher Education and Adult Learning of the Office of Educational Research and Improvement of the U.S. Department of Education, Washington, DC (Contract No. OERI-P-86-3015).

Darkenwald, G., & Valentine, T. (1984). *Outcomes and impact of adult basic education.* New Brunswick, NJ: Center for Adult Development, Rutgers University.

Darling, S. (1981). *Final report: Jefferson County adult reading project.* Department of Adult and Continuing Education, Jefferson County Board of Education, Louisville, KY.

Dessauer, J. (1982, April 8). Estimated book industry sales: First quarter 1982. *Publisher's Weekly,* pp. 23-26.

Diehl, W., & Mikulecky, L. (1980). The nature of reading at work. *Journal of Reading, 24,* 221-227.

Digest of Educational Statistics (1979). Washington, DC: National Center for Educational Statistics, U.S. Department of Health, Education, and Welfare.

Fisher, D. L. (1978). *Functional literacy and the schools.* Washington, DC: National Institute of Education.

Fowler, F. J. (1986). *Survey of literacy resources: A report of methods and basic estimates.* Boston: Center for Survey Research, University of Massachusetts.

Gadway, C., & Wilson, H. A. (1975). *Functional literacy: Basic reading performance.* Denver, CO: National Assessment of Educational Progress.

Gambrell, L. B., & Heathington, B. S. (1981). Adult disabled readers' metacognitive awareness about reading tasks and strategies. *Journal of Reading Behavior, 13,* 215-221.

Gray, W. S. (1956). *The teaching of reading and writing* (Monographs on fundamental education, No. 10, p. 24). Paris: UNESCO.

Guthrie, J. T. (1983). Equilibrium of literacy. *Journal of Reading, 26,* 668-670.

Harmon, D. (1986). Keeping up in America. *The Wilson Quarterly, 10*(2), 116-131.

Harmon, D. (1987). *Illiteracy: A national dilemma.* New York: Cambridge Book.

Harris, L., & Associates (1970). *Survival literacy: Conducted for the National Reading Council.* New York: Louis Harris & Associates.

Harste, J., & Mikulecky, L. (1984). The context of literacy in our society. In A. Purves & O. Niles (Eds.), *Becoming readers in a complex society* (pp. 47-78). Eighty-third Yearbook of the National Society for the Study of Education, Part I. Chicago, IL: University of Chicago Press.

Hodgkinson, H. L. (1985). *All one system: Demographics of education.* Washington, DC: Institute for Leadership in Education.

Johnston, P. H. (1985). Understanding reading disability: A case study approach. *Harvard Educational Review, 55,* 153-177.

Kent, W. (1973). *A longitudinal evaluation of the adult basic education program.* Falls Church, VA: Systems Development Corp.

Kirsch, I., & Guthrie, J. T. (1977-1978). The concept of measurement of functional literacy. *Reading Research Quarterly, 13,* 485-507.

Kirsch, I., & Jungeblut, A. (1986). *Literacy: Profiles of America's young adults.* Princeton, NJ: National Assessment of Educational Progress at Educational Testing Service.

Kozol, J. (1985). *Illiterate America.* Garden City, NY: Anchor Press/Doubleday.

Larson, G. (1980). The effects of basic literacy training on performance in occupational training programs in the U. S. Army (Rutgers University). *Dissertation Abstracts International, 40,* 3697A.

Leibert, R. E. (1983). Performance profiles of ABE students and children on an informal reading inventory. *Reading Psychology: An International Quarterly, 4,* 141-150.

Lytle, S. L., Marmor, T. W., & Penner, F. H. (1986, April). *Literacy theory in practice: Assessing reading and writing low-literate adults.* Paper presented at the annual meeting of the American Educational Research Association, San Francisco.

Mezirow, J., Darkenwald, G., & Knox, A. (1975). *Last gamble on education: Dynamics of adult basic education.* Washington, DC: Adult Education Association.

Mikulecky, L. (1982). Job literacy: The relationship between school preparation and workplace actuality. *Reading Research Quarterly, 17,* 400-419.

Mikulecky, L., & Ehlinger, J. (1986). The influence of metacognitive aspects of literacy on job performance of electronics technicians. *Journal of Reading Behavior, 18,* 41-62.

Mikulecky, L., & Winchester, D. (1983). Job literacy and job performance among nurses at varying employment levels. *Adult Education Quarterly, 34,* 1-15.

Murphy, R. T. (1975). Assessment of adult reading competence. In D. M. Nielson & H. F. Hjelm (Eds.), *Reading and career education* (pp. 50-61). Newark, DE: International Reading Association.

Naisbitt, J. (1982). *Megatrends.* New York: Warner Books.

Negin, G., & Krugler, D. (1980). Essential literacy skills for functioning in an urban community, *Journal of Reading, 24,* 109-115.

Newman, A. P. (1986). *An evaluation of the impact of the Advertising Council's volunteer against literacy campaign on public awareness of and resources devoted to adult literacy for 1985.* Washington DC: Coalition for Literacy.

Northcutt, N. (1975). Functional literacy for adults. In D. M. Nielson & H. F. Hjelm (Eds.), *Reading and career education* (pp. 43-49). Newark, DE: International Reading Association.

Pasch, M. (1985). *An evaluation study of project LEARN students and tutors 1982-1984.* Ypsilanti: Eastern Michigan University.

Rush, T., Moe, A., & Storlie, R. (1986). *Occupational literacy.* Newark, DE: International Reading Association.

Scribner, S., & Cole, M. (1978). Literacy without schooling: Testing for intellectual effects. *Harvard Educational Review, 48,* 448-461.

Smith, P. H., Balian, L., Brennan, D., Gorringe, J., Jackson, M., & Thone, R. (1986) *Illiteracy in America: Extent, causes, and suggested solutions.* A report of the National Advisory Council on Adult Education. Washington, DC: U.S. Government Printing Office.

Sticht, T. G. (1975). *Reading for working: A functional literacy anthology.* Alexandria, VA: Human Resources Research Association.

Sticht, T. G. (1980). *Literacy and human resources development at work.* Alexandria, VA: Human Resources Research Organization.

Sticht, T. G. (1982a). *Basic skills in defense.* Alexandria, VA: Human Resources Research Organization.

Sticht, T. G. (1982b). *Evaluation of the reading potential concept for marginally illiterate adults.* Alexandria, VA: Human Resources Research Organization.

Sticht, T. G., Caylor, J. S., Fox, L. C., Hauke, R. N., James, J. H., Snyder, S. S., & Kern, R. P. (1972). Project REALISTIC: Determination of adult functional literacy skills levels. *Reading Research Quarterly, 7,* 424-465.

Sticht, T. G., Amijo, L., Weitzman, R., Koffman, N., Roberson, K, Chang, F., & Moracco, J. (1986). *Teachers, books, computers, and peers: Integrated communications technologies for adult literacy development.* Monterey, CA: U.S. Naval Postgraduate School.

Sticht, T. G., Armstrong, W., Hickey, D., & Caylor, J. (1986). *Cast-off youth.* New York: The Ford Foundation.

Tyler, R. W. (1978, June). *Education for functional literacy: Old problems, new problems.* Paper presented at a conference on functional literacy, Indiana University, Bloomington.

Valentine, T. (1986). *Issues central to the definition of adult functional literacy.* Paper prepared for the Office of Higher Education and Adult Learning of the Office of Educational Research and Improvement of the United States Department of Education (Contract No. OERI-P-86-3014).

Wheat, T., Lindberg, M., & Nauman, M. (1977). An exploratory investigation of newspaper readability. *Illinois Reading Council Journal, 5,* 4-7.

COPING STRATEGIES OF FOUR SUCCESSFUL LEARNING DISABLED COLLEGE STUDENTS: A CASE STUDY APPROACH

William G. Brozo
Northeastern Illinois University

Carol L. Curtis
Highland Park High School

Learning disabled students are often characterized by their lack of self-awareness with regard to their learning disability and learning strategies (Brown & Palincsar, 1982; Torgesen, 1982; Weiner, 1983) and by their tendency to attribute success and failure to causes outside their control (Diener & Dweck, 1978; Dweck, 1975; Johnston & Winograd, 1985). Together, these characteristics can be so debilitating as to all but ensure failure on academic tasks and limit career and life options (Johnston, 1985).

Central to metacognitive theory is that students actively participate in the learning process through planning, monitoring, and recovering (Armbruster, Echols, & Brown, 1984; Harter, 1982). Learning disabled students are often described as inactive learners who fail to use efficient, organized strategies (Johnston & Winograd, 1985) and who lack self-knowledge about the nature of their disability, its limitations, and general strategies for coping with their disability (Licht, 1983).

Attribution theory (e.g., Covington & Omelich, 1979; Weiner, 1979) suggests that a student's performance on a task is influenced by his/her perceptions of the causes of past behavior. Researchers investigating attributions made by students in learning situations (Butkowsky & Willows, 1980; Diener & Dweck, 1978) have found that students who attribute their performance to a stable, controllable factor (such as effort) maintain their effort in the face of failure, while those who attribute performance to uncontrollable factors (such as luck, the task, the teacher, ability) are likely to show deterioration of effort in the face of failure.

This study investigated the extent to which these characteristics applied to a unique population of successful learning disabled college students. This paper presents selected findings from four case studies designed to determine how juniors and seniors in college, who had been identified in high school as learning disabled, managed to persist. Attributional and metacognitive theories were the frameworks used to guide the development and selection of interview questions and stimuli for obtaining verbal reports.

METHOD

Subjects

Junior and senior level college students who had been diagnosed as learning disabled were recruited for the investigation. Students were required to document their disability with high school records. Selection procedures resulted in a pool of five students, four of whom were chosen, three juniors and one senior. Junior or senior level status was used as the criterion for persistence. The fifth student was eliminated because he did not meet this criterion. All four subjects were currently holding a "C" average or better in their academic coursework.

Of the four students selected, one was female and three were male. The following disabilities and behavioral characteristics were taken directly from the documentation provided by the students: (a) all were described as possessing difficulties with memory (i.e., unable to recall information presented visually or orally); (b) three with writing (i.e., difficulties with handwriting, spelling, and composition); (c) two of the males had attention disorders (i.e., distractable, unable to focus on a task, and hyperactive); and (d) all possessed some form of social/emotional difficulty (i.e., inappropriate feelings of anger and resentment toward teachers and peers, and anxiety). All of the subjects had received special education services in high school; none had been involved in special education services at the college level. One male subject was continuing drug therapy for hyperactivity.

Materials and Procedure

Each subject met with the researchers for a total of three one-hour sessions. In the first session, interview data were collected. Sessions two and three were primarily devoted to obtaining verbal reports on reading comprehension and summarizing strategies. The verbal report methodology is gaining acceptance as a valid data source (Afflerbach, 1986; Afflerbach & Johnston, 1984; Johnston, 1985).

Two college level passages of similar length from the *Advanced Reading Inventory* (Johns, 1984) were used. With the first text, "The American" (238 words), subjects were directed to read aloud and report on the processes they used for constructing an interpretation of the text. Subjects were asked to stop after each sentence and report on their processes, although they could verbalize any time. With the second text, "Beards" (250 words), subjects were asked to construct a written summary and verbalize thought processes while constructing the summary.

Transcriptions from these sessions yielded over 250 pages of data. A complete record of all interview and verbal report data cannot be presented here; therefore, we included only those excerpts that represent similar statements made on at least two occasions by all subjects.

RESULTS AND DISCUSSION

Text Processing Strategies: Evidence of Metacomprehension

Word attack strategies. When the readers encountered an unfamiliar word or phrase, they made extensive use of their general knowledge and the context in order to figure it out. In this way, our learning disabled college readers were characteristic of good comprehenders who use context-driven strategies as much as possible in constructing interpretations of the text (Baker & Brown, 1984).

> Example 1: Divan—I don't know what that is. How would I try to figure it out? Um, well I'm definitely looking at the context because that's the only thing that's going to give me the clue. Somewhat it looks like it's a—he is in a reclining position on this—whatever it is. I would say he's relaxing and looking up, it seems like he's on a soft chair or couch or something.

For the words which were impossible to figure out through framing them in context, some readers combined a form of phonics or word-part analysis to facilitate word recognition. This combination of strategies is consistent with mature reading (Holdaway, 1979).

> Example 2: As-ker-ist, no, yeah, asterisk. That's the little star, asterisk sign, um, it doesn't look familiar but once I sounded it out, um, when I heard it it make sense to me.
>
> Example 3: Um, atomy sorta sounds like autonomy, so I figure that it was talking about the body.

Making use of text structure cues. Efforts to understand and learn from reading material will be aided if one is able to recognize and capitalize on any structure in the text (Meyer, Brandt, & Bluth, 1980). Text structure cues are often signaled by the repetition of words, phrases, and concepts. Good readers can use their textual schemata or general knowledge of conventions of discourse to help them determine important ideas in a text (Afflerbach, 1986; Anderson, Pichert, & Shirey, 1983). Our readers exhibited knowledge and use of text structure cues.

> Example 4: Well, I'm going to go on and see if it was mentioned again or described in more detail, you know, mentioned again someplace. And if it's mentioned again I would get a better grasp of what is meant.

Use of prior knowledge. The ability to activate appropriate prior knowledge during reading is an important metacognitive component of sophisticated reading (Spiro, 1979). Our readers made extensive use of their prior knowledge for understanding the passages.

> Example 5: Well, this is just a, um, "a new kind of arithmetic," that is a, that's a monkey wrench in the whole sentence because Raphael, Titian and Rubins are all artists. How do I know that? Because of general knowledge. It's a monkey wrench because arithmetic is the antithesis of art, you know, that's what I think.

Strategic learning. Mature reading involves modifying strategies to suit goals and purposes (Gray, 1917; Rothkopf & Billington, 1979) and knowing when remedial action is necessary (Alessi, Anderson, & Goetz, 1979). The learning disabled subjects often verbalized an understanding of the importance of using different approaches to processing the text relative to their goals.

Example 6: If this was an English class and I had to know specific dates and specific, um, you know, like writer's style or something, I'd sure go back on it, but if I was reading this for a different type of class, I'd probably—for leisure reading I'd whip right through it, you know, like right now I'd say for leisure reading I would have a grasp.

Macrorules for Summarizing Text

Recently, Brown and her associates (Brown & Day, 1983; Brown & Palincsar, 1982) and others (Torgesen, 1982; Weiner, 1983; Wong, in press) have proposed that learning disabled readers and poor college readers are unable to employ effective macroprocesses for summarizing text. Competent readers, on the other hand, perform macroprocesses of deletion and generalization for determining important information in text and deriving gists (Kintsch & van Dijk, 1978). We found evidence that our learning disabled college readers could successfully use the macroprocesses of deletion and generalization in summarizing text and determining important ideas.

Example 7 (Deletion):
You need to understand the gist first—then I read this short paragraph, this two-sentence paragraph and it doesn't add anything startling or new to what I already know, so I can skip that paragraph and get more information from this first one and last one.

Example 8 (Generalization):
I'm going to see which ones are similar and then group them. In the last paragraph they said two or three different situations but were similar, like king of France and Spain and the Queen of England. They also had similar effects on the people who were wearing beards, so maybe I will summarize it by saying royalty said this—instead of saying the queen said this and the Spanish king said this and the French king said this.

Self-awareness: Attribution Patterns and Coping Strategies

Attributions. Attribution theory posits that learning disabled students tend to see their success and failure as caused by factors beyond their control (Diener & Dweck, 1978, 1980). The students we interviewed often assigned uncontrollable factors such as teachers, the task (ease or difficulty), and luck as causes for their academic successes and failures.

Example 9: Teachers have failed me.
Example 10: I had a high school math teacher that liked me, he . . . got me through.
Example 11: My success so far is due to luck . . . it's catching up with me now, though.
Example 12: I have problems reading because the textbook isn't clear.
Example 13: If I don't understand a math problem it's because they're too difficult.

Our subjects also saw themselves as lacking ability, a very stable, uncontrollable attribution (Covington, Spratt, & Omelich, 1980). This perception has been linked with the phenomenon of learned helplessness, a maladaptive behavior pattern in which students who repeatedly encounter failure become inactive learners and view themselves as failures in academic contexts in general (Diener and Dweck, 1978).

Example 14: I see it as stuff I wasn't born with.
Example 15: I'm not smart.
Example 16: There's not a lot I can do to change myself.

However, our findings regarding the students' global self-perceptions were revealing. While it is true that they saw themselves as lacking ability in their deficit areas, the perception was not transferred to their academic self-concepts in general. That is, they were each able to speak confidently about a skill area in which they excelled.

Example 17: I am very good in art.
Example 18: Math is no problem for me.
Example 19: I'm really good at assembly language, programming.
Example 20: I've become a good speaker.

We can assume, therefore, that any potentially debilitating effects of seeing oneself as helpless with regard to one aspect of academic performance does not, at least for these students, preclude the possibility of a healthy global self-concept.

It has been demonstrated in recent attributional literature that when introduced to failure, learning disabled students have been found to decrease their effort on a task and avoid similar learning situations in the future (Diener & Dweck, 1978, 1980). We found it significant that the learning disabled students we interviewed tended not to be passive, inactive learners. Nor did they decrease their effort in the face of failure. Instead these students tended to persist in their efforts, in spite of continued depressed affect and negative feelings associated with their failure. Statements that follow demonstrate this intention to keep going:

Example 21: You just keep at it.
Example 22: I just work real hard.
Example 23: I keep going with what works.
Example 24: Just keep hammering away.
Example 25: I suppose I'm stubborn, if I weren't, I wouldn't be here.

Thus, despite feelings of helplessness and lack of control in their disability areas, these students stated that persistence was a major reason for their successes.

Coping strategies. It is clear that the students with whom we spoke would not continue to persist if they were merely exposing their most vulnerable areas again and again in the classroom. We reasoned that there must be other characteristics that separate them from their unsuccessful disabled peers. Indeed, throughout the course of the interview process, our subjects described several strategies that they routinely used for coping with the academic demands of college.

1. *Utilize strengths.* Each of the students was able to talk enthusiastically about a skill that was enjoyable, required less effort, and brought them feelings of success. Similarly, each was pursuing a program of study that related at least indirectly to the favored skill area. One student described his most successful learning as involving "touching, doing, seeing" and was enrolled in a program in industrial education. Similarly, a student, whose self-identified strengths lay in art, was pursuing a degree

in the field. And another who preferred math over reading was finishing a degree in computer science.

2. *Limit the use of the deficit area.* Each subject was able to clearly and consistently describe the nature of their learning disability, and each made statements emphasizing the necessity of working around the deficit area. This was true despite differences in the nature of each disability. For instance, one student whose disability included hyperactivity, which made it difficult to study for long periods of time without extreme frustration, gave us one of his strategies for coping: "Most often is, I just put it down and come back to it. A lot of tasks seem big all at once but if you break them down and make small hunks out of it, a little at a time it gets done." In contrast, a subject whose greatest difficulty was writing, especially term papers, told us: "I avoid classes that involve lots of writing . . . anything to avoid failure is positive." Another subject simply put it this way: "I have to find a creative way to get around it [the disability]."

3. *Get help.* Although the preceding strategies have been useful to these students, there have unfortunately been instances when they were of no use. In these cases our subjects offered one answer unanimously: get help, and get it early. Each subject sought a tutor or mentor, someone who did more than read their papers or reviewed math homework and who also provided guidance and personal attention. One student stated: "I need someone who can give me instant rewards, or at least instant feedback so I can try it again." Another student described his fear of not finding the kind of help he needs: "I'm . . . afraid to go away (to college) again. People could take advantage of me. Having a good relationship with a teacher is a very high priority for me." One of our subjects described her experience in high school with a person who helped her as "Mostly an experience in organizing my life and values." Thus, for our students, a helping person is much more than one who simply bolsters weak skill areas; he or she clearly provides emotional support as well.

SUMMARY

Taken together, the metacognitive and attributional literature offers little hope of academic success for learning disabled students. They are characterized by their inability to use organized, sophisticated learning strategies, their low expectations for success, and their lack of persistence in the face of failure. Yet, for our unique group of four students, we discovered that in spite of their disabilities they have found ways to surmount these formidable barriers to learning. Their success appears to be attributable to sound reading skills, and a range of strategies for exploiting their strengths and coping with their disabilities.

While we strongly endorse early detection and remediation, alternatives must be considered for students who have been provided unsuccessful instruction or whose learning disabilities have gone undetected beyond the early grades. Although this exploratory study should be regarded as tentative, given the limited number of subjects interviewed, the results suggest that LD students can succeed. Therefore, we strongly urge that future research examine the value of training high school and college learning disabled students to (a) become more self-aware not only in terms of their reading and learning processes but also about the nature of their disabilities, (b) eliminate unrealistic expectations in deficit areas, (c) become personally responsible for learning outcomes by developing healthy, internal attributions for academic success and failure, and (d) exploit their strengths, and develop appropriate coping strategies for their disabilities.

REFERENCES

Afflerbach, P. (1986). The influence of prior knowledge on expert readers' importance assignment processes. In J. Niles & R. Lalik (Eds.), *Solving problems in literacy: Learners, teachers, and researchers* (pp. 30-40). Thirty-fifth Yearbook of the National Reading Conference. Rochester, NY: National Reading Conference.

Afflerbach, P., & Johnston, P. (1984). On the use of verbal reports in reading research. *Journal of Reading Behavior, 16,* 307-322.

Alessi, S. M., Anderson, T. H., & Goetz, E. T. (1979). An investigation of lookbacks during studying. *Discourse Processes, 2,* 197-212.

Armbruster, B. B., Echols, C. H., & Brown, A. L. (1984). The role of metacognition in reading to learn: A developmental perspective. *The Volta Review, 84,* 45-55.

Anderson, R., Pichert, J., & Shirey, L. (1983). Effects of readers' schema at different points in time. *Journal of Educational Psychology, 75,* 271-279.

Baker, L., & Brown, A. L. (1984). Cognitive monitoring in reading. In J. Flood (Ed.), *Understanding reading comprehension* (pp. 21-44). Newark, DE: International Reading Association.

Brown, A. L., & Day, J. (1983). Macrorules for summarizing texts: The development of expertise. *Journal of Verbal Learning and Verbal Behavior, 22,* 1-14.

Brown, A. L., & Palincsar, A. (1982). Inducing strategic learning from texts by means of informed, self-control training. *Topics in Learning and Learning Disabilities, 2,* 1-17.

Butkowsky, I., & Willows, D. (1980). Cognitive-motivational characteristics of children varying in reading ability: Evidence for learned helplessness in poor readers. *Journal of Educational Psychology, 72,* 408-422.

Covington, M., & Omelich, C. (1979). Effort: The double-edged sword in school achievement. *Journal of Educational Psychology, 71,* 169-182.

Covington, M., Spratt, M., & Omelich, C. (1980). Is effort enough or does diligence count too? Student and teacher reactions to effort stability in failure. *Journal of Educational Psychology, 72,* 717-729.

Diener, C., & Dweck, C. (1978). An analysis of learned helplessness: Continuous changes in performance, strategy, and achievement cognitions following failure. *Journal of Personality and Social Psychology, 34,* 451-462.

Diener, C., & Dweck, C. (1980). An analysis of learned helplessness: II. The processing of success. *Journal of Personality and Social Psychology, 36,* 940-952.

Dweck, C. (1975). The role of expectancies and attributions in the alleviation of learned helplessness. *Journal of Personality and Social Psychology, 31,* 674-685.

Gray, C. T. (1917). Types of reading ability as exhibited through tests and laboratory experiments. *Supplemental Educational Monographs, 5.* Chicago: University of Chicago.

Harter, S. (1982). A developmental perspective on some parameters of self-regulation in children. In P. Karoly & F. Kanfer (Eds.), *Self-management and behavior change: From theory to practice* (pp. 165-204). New York: Pergamon.

Holdaway, D. (1979). *The foundations of literacy.* New York: Ashton Scholastic.

Johns, J. L. (1984). *Advanced reading inventory.* Dubuque, IA: Wm. C. Brown.

Johnston, P. (1985). Understanding reading disability: A case study approach. *Harvard Educational Review, 55,* 153-177.

Johnston, P., & Winograd, P. (1985). Passive failure in reading. *Journal of Reading Behavior, 17,* 279-301.

Kintsch, W., & van Dijk, T. (1978). Toward a model of text comprehension and production. *Psychological Review, 85,* 363-394.

Licht, B. (1983). Cognitive-motivational factors that contribute to the achievement of learning disabled children. *Journal of Learning Disabilities, 16,* 483-490.

Meyer, B., Brandt, D., & Bluth, G. (1980). Use of top-level structure in text: Key for reading comprehension of ninth grade students. *Reading Research Quarterly, 15,* 72-103.

Rothkopf, E., & Billington, M. (1979). Goal-guided learning from text: Inferring a descriptive processing model from inspection times and eye movements. *Journal of Educational Psychology, 71,* 310-327.

Spiro, R. (1979). Etiology of reading comprehension styles. In M. Kamil & A. Moe (Eds.), *Reading research: Studies and applications* (pp. 118-122). Twenty-eighth Yearbook of the National Reading Conference. Clemson, SC: National Reading Conference.

Torgesen, J. (1982). The learning disabled child as an inactive learner. *Topics in Learning and Learning Disabilities, 2,* 45-52.

Weiner, B. (1979). A theory of motivation for some classroom experiences. *Journal of Educational Psychology, 71,* 3-25.

Weiner, B. (1983). Speculations regarding the role of affect in achievement change programs guided by attributional principles. In J. Levine & M. Wang (Eds.), *Teacher and student perceptions: Implications for learning* (pp. 57-74). Hillsdale, NJ: Erlbaum.

Wong, B. (in press). Metacognition and learning disabilities. In T. Waller, D. Forest, & E. MacKinnon (Eds.), *Metacognition, cognition, and human performance.* New York: Academic Press.

ASSESSMENT

EMERGENT LITERACY

COMPREHENSION

INSTRUCTIONAL EFFECTIVENESS

ADULT LITERACY

WRITING

WRITING IN CONSTRAINED GENRES: PUSHING THE LIMITS OF WRITING MODELS

Gary M. Schumacher, Byron T. Scott, George R. Klare, and Frank C. Cronin
Ohio University

Wendy Schweigert
Plymouth State College

Ronald J. Foos
Ohio University

The current interest in writing development and writing instruction has led to extensive research on writing processes. As the results of this research activity have become available, there has been a growing press to create models and theories which capture the essence of this work. Thus, we have developmental models emphasizing writing as an information-relating or knowledge-telling process (Scardamalia & Bereiter, 1982); models of subprocesses in writing such as the revision processes (Flower, Hayes, Carey, Schriver, & Stratman, 1986) and general models of the cognitive processes involved in writing (Flower & Hayes, 1981). Generally, the models of adult writing seem to concur on some of the major characteristics of writing; that is, writing is viewed as being a problem-solving activity, as being recursive and nonlinear, and as involving extensive planning and goal-setting activities.

Unfortunately, as Schumacher, Klare, and Scott (1985) have noted, the large majority of the work upon which the models and theories of writing are based represents a quite limited range of writing genres—mainly expository and narrative genres. It is rare to find extensive work on other genres such as letters, advertising copy, news stories, business reports, poetry, editorials, and music. It is possible that this restriction in genres has led to a constrained understanding of the cognitive processes involved in writing. It is, therefore, unclear whether the current models of writing based on this research will generalize to other writing genres and writing conditions. One particular concern arises because of the relatively few restrictions which are imposed on the writer by expository and narrative genres. These genres allow for a substantial latitude of approach by the writer, thus necessitating wide ranging and possibly highly varied decisions during writing. In contrast, more constrained genres may change the nature of the cognitive processes appreciably, perhaps resulting in different patterns or types of cognitive processes. It would be fruitful, therefore, to investigate writing genres of differing levels of constraints so the effects of these constraints can be understood.

One area that offers much promise is journalism, for it includes a wide variety of genres. Some of the journalistic genres involve many specific constraints while others involve few and relatively nonspecifc constraints. Genres in the former category include news stories and obituaries. News stories, for example, are highly structured genres involving the *inverted pyramid* form. In this form the first lines contain the summary lead which includes the most important information in the story. This is followed by paragraphs dealing with less and less important information (Izard, Culbertson, & Lambert, 1977).

In contrast, journalistic genres in the less constrained category include editorials and feature stories. Editorials, for example, may refer to facts, but the major purpose is not to introduce them to the reader. Instead, the editorial involves a persuasive explanation of the writer's point of view. The style thus is much less restricted than the news story and may necessitate greater concern with how to present a case in the most convincing manner (Alexander, 1975).

Schumacher et al. (1985) tested the effects of different types of journalistic genres to see if the processes writers used were the same. They monitored the cognitive processes of journalism students from advanced undergraduate journalism classes as they produced news stories or editorials based on one of two fact sheets. One fact sheet dealt with the theft of a police car by an intoxicated man and the other involved a strike by mine construction workers. The subjects produced their papers during a 30-minute time period on a typewriter placed in a special platform. The platform had a sheet of semisilvered glass placed about six inches above the keyboard. With appropriate lighting this glass appeared transparent. This apparatus was similar to that used by Schumacher, Klare, Cronin, and Moses (1984). A videotape camera recorded the developing paper *through* the glass and a reflection of the writer's face *from* the glass.

After completing their writing, the subjects reviewed the videotape with the experimenter. The videotape machine was linked to a set of timers so that all writing pauses could be timed. If subjects paused for five seconds or longer, they were asked to indicate which of 19 different cognitive activities they were carrying out. The list, used previously in a slightly different form by Schumacher et al. (1984), described the activities and, for each activity, gave two examples of the kinds of questions subjects might have asked themselves during writing.

Schumacher et al. (1985) reported that news story writers paused more often and showed more cognitive activities per writing session than did editorial writers. In contrast, the subjects who were writing editorials had marginally longer pauses than subjects writing news stories. They suggested that the greater number of pauses may have been related to the tight constraints of the news story genre. The fact that some of the major categories reported more frequently by the news story group were *standards, evaluation,* and *sound* supports this interpretation. In contrast, the lower use of these same categories and the marginally longer pauses by the subjects writing editorials suggested a more open-ended task. Editorial writers seemed less concerned with determining whether a particular format was being followed than did news story writers, but this more open format appeared to require more time to reach decisions.

Unfortunately, the pausal technique used by Schumacher et al. (1985) provides only limited support for this interpretation since it only indicated the length of pauses and the general categories of activities (e.g., global planning, planning to say, reviewing the content) which subjects reported doing in the two writing conditions. This technique was not sensitive to strategies or heuristics which the writers employed while writing. The purpose of the present study was to investigate more specifcally the strategies subjects used in writing tasks involving varying levels of constraints.

METHOD

Subjects

Eight students from a senior level writing class in a university journalism school served as subjects. All the subjects had taken prior journalism classes and all were trained to write on typewriters. The subjects were divided into two groups of four students—a pausal interview group and a protocol group. The subjects in the pausal interview group (three female, one male) described their activities during each pause of at least five seconds; the subjects in the protocol group (three female, one male) talked aloud while doing their writing.

Materials

Two types of materials were used during the study. The first provided the writing assignment and facts for the subjects. All subjects were given either a fact sheet describing a theft of a police car by an intoxicated man or a fact sheet describing a strike by mine construction workers. The second provided a list of cognitive activities which judges used in describing what writers were doing during pauses in writing. This list was the same as used by Schumacher et al. (1985) and included the following 19 categories (in the random order in which they were presented to the subjects in that study): support, illustrations, sentence structure, standards, reorganizing, sound, evaluation, spelling, planning to do, reviewing the content, punctuation and capitalization, planning to say, mood, reviewing own experience, transitions, word choice, reviewing the assignment, global planning, and effect on reader. The apparatus used for the study was the same as that used by Schumacher et al. (1985). It included a special platform which had a sheet of semisilvered glass mounted about six inches above a typewriter keyboard. With appropriate lighting, the glass was transparent to the writer. A videotape camera recorded the developing paper through the glass and a reflection of the writer's face from the glass.

Procedure

Subjects came individually to the testing room and were randomly assigned to either the pausal interview group or the protocol group. Subjects in both groups were told that their writing would be recorded, that they would not have to have a finished paper by the end of the writing session, and that the experimenter would leave the room while they wrote to avoid disturbing them. Half the subjects in each group were asked to write an editorial and half a news story on whichever fact sheet they received. Subjects in the pausal interview study were seated in front of the writing platform and told that they would have 30 minutes to write their paper. After giving these subjects their instructions and fact sheet, the experimenter started the videotape and left the room. The experimenter returned after 30 minutes, rewound the videotape, and gave further instructions. The subjects were asked for their help in telling in as much detail as possible what they had been thinking at each pause in their writing (i.e., periods during which they were not producing text) which lasted five seconds or longer during the writing session that had been completed earlier. The subjects had their written paper available as they reviewed the tape showing the developing paper and their facial expressions and eye movements. Subjects in the protocol group were told that they had 45 minutes to write their papers. They were given more time than the pausal interview subjects since they had to talk as they wrote. The protocol subjects were given standard protocol instructions. Specifically, they were told to say everything aloud that they read, wrote, or thought, no matter how unimportant they thought it might be. They were also given a brief practice period on another writing assignment before they were given the experimental task to make them feel more comfortable with the task. After the practice period was completed, the subjects were given the assignment and the fact sheet. The experimenter started the videotape machine and left the room. After the writing period was complete, the experimenter returned to the room and dismissed the subject.

Scoring. The verbal comments from both the pausal interview and protocol conditions were transcribed. For the pausal interview transcripts, the comments reported by subjects about each pause lasting at least five seconds were treated as one scoring unit. Two judges coded these comments into the 19 different cognitive activity categories described above. The average coding reliability was 92.6%. In addition, the judges looked for comments describing strategies and processes used by the subjects in completing the two writing tasks. For the protocol subjects, three judges reviewed the transcripts independently for global strategies and processes used by the subjects.

RESULTS AND DISCUSSION

Schumacher et al. (1985) reported results indicating that subjects writing news stories carried out more activities per writing session than did subjects writing editorials. They suggested that this greater number of activities may have been related to the tight constraints of the news story genre. The subjects writing news stories in the pausal interview condition in this study again were found to carry out more activities per writing session than did those in the editorial condition (177 vs. 145, respectively). The difference in category use was especially prominent in the categories found to be more heavily used by the news story writers than the editorial writers in Schumacher et al. (1985). In particular, the categories of *sound, standards, evaluation, reviewing the assignment, reorganizing,* and *planning to do* were used 72 times by the news story writers but only 48 times by the editorial writers.

In addition, analyses of the pausal interview comments and the protocols indicated that the subjects writing news stories operated with a very different set of strategies, assumptions, and processes than those writing editorials. News story writers used a highly constrained, preorganized, genre-controlled strategy. The major elements of this strategy were as follows:

1. the use of a preorganized structure into which information was inserted.
2. the use of a priority list of information to determine the order of mention of information.
3. the use of a tight set of linguistic and rhetorical constraints.
4. a considerable concern with accuracy.

Each of these elements is considered in greater detail with supporting evidence drawn from the analyses of the pausal interviews and the protocols.

Preorganized structure. News story writers appeared to have a well-detailed schema for the organization of news stories and the writing of such a story was very much like instantiating a schema. Some of the properties of the news story schema included a lead sentence which summarized the story, a necessity for frequent direct quotes, and a pattern for less important information to be listed in later paragraphs in the story. This interpretation is supported by the fact that news story writers rarely considered structural issues in their protocol observations. The following observations from news story writers show the flavor of the news story task and show the similarity of this task to schema instantiation: "It's just like a puzzle you build—its got to all fit"; and "It was time for a good quote to break up the copy." Observations such as these were not found in the editorial protocols.

Use of a priority list. The use of a preorganized structure reduced the need for extensive consideration of structural issues in writing news stories. As a consequence, some of the problem-solving flavor which is normally seen as writers struggle with organizational issues disappeared in the news story writers. However, another type of problem arose for these writers—namely, which information fit in which location in the news story schema. To handle this problem, news story writers seemed to have had some internal priority list which aided them in making these decisions. Three elements of this priority list abstracted from the pausal interviews and protocols are indicated below; protocol and interview segments supporting these elements are indicated.

1. Personal injury is a high priority issue.
   "Were these kids hurt? And the answer was obviously, if they were injured, that would be more significant, which would be newsworthy, which would, which would fall higher up in the story."
2. Names and addresses need to be included but they are less important.
   "I remember I wanted to be sure I had, uh, presented the people in a good way, and that I has put their names, addresses and cities, I wasn't sure that was so important . . ."
3. Reasons for actions should be presented early in a story.
   ". . . it would help if I put the reason why they striked [sic] up higher and reiterate it so it would be more understandable to the reader."

Existence of tight linguistic and rhetorical constraints. News story writers operated under a set of tight linguistic and rhetorical constraints many of which are specified in the Associated Press and United Press International style books. Observations derived from the protocols and interviews indicated that a substantial number of these were operative when subjects were writing news stories. Five specific types of these constraints are noted below with specific observations from the pausal interviews and protocols of news story writers showing their use.

1. Use active voice.
   "I wanted to be sure I was in the active not the passive voice."
2. Use agreed-upon punctuation and capitalization conventions.
   "I was wondering about my capitalization, whether if the title in front of the name should get capitalized . . ."
3. Use only appropriate abbreviations.
   ". . . here I decided I should spell it out so I circled it."
4. Be interesting.
   "I have to start with an interesting lead so I don't bore the reader."
5. Present a balanced view to the reader.
   "This article sounds kind of one-sided to me."

The character of the first three elements of the news story strategy seemed aimed at allowing the writer to write with increased speed in order to meet the tight time constraints frequently imposed on journalistic writers. The fourth element of this strategy appeared to serve a different function.

Concern for accuracy. News story writers showed a considerable concern that the information presented in the story be accurate. This appeared to be related to the function of news stories as conveyors of information. The concern for accuracy may be linked to concerns about litigation but, for whatever reason, that concern was commonly expressed in comments in the pausal interview and protocols such as the following:

1. "You know you have to be accurate, accurate, accurate."
2. "It's the key, you've got to be accurate."

Comments such as these were not found in the editorial condition.

In contrast to the news story writers, the editorial writers did not have as clear a strategy to draw on for their writing. This resulted in greater wrestling by the editorial writers in the early portions of the writing periods with structural issues as seen in the following interview and protocol excerpts:

1. "I was thinking about the structure of it. I wasn't sure whether or not, like in the first paragraph to give a brief overview."
2. "First of all, (its) unnatural for me to deal with an editorial like this."

These types of observations were not made by the news story writers, even though they were still in a training program for journalists. In lieu of the tightly organized writing structure used by the news story subjects, the editorial subjects appeared to adopt one of two strategies. The first was to treat the editorial as a news story with a tag opinion paragraph as seen in the following observation from an editorial subject:

"I did give a brief overview of exactly what happened."

Subjects using this strategy basically wrote a news story and then added their ideas and opinions about the topic. This had the advantage of drawing on a well-known genre by analogy. The second strategy for handling the editorial was to search for some aspect of the story which could be made personal to the writer. As one writer expressed it, "I was trying to think of some way to make it personal." This approach seems to be linked to a somewhat simple view of an editorial as a set of personal beliefs about a given topic. Nevertheless, it did serve the purpose of providing an initial approach to the writing task.

Although the results reported here were based on a small number of subjects drawn from one journalism school, they fit very well with those reported by Schumacher et al. (1985). The tight constraints noted in the news story condition in the pausal interview and protocol groups necessitated constant monitoring to determine if these constraints were being met. This resulted in numerous pauses by the writer during which a number of issues were checked to determine if all aspects of the constraints were being met. Thus, subjects might be checking to determine if they were using the active voice consistently, if their facts were accurate, if a quote should go at the current spot, if a particular fact should occur at this spot or another, or whether all facts had been covered. An increased number of pauses and more activities were the specific findings reported by Schumacher et al. (1985). Editorial subjects, in contrast, lacking the tight constraints of the news story genre, may need longer time periods to consider these organizational issues. Schumacher et al. (1985) reported marginally longer pauses by the editorial subjects.

What implications do these findings have for the existing models of the writing process? These results tend to suggest that the general cognitive processes model of writing as proposed by Flower and Hayes (1981) may be best characterized as a generic model of writing. That is, this model appears to be descriptive of writing primarily when subjects are unfamiliar with or unpracticed on a writing task, or the task is one in which the constraints are very loose allowing the writer a number of options. This would be the case in genres dealing with exposition or narration. However, in genres presenting tight constraints such as news stories, letters of recommendation, and case reports, writers may develop highly detailed knowledge structures which guide much of the writing process. These detailed knowledge structures allow for faster writing; in these cases the writing process takes on much of the character of highly automated cognitive tasks. A complete writing model must take this type of writing into account.

REFERENCES

Alexander, L. (1975). *Beyond the facts: A guide to the art of feature writing.* Houston, TX: Gulf Publishing.

Flower, L., & Hayes, J. R. (1981). A cognitive process theory of writing. *College Composition and Communication, 32,* 365-387.

Flower, L., Hayes, J. R., Carey, L., Schriver, K., & Stratman, J. (1986). Detection, diagnosis, and strategies of revision. *College Composition and Communication, 37,* 16-55.

Izard, R. S., Culbertson, H. M., & Lambert, D. S. (1977). *Fundamentals of news reporting* (3rd ed.). Dubuque, IA: Kendall/Hunt.

Scardamalia, M., & Bereiter, C. (1982). Assimilative processes in composition planning. *Educational Psychologist, 17,* 165-171.

Schumacher, G. M., Klare, G. R., Cronin, F. C., & Moses, J. D. (1984). Cognitive activities of beginning and advanced college writers: A pausal analysis. *Research in the Teaching of English, 18,* 169-187.

Schumacher, G. M., Klare, G. R., & Scott, B. T. (1985, April). *Writing genre: Its influence on writing process.* Paper presented at the annual meeting of the American Educational Research Association, Chicago.

THE RELATIONSHIP BETWEEN TEACHERS' BELIEFS AND INSTRUCTION AND STUDENTS' CONCEPTIONS ABOUT THE WRITING PROCESS

Kathleen L. Fear, Linda M. Anderson, Carol Sue Englert, and Taffy E. Raphael
Michigan State University

Current research in writing has focused on the writing process itself (e.g., Flower & Hayes, 1981), on students' knowledge about the writing process (e.g., Raphael, Kirschner, & Englert, 1986), and on instruction in writing (e.g., Applebee & Langer, 1984). However, little research has been conducted that describes relationships between and differences in teachers' and students' underlying assumptions and conceptions about the writing process.

This study was conducted as part of a three-year project, Cognitive Strategy Instruction in Writing (Englert, Raphael, & Anderson, 1985). The purpose of the current study was to focus on the relationship among teachers' beliefs about writing, their instructional practice, and their students' beliefs about writing and their writing performance. Examining student beliefs provides an important source of information for documenting teacher effects. For example, Rohrkemper (1984) found that students' perceptions of schooling and self-perceptions are strongly influenced by teachers' beliefs and behaviors. Further, Anderson and Smith (1983) found that less effective teachers were unaware of and did nothing to address students' preconceptions. That is, less effective teachers provided infrequent opportunities for the identification of student (mis)conceptions, resulting in little or no action on the part of these teachers to modify their instruction. This is particularly relevant in light of the potentially debilitating effects of students' misconceptions on their learning and comprehension. This effect has been demonstrated in content area reading (Roth, 1985) and in general comprehension of text (Maria & MacGinitie, 1981). Thus, it is important to identify the potential effects of teachers' instructional beliefs on the formation of students' beliefs about writing and their own abilities as writers.

In the present study, we examined the relationship between two teachers' instructional styles and belief systems as inferred from observational data and from teachers' self-reports, respectively, and their influence on students' perceptions of writing. Two disparate belief systems (structuralism and post-structuralism) were adapted from literary theory (Eagleton, 1983). Teachers with a structural perspective interpret writing instruction as a process of informing the writer of formal rules, procedures and strategies that can be decontextualized from the writing process without regard for purpose or audience. Instruction within this view tends to be didactic (e.g., lecture or declaratives predominant in the teachers' instruction, with evaluation of student composition based on comparisons with expert models). Thus, teachers within this perspective tend to view their role as that of informant.

In contrast, teachers with a post-structural perspective interpret writing instruction as establishing a writing context so that the writer can identify procedures and strategies that fit the context of their writing problem. Formal rules and procedures are questioned in light of purpose and audience. Within this perspective, the mode of instruction is interactive, featuring interrogative dialogue that guides students to understand, question, and select strategies. Thus, a teacher with this perspective tends to view the students' role as that of the informant. The evaluation of the writer's performance focuses on student self-evaluation of strategy use based on the intended writing purpose, writing audience, and the situational context in which students compose.

Prior research suggests that teachers' assumptions about writing and student evaluation produce different effects (Langer, 1985). Therefore, it was hypothesized that teachers who differed in their conceptions of writing, their beliefs about students' control of various aspects of the writing process, and their perceptions of appropriate instructional responses would have students whose beliefs also differed in their perceptions of themselves as writers and their willingness to take control of and monitor the effects of writing strategies.

METHOD

Subjects

From a pool of 16 teachers (eight regular and eight special education) participating in the original study (Englert, Raphael, & Anderson, 1985), two upper elementary regular education teachers were identified who seemed to illustrate very different views of writing. The two teachers taught at the same school, had students from the same population, had similar management styles, similar class sizes, and they both had participated in the same staff development process-writing program. These teachers were identified after five formal observations. The teacher who represented the structural perspective (Teacher S) focused on external standards and form. She exemplified didactic presentation in terms of her stress on teacher-selected topics and in the predominance of declaratives in her teacher dialogue. The second teacher, who exemplified the post-structural perspective (Teacher P), stressed self-evaluation and used interrogatives as a mechanism for introducing students to writing strategies.

From each of the two teachers' classrooms, six students were randomly selected within ability levels for in-depth study. To represent a continuum of ability, two students each were selected from high-achieving, low-achieving, and special education students. The two high-achieving students were randomly selected from students scoring at the 69th percentile and above on the language subtest of the Stanford Achievement Test (1973), the two low-achieving students were selected from students scoring at the 39th percentile and below, and two learning disabled students were selected from students who were receiving part-time special education services in resource rooms for the learning disabled.

Materials

Teacher interview. A teacher interview was developed to evaluate teachers' beliefs and conceptions about writing instruction and their students' abilities. The one-hour interview focused on their writing curriculum, including (a) teachers' writing goals, (b) selection of writing topics, (c) students' writing problems, and (d) instructional responses to high-achieving, low-achieving, and special education writers.

Teacher observation. Prior to the interview, five observations of each teacher were conducted and used to establish differences in instructional syles. These observations included two half-day observations, two observations of writing lessons, and one observation of a content area subject (e.g., social studies). Observations were recorded in narrative form, and specific attention was given to teacher statements or dialogue regarding (a) expectations or attributions for students' success and failure on academic tasks, (b) feedback about individual performance and how progress was defined, (c) procedures that furthered student independence and self-regulation in performing tasks (i.e., think-aloud, emphasis on self-monitoring routines or student control in selecting or monitoring strategy use), (d) selection of content (i.e., writing mechanics, grammar, composition), (e) selection of writing topics (e.g., teacher-selected, child-selected, or textbook-determined), (f) audience for children's writing (e.g., teacher, self, peer, parents), (g) evaluation of children's writing, including teacher dialogue concerning who performs the evaluation (e.g., teacher, self, peer), and the focus of the evaluation (e.g., mechanics, grammar, text structure, vocabulary, etc.), and (h) writing processes (e.g., prewriting, drafting, editing, and revising).

Student interview. A student interview was developed to parallel the teacher interview and portions of the observation instrument. Specifically, the interview tapped students' perceptions of (a) writing goals, (b) selection of writing topics, (c) identification of sources of writing problems, (d) evaluation of written products, and (e) selection/monitoring of writing strategies. This information was gathered by providing students with a series of vignettes that required them to give advice to hypothetical students with various writing problems and concerns.

Student written products. Three writing measures were developed to analyze (a) number of ideas that students were able to generate given a specific text structure, (b) presence of key words and phrases signaling text structure, (c) provision of relevant detail corresponding to the given text structure, and (d) ratings of coherence or logical sequence. These were totaled to provide a *productivity* score.

Procedure

Following the identification of the participating teachers based on observational data about writing instruction, the related teacher interviews were coded and analyzed. First, the two teacher interviews were examined in terms of the eight categories described above. Specific statements from the eight categories were further differentiated as they related to beliefs about instructional goals, characteristics of good and poor writers, identification of appropriate instructional responses to students, and methods for teaching students about topic selection and problem identification. Second, a parallel subset of student interview responses was examined and responses were categorized. Specific questions were analyzed that described types of knowledge about topic selection, strategies for decision-making, sources of information, and methods of evaluating writing products.

Finally, student topic selections were coded as personal versus school-related. Personal topics were defined as any topic and subordinating details that dealt with reports of people, pets, favorite TV characters, and events that were described by students as present in their daily lives. School-related topics were identified as those topics and subordinating details that appeared in the curriculum guide and in the current year's textbook.

Teachers' responses to hypothetical classroom situations and students were coded as declarative and interrogative. Declarative statements were defined as statements that told the students what to do next. Interrogative statements were defined as statements that asked students for further information.

RESULTS

A brief summary of the major findings related to teacher beliefs about writing goals and responses to students is reported first. Then specific teacher beliefs about instructional practices are presented in two areas: topic selection and problem identification. Illustrative comments from the teacher interview are reported to illustrate these teachers' belief systems, followed by representative responses from student interviews to illustrate the potential effects of teachers' perspectives on students' conceptions of the writing process and on their writing performance with specific attention to topic selection and problem identification.

Teacher Beliefs: Writing Goals

Throughout the interviews, both teachers state similar beliefs about the importance of basing writing activities on students' personal experiences and the importance of teaching sentence structure and mechanics. However, their instruction and responses to students take two different forms. Teacher S views her role as informing students of what and how to write by giving them structured rules and algorithms. The following example illustrates how she provides students with structured algorithms to guide their writing, invoking formal rules regarding structure and mechanics: "I use the acronym CUPS. It acts as an editing facility for the child. CUPS, that's C for capitalization, U is usage, P is punctuation, and S is spelling."

On the other hand, Teacher P views her role as helping students to assume an informant role in communicating to their audience by interpreting the writing context and situation. Instead of having stable goals, she emphasized that her goals were situationally specific and sensitive to individual needs. She demonstrates a concern for individual differences and she identifies goals that fit the context of the writing situation. She explains that her goals change ". . . when teaching writing in social studies, math, reading, spelling and poetry, it depends on the lesson and it depends on their (students') mood."

Teacher Beliefs: Writing Responses

When teachers were asked how they respond to students' composition, Teacher S said that she responds to students by emphasizing her evaluation of structure and form that are indicators of expert writing. For example, she described one of her typical responses as "Oh, you had a compound, complex sentence . . . lots of descriptive words . . . Is that what you want to turn in to me?"

Teacher P indicated she asks questions about the meaning of the paper as it will be understood by an expanded audience. She described one of her typical responses as "I will ask them to go back and make sure it makes sense to them. Pretend that they are a neighbor, pretend that they are a friend and a friend is reading the paper . . ." Teacher P was aware that her questions are instrumental in helping students to develop meaning: "I ask questions so often, and they look at me and think, 'Oh no, not again!' But I have a couple kinds of comments that I use that they pick up on, . . . 'This is an *I went to the store, and then I came home story,'* 'How did the character change?,' 'Can you tell me the cartoon you remember this happening in?' " Thus, Teacher P responds to students' written pieces by asking them for information that will improve her and the audience's comprehension of the paper. Throughout the process, she conveys to students that they own the paper and, therefore, need to self-evaluate for effective audience communication.

Instructional Practices: Topic Selection

The two teachers were asked to describe classroom procedures for topic selection. Teacher S preferred to maintain control for selecting writing topics, whether these topics were selected from history or science books: "I just picked the Revolutionary War because that's what we're studying currently. What we teach in social studies is predetermined, not by us. So consequently, I get within an area . . . and I will just brainstorm, pick my own mind . . . and even in science, it's the same kind of thing."

When asked specifically about student-generated topics, Teacher S defined the topic selection task limiting both the time and range of topics from which students may choose. "This can be done in 10 minutes. 'Would you write: . . . three places that you have visited this summer, . . . the names of three animals, . . . three times when you were happy, . . . three times when you were sad.' " Teacher S summarized where students usually get their topics, stating "I usually give it to them."

In contrast, Teacher P's comments suggested that students in her classroom have far greater control over topic selection. For example, she had her students generate a list of ideas that they continually referred to in selecting writing topics: "One of the first things we do is make a list of all the different kinds of things we would like to tell someone about. We keep that list stapled in front of their writing folders. So they have that to refer to. The list comes from their heads."

Teacher P also indicated broader choices for writing topics than those identified by Teacher S. Teacher P emphasized the importance of current events: "I've had some marvelous reports, when Christa McAuliffe was killed in the space shuttle . . . two boys came and said 'We'd like to do a special report on the space shuttle.' I guess I bring in the news quite a bit . . . and I have kids bring it in . . . if someone's interested in learning more about the subject and would like to share it with us." Her emphasis on personal interest is further apparent even in a more constrained writing task. She noted that "(For famous person report . . . I give them a specific outline . . . and they choose the person they want to write on."

Interviews with students suggested a positive relationship between these teachers' belief systems and students' chosen strategies. When Teacher S's students were asked what they wanted to write about, they mentioned 34% fewer ideas than Teacher P's students and they chose school-related topics that a teacher might assign. For example, Dan—a student who won a school-wide award for creative writing—mentioned many interesting topics that he could write about, for example, his evicted relatives and an uncle who "mounts dead fish," but his final selection of a writing topic was the "nine planets in the solar system." Furthermore, when Teacher S's students were asked how to select writing topics, their responses reflected a reliance on external sources, for example, "ask the teacher."

In contrast, Teacher P's students chose personal topics 25% more of the time than Teacher S's students. For example, one student chose to write about his cousins and personal relations. When they were asked how they selected writing topics, they showed a reliance on their personal experience, as typified by one student who responded ". . . by doing things . . . like playing and let's see, by my experience." Students' control over topic selection was especially evident in Corky's response. When he was asked to generate ideas for a compare/contrast paper on Florida and Michigan, he attempted to negotiate with the interviewer to change the topic to Michigan and Texas: "I know about Texas. I like Texas. Everbody I know is there."

One might predict a positive relationship between student control of topic selection and the number of ideas that students included in their papers. Teacher P's students were able to generate 1.5 times the number of ideas generated by students in Teacher S's classroom on three writing measures. When a t test was performed on students' productivity scores, the results showed that the idea units included in students' papers differed in a statistically significant manner, $t(43) = 2.15, p < .05$.

Instructional Practice: Problem Identification

Teachers also were asked to identify writing problems that characterized students in their classroom. Teacher S responded to this question by referring to internal and stable characteristics when she described good and poor writers. For example, her evaluation of good writers—individuals "who are sharp," "think systematically," and "have the mechanics of writing"—not only places stress on the importance of mastery of formal structures or rules but on traits not as amenable to instruction.

Similarly, her assessment of poor writers—children "who don't want to write" or who "have a poor grasp of the English language"—places emphasis on traits acquired outside the school setting. "Poor writers are poor because of a lack of writing. We have bilingual children, so they don't have a real grasp of the English language . . . Children who don't read, who watch TV all the time." She states that her most serious problem is students' "copying word for word."

Good writers, from her perspective are successful because "It's very easy for anyone to do something that they're good at . . . good writers take the time . . . write a lot. I get good students or a sharp child, they think systematically, and they have the mechanics of spelling.''

She mentions that she does not write with students in school because she has limited time: ''. . . you must remember, I have children of my own at home.'' Most of the causes of her problems and her students' problems are located outside the school context.

When Teacher P described poor writers, she identified four problems within the context of the classroom (unorganized, poor readers, inability to ask questions, self-evaluation). Strikingly, her conceptualization of poor writers as students who do not ask questions and who do not self-evaluate conveyed a belief that student self-evaluation and control of writing are important traits that distinguish good from poor writers. ''Poor writers really don't have very many questions. They just kind of think, ask 'Well, is that good enough? . . . What do you think? . . . I don't know if this is very good.' '' Her view of good writers seems based on more internal characteristics: ''My best writers are probably the most thoughtful people, I mean thoughtful of others and thoughtful when we're having discussions. They're the people that raise their hands last . . . they seem to be able to see things in a situation that other children can't see.''

Furthermore, Teacher P writes with her students and questions her own writing with her students. In reporting her classroom discussions with students, she again emphasized the importance of student control of learning rather than dependence on the teacher for answers. She stated, ''I just tell them that teachers don't know everything, and that they have to know where to find the information quickly, and that's one of the best things they can do.''

Not surprisingly, students in the two classrooms differed markedly in their diagnosis of and responses to writing problems. Teacher S's students were reliant on external criteria or formal structures when they were asked to prescribe strategies for students with difficulties. For example, as did their teacher, they mentioned mnemonics such as ''CUPS'' to aid them in writing. Similarly, they referred to the teacher or other external criteria (e.g., page length) in making decisions about how much to write and when or why they should rewrite first drafts. Seldom did self-evaluation appear in their dialogue, and Teacher S's students did not refer to internal standards or criteria in determining the completeness or adequacy of papers. Typically, students stated, ''I write until I get to the bottom of the page . . .'' ''I draft to complete assignments . . .,'' ''recopy for the teacher,'' or ''. . . draft in case the teacher loses my paper.''

In contrast, Teacher P's students referred to internal standards such as purposes that addressed the needs of the audience. Teacher P's students were aware of their own writing problems, for example, ''I have trouble with writing about Florida because I've never been there. I need more experience. I need to know more.'' In such cases, the dialogue of Teacher P's students suggested that they were more aware of knowing both what they knew and what they needed to know. They were more capable of conducting a self-analysis and prescribing writing strategies to overcome their perceived deficiencies.

DISCUSSION

The structural and post-structural perspectives are used to examine the relationship between teachers' beliefs about instructional practice and their students' beliefs about the writing process. The teacher representing the structural perspective focused on declarative statements and questions that directed students to focus on decontextualized external criteria to evaluate writing products. Her responses were evaluative of student's ability to meet these criteria. Based on an analysis of the teacher interview, examples of types of responses confirm these differences. The teacher representing the post-structural perspective indicated 63% more questions as a type of response than did the teacher representing the structural perspective. Her questions were designed to stimulate students to reflect back on their paper, their topics, the audience, and internal criteria to evaluate the interaction between the product and the reader. Her responses were designed to focus students' attention on the success of the written piece to communicate.

When students' responses were examined, they differed in predicted directions with respect to their perceptions of control of the writing process. Students who were presented with decontextualized procedures (structural perspective) relied on external sources for topic selection and for solutions to writing problems. On the other hand, writing instruction that placed the student in the role of the informant (post-structural perspective) encouraged greater control of the writing process by directing students to rely on internal strategies for topic selection and problem identification.

In summary, while an obvious limitation of this study is that only two teachers representing the two different perspectives were studied, the data suggest a positive relationship between teachers' belief systems, their instructional practices, and the impact of these beliefs on student perceptions about writing, particularly as it relates to students' perceived control of the writing process. The teacher representing a structural perspective tended to have students who held a (mis)conception of writing as an externally driven activity that must be completed for school tasks. In contrast, the teacher representing a post-structural perspective tended to have students who held a conception of writing as an internally driven activity that must be completed to communicate with different audiences in different contexts. This confirms and extends the research of Rohrkemper (1984) by describing how students' perceptions of writing and their self-perceptions are influenced by teachers' beliefs and behaviors. This is also consistent with, and extends to writing, existing research on teacher explanation (Roehler, Duffy, & Meloth, 1984) that has found a strong relationship between what teachers explain and what is learned. Future research would make useful contributions to our understanding of writing instruction by systematically examining the relationship between teacher and student beliefs and practices in writing and by documenting the mechanisms by which students acquire the beliefs that guide their writing.

REFERENCES

Anderson, C. W., & Smith, E. L. (1983, April). *Teacher behavior associated with conceptual learning in science.* Paper presented at the annual meeting of the American Educational Research Association, Montreal, Canada.

Applebee, A. N., & Langer, J. A. (1984). Instructional scaffolding: Reading and writing as natural language activities. In J. M. Jensen (Ed.), *Composing and comprehending* (pp.183-190). Urbana, IL: ERIC Clearinghouse on Reading and Communication Skills.

Eagleton, T. (1983). *Literary theory.* Minneapolis: University of Minnesota Press.

Englert, C. S., Anderson, L. M., & Raphael, T. E. (1985). *Teaching cognitive strategies to the mildly handicapped: A classroom intervention study* (G008530201). Washington, DC: U.S. Dept. of Education, Special Education and Rehabilitative Services.

Flower, L. S., & Hayes, J. R. (1981). Problem-solving and the cognitive process of writing. In C. H. Frederiksen & J. F. Dominic (Eds.), *Writing: The nature, development and teaching of written communication* (pp. 39-58). Hillsdale, NJ: Erlbaum.

Langer, J. A. (1985, May). *A study of the impact of teacher education.* Paper presented at Michigan State University, East Lansing.

Madden, R., Gardner, E., Rudman, H., Karlsen, B., & Merwin, J. (1973). *Stanford achievement test.* New York: Harcourt Brace Janovich.

Maria, K., & MacGinitie, W. (1981, December). *Prior knowledge as a handicapping condition.* Paper presented at the National Reading Conference, Dallas.

Raphael, T. E., Kirschner, B. W., & Englert, C. S. (1986). *Students' metacognitive knowledge about writing* (Research Series No. 177). East Lansing: Michigan State University, Institute for Research on Teaching.

Rohrkemper, M. M. (1984). The influence of teacher socialization style on students' social cognition and reported interpersonal classroom behavior. *The Elementary School Journal, 85,* 245-275.

Roehler, R. R., Duffy, G. G., & Meloth, S. M. (1984). What to be direct about in direct instruction in reading: Content-only versus process-into-content. In T. E. Raphael (Ed.), *The context of school based literacy.* New York: Random House.

Roth, K. (1985, April). *Conceptual change learning and student processing of science texts.* Paper presented at the annual meeting of the American Educational Research Association, Chicago.

AN INSTRUCTIONAL INVESTIGATION OF STUDENTS' IDEAS GENERATED DURING CONTENT AREA WRITING

Michael A. Martin
Eastern Michigan University

Bonnie C. Konopak
Louisiana State University

In many content areas, the primary source of information is the class textbook because it provides both a structure for and facts about a particular subject area. However, many students have problems learning from these materials, often due to a mismatch between the conceptual and stylistic demands of text reading and the students' content reading skills. That is, the students have not developed those reading skills needed to organize and synthesize new text information or the ability to integrate this information with their own background knowledge.

Unfortunately, recent research has shown that reading may not be a well-applied component of either teaching or learning in the content classroom. Rather than direction in how to think about text content, instructional practices appear to emphasize postreading, unguided practice and/or assessment of literal information (Neilsen, Rennie, & Connell, 1982). In reponse, students learn to "get by" with attending to the teacher's lecture and answering short-answer comprehension questions to acquire information (Smith & Feathers, 1983). Given such circumstances, students rarely develop those reading skills needed for in-depth study. The purpose of the present study was to investigate the effects of an integrated approach—content area writing—as an aid to learning content information.

In recent years, various strategies such as the Guided Reading Procedure (Manzo, 1975) have been introduced that emphasize an integrated active learner approach, focusing on holistic methods to facilitate comprehension. While many of these strategies have primarily used speaking and listening activities, they have not offered students the opportunity for the expressive synthesis and organization that writing can provide (Emig, 1977; Graves, 1978). One strategy that has been developed to promote this synthesis of ideas through writing is the Guided Writing Procedure (Smith & Bean, 1980).

The Guided Writing Procedure (GWP) is an instructional strategy designed to enhance students' comprehension of content material through the integration of activities involving all four of the communication arts. The emphasis is on developing proficiency in explanatory writing to facilitate the synthesis and retention of content material. The two-day procedure includes activities to activate students' prior knowledge through the use of the four communication arts, to improve expository writing skills, and to enhance the comprehension of text material.

The procedure includes the following seven sequential steps, carried out over a two-day period: on day one, (a) activate students' prior knowledge of a given topic, (b) have students list, organize, and label their collective ideas, (c) have each student write two paragraphs using this information, (d) assign text reading on the topic; on day two, (e) provide a diagnostic checklist as to the structure, spelling, and punctuation of the students' first drafts, (f) have the students revise their drafts according to the checklist and the material read, and (g) give a follow-up quiz on the text material.

Searfoss, Smith, and Bean (1981) conducted a study based on the GWP utilizing eighth-grade second-language students enrolled in content area classes. They found the procedure to be effective in providing these learners with the opportunity of using and integrating reading, writing, speaking, and listening while simultaneously acquiring content area information.

Martin, Konopak, and Martin (1986) and Konopak, Martin, and Martin (in press), in an effort to test the usefulness of this strategy, conducted two experimental studies which examined a modified version of the GWP. The major change in both studies was the deletion of the diagnostic checklist; rather than concentrating on spelling and punctuation, the emphasis was upon the fluency and coherence of ideas.

Both studies involved eleventh graders selected from U.S. history classes in which the GWP was used to enhance the learning/comprehension of a text passage on the California gold rush. The treatment groups received writing activities to aid their synthesis and retention of information, while the control groups participated in *business as usual* activities. That is, the latter group merely was asked to read and complete text-based tasks, including word identification and short-answer comprehension questions. Results from both studies indicated that the treatment group subjects used fewer text-based ideas in their posttest writing, were better able to synthesize information from a variety of class activities, and improved their writing with regard to the quality of ideas generated and overall writing ability.

The present study was an attempt to further investigate the effects of writing activities on secondary students' comprehension of content area material. However, rather than focus only on a quantitative assessment of the product of these activities (Konopak et al., in press; Martin et al., 1986), the present descriptive study attempted to explore the idea units generated by each class activity to determine a flow pattern of ideas across instructional tasks. Such an analysis is important as it focuses on the genesis and evolution of ideas reported by students during the learning process. It is through this type of process that the students' organization and synthesis of new information, as well as integration with prior knowledge, is made evident.

METHOD

Subjects

Subjects participating in this study included 13 average and above average eleventh graders enrolled in an American history class at a southeastern university laboratory school. Their mean reading percentile (Comprehensive Test of Basic Skills, 1973) was 74.77 (*sd* = 22.83), with a range from 25–97.

Materials

Materials included both instructional and assessment tools. A passage of approximately 500 words on the topic of the California gold rush was extracted from a high school U.S. history text (Bass, Billias, & Laponsky, 1979, pp. 483–485) not used by the lab school. This topic was deliberately chosen as one that had been previously studied by these subjects, so as to ensure some existing prior knowledge with which to integrate new information. However, the passage used in this study contained facts and ideas not included in the subjects' own text or class discussions, as verified by examination of the original text and by the classroom teacher. That is, the subjects' original study of the California gold rush, several months prior to this experiment, included a survey of western gold rushes, while the experimental text contained specific details as to the California rush in 1848–1849.

Assessment instruments included a pretest, two writing activities, and a posttest. The pretest asked for each subject to individually generate a list of ideas on the California gold rush (adapted from Langer & Nicolich, 1981). This task functioned as an assessment of each of the students' prior knowledge. The two writing activities asked for explanatory writings of information on the topic, based on immediate and previously conducted class activities. The posttest also included an explanatory writing but was based on recalled information. The two writing activities and the posttest served both as measures of acquired knowledge as well as samples of writing quality.

Procedure

The experiment was conducted during three 50-minute class periods over three consecutive days. During this time, the two researchers alternated as instructors to account for possible experimenter bias. Prior to testing, the subjects were told by their classroom teacher that they would be participating in a university study to examine learning in the content areas. However, they were not given specific purposes for the investigation or descriptions of the activities required of them.

On day one, the subjects generated individual lists of ideas on the California gold rush as a pretest measure. This task was followed by a class activity, a collective brainstorming of all the ideas. These ideas were written on the chalkboard by the experimenter and then grouped and labeled by class consensus. Following this activity, each subject individually prepared an explanatory writing sample on the topic, based on ideas from the individual pretests and the group brainstorming. Both the pretest and classification of ideas were available for the students' use.

On day two, the subjects read the text passage on the California gold rush. Then, with text available, they revised their day one writings to include any newly acquired information. On day three, they were administered the explanatory writing posttest, without any information aids available. Again, they were encouraged to include any information gained over the two days of class activities.

Scoring. In this study, the major areas of interest were the sources of ideas used in the three explanatory writings and flow pattern of ideas across instructional tasks. For this study, an idea was defined as one autonomous bit of information without regard to sentence structure. For example, ''panning for gold'' was considered one idea, while ''panning for gold in mountain streams'' was counted as two ideas (Konopak et al., in press). A preliminary step, then, was to parse each writing into idea units.

The first area of interest focused on the original source of each idea included in each writing sample. For the brainstorm writing, possible sources of ideas were the students' individual pretests and the collective brainstorming activity. For the passage writing and posttest writing, possible sources also included the text passage. For each writing sample, then, an idea was assigned to the information source where it had originally surfaced. Scores were determined by summing the number of ideas assigned to each source and then calculating percentages, based upon the total number of ideas generated for that writing.

The second area of interest concerned the flow of ideas carried over the three explanatory writings. Here, the focus was on each idea as it appeared in successive writings, rather than on the original information source. For the brainstorm writing, the pretest was examined. For the passage writing, both the pretest and the brainstorm writing were studied. For the posttest writing, the pretest, brainstorm writing, and passage writing were considered. For each writing sample, then, an idea was assigned to that writing activity where it was first used. Scores were again determined by summing the number of ideas assigned to each original writing activity and then calculating percentages, based on the total number presented for the writing sample.

RESULTS AND DISCUSSION

Descriptive statistics first were calculated for the assessment data. In looking at the sources of ideas for the three writing samples, percentages were calculated for each source. As seen in Table 1, the subjects used ideas from a variety of sources for each writing, a pattern that supports the findings of Martin et al. (1986) and Konopak et al. (in press). One trend in particular appeared to be similar; the subjects seemed to use the ideas most often from the activity which preceded the writing. On the brainstorm writing, more emphasis was placed on this categorization activity, while for the passage writing, stress was placed on the text reading. In contrast, the posttest writing integrated more information from all possible sources. This latter finding indicates a synthesis of ideas necessary for in-depth learning, rather than reliance on one particular source of information. The *Other* category used in Table 1 was a source for those ideas that had not been previously mentioned in the pretest, brainstorming, or text.

Table 1

Percentage of Ideas by Original Information Source Across Writing Activities

	Original Information Source			
Writing Activity	**Pretest (%)**	**Brainstorming (%)**	**Passage (%)**	**Other (%)**
Brainstorming Writing	21	64		15
Passage Writing	11	28	59	2
Posttest Writing	12	36	45	7

The second assessment focused on the percentage of ideas as they appeared in the writing activities themselves. As seen in Table 2, the subjects carried a number of ideas across the various writings. Of particular interest here was the discrepancy between the percentage of ideas by original information source (Table 1) and how they appeared in the various writing activities (Table 2). For example, on the passage writing, 28% of the ideas were originally from the brainstorming activity, while 22% had appeared on the brainstorm writing. That is, 6% of the brainstorming ideas were recalled from the first day's activity that had not been included in the brainstorm writing immediately following. Similar results were found for the posttest writing where 36% of the ideas were originally from the brainstorming activity, a 9% gain over the percentage of ideas appearing on the brainstorm writing. This shows some activation of knowledge beyond the ideas used in the writing at that time. In contrast, on the posttest writing, the percentage of ideas originally from the text passage and from the passage writing were relatively similar (45% and 43%, respectively). This latter finding may indicate a reliance for information on the writing sample, done just the previous day, rather than the text itself.

Table 2

Percentage of Ideas by Original Writing Source Across Writing Activities

	Original Writing Source		
Writing Activity	**Pretest (%)**	**Brainstorm Writing (%)**	**Passage Writing (%)**
Brainstorming Writing	21		
Passage Writing	11	22	
Posttest Writing	12	27	43

In addition to analyzing the percentage of ideas by source, the content of ideas, in terms of commonality, was also examined as the ideas appeared across writing samples. On the brainstorm writing, 85% of the ideas generated originated on the individual pretests and on the collective brainstorming activity. These ideas, as categorized by student groupings, included the major topics of (1) gold discovery in the western states, (2) the prospectors' travel efforts, (3) the conflict that arose out of greed and lawlessness, (4) the beneficial results regarding advances in transportation, technology, economy, and western settlement, and (5) the harmful results including Indian conflicts, harsh environments, disease, and mining catastrophes. The additional 15%, indicated under the Other category, generally included details contained in the course textbook but not previously reported, such as the development of natural resources.

On the passage writing, almost 40% of the ideas used were from the pretests and brainstorming activity. Generally, these ideas were those supported by the text passage, including the discovery of gold, the lawlessness in mining camps, and the settlement of the west; nontext topics such as transportation and Indian conflicts were not included. On this writing, only 2% of the ideas were in the Other category; nearly all were included on the brainstorm writing. Those ideas taken from the text passage included specific information as to the discovery of gold, immigration/emigration, placer mining, success for business people but not for miners, the later take-over by large mining companies, and the gradual settlement of the west.

On the posttest writing, the ideas selected from various sources were well integrated. The majority of ideas from the pretest and brainstorming activity were those used on the passage writing but included more detail (a gain of 8%) regarding the prospectors' efforts/hardships and the overall benefits of the various gold rushes. The ideas selected from the text dropped 14% from the passage writing to the posttest writing. Generally, those ideas deleted included specific details of the major topics, while the main ideas were left intact. The 7% in the Other category included those ideas carried over from the brainstorm writing.

In conclusion, the results of this study are limited by the fact that the data were collected only over a three-day period and by the use of such a small sample. However, two important conclusions can be drawn from the results of this study. First, the results indicate that, when provided with guided practice in a variety of activities associated with a strategy such as the Guided Writing Procedure, students have a tendency to synthesize information from a variety of sources. Secondly, an activity such as a class brainstorming session, followed by writing on the topic, enhances subjects' abilities to integrate prior knowledge and new information across various writing activities. Of all the activities utilized in the present study, this one seemed to have had the most dramatic effect with regard to the utilization of ideas across instructional activities. Such findings have implications for the classroom educator who wants to enhance in-depth understanding of the topic under study. Various student activities should be provided at all stages of the instructional lesson; in addition, these activities should include utilization of all language processes to promote active learning.

REFERENCES

Bass, H. J., Billias, G. A., & Laponsky, E. J. (1979). *Our American heritage.* Morristown, NJ: Silver Burdett.

Comprehensive test of basic skills (1973). New York: McGraw-Hill.

Emig, J. (1977). Writing as a mode of learning. *College Composition and Communication, 28,* 122-128.

Graves, D. (1978). Balance the basis: Let them write. *Learning, 6,* 30-33.

Konopak, B. C., Martin, S.H., & Martin, M. A. (in press). An integrated communication arts approach for enhancing students' learning in the content areas. *Reading Research and Instruction.*

Langer, J. A., & Nicolich, M. (1981). Prior knowledge and its relationship to comprehension. *Journal of Reading Behavior, 13,* 373-379.

Manzo, A. V. (1975). Guided reading procedure. *Journal of Reading, 18,* 287-291.

Martin, M. A., Konopak, B. C., & Martin, S. H. (1986). Use of the guided writing procedure to facilitate reading comprehension of high school text material. In J. A. Niles & R. V. Lalik (Eds.), *Solving problems in literacy: Learners, teachers, and researchers* (pp. 66-72). Thirty-fifth Yearbook of the National Reading Conference. Rochester, NY: National Reading Conference.

Neilsen, A., Rennie, B., & Connell, A. (1982). Allocation of instructional time to reading comprehension and study skills in intermediate grade social studies classrooms. In J. Niles & L. Harris (Eds.), *New inquiries in reading research and instruction* (pp. 81-84).Thirty-first Yearbook of the National Reading Conference. Rochester, NY: National Reading Conference.

Searfoss, L. W., Smith, C. C., & Bean, T. W. (1981). An integrated language strategy for second language learners. *TESOL Quarterly, 15,* 388-389.

Smith, C. C., & Bean, T. W. (1980). The guided writing procedure: Integrating content reading and writing improvement. *Reading World, 19,* 290-294.

Smith, F., & Feathers, K. (1983). Teacher and student perceptions of content area reading. *Journal of Reading, 26,* 348-354.

RELATING READING AND WRITING VIA COMPREHENSION, QUALITY, AND STRUCTURE

Annette Schewe
Child Guidance Clinic of Greater Winnipeg

Victor Froese
University of British Columbia

While there has been recent emphasis on the whole language approach, communicative competence, and process writing, the precise nature of the relationship among language components which constitute these global concepts remains obscure (Hammill & McNutt, 1981; Stotsky, 1983), and only minimal empirical evidence exists to support teaching and testing practices. Early studies examining the relationship among the language arts components were largely correlational in nature and yielded very general conclusions regarding that relationship (Stotsky, 1983). More recently, however, it has been suggested that reading and writing specifically are both processes whereby the reader or writer strives to construct meaning (Squire, 1984). This premise has permitted a more definitive analysis of the reading-writing relationship.

Kintsch and van Dijk's (1978) text analysis at the idea level has made it possible to segment text into small meaningful idea units which can be tabulated and analyzed for recall of reading comprehension, as well as for ideas produced in writing. Story grammarians have provided an overall structuring of the propositional units into basic elements of narrative text (Mandler & Johnson, 1977; Stein & Glenn, 1977). This text analysis research has provided the tools for studying the reading-writing relationship using dependent measures considering tasks of similar processing demands. Previous research reviews have concluded that the dependent measures used in studies dictated the nature and degree of the reading-writing relationship findings (Straw, 1979). Further developments in research that contributed to the clarification of the reading-writing relationship emanated from the field of cognitive psychology. The proposal of schema theory (Rumelhart, 1975) and, specifically, story schema theory (Mandler & Johnson, 1977) have enabled more useful parallels to be drawn between the language user's text processing and the actual text organization. In this way the effects of text variables, content and organization, could be separated from the reader/writer variables such as prior knowledge, recall, comprehension, and structure imposed upon text.

Given that reading and writing involve a constructive process whereby meaning is created through text, along with the systematic means for text analysis and a well-defined story schema theory, the reading-writing relationship can be further analyzed. The basic goal of this study was to further define the nature of the reading-writing relationship. The purpose of this research, therefore, was to explore a variety of variables linking fourth graders' reading comprehension and writing ability. Four main questions were addressed:

1. What is the relationship between free recall and comprehension probe scores in reading and analytic scale scores in writing?
2. What are the effects of reading and writing competence on the production of story grammar categories in writing?
3. What is the relationship among writing scores and the components of the analytic writing scale?
4. What qualitative differences can be observed in the students' use of story grammar categories in their reading recall protocols and in their independent writing samples?

METHOD

Subjects

The subjects in this study were 36 fourth-grade students from two schools in the same suburban school division in Winnipeg, Manitoba, Canada. All subjects comprising the fourth-grade population of the two schools were included in the study. The high, average, and low ability grouping was determined by dividing the reading scores (PCTOT) into quartiles and then assigning those in the first quartile to the high group, those in the second and third quartiles to the average group, and those remaining to the low ability group.

Materials

Reading assessment. The measures of reading ability were specifically designed for this study. The text consisted of two ideally structured passages of 15 propositional units which represented all seven story grammar categories defined by Mandler and Johnson (1977). A recall analysis protocol listing the propositions was used to record both unaided and aided recall of text. Further, the score was combined to represent total comprehension and was labeled *PropR.* The recall analysis protocol further segmented the propositions according to the appropriate story grammar category (i.e., initiating event, etc.).

A second measure of reading ability (COMP) involved a five-item inferential comprehension probe check on the two *ideally structured* stories. The paragraph comprehension total scores (PCTOT) represented the combined PropR and COMP scores.

Writing assessment. A three-point analytic writing scale (a modification and extension of the *Glazer Writing Scale* [Glazer, 1971]) was designed to assess writing quality. Components assessed in the writing scale included (a) story grammar category, (b) characterization, (c) mechanics, (d) sentence structure, (e) style, and (f) word usage.

Procedure

Data collection. The reading assessments were conducted on an individual basis. Each subject silently read the passage, retold the story to the examiner, responded to aided recall questions for propositions not included in the initial retelling, and orally responded to the comprehension probe questions asked. The second passage was similarly presented. The sessions were audiotaped and the tapes were later transcribed and analyzed.

The writing samples were collected within the classroom setting over a period of four weeks. A prewriting session was given prior to data collection to familiarize the subjects with the task requirement. A writing process (think, write, edit) was modeled and practiced during this session to minimize influence of previous teaching. No reference was made to the components of the analytic scale used in the study. Once a week for the following three weeks, each subject was provided with a picture stimulus and asked to write a story relating to that picture. The samples were collected and copied; one copy was returned to the students for sharing. The other copies were segmented into *t* units and propositions. They were then analyzed for story grammar categories. Quality ratings were done by three independent raters using the analytic writing scale (the third rater's score was used to arbitrate final decisions). The resulting interrater reliability was calculated to be .82.

RESULTS

The results are reported in the order of the four main questions presented earlier and the significance level was set at $p \leq .05$.

Question One

The overall findings of the study indicated that many aspects of reading comprehension and writing ability were related. Reflecting the type of data collected, Table 1 provides important means. Correlation calculations computed on the three reading

Table 1

Means and Standard Deviations of Dependent Variables*

Variable	Mean	*SD*	Minimum Score	Maximum Score
Comprehension	6.92	2.0	3.0	7.0
Propositions Recalled	22.44	4.1	15.0	29.0
Propositions Produced	40.64	18.4	17.0	99.0
Total Writing Score	32.08	6.4	19.0	46.0
Story Grammar Category	11.32	2.5	7.0	18.0
Mechanics	0.66	0.2	0.3	1.0
Sentence Structure	0.53	0.5	0.3	0.8
Style	0.55	0.1	0.3	0.7
Characterization	0.42	0.1	0.2	0.7
Word Usage	0.58	0.1	0.3	0.8

*n = 36.

ability scores and writing quality scores were significantly correlated (*r* COMP = .45, *p* = .006; *r* PCTOT = .42, *p* = .01; *r* PropR = .36, *p* = .03). A statistically nonsignificant correlation was found between the total number of propositions recalled in reading and the total number of propositions produced in writing (*r* = .09; *p* = 0.6). Correlational calculations revealed that the only statistically significant correlated story grammar category to be recalled in reading and produced in writing was internal reaction (*r* = .38, *p* = .02). The remaining six categories showed statistically nonsignificant relationships. Further correlation calculations indicated that inferential comprehension abilities in reading and evidence of story grammar elements in writing were related (*r* = .45, *p* = .0059) at a statistically significant level.

In response to question one, it would seem that, while all measures of reading ability used here were valid predictors of writing quality, inferential probes were the best predictors of overall writing performance. Further, inferential probes were valid predictors of story grammar usage in writing. On the other hand, the propositional units and story grammar elements were not valid predictors of the reading/writing relationship when analyzed through correlation.

Question Two

Analysis of variance revealed that the subjects' writing ability was different from their production of story grammar categories, *F*(1, 35) = 4.57, *p* = .017, at a statistically significant level, whereas their reading ability was not, *F*(1, 35) = 2.18, *p* = .129. Results of a follow-up *t* test indicated that the high ability writing group was different in story grammar usage from both the middle and low ability groups, *t* (35) = 2.54, *p* = .005; *t*(35) = 1.94, *p* = .05, at a statistically significant level, respectively.

That is, those students who were more proficient writers tended to use their story grammar knowledge more efficiently in structuring their written products than did their less proficient counterparts, both average and low writing ability groups. This was not true of the most capable readers as their use of story grammar knowledge did not differ statistically from that of their less capable counterparts.

Question Three

As shown in Table 2, correlation calculations revealed that all components of the writing scale were related to the overall writing quality score at a statistically significant level. Mechanics (*r* = .87, *p* = .0007) and story grammar category (*r* = .86, *p* = .0001) were the best predictors of writing ability results in that they accounted for 91% of the variance in writing scores.

Results of the factor analysis (maximum likelihood method with varimax rotation—SAS 82.4) in Table 3 indicate that two dimensions represented by style and characterization were being assessed by the analytic scale. Style evaluated originality of written content and selection of title, and characterization was mainly concerned with the development of a central character within the written narrative. The remaining four components aligned themselves with one of these two dimensions.

Table 2

Stepwise Regression for Writing Ability and Components of the Analytic Scale*

Step	Variable	*R*	R_2	Significance	*SE*
1	Mechanics	.87	0.75	0.0001	3.2060
2	Story Grammar Category	.86	0.91	0.0001	0.1687
3	Sentence Structure	.86	0.95	0.0001	2.3972
4	Word Usage	.67	0.96	0.0001	2.7561
5	Style	.77	0.97	0.0001	2.5795
6	Characterization	.52	0.97	0.0001	2.1828

*n = 36.

Table 3

Factor Analysis Computed on the Six Variables of the Analytic Writing Scale*

Variable	Factor 1	Factor 2
Style	.88	.09
Sentence Structure	.76	.35
Story Grammar Category	.73	.37
Mechanics	.63	.49
Characterization	.14	.81
Word Usage	.45	.58

*n = 36.

Question Four

A qualitative analysis of subjects' story grammar usage indicated that, while the most proficient readers recalled more propositions per story grammar category, it was the average ability writers who recalled and produced the greatest number of propositions when compared to the other two groups. Analysis of syntactic complexity of the writings produced indicated that the most proficient writers' average *t* unit length surpassed that of the average group by 3.3 words (H = 10.7, A = 7.4, L = 7.6 words per *t* unit). Analysis of the organization of propositions into story grammar categories in writing indicated that internal response, goal, attempt, and end structures appeared less than once per story. Story grammar categories most frequently recalled per story included internal response (89%), setting (84%), and initiating event (82%). Those recalled least frequently were goal (54%) and attempt (59%). It would appear that the quantity of propositional units recalled and produced is not a valid indicator of reading and writing ability.

In addition, although use of story structure knowledge was apparent in the subjects' writings and readings, the frequency of usage varied according to the type of story grammar element and the task being performed (reading recall or written production).

DISCUSSION AND CONCLUSIONS

In addressing the four questions posed, the following four main conclusions were drawn based on the results of this study. Reading comprehension measures and writing ability measures were significantly related. The subject's ability in responding to inferential probes on reading passages was the best predictor of writing ability and the ability to effectively use story structure in writing. The total number of proposition units was not an accurate predictor of either reading or writing ability. It may well be that the level of processing required in responding to inferential questions is similar to the depth processing required in forming macrostructures (Kintsch, 1977). Written language production may well be a reciprocal act demanding an equal level of in-depth processing (as opposed to the task demands made in reading recall and written production). This suggests a need for caution in future research to ensure that task requirements are equated when comparing the various language processes.

The ability to recall story grammar elements during reading was not indicative of the ability to produce the same elements in writing. Further, writing ability, but not reading ability, was a valid predictor of story structure production in writing. It was felt that knowledge of story structure had fully emerged in its influence on reading recall but not on writing performance at the fourth-grade level. Previous research has suggested that story structure usage is developmental (Hansche & Gordon, 1983; Mandler & Johnson, 1977). It would appear that the use of story schema in recalling text emerges well in advance of the use of story schema in producing text.

The mechanics and story grammar category components of the analytic writing scale were the best predictors of writing quality. It may well be that those fourth graders who have mastered the mechanical conventions of writing are also the ones who have developed efficient organizational patterns in story production. Of the writing aspects measured in this study, mechanics and story structure were the best correlates of writing quality. Many aspects of the writing process (awareness of audiences, teacher influence, social context), however, were not assessed in this study. These variables do not readily lend themselves to assessment, but may be equally influential in their impact on writing quality.

Good readers and good writers, as assessed by the number of propositions recalled in reading and produced in writing samples, are not necessarily one and the same. Moreover, fourth graders apparently used an internalized story schema, with varying levels of success, to aid in recalling and producing text. It may well be that less proficient writers have not fully developed the ability to incorporate all components of their internalized schema in their independent writings, whereas, even the least proficient readers have developed their story schema knowledge to effectively aid reading recall.

REFERENCES

Glazer, J. (1971). *Glazer narrative composition scale.* Urbana, IL: National Council of Teachers of English. (ERIC Document ED 091 763)

Hammill, D., & McNutt, G. (1981). *The correlates of reading.* Austin, TX: Pro-Ed.

Hansche, L., & Gordon, B. (1983). An investigation of the relationship of story schema to reading ability and grade level. In J. Niles & L. Harris (Eds.), *Searches for meaning in reading/language processing and instruction* (pp. 255-259). Thirty-second Yearbook of the National Reading Conference. Rochester, NY: National Reading Conference.

Kintsch, W. (1977). On comprehending stories. In M. Just & P. Carpenter (Eds.), *Cognitive processes in comprehension* (pp. 33-62). Hillsdale, NJ: Erlbaum.

Kintsch, W., & van Dijk, T. (1978). Toward a model of text comprehension and prediction. *Psychological Review, 85,* 363-394.

Mandler, J., & Johnson, N. (1977). Remembrance of things parsed: Story structure and recall. *Cognitive Psychology, 9,* 111-151.

Rumelhart, D. (1975). Notes on a schema for stories. In D. Bobrow & A. Collins (Eds.), *Representations and understanding studies in cognitive studies* (pp. 211-236). New York: Academic Press.

Schewe, A. (1986). *Relating reading and writing: A study of fourth-graders' use of story schema.* Unpublished master's thesis, University of Manitoba.

Squire, T. (1984). Composing and comprehending: Two sides of the same basic process. In J. Jensen (Ed.), *Composing and comprehending* (pp. 23-31). Urbana, IL: National Conference on Research in English.

Stein, N., & Glenn, C. (1977). An analysis of story comprehension in elementary school children. In R. Freedle (Ed.), *New directions in discourse processing* (pp. 53-120). Norwood, NJ: Ablex.

Stotsky, S. (1983). Research on reading/writing relationships: A synthesis and suggested directions. *Language Arts, 60,* 627-642.

Straw, S. (1979). Measuring the effect of sentence-combining instruction on reading instruction. In D. Daiker, A. Kerek, & M. Morenberg (Eds.), *Sentence-combining and the teaching of writing* (pp. 43-49). Conway, AR: University of Central Arkansas.

TWO YOUNG WRITERS: THE RELATIONSHIP BETWEEN TEXT REVISIONS AND TEACHER/STUDENT CONFERENCES

Carol Vukelich
University of Delaware

LuAnn D. Leverson
West Chester School District

Several researchers (Beach, 1976; Bracewell, Scardamalia, & Bereiter, 1978; Bridwell, 1980, 1981; National Assessment of Educational Progress, 1977; Perl, 1979; Pianko, 1979; Rubin & Piché, 1979; Sommers, 1978, 1980) have concluded that students engage in little substantive text revision. While some researchers, like Bracewell, Scardamalia, and Bereiter (1978), have suggested that the observed failure to revise is related to the students' lack of attainment of a particular stage of cognitive development, others' findings (Calkins, 1983, 1986; Fitzgerald & Markham, 1985; Graves, 1981, 1983; Kamler, 1981; Vukelich, 1986) have suggested that students' failure to revise is the result of lack of participation in an instructional program in which writers are taught to revise in order to communicate more clearly with their audiences.

Archie E. Lapointe (1986), Executive Director of the National Assessment of Educational Progress (NAEP), identified a specific aspect of this instructional program—teachers and students discussing the content of the students' pieces—which he believes the analysis of NAEP's recently collected writing data suggests can have a significant impact on students' ability to revise texts to make the message more clear. While Calkins (1983, 1986), Estabrook (1982), and Graves (1983) would agree with Lapointe, none provide descriptions of the specific relationship between conference discussions and students' text revisions. It was the purpose of the present study to describe the relationship between the revisions made by young writers in their texts following the conferences and the unclear aspects of the texts discussed during the conferences.

METHOD

Subjects

The subjects were two seven-year-old children, both females, from a second-grade classroom located in a middle-class neighborhood in a mideastern state. These two subjects were randomly selected from the available pool of 19 children.

Materials and Procedure

This study was conducted in a classroom where the Graves' (1983) process approach to teaching writing had been implemented twice per week for three months prior to the initiation of this investigation.

The writing program was implemented by the classroom teacher and the two authors. Consistent with Graves' recommendations, each writing session began with a mini-lesson of approximately ten minutes. The writing workshop of approximately 35-40 minutes followed. Following the writing workshop, the children were divided randomly into three small groups and interested children shared their drafts within a group sharing conference; these sharing sessions lasted 10-15 minutes.

The teacher/student conferences with the two subjects were held during the writing workshop time. Nondirective conferencing procedures, as recommended by Graves (1982, 1983), were used because of their reported success with young children.

The teacher's task during a Graves-type conference is to question and wait. Graves has identified at least five kinds of questions—process, basic structure, following, opening, and questions about development—which the teacher can use as he or she receives the child's piece and helps the child value and assess the work. While the teacher may ask many questions, the focus of these questions should be the clarification of the meaning, the elaboration of the information, or the relationship of the information known by the child regarding one or two aspects of the piece.

The teacher in all the conferences with the two young writers was the second author. During the five-month data-collection period, six content conferences were held with Susan while seven conferences were held with Angela. All conferences were audiotaped and transcriptions were prepared. All drafts were photocopied after the child had at least one writing workshop to revise her piece and before the next conference.

Data analysis. Each question or comment during a conference is *not* a recommendation for a separate revision. Typically several questions or comments explore one confusing aspect of the text. Collectively, these several questions and comments identify an aspect of the text which is confusing to the audience. Consequently, each interactional unit identifies an area of the text which needs to be reconsidered and perhaps revised. For purposes of this investigation, each set of interactions—questions, comments, and responses—focusing on one aspect of the text was labeled an interactional unit. The following example of one interactional unit is provided for clarification.

Adult: Your mom is going back to the hospital?
Child: Yes, to get some tests.
Adult: I wonder what kinds of tests will be done.
Child: They do an x-ray and then do a check on her neck and put a needle in her arm.
Adult: I wonder what will the tests tell the doctors?
Child: On the x-rays it shows her neck and then they could see what the problem is.
Adult: Oh, I see. And your mom will have the tests tonight?
Child: No, I'm not sure, maybe today.

The focus of this series of comments, questions, and responses was the tests the child's mother was to receive in the hospital. The interactional unit helped the child reconsider the information in her piece about her mother's hospital visit.

Two trained raters analyzed the transcript of each conference to identify the interactional units present. Interrater reliability was .93.

To identify the revisions made by the children in their texts, two trained raters compared the text of each draft, as it was read by the child at the beginning of the conference, with the photocopy of the appropriate draft. Revisions made in the text of each draft were noted. Then each conference transcript, with each interactional unit identified, was compared with the appropriate draft with the revisions noted. This comparison permitted the raters to identify which interactional units had been used by the child to guide her text revisions. Finally, the oral language used by the child in each interactional unit was compared with the appropriate text revision. Each text revision was judged to be in one of four categories: (a) revision did not clarify the confusing aspect of the text, (b) revision clarified the confusing aspect of the text but used language different from that used in the conference, (c) revision used some of the exact language of the conference but was not as elaborated, and (d) revision was directly related to the child's oral language. Interrater reliabilities for these various analyses ranged from .83 to total agreement. Discrepancies were resolved by a third rater.

RESULTS

Across the 13 conferences, there were 24 interactional units, an average of 1.8 interactional units per conference. This is consistent with Graves' (1983) recommendation that no more than one or two confusing aspects of the text be considered in each conference.

Susan and Angela used 79% of the interactional units to guide their text revisions. To clarify the conference-identified confusing aspects of their texts, they added new information (68% of the conference-related text revisions) or they deleted a piece of the text (26% of the conference-related text revisions). In addition, Susan substituted one word for another, "Holly" for "her."

The greatest percentage (37%) of the text revisions clarified the aspect of the text identified as confusing with language different from that used by the child in the conference. In some instances, the clarification provided by the child during the interactional unit was greater than that provided in the text revision. For example, during the conference on "Holly's Birthday," the teacher said, "I see you celebrated Holly's birthday on April 30th." Susan responded, "We had her party then because my mom had to work on May 2. Also I had school and so did John-John." Susan revised her text by adding the sentence "We had to celebrate on April 30th because if we didn't, we couldn't celebrate it." Her oral text had identified more clearly the reason for the change in the date of celebration. In other instances, the text revision clarified the confusing aspect of the text more fully than the oral discussion. For example, during the conference on "The Minibike," the teacher said, "I wonder why John-John wears a helmet while riding the minibike." Susan responded, "To keep from bumping his head on rocks." Susan revised her text by adding "just in case he falls off and hits a rock" onto the end of the sentence "John-John wears a helmet while riding the minibike."

Thirty-two percent of the text revisions of the conference-related clarifications of the confusing aspects of the texts used the exact language the child had used during the conference or were made exactly as the child had prescribed during the conference. One interactional unit during Angela's conference on "It Snowed" and the subsequent text revision illustrates the use of the same language used in the conference to revise the text. The teacher said, "I see you went to the bus stop and you said, 'It was fun!' I wonder why it was fun." Angela responded, "Because I had a snowball fight." Angela clarified her text by inserting the exact words "I had a snowball fight" after the sentence "It was fun!" Examples from Susan and Angela illustrate the revision of texts as prescribed during the conferences. Susan made two revisions—both deletions—which she had identified as being needed during two different conferences. She said, "I shouldn't put that there" and "I don't know why I said it there." In both cases, she deleted the misplaced sentences. Angela made one similar prescription. During one of the three conferences on "My Mommy's Neck Hurts," she said, "I'm going to throw out this part because it's a lie." She deleted "She might go to the hospital. I might go to my friend's house. It's very hard to see my mom in the hospital. My daddy might take me to the hospital tonight to see my mom. She is very ill. Because she might have an infection in her neck or a sinus problem in her neck or a tumor in her neck."

Sixteen percent of text revisions used some of the child's exact language from the conference but the text revision was not as elaborated as the conference discussion. For example, during the conference on "My Cats," Susan described her cat, Whiskey, as "She's black all over and she has white paws and a white back and she has white on her neck." She revised her text by inserting the sentence "Whiskey is black all over."

Sixteen percent of the text revisions were made to aspects of the texts which had been identified as confusing during a conference but were made in a way which did not clarify the confusion. For example, during the conference on "It Snowed," the teacher said, "I was wondering what this meant. 'Then I made one in the front.' I'm not quite sure what it is you made." Angela responded, "Snowball." She revised her text by inserting "yard" into the sentence, "Then I made one in the front yard."

DISCUSSION

Contrary to the findings of previous researchers (e.g., Beach, 1976; Bracewell, Scardamalia, & Bereiter, 1978), this study suggests that students are able to engage in substantive text revision. Contrary to the findings of such researchers as Bracewell, Scardamalia, and Bereiter (1978), young writers, at least some young writers, seem able to revise their texts in response to their audience's requests for additional information. The present study's data seem to lend support to the findings of earlier researchers (Calkins, 1983, 1986; Fitzgerald & Markham, 1985; Graves, 1981, 1983; Kamler, 1981; Vukelich, 1986) who suggested that students' failure to revise is the result not of these students' age or inability to revise but of their failure to participate in an instructional program which teaches them how and why to revise.

Lapointe (1986) suggested that a critical component of such an instructional program is teacher/student conferences. The discovery of the strong relationship between the conference discussion and the text clarifications (84% of the interactional units used resulted in the clarification of the text's message and 79% of the interactional units were used) not only lends support to his contention but also provides empirical evidence to support the general descriptions of the relationship between conference discussions and students' text revisons provided by Calkins (1983, 1986), and Graves (1983).

Unlike these previous general descriptions of the link between conference discussions and students' text revisions, the present study provides a detailed accounting of two young writers' use of the interactions during nondirective teacher/student conferences to guide their text revisions. This description indicates that when young writers use the conference discussions to guide their text revisions, they typically make additions to their texts. Since the adult during the teacher/student conference frequently is indicating confusion and requesting additional information through her questions and comments, the addition of new information to the texts seems an appropriate response. Further, this description identifies four possible links between children's conference oral language and written text revisions. The written text revisions used the exact oral conference language or a portion of the exact oral conference language in nearly one half of the interactional units used. Clearly the link between the oral and written text revision language is strong.

While the message of the texts may be clarified through the use of nondirective teacher/student conferences, use of conferencing does not guarantee the elimination of all confusing aspects of texts. Sometimes the student ignores the teacher's request for clarification. Sometimes, upon independent after-conference rereading of the text, the writer revises the text in a manner which fails to clarify the reader's confusion. In addition, Graves (1983) warns teachers that one conference cannot address all problems with a piece of writing. With these young writers, writing on a topic often was sustained for only one writing workshop. Only one conference, on one or two confusing aspects of the text, was possible. It should be noted that these young writers sometimes did make revisions to their texts which were unrelated to any conference discussions, but that phase is beyond the scope of this paper.

REFERENCES

Beach, R. (1976). Self-evaluation strategies of extensive revisers and non-revisers. *College Composition and Communication, 27,* 160-164.

Bracewell, R., Scardamalia, M., & Bereiter, C. (1978, April). *The development of audience awareness in writing.* Paper presented at annual meeting of American Educational Research Association, Toronto, Canada.

Bridwell, L. (1980). Revising strategies in twelfth grade students' transactional writing. *Research in the Teaching of English, 14,* 197-222.

Bridwell, L. (1981). Rethinking composing: Implications from research on revising. *English Journal, 77,* 96-99.

Calkins, L. (1983). *Lessons from a child.* Portsmouth, NH: Heinemann.

Calkins, L. (1986). *The art of teaching writing.* Portsmouth, NH: Heinemann.

Estabrook, I. W. (1982). Talking about writing developing independent writers. *Language Arts, 59,* 696-706.

Fitzgerald, J., & Markham, L. (1985, December). *Effects of instruction in revision on children's story writing.* Paper presented at the National Reading Conference, San Diego, CA.

Graves, D. H. (1981). A case study observing the development of primary children's composing, spelling, and motor behaviors during the writing process. In D. H. Graves (Ed.), *A researcher learns to write* (pp. 141-166). Portsmouth, NH: Heinemann.

Graves, D. H. (1982). Six guideposts to a successful writing conference. *Learning, 11,* 76-77.

Graves, D. H. (1983). *Writing: Teachers and children at work.* Portsmouth, NH: Heinemann.

Kamler, B. (1981). One child, one teacher, one classroom. In R. D. Walshe (Ed.), *Donald Graves in Australia: Children want to write* (pp. 73-88). Portsmouth, NH: Heinemann.

Lapointe, A. (1986, April 9). Student's writing skills found distressingly poor by NAEP. *Education Week.*

National Assessment of Educational Progress (1977). *Write/rewrite: An assessment of revision skills.* Denver: Educational Commission of the States.

Perl, S. (1979). The composing process of unskilled college writers. *Research in the Teaching of English, 13,* 317-336.

Pianko, S. (1979). A description of the composing processes of college freshmen writers. *Research in the Teaching of English, 13,* 5-21.

Rubin, D., & Piché, G. (1979). Development in syntactic and strategic aspects of audience adaptation skills in written persuasive communication. *Research in the Teaching of English, 13,* 293-316.

Sommers, N. (1978). *Revision in the composing process: A case study of college experienced adult writers.* Unpublished doctoral dissertation, Boston University.

Sommers, N. (1980). Revision strategies of student writers and experienced adult writers. *College Composition and Communications, 31,* 378-387.

Vukelich, C. (1986). The relationship between peer questions and seven year olds' text revisions. In J. A. Niles & R. Lalik (Eds.), *Solving Problems in Literacy: Learners, Teachers, and Researchers* (pp. 300-305). Thirty-fifth Yearbook of the National Reading Conference. Rochester, NY: National Reading Conference.

THROUGH TEACHERS' EYES: REFLECTIONS ON ETHNOGRAPHY AND WRITING*

Sondra Perl
Lehman College

> . . . it is the business of writing and the responsibility of the writer to disentangle the significant—in character, incident, setting, mood, everything—from the random and meaningless and irrelevant that in real life surround and beset it. (Eudora Welty, date unknown)

In 1981, when I invited two teachers to join me as researchers on an ethnographic study of the teaching of writing in the Shoreham-Wading River school district on Long Island (Perl, 1981), I knew that we too would be looking to *disentangle* the significance of classroom life from the many *random* and extraneous events that surround it. I knew that we would be looking for the core of teaching, for what allows a writing-process approach to flourish and what, on occasion, hinders it. I knew we wanted to be inside classrooms, to come to know them the way the students and teachers who spend 180 school days in them do. But I was not at all certain, when we began our inquiry, just exactly what direction the research would take.

ETHNOGRAPHY AND WRITING

We began, naturally, by schooling ourselves in the principles and procedures of ethnography, by reading, talking to ethnographers, and trying to prepare ourselves for the work which lay ahead. We were all well aware of the pitfalls of what Ray Rist (1980) calls "blitzkrieg ethnography"—the tendency for researchers to rush into schools, collect their data, and hurriedly leave—and we knew that we wanted to act differently. As a result, long before our study officially began, we met with ethnographers, visited classrooms together, studied samples of fieldnotes, read anthropologists' accounts of fieldwork, and prepared lists of questions and checklists of items that we wanted to study. In addition, we met with the 10 teachers who volunteered to participate in the study to discuss with them what to expect when we began to study their teaching.

*Plenary Address.

The more we came to understand ethnography, the more comfortable we became with its assumptions. We found that many of the notions we hold to be true about writing have counterparts in ethnography, and it was often our understanding of the writing process that helped guide us in making decisions when we were faced with methodological issues. As we began to articulate the implicit assumptions about writing which were guiding our thinking, we generated seven principles that have proven useful through the course of study.

We came to see first that ethnography, like writing, is both a product and a process (Agar, 1980). While it usually results in a report or a book, it begins with a series of activities—looking, asking questions, speculating, making observations, drawing inferences. And, just as the last decade of work on composition shows that we will not discover how writers write solely by analyzing their products, we assert that we will not discover how teachers teach merely by analyzing their grade books or their lesson plans. In order to discover how a process unfolds, whether it is writing or teaching, we have to observe it, and to do this we benefit when we use a method that is itself concerned with how things evolve.

A second feature common both to writing and ethnography is that we learn by doing. It is commonplace to say that we will never learn how to write solely by reading about it or studying what writers say about it; similarly, budding ethnographers will not learn the methods and procedures of ethnography merely by reading or studying accounts of other anthropologists. While we are not advocating the abandonment of careful study and preparation, the advice we received, which echoes again and again in the books we read and in the talks we had with different consultants, was that we learn to do ethnography by rolling up our sleeves and getting our hands dirty. In other words, there is no substitute for going into the field, collecting one's own data, learning to follow one's own hunches, and learning how to let one's own questions be one's guide.

Third, a notion common to many teachers of writing is that writing leads to discovery. As writers, we do not plan ahead of time everything we will say. More often, we discover what we want to say as we go along. So, too, in ethnography. We don't enter a setting deciding ahead of time what events will mean; rather, we allow the meaning to emerge from our observations and repeated reflections. While we may enter the setting with certain guiding questions, we do not impose our answers. We allow them to emerge from the process of looking.

Fourth, from writing process research has come the notion that writing is a recursive process. When writers write, we often repeat certain patterns or routines: we literally go back to go forward. We often go back to words, we reread, we go back to the topic, or we even return to what we sense about the topic that is not yet in words. Similarly, ethnography is a recursive process. Researchers return to fieldnotes, for rereading and study, to informants for verification and elaboration, and even more importantly to their hunches, to random thoughts that recur, to their sense of what is occurring in the field so that they can begin to discern patterns and themes. And just as in writing, when we go back to the text and let our sense of it tell us where we need or want to go next, so in ethnographic research, when we return to our notes and to the classrooms themselves, our sense of what is occurring deepens and we see where next to direct our observations.

Fifth, in the writing process approach we advocate, writers shape their ideas, experiences, thoughts, perceptions, and arguments in many different forms and from many different points of view. By doing so, they begin to see not only how rich experience is and how most ideas or experiences lend themselves to a variety of interpretations but also how they, themselves, play an active role in constructing what experiences mean. Similarly, ethnographers recognize the multiplicity of views inherent in human experience. The researcher's perspective is seen as one among many—not as *the one* representing *the truth.* In fact, ethnographers understand that no single ethnographic account is the truth. Rather, ethnographers present a version of reality one they have lived, which represents their own biases, prejudices and preferences, one marked by the stamp of their own personalities.

Sixth, ethnography is a model which relies primarily on human perception—on the ethnographer himself or herself. Born out of anthropology as a way for the lone anthropologist to become immersed in and come to understand a foreign culture, it now enables us to approach classrooms (something with which we are very familiar) with freshness and clarity. In ethnography researchers tend not to discuss classrooms in terms of lesson plans or test scores; rather, we seek to bring to the surface what we sense as intangible, hidden, often overlooked in the unfolding of classroom dynamics. The reason why we have been comfortable using ethnography in our study is because our view of teaching and writing is that both are human processes that ought *not* be reduced to linear schemes or checklists. In this sense, writing and teaching are both seen as complex personal and social acts created by individuals within particular contexts; such complex processes, in fact, that only a human being would be capable of grasping their significance. When we take this kind of approach to phenomena, we do not end up with neat research designs, clear-cut boundaries and controlled variables. But we do find ourselves involved in an enormously rich task that requires us to respond on a human level.

And, finally, what we have discovered that makes writing and ethnography so similar, and what must be there for each one to flourish, is the development of trust. In classrooms, we have seen that what allows for writing that has voice is a trusting relationship among the students and between students and teachers—where students feel comfortable about taking risks. Similarly, we have come to see that ethnography, like writing, offers us the opportunity to go beneath the surface and study what is most intimate in teaching, and that, too, requires the development of trust.

THE STORY OF A RESEARCH PROJECT

We were not aware of these connections when we began our study on the first day of school in September of 1981. The connections came later, with time to stand back and reflect. In the beginning, we were conscious only of the day-to-day work of taking fieldnotes in 10 different classrooms. Initially, one research assistant, James Carter, divided his time among four elementary school teachers, from first, second, fourth and fifth grades; a second research assistant, Nancy Wilson, followed three high school teachers in grades 10, 11 and 12; I spent my days in one sixth-grade and two eighth-grade classrooms in the middle school. Each of us had field notebooks, pens, personal journals, maps of each building and, barely, a lunch break. We saved after-school time for meeting and comparing notes. Tuesday afternoons were used for our study group meetings—a time for the 10 teachers to meet with us, to write, to question, to read, and reflect.

As ethnographic researchers, our goal was to immerse ourselves as fully as possible in these classrooms, the schools, the community, to come to know from our own experience both the culture within each classroom and the culture which surrounded it. We looked to blend in, to become a part of what was going on, to become familiar figures to school and community members. When secretaries began to call us by our first names or when they had saved some xerox paper for us, when janitors offered us leftover milk or unlocked a door for us, when we knew which entrance to a school was left open late or who would be likely to give us a lift to the local gas station, we knew we had begun to fit in.

Our living situations helped us in becoming community members. Since Shoreham was too far away from New York City for us to commute, we lived in the homes of teachers. For the entire first year of the study, we would arrive in Shoreham on Sunday night or Monday morning and not return home until Thursday night or Friday. As a result, we had hours of after-school time to meet with teachers, attend faculty meetings, interview parents, students, and administrators, to meet together, to talk, and to write. We attended community hearings on the Shoreham Nuclear Power Station, took walks on the beach, ate Chinese food or pizza in local shopping centers; more often than not we worked late in the middle school reading fieldnotes to one another.

In fact, after spending six hours in school each day, writing and reading took up most of our remaining time. We were all diligent notetakers, writing down as much classroom dialogue as we could in each class we visited. Then, as a way to keep track, to review for ourselves and to learn from one another, we would read our fieldnotes aloud. We would list points of interest—commonalities, differences—in a log, initiating a process we were to use over and over, using one set of data (fieldnotes) to generate another (a log book with emerging themes).

Six weeks into the study we knew it was time to review notes, to synthesize, to step back and see what we had been learning. We knew no better way to do this than to write. We did not, however, want to produce *analytic memos,* the traditional ethnographic term used to describe this type of writing, for we felt it was too early to set ourselves up as analysts of another teacher's teaching. As a result, we coined a term to fit our sense of what we were doing: we wrote *thinking-aloud memos.* These documents represented our thoughts and perceptions in response to the question What have I learned about this teacher, this class, so far?

In the midst of writing, we stopped short. It struck us that we had only been in these classrooms for a month or so; the teachers had been in them for years. And so we set in motion another process that was to continue for the next three years: we asked the teachers to join us, to write their perceptions of their classroom, this time in response to this question: What are my implicit assumptions about teaching? or Why do I do what I do? Then, in our study group, we met to explore, to construct together from their papers and our memos a shared view of the classrooms we were now all inhabiting.

In addition to answering our particular questions, the teachers were also writing about their *own* concerns in teaching. They kept teaching journals in which they recorded their perceptions of classroom events, their students, and their thoughts about teaching. They conducted case studies of students in their classes. Some revised these case studies for publication in professional journals; others wrote and revised articles on other aspects of classroom life. They wrote about their reactions to research in the field. They wrote about their reactions to having us in their classrooms. And we wrote back to them.

Over the course of the year, our writing and theirs changed both in tone and scope. Our thinking-aloud memos became longer and more complex. From initial two- to six-page reports on what teachers said and did, they became more thoughtful analyses (some of them 30 to 40 pages long) of what teachers' behaviors meant. We began to ask questions, to clarify areas we did not feel comfortable about, to probe. And with each new round of writing, we included more. We wrote first of our perceptions, sprinkled with direct quotes from the teachers. Then we began to include excerpts from the teachers' journals. By spring, we quoted student writing as well. We kept widening our frame of reference, attempting to explore a broader range of issues from a more varied set of perspectives. We often likened memo writing to panning for gold—dipping the pan into the water, shifting and shaking until something appeared, saving what was useful, discarding what was not useful, and dipping back into the source, over and over again.

As the school year wore on and the teachers began to trust us, to see us not as university researchers or classroom evaluators but as fellow inquirers, their writing changed, too. In the early journals, we researchers appeared as outsiders looking in: "Sondra visited English A today . . ." "Nancy sat with Dave's group. She reported that . . ." Within a few months, however, and in some cases almost immediately, the "shes" gave way to "yous": "Did you notice . . .?" or "I've been meaning to ask you . . ." As the journals passed back and forth, and we began, gradually, to form partnerships in the classrooms, our replies, written in the margins or on sheets of paper stuck between pages, became part of the dialogue, and the journal entries themselves began to sound like letters. By the end of the year, the "shes" had often turned to "wes": "Tomorrow maybe we should consider . . ."

In fact, the study group itself became an extended partnership. Writing back and forth in the journals, circulating notes and memos, studying the data together, we were forging a research team. As researchers, we saw our task as different from the teachers', but we did not necessarily see ourselves as knowing more than they did. In fact, when it came to understanding their classrooms, we thought that the teachers knew more than we did but often without knowing that they knew it. Our job was to tap their implicit knowledge and to work with them to make that knowledge explicit. To accomplish this, we needed to check our perceptions, again and again, against theirs. Memos, comments in journals, chats over coffee and discussions in the study group—all these became ways for each of us to ask each teacher we studied: Does my vision match yours? Am I seeing your classroom the way you see it yourself? If so, what can we add to this shared view? If not, why not?

Furthermore, we were doing ethnography not on a far-away island but in Long Island, close to home; we were studying not members of a culture strange to us but teachers like ourselves. We could not imagine behaving like traditional researchers, keeping our theories and interpretations to ourselves until the publication of a final report. We felt accountable to the teachers we studied. We thought they had a right to know what we were thinking as we sat in their classrooms. And we knew that, although at times it would have been easier for us to remain silent, had we done so we would have been giving up one of the most valuable aspects of our collaboration: the dialogue which would enable us to arrive at a common understanding of the classrooms, an understanding that would make sense not only to us but also to the teachers.

As the weeks passed, and then the months, our understanding of each classroom grew and balances shifted. We researchers found ourselves spending more time in some rooms than others, forming closer ties to some teachers than to others. In some classrooms, we remained primarily observers; in others, more and more, we became participants.

I was most comfortable and most deeply immersed in Diane Burkhardt's eighth-grade classroom; Nancy was most at home in Audre Allison's seventh grade. Was this a problem? we asked ourselves in research meetings. Should we be dividing our time more equally? Or should we let ourselves be drawn to these particular teachers by affinities we could not yet explain? We decided, in the end, that we were facing not so much a problem as another subject for study.

Believing that each of us would learn more by studying one classroom and one teacher deeply than by studying three or four classrooms superficially, we let our inclinations guide us. But always, we examined them. Why these pairs? we asked ourselves. What shared beliefs or sympathies have formed these partnerships? And since, in ethnography, the ethnographer is the primary research tool, we took notes on our answers. We could not and did not try to leave ourselves behind when we sat in classrooms, but we kept on questioning and testing our biases, to try to understand how they influenced what we saw.

By the end of the first year of study, we realized that we had begun to put down roots in Shoreham. We found ourselves sitting in the sun at softball games, making plans to attend school graduations, handing out our addresses to seniors who were graduating or second graders who wanted to send us postcards. We spent hours in front of the district's copying machines, duplicating teachers' journals and students' writing. Preparing to return to the city, we collected audiotapes and videotapes, interview notes, fieldnote books, and our own personal journals. As we loaded boxes of data into our cars, we wondered how we had made sense of it all. What events would emerge as important?

During the second year of our study, data analysis took precedence over data collection. We still visited classrooms (every other week) to keep looking, to follow leads, hunches and even students from last year; but our primary focus was on writing. In fact, by the fall of 1982, our file cabinets were bursting with data: two to three notebooks filled with fieldnotes for each of the 10 teachers, volumes of teaching journals, one year's worth of writing samples from each of the 10 classes, notes and tape recordings from our study group meetings, research papers and personal writing completed by the teachers, our personal journals, interview notes, and audio- and videotapes of selected writing classes and writing groups. In addition, we had all of the writing we had done the first year to help us make sense of what we were collecting while we were collecting it: monthly calendars of events for each class, time sheets logging the number of days and hours spent in class, thinking-aloud memos, a log book of themes, teachers' written responses to what we had written.

Masses of data; bulging file cabinets; how to make sense of it? Where to begin? Ethnographic textbooks speak of triangulating; we felt like drowning! We began though, however hesitantly, to make our way through it.

First, we worked chronologically, writing narrative accounts of classroom events that combined our view (taken from our fieldnotes), the teacher's view (taken from his or her journal), and the students' responses (taken from their written products). In this instance, our fieldnotes and the flow of time served as the main organizer; all other data fit into the chronological scheme.

Then we took a logical approach. We let the writing process principles be the main organizer and we examined how each principle was played out in each classroom. We asked, for instance, how the notion of collaboration worked in each classroom. What collaborative acts occurred in a first- or a fifth-grade class which resembled or differed from collaborative acts in an eighth- or eleventh-grade class? We looked, as another example, at the concept of ownership, and asked how ownership worked in the 10 classrooms we had studied. Here, categories which we derived from our understanding of the writing process formed the basis of our analysis.

Finally, we took the teachers' journals as the main vehicle and asked: What, by virtue of being written about over and over, seems to matter to each teacher? What themes, if any, seem to recur in a particular teacher's journal? Once we found a recurring theme, we asked: Are there examples of this theme being played out in the teacher's behavior? Our answers led us to produce portraits of each teacher, three- to four-page analyses capturing what for us was the particular and unique core of each teacher's teaching.

None of this writing is what we finally produced either in our report to the National Institute of Education (Perl, Wilson, & Carter, 1985) or in our book (Perl & Wilson, 1986). It was all preliminary, a way of immersing ourselves, coming to understand, discovering connections, deepening our understanding. We needed to write and write until we saw what we had. We needed many cuts through the data until moments that mattered, the key classes, and the telling incidents emerged.

We discovered that chronologies were useful, but they went on too long. Who wants to read what happens *every* day in *every* class? The writing process principles were interesting, we felt, but too dry. Imposing categories from without did not capture the life we knew we had experienced by living in those classrooms. And the portraits? Here we surprised ourselves: We went into Shoreham with the purpose of studying how teachers teach writing. We discovered that we had collected data on how teachers teach where, in this case, the subject *happens to be* writing. We saw that these teachers would teach any subject according to who they were—that their beliefs, biases, preferences, and predilections make them the teachers they are, and that any analysis of their teaching of writing would have to include a description of the particular presence they bring with them into the classroom. We came to see that the culture of writing instruction in any given class consists not only of the particular approach or theories guiding the teacher, nor simply the histories and personalities of the students, but also—perhaps especially—the personal stance of the teacher.

During this second year of the study, we brought our analyses and classroom write-ups to the study group. The teachers read them, responded, poked fun at our categories and were sometimes made uncomfortable by being so carefully examined. They smiled at our preoccupation with *understanding*. They, as they often reminded us, were content to teach. We often were torn: wanting to join them fully in appreciating and following the growth of students this second year, versus the need to focus in on the previous one, trying to understand, to get at the core. In fact, the second year was a divided one for us. In New York, at Lehman College, we would write and think, sift and sort, question and analyze. The following week, in Shoreham, we would observe and take notes, Xerox writing and interview; at times we would return to the classrooms we were in the year before; more often than not, we pursued new interests. I switched my focus to the elementary school, visiting a first-grade class; Nancy followed her eleventh-grade students into twelfth-grade and also spent time in a combined fourth- and fifth-grade class.

By our third year, we found ourselves on firmer ground. All the writing we had done, the going back and reviewing, the looking and looking again, had taught us something. When we first entered classrooms, looked at a teacher's or a student's behavior and asked the most basic ethnographic question, What does this mean? all we could answer was: We do not know. We were outsiders. Three years later this had changed. We knew when a teacher we studied did something, what it meant—to her, to her students. Glances, raised eyebrows, sitting, standing, moving, being quiet or talking, the most minute pieces of behavior and the largest actions—all had accumulated meaning, significance. When we now asked, What does this mean?, we answered with an insider's perspective.

Thus, in the third, fourth, and fifth years of turning thousands of preliminary pages into a book, we were faced with the task of showing how the teachers we had studied taught writing. And, at the same time, we were conveying all that we knew—about them, their lives, their students—to provide readers with an insider's view of the writing process approach and still to bring these classrooms to life.

To capture the life of the classroom, to show what teaching was like, we eventually decided to write our research as a story. We did so for many reasons. First, we believe in the inherent power of narrative. To us, nothing teaches as well as a story. For as readers, we learn from stories and go on to construct our own.

Second, we believe that ethnography is strongest when it is not trying to prove anything. This is not to say that we were not rigorous, but we think that our rigor can best be measured by readers who ask themselves Does this story ring true?, or Are these teachers and students believable?

Third, we are not looking to create an *exportable classroom*. We are hoping that just as readers of literature come to examine themselves in the light of characters whose lives and thoughts speak to them, so teachers who read our report will use the particulars of details we have amassed to illuminate both the teachers they are reading about and their own teaching lives.

Fourth, more than anything else, we have come to see that each classroom is a world unto itself; each year has its own integrity, its own story. To cut each classroom up into little bits to serve some general point seemed, to us, to run counter to everything we had learned. As a result, we chose to let the story of each classroom unfold, not in brief anecdotes but in year-long tales of each teacher's teaching year.

We tell, for instance, the story of a first-grade teacher who is scared of writing yet who finds a way to let her fear guide her in teaching six- and seven-year-olds to write. We tell the story of an eleventh-grade teacher whose values about teaching writing and literature are in conflict with the traditional eleventh-grade curriculum which emphasizes test preparation for college placement examinations.

We tell the story of an eighth-grade teacher who forms partnerships with her 13- and 14-year-old students; of a fourth- and fifth-grade teacher who turns his classroom into a laboratory for the study of children's thinking; of a twelfth-grade teacher who finds ways to interest his underachieving seniors in their own growth by encouraging them to observe it and write about it. And, finally, we tell the painful story in the book, the story of another eighth-grade teacher who, after 20 successful years of teaching, experiences failure as a teacher; who sadly concludes that his classroom, the year we studied it, had become a battlefield.

It seemed important to us to let each story unfold, to encourage readers to enter each classroom and immerse themselves in the lives we presented; as researchers, however, we also felt we had another task to complete. We felt that as much as we had disentangled the significant in each classroom, we needed further to ask "What do these six stories, taken together, mean?"

In one final chapter, then, we stand back and discuss what we learned about teaching and writing. We discuss the ways classroom communities are formed and the ways teachers can use or abuse their authority in their quest to enable students to write. We look at the notions of reflection and collaboration and the ways each can help teachers see more clearly what they are doing. And, finally, we look at what we call the act of seeing the way in which how we see affects how we teach.

This final point brings me to my conclusion. *Through Teachers' Eyes,* the title of this paper as well as the title of our book, refers not only to the six teachers we described or to our own eyes which examined them, but also to the eyes of our profession. It refers to all readers and writers who are also teachers and researchers, and to how all of us see or perceive our students, our classrooms, and our work. It seems to me that our professional lives would be enhanced if we could look more closely at, and let one another in on, our own stories, on the decisions which guided our research and on what we see when we study and teach.

REFERENCES

Agar, M. H. (1980). *The professional stranger: An informal introduction to ethnography.* New York: Academic Press.

Perl, S. (1981). *How teachers teach the writing process.* Grant proposal submitted to the National Institute of Education.

Perl, S., Wilson, N., & Carter, J. (1985). *How teachers teach the writing process* (Final Rep., Grant No. G-82-0011). Washington DC: National Institute of Education.

Perl, S., & Wilson, N. (1986). *Through teachers' eyes: Portraits of writing teachers at work.* Portsmouth, NH: Heinemann.

Rist, R. (1980). Blitzkrieg ethnography: On the transformation of a method into a movement. *Educational Researcher, 9,* 8-10.

COHESIVE HARMONY ANALYSIS: ISSUES OF TEXT PRAGMATICS AND MACROSTRUCTURE

Lawrence B. Friedman
North Central Regional Educational Laboratory

Elizabeth Sulzby
University of Michigan

A variety of analytic tools are being used to chart the development of children's written language abilities. To our knowledge, nobody has perfected a completely satisfactory analytic tool for any purpose prior to application. Rather, the tools are refined recursively in the research process. One collects data that appear appropriate to the tool, analyzes the data, talks with other researchers about the tool and its features, refines the tool, and begins the process again if need be. Above all, one attempts to communicate the analytic difficulties encountered to other researchers so that further research can address them.

Cohesive harmony analysis (Hasan, 1984; Pappas, 1981) is one analytic tool which has been developed and refined through use. Hasan developed cohesive harmony analysis because she found that cohesion analysis did not capture all the coherence of a written text. She and others (Hasan, 1984; King & Rentel, 1981; Rentel & King, 1983) have continued to refine cohesive harmony analysis, making it an increasingly powerful tool for analyzing written text.

Cox (1986) used cohesive harmony analysis in a study comparing narrative and expository texts written by 24 good and 24 poor readers from third and fifth grades. She found significant correlations between cohesive harmony scores and reading ability and between cohesive harmony scores and grade level. The first author served as a second scorer and the second author as consultant in Cox's study. During the course of the analysis, we found some problems with cohesive harmony analysis that may contribute to its refinement. In this article, we briefly describe cohesive harmony analysis, discuss three problems and their implications, and suggest solutions to make the analysis more accurate. The problems indicate that the lexical and grammatical sources of textual coherence identified by cohesive harmony do not exhaust the sources of textual coherence. Pragmatic and macrostructural factors also play a role.

THE PROPERTY OF COHESIVE HARMONY

Cohesive harmony is a property of oral and written texts. It is easiest to understand the property of cohesive harmony through its relation to coherence, another property of oral and written texts. Coherence, according to Hasan (1984) is the ". . . property of 'unity', of 'hanging together' " (p. 181). This unity is the semantic or the representational unity of the text's clauses. The more a text's clauses hang together, the greater is its cohesive harmony. In short, a text's cohesive harmony is its clausal-level coherence, a substantial part of its overall coherence.

A high degree of cohesive harmony is a necessary, but not sufficient, condition for a high degree of textual coherence. However, data suggest a strong correlation between a text's cohesive harmony and its coherence. Hasan's (1984) data support the hypothesis that ". . . ranking by cohesive harmony will match the ranking of the texts on a cline of coherence by reference to reader/listener reaction . . ." (p. 218).

Hasan says the clauses of a text display cohesive harmony, or hang together when ". . . similar 'things' are said about similar/same 'entities', 'events', etc." (p. 212). For simplicity's sake, we will use the term *subjects* in place of *entities, events,* etc. Unpacking Hasan's gloss of cohesive harmony, clauses hang together when three conditions are met:

1. The clauses contain terms saying similar things;
2. The clauses contain terms mentioning similar/same subjects; and,
3. These terms are related so that the similar things are said about the similar/same subjects.

Cohesive Chains: Saying Similar Things and Mentioning Similar/Same Subjects

Terms say similar things when they stand in certain grammatical and/or lexical relations to each other. Similarly, terms mention similar/same subjects when certain lexical and/or grammatical relations hold among them. These lexical and grammatical relations establish semantic bonds between terms. These semantic bonds constitute most of a text's *cohesion.* (A third category of grammatical relations, *conjunction,* contributes to a text's cohesion but does not figure in the text's cohesive harmony.)

Table 1 lists the lexical and grammatical relations which can hold among terms saying similar things and among terms mentioning similar/same subjects. Note that lexical relations 1–5 are text-independent; that is, they hold between terms in any text. Lexical relations 6–8 are text-dependent; they hold only within particular texts. It also should be noted that the eight lexical relations do not exhaust the lexical relations contributing to cohesive harmony. However, they come close and those not included are very difficult to operationalize (Cox, 1986; Hasan, 1984).

Cohesive chains are formed through the text by terms saying similar things and terms mentioning similar/same subjects. The links of such chains are the grammatical and lexical relations holding among the terms in the chains. There are two kinds of chain. A chain which contains only terms referring to the same subject is an *identity chain.* All other chains are *similarity chains.* A similarity chain contains terms mentioning similar subjects or terms saying similar things. Thus, two terms say similar things when the terms belong to the same similarity chain and two terms mention similar/same subjects when the terms belong to the same similarity chain or identity chain.

Table 1

The Grammatical and Lexical Relations of Cohesive Harmony*

Grammatical Relations	
1. Reference	
a. Pronominal	*A cat* is on the mat. *It* is sleeping.
b. Definite article	*A cat* is in the house but I cannot find *the cat.*
c. Demonstrative	*Larry's cat* is difficult. *That cat* is incorrigible.
d. Comparative	Leslie is *5'11''*. Chris is *taller.*
2. Substitution	
a. Nominal	*My cat* is friendly. *The animal* is too friendly.
b. Verbal	My cat *stays out all night.* Mine *does,* too.
c. Clausal	*Larry's cat is incorrigible.* Perhaps *so.*
3. Ellipsis	
a. Nominal	*My cat* stays out all night and *(it)* sleeps all day.
b. Verbal	My cat can *sing.* Really, it can *(sing).*
c. Clausal	*Can my cat sing?* You bet *(my cat can sing).*
Lexical Relations—Text-independent	
1. Repetition	The cat *left* the house. The dog *left,* too.
2. Synonymy	The cat *slept* in the sun. The dog *napped,* too.
3. Antonymy	My cat is *awake.* My dog is *asleep.*
4. Hyponomy (class inclusion)	*Alley cats* have character. Most *cats* do.
5. Meronomy (part/whole)	My *cat* is black and white. Its *paw* is black.
Lexical Relations—Text-dependent	
6. Equivalence	My *cat* is *my best friend.*
7. Naming	*My cat* is named *Leslie.*
8. Semblance	My cat *climbs* like an infant *crawls.*

*Adapted from Hasan (1984).

Chain Interaction: Saying Similar Things about Similar/Same Subjects

According to Hasan (1984), two clauses say similar things about similar/same subjects when the similarity chain containing the terms saying similar things *interacts* with the similarity or identity chain mentioning similar/same subjects. Her account of chain interaction is based on a second set of grammatical relations borrowed from Halliday's (1985) account of the representational meaning of clauses.

Central to Halliday's account of the representational meaning of clauses is the semantic thesis that a clause represents at least one process and the participant(s) in that process; it also may represent the circumstances of that process. The grammar of a clause mirrors this semantic thesis. A term in a clause may play the grammatical role of process, participant, or circumstance. Process roles typically are filled by verbs or verbal groups, participant roles by nouns, noun groups, or pronouns, and circumstance roles by adverbs, adverbial groups, or prepositional phrases. For example, in the clause *The dog barked for an hour,* the process is represented by *barked,* the participant is represented by *The dog,* and *for an hour* represents a circumstance of the barking.

Table 2 lists the various process roles, participant roles, and circumstance roles. Notice that particular participant roles are associated with particular process roles. This is not the case for circumstance role; each circumstance role is associated with each process role, although some of the associations rarely occur (Halliday, 1985).

Participant/process role pairs, such as recipient/material process and sensor/

Table 2

Grammatical Roles: Processes, Participants, and Circumstances*

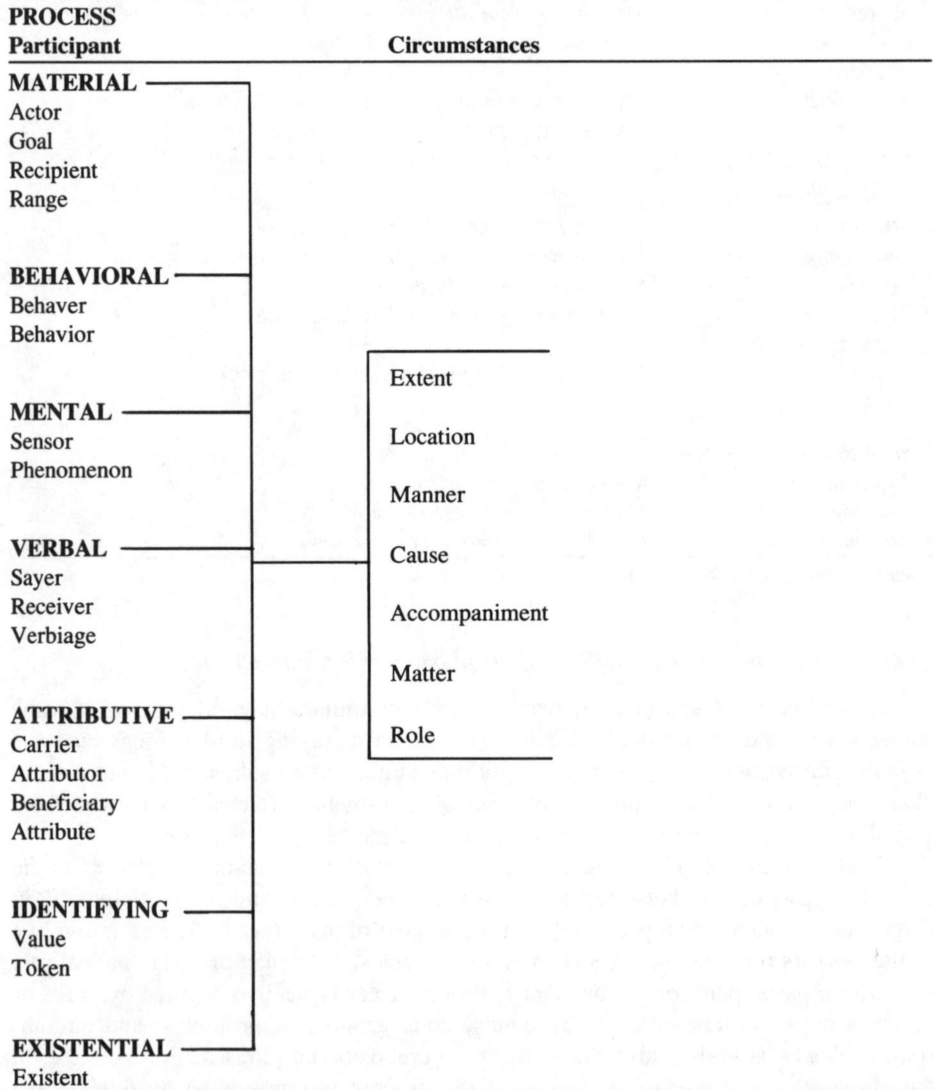

PROCESS **Participant**	**Circumstances**
MATERIAL Actor Goal Recipient Range	
BEHAVIORAL Behaver Behavior	
MENTAL Sensor Phenomenon	Extent Location Manner
VERBAL Sayer Receiver Verbiage	Cause Accompaniment Matter Role
ATTRIBUTIVE Carrier Attributor Beneficiary Attribute	
IDENTIFYING Value Token	
EXISTENTIAL Existent	

*Adapted from Halliday (1985).

mental process, and process/circumstance role pairs, such as behavioral process/extent and identifying process/location, specify grammatical relations. For example, the clause *The dog barked for an hour,* contains two grammatical relations. The actor/material process relation holds between *The dog* and *barked* and material process/extent relation holds between *barked* and *for an hour.*

Hasan also uses one grammatical relation, epithet/thing, occurring *within* a participant role or a circumstance role in her account of chain interaction. Epithets represent qualities of things. In the clause *The gray dog barked at the silver moon, gray* is an epithet of *dog* as is *silver* of *moon.* We hypothesize that Hasan included this third kind of about-relation because, without it, some adjectives belonging to cohesive chains would not figure in the cohesive harmony of a text.

Cohesive chains interaction takes place when two terms in one chain stand in the same grammatical relation to two terms in the other chain. Thus, two clauses C1 and C2 say similar things about similar/same subjects when

1. C1 contains a term *a* and C2 contains a term *b* such that *a* and *b* belong to one cohesive chain;
2. C1 contains a term *c* and C2 contains a term *d* such that *c* and *d* belong to a second cohesive chain; and,
3. The *same* grammatical relation holds between *a* and *c* and between *b* and *d.*

Consider the following three clauses.

C1. The dog chased the robot.
C2. The cat chased a string.
C3. The robot chased the mouse.

C1 and C2 say similar things about similar subjects. The terms *dog* in C1 and *cat* in C2 form a similarity chain. The *chased*s in C1 and C2 form a similarity chain. (The two *chased*s do not form an identity chain because an identity chain is formed when two terms *refer* to the same subject. The term *chased* does not refer.) The same grammatical relation, actor/material process holds between *dog* and *chased* and between *cat* and *chased.* C2 and C3 say similar things and mention similar subjects but do *not* say similar things about similar subjects. The terms *cat* in C2 and *mouse* in C3 mention similar subjects because they form a similarity chain. The two *chased*s say similar things because they form a similarity chain. However, the grammatical relation actor/material process holds between *cat* and *chased* while the grammatical relation, material process/goal holds between *chased* and *mouse.*

THREE PROBLEMS WITH COHESIVE HARMONY ANALYSIS

In this section, we argue that cohesive harmony analysis is an incomplete analysis of the representational unity of a text's clauses. Cohesive harmony analysis locates the sources of a text's representational unity in the lexis and grammar of the text. We agree that a text's lexis and grammar are sources of the text's representational unity. However, we question that they are the *only* sources. The problems presented below indicate that the pragmatics and macrostructure of a text are additional sources of representational unity.

The Problem of Hyponomy

Hyponomy, or set inclusion, is one of the lexical relations of cohesive harmony. The lexical relation of hyponomy is a text-independent relation. Two terms are hyponyms if the extension of one of the terms is a subset of the extension of the other term or the extensions of the two terms are subsets of a larger set. If two terms in different clauses are hyponyms, the terms belong to the same similarity chain and, hence, count for or against cohesive harmony and representational unity.

The problem of hyponomy is that the definition of *hyponomy* is overly liberal. It allows terms such as *artichoke, virus,* and *person* to be hyponyms since their extensions are subsets of the set of living things. Similarly, *carnation* and *living thing* are hyponyms because the set of carnations is a subset of living things. Revising the definition to exclude such cases for nonarbitrary reasons while keeping hyponomy a text-independent, lexical relation is difficult if not impossible, especially in nontaxonomic semantic networks. However, unless this can be done, hyponomy is an indeterminate relation. The indeterminacy of hyponomy infects similarity chain membership. Therefore, the indeterminacy of hyponomy results in indeterminacy of cohesive harmony and representational unity.

We think the solution to the problem of hyponomy is to leave its definition alone and treat hyponomy as a text-dependent, pragmatic relation. What counts as hyponomy *in a particular text,* and thus, what counts as similarity chain membership in that text, depends on the *purpose* of the text. Consider two texts which discuss dogs and cats. One text contrasts dogs and cats. The other text discusses animals and uses dogs and cats as examples. In the text which contrasts dogs and cats, *dog* and *cat* do not function as hyponyms because the purpose of the text is to contrast the mutually exclusive sets of cats and dogs. In the text which discusses animals and uses dogs and cats as examples, *dog* and *cat* function as hyponyms because the purpose of the text is to discuss the set of animals of which the set of dogs and cats are subsets. Our solution to the problem of hyponomy introduces a pragmatic aspect into the concept of cohesive harmony to capture a pragmatic aspect of representational unity.

The Problem of Clausal Order

The problem of clausal order for cohesive harmony analysis is that a text's representational unity is always a function of the order of its clauses while the text's cohesive harmony need not be. Two texts containing the same clauses in different order display the same degree of cohesive harmony as long as they contain the same failures of reference, illegitimate ellipses, and illegitimate substitutions. The texts display equal degrees of cohesive harmony because clausal order only affects the cohesive harmony relations of reference, ellipsis, and substitution. However, as the two texts below show, identity of cohesive harmony does not ensure identity of representational unity. There is a difference between the two text's representational unity because the two text's develop their representations differently.

Text 1. Almost everyone can tell an animal from something that is not an animal. How can we tell? We know that an animal is a living thing or an organism. We know that rocks, stars, and houses are not animals because they are not organisms. However, some organisms are not animals. There are three differences between plants and animals. One difference is that an animal can move voluntarily, or on its own, but a plant cannot. Another difference between a plant and an animal is that an animal has specialized sense organs, such as eyes and ears, while plants do not. The final difference between a plant and an animal is that animals cannot make their own food but plants can through the process of photosynthesis.

Text 2. There are three differences between plants and animals. One difference is that an animal can move voluntarily, or on its own, but a plant cannot. Almost everyone can tell an animal from something that is not an animal. How can we tell? Another difference between a plant and an animal is that an animal has specialized sense organs, such as eyes and ears, while plants do not. We know that an animal is a living thing or an organism. We know that rocks, stars, and houses are not animals because they are not organisms. However, some organisms are not animals. The final difference between a plant and an animal is that animals cannot make their own food but plants can through the process of photosynthesis.

A solution to the clausal order problem is to include the relations which figure in representational development in the relations of cohesive harmony. Two examples of relations which play a role in representational development are relations between a text's macrostructure and clausal order and relations between the intended audience's relevant knowledge base and clausal order. For instance, presenting the solution to a problem in the midst of describing the problem harms representational development as does presenting unfamiliar concepts before presenting familiar examples. Including these relations in the relations of cohesive harmony expands the sources of cohesive harmony to include the macrostructure and pragmatics of text as well as its lexis and grammar.

The Problem of Clausal Redundancy

Clausal redundancy can be characterized as saying similar things about the same subjects with a vengeance. Clausal redundancy occurs when two or more clauses repeat the same information. The clauses may repeat the information word for word or use different words in different orders to repeat the information. The clausal redundancy problem, in brief, is that clausal redundancy can increase the cohesive harmony of a text while diminishing the text's representational unity.

Clausal redundancy increases the cohesive harmony of a text in all cases in which the redundant clause occurring first in the text does not contain a referring term which fails to establish reference, an illegitimate substitution, or an illegitimate ellipsis. (When the first redundant clause contains such terms, cohesive harmony may increase or decrease.) Terms in the later redundant clause(s) enter into cohesive chains to which terms in the first redundant clause belong and/or form new cohesive chains with terms in the first redundant clause. The terms from the later redundant clause(s) in cohesive chains will stand in the same grammatical relations as terms from the first redundant clause, thereby increasing chain interaction and cohesive harmony.

Clausal redundancy which increases cohesive harmony diminishes representational unity when the redundancy increases representational confusion. Consider two examples.

First, consider a three-paragraph text which compares and contrasts dogs and cats. The first paragraph discusses dogs, the second cats, and the third similarities and differences between dogs and cats. The cat-paragraph contains two clauses about dogs which repeat information in the dog-paragraph and increase the cohesive harmony of the text. Most, if not all, readers/listeners would judge that these two clauses do not increase the representational unity of the text. Rather, they would judge that the clauses reduce representational unity because they create representational confusion in the cat-paragraph. However, if the redundant clauses were located in the paragraph discussing similarities and differences of cats and dogs, they would remind readers/listeners of information useful for understanding the similarities and differences. Locating the redundant clauses in this paragraph increases representational clarity, thereby increasing representational unity.

Next, consider a text which contains the clause *A dog chased a cat* followed by the clause *In other words, a domestic canine pursued a domestic feline.* The presence of the second redundant clause increases the cohesive harmony of the text. However, the second clause would cause representational confusion and, hence, decrease representational unity, for readers/listeners who do not understand it and/or the purpose for its inclusion. Notice that, for these readers/listeners, the representational clarity of a text containing the clause *A domestic canine pursued a domestic feline* increases if that clause is followed by the clause *In other words, a dog chased a cat.*

These examples show that the problem of clausal redundancy arises for cohesive harmony analysis because the grammatical and lexical relations of cohesive harmony do not distinguish between redundancy which increases, and redundancy which diminishes, representational unity and clarity. The compare and contrast example suggests that one textual feature involved in the distinction is the location of the second redundant clause in the macrostructure of the text. The adjacent redundant clauses example suggests that a pragmatic textual feature, audience appropriateness, also is involved in the distinction.

SUMMARY

While cohesive harmony analysis measures an important part of a text's representational unity, it is not without problems. It does not produce a determinant measure of a text's representational unity (the problem of hyponomy) and, in some cases, inaccurately measures a text's representational unity (the problems of clausal order and clausal redundancy). The problems arise because the lexical and grammatical relations upon which cohesive harmony analysis is based are not the only textual features which contribute to a text's representational unit. The pragmatic and macrostructural features of a text also contribute.

Research using cohesive harmony analysis has revealed developmental patterns in children's use of lexical and grammatical resources to produce coherent written texts (e.g., Cox, 1986; Pappas, 1981; Rentel & King, 1983). The problems we have raised for cohesive harmony analysis do not call into question this research. However, they suggest that a *necessary* supplement to this research is research into the developmental patterns of children's use of the pragmatic and macrostructural resources to produce coherent written texts.

The impact of pragmatic and macrostructural factors on textual coherence has implications for the methodology of research on the development of children's abilities to produce coherent texts. The pragmatic impact, on one hand, is one more reason why such research must tap other sources of data, such as the text's author and context, in addition to the paper or tape with the *text* on it. On the other hand, if the research analyzes only the paper- or tape-text, the research design must control for pragmatic variables (cf. Cox & Tinzmann, 1986; Kamberelis & Sulzby, 1986). The impact of macrostructural factors reminds us that generalizations about the development of children's abilities to produce coherent text often only hold for particular kinds of text. It also reminds us of how important it is for the research upon which such generalizations are made to specify, and control for, those writing/speaking task variables which influence macrostructure.

REFERENCES

Cox, B. (1986). *Cohesion and content organization in the narrative and expository writing of children.* Unpublished doctoral dissertation, Northwestern University, Evanston, IL.

Cox, B., & Tinzmann, M. B. (1986, December). *The development of the literate voice.* Symposium paper presented at the annual meeting of the National Reading Conference, Austin, TX.

Halliday, M. A. K. (1985). *An introduction to functional grammar.* Baltimore, MD: Edward Arnold.

Hasan, R. (1984). Coherence and cohesive harmony. In J. Flood (Ed.), *Understanding reading comprehension* (pp. 181-219). Newark, DE: International Reading Association.

Kamberelis, G., & Sulzby, E. (1986, December). *Emergent and polyphonic voices in adolescent writing.* Symposium paper presented at the annual meeting of the National Reading Conference, Austin, TX.

King, M. L., & Rentel, V. M. (1981). *How children learn to write: A longitudinal study* (RF Project 761861/12383 and 761513/711748, Final Rep., June). Columbus, OH: Ohio State University.

Pappas, C. G. (1981). *The development of narrative capabilities within a synergistic, variable perspective of language development: An examination of cohesive harmony of stories produced in three contexts—retelling, dictating, and writing.* Unpublished doctoral dissertation, Ohio State University, Columbus, OH.

Rentel, V. M., & King, M. L. (1983). *A longitudinal study of coherence in children's written narratives* (Grant No. NIE-G-81-0063). Washington, DC: National Institute of Education.

NRC YEARBOOK SURVEY
NRC PROGRAM
INDICES

YEARBOOK OF THE NATIONAL READING CONFERENCE MEMBERSHIP SURVEY AND RESULTS

Jill Fitzgerald and Dixie Lee Spiegel
University of North Carolina at Chapel Hill

The 1985 Board of Directors of the National Reading Conference (NRC) authorized the Publications Committee to review the *Yearbook of the National Reading Conference* by means of a membership survey. The main purposes of the survey were (a) to determine NRC members' perceptions of the *Yearbook* with regard to its importance, potential utility, and quality; (b) to determine if NRC members use the *Yearbook* and, if so, how the *Yearbook* is used; and (c) to determine NRC members' opinions about changes with regard to the *Yearbook.*

METHOD

Materials and Procedure

The NRC Publications Committee met with us at the May 6, 1986 annual meeting of the International Reading Association to offer guidance, make comments, and suggest questions for the survey. We then developed a statement of the purpose of the survey and the format and items for the questionnaire. The questionnaire was distributed among Publications Committee members for review and was then edited and revised. Surveys were mailed to the 804 NRC members in July 1986, with a second wave sent to members who had not so far responded in early August.

The survey contained three major sections, one corresponding to each of the three main purposes. Minimal demographic information was also collected. Most items were Likert-type (with possible responses ranging from strongly disagree to strongly agree, scored from one to 11). One item required respondents to rank entries. Another set of questions was open-ended, and a final set was multiple choice. The survey items (excepting the two demographic items) are shown in Tables 1 through 4.

Analyses. To address the main purposes of the survey, several types of analyses were done. First, descriptive statistics were compiled for each item except the open-ended responses. Second, to aggregate information, eight scales were created by averaging selected items. (Items worded negatively were reverse scored when used in scales.) Four of the scales revealed the extent to which respondents agreed with positive statements about (a) overall quality of the *Yearbook,* (b) quality of the style and format of the *Yearbook,* (c) quality of the content of the *Yearbook,* and (d) quality of the review procedures used for the *Yearbook.* The other four scales revealed the extent to which respondents agreed there should be changes in (a) the *Yearbook* in general, (b) style and format of the *Yearbook,* (c) content of the *Yearbook,* and (d) review procedures used for the *Yearbook.* Coefficient alphas for reliability of the eight scales were moderately positive for seven of the scales, ranging from .70 to .86. The coefficient alpha was somewhat low (.63) for the scale dealing with the extent to which respondents agreed there should be changes in content of the *Yearbook.* Third, relationships between selected variables were examined. Fourth, responses to the open-ended questions for suggested changes were categorized and tabulated. For each of the 14 open-ended questions (items 36a through 36n), subcategories of possible responses were created. For example, for item 36b, changes suggested regarding number of reports, the subcategories were "more," "fewer," "fewer but better," "fewer but longer," and "fewer but more important." An answer was counted as containing as many responses as could be placed in unique categories. For example, a response to changes regarding durability (item 36d) such as "hardcover if content is improved," was coded as one response for the "hard binding" subcategory under "appearance" and one response for the "improve level of scholarship" category. Interrater reliability for assignment of responses to subcategories was .83.

RESULTS

Summary data for items and scales are shown in Tables 1 through 5.

Respondents

Five hundred seven members responded to the survey, constituting a 63% return rate. In all, there were 492 usable questionnaires. (Not all members responded to each question. Also, missing cases for items or for combinations of items caused subjects to be dropped during computer analyses.)

Of the respondents, 41.08% (N = 198) were NRC members for one to three years, 41.91% (N = 202) were members for four to nine years, and 17.01% (N = 82) were members for 10 or more years. Most respondents held university teaching and research positions (70.07%, N = 323). The remaining respondents were fairly evenly dispersed across six remaining categories: public school administration, work in a research facility, public or private school teaching, work within a publishing company, graduate student status, or other (range of percentages = 1.30 to 8.03, range of Ns = 6 to 29).

Perceptions of the Yearbook

Is it important? The membership tended to think the *Yearbook* is important, but appeared to feel it has more potential to make an impact on the field than it currently does. The responses to item 1 indicated the membership tended to agree that the

Table 1

Summary Data for Items on the *Yearbook*'s Importance, Potential Utility, and Quality

Item	Mean	*SD*	Number of Responses
1. The *Yearbook* has the potential to be an important contribution to the literature on language/literacy/reading research.	9.52	1.70	484
2. The *Yearbook* is an important contribution to the literature on language/literacy/reading research.	8.39	2.17	488
3. The *Yearbook* could/should be used for:			
a. reproduction for class handouts	7.62	2.69	468
b. one's personal library	9.82	1.62	468
c. an outlet for research dissemination	9.74	1.63	468
d. resource for brief research reports	9.15	2.12	468
e. a representation of the NRC annual meeting	8.78	2.29	468
4. The length of reports is appropriate.	7.92	2.50	478
5. The number of reports in the *Yearbook* is just about right.	7.91	2.28	476
6. The durability of *Yearbook* paper and binding is good.	8.42	1.87	485
7. I like the *Yearbook*'s general appearance.	8.46	1.80	485
8. I like the Oscar Causey Award section.	7.22	2.26	413
9. The content of the *Yearbook* reflects the content of the annual meeting very well.	8.05	1.83	436
10. The content reflects current thinking and research.	8.63	1.88	482
11. The listing of the NRC annual meeting program is a valuable feature.	8.21	2.47	476
12. The current quality of scholarship in reports is high.	7.97	2.02	486
13. Generally the reports make a substantial contribution to the literature.	7.89	2.13	486
14. Generally reports are well-written.	8.10	1.79	487
15. The review(s) I received was (were) adequate.	7.72	2.33	178
16. The review(s) was (were) fair.	8.21	1.96	177
17. The review(s) was (were) not timely.	4.75	2.94	166
18. The reviewer's comments were helpful.	7.14	2.48	174
19. Two reviewers per report is sufficient.	7.53	2.60	177
20. The reviewers are not representative of NRC membership.	4.02	2.38	159
21. Most of the reviewers are recognized scholars.	7.83	1.97	152

Note. Respondents were asked to answer items 15 through 21 only if they had submitted at least one report to the *Yearbook* during the last three years. The mean number of reports submitted was 1.74 (*SD* = 1.05), and the personal acceptance rate averaged .70 (*SD* = .40).

Table 2

Summary Data for Items on Use of the *Yearbook*

Item	Mean	*SD*	Number of Responses	Median Rank
22. I don't use the *Yearbook* much.	4.94	2.81	471	
23. I use the *Yearbook* for:				
a. reproduction for class handouts	4.65	3.23	382	
b. my personal library	9.62	1.76	468	
c. an outlet for research dissemination	7.56	3.10	409	
d. resource for brief research reports	8.54	2.42	443	
e. a representation of the NRC annual meeting	7.67	2.78	430	
24. Please rank order the following entries, using 1 for the entry you feel is the main way you use the *Yearbook,* 2 for the next greatest use, etc.				
_____a. reproduction for class handouts				4.61
_____b. my personal library				1.23
_____c. an outlet for research dissemination				3.10
_____d. a resource for brief research reports				2.22
_____e. a representation of the NRC annual meeting				3.71

Note. Respondents were asked to answer item 24 only if they used the *Yearbook.*

Yearbook has the potential to be an important contribution to the field. It is useful to know also that responses to this item were negatively skewed with 86% of the respondents either agreeing or strongly agreeing that the *Yearbook* has the potential to be an important contribution to the field.

Responses to item 2 indicated a tendency to agree that the *Yearbook* does make an important contribution to the field. However, the mean response was slightly lower than for item 1, and although still negatively skewed, only 61% of the respondents either agreed or strongly agreed with the statement.

How might the Yearbook be used? Responses to item 3 showed that individuals tended to mildly agree or agree that the *Yearbook* could or should be used for class handouts, one's personal library, an outlet for research dissemination, a resource for brief research reports, and a representation of the NRC annual meeting.

What is the quality of the Yearbook? The first four means in Table 5 are for the four scales on the extent to which respondents agreed with positive statements about the quality of the *Yearbook.* The means indicated that individuals were moderately positive about the quality. The average for the quality of review procedures was lowest, but still positive.

It is of interest to know that, of those who had submitted reports to the *Yearbook,* the average number of reports submitted during the last three years was 1.74, and the personal acceptance rate was .70, with 57% of those who had submitted reports having personal acceptance rates of 1.00. Most importantly, as might be expected, there was a statistically significant correlation between personal acceptance rate and the extent to which respondents viewed review procedures positively (r = .48, p = .01).

Table 3

Summary Data for Items on Changes for the *Yearbook*

Item	Mean	*SD*	Number of Responses
25. The *Yearbook* should be eliminated.	1.84	1.83	467
26. There should be changes in the *Yearbook* in:			
a. length of reports	5.24	3.03	436
b. number of reports	5.10	2.91	437
c. special features	4.77	2.65	406
d. durability	4.21	2.51	434
e. appearance	4.14	2.41	435
f. print size	4.00	2.36	430
g. the extent to which reports reflect the annual meeting	4.52	2.49	415
h. level of scholarship of reports	4.95	2.76	436
i. the degree to which reports contribute to the field	5.12	2.93	422
j. fairness of reviews	4.57	2.52	367
k. timeliness of reviews	4.46	2.43	363
l. quality of responses to authors	4.94	2.64	358
m. capability of reviewers	4.50	2.53	355
27. I think the annual debate should be included in each *Yearbook.*	6.52	3.26	452
28. I think the Plenary Sessions presentations should be included every year.	6.28	3.07	440
29. The Annual Review of Research should be included every year.	7.92	2.79	452
30. A topic index would be useful.	9.19	2.25	479
31. Dual publication in the *Yearbook* and other outlets should be encouraged.	6.58	3.46	456
32. There should be an option of submitting extended abstracts instead of reports.	5.70	3.36	466
33. There should be section headings within the body of the *Yearbook.*	7.63	2.65	462
34. There should be a brief introduction for each section of the *Yearbook.*	6.26	2.95	466
35. Submitted manuscripts should be reviewed with authors' names removed.	9.12	2.60	475

Use of the Yearbook

The responses to item 22 indicated that the *Yearbook* is used to a moderate extent. For items 23 and 24, the responses showed that, for those who use the *Yearbook,* certain uses predominated. The *Yearbook* was used mainly as a personal library, next as a resource for research reports, as an outlet for dissemination, as a reproduction of the NRC annual meeting, and last for class handouts.

Table 4

Frequencies and Percentages for Open-ended Items and Selected Subcategories of Suggested Changes for the *Yearbook*

Item	Selected Subcategories of Suggested Changes	No. of Sugges-tions	Percentage of Total Codable Suggestions	Percentage of Sug-gestions for Item
Style and Format		334	53.8	
36a. length		159	25.6	
	lengthen (in unspecified way)	28[a]		17.6
	lengthen methods or procedures	34		21.4
	lengthen results, conclusions, implications	35		21.4
	shorten (in unspecified way)	17		10.7
b. number of reports		76	12.2	
	more	22		28.9
	fewer	54		71.1
	fewer but longer	26[b]		34.2[b]
c. special features		35	5.6	
	more	24		68.6
	fewer	11		31.4
d. durability		23	3.7	
	better/sturdier binding	17		69.6
e. appearance		17	2.7	
f. print size		24	3.9	
	larger	20		83.3
Content		188	30.3	
g. degree to which the *Yearbook* reflects annual meeting		60	9.7	
	should not necessarily reflect	15		25.0
	include most/all reports from meeting in some form	14		23.3
h. level of scholarship of reports		66	10.6	
	improve (in unspecified way)	38		57.6
i. contribution to the field		62	10.0	
	reports are too short to make an important contribution	11		17.7
	include a broader variety of reports	15		24.2
Review Procedure		99	15.9	
j. fairness of reviewers		37	6.0	
	need a blind review	15		40.5
k. timeliness of reviews and distribution of *Yearbook*		19	3.1	
	improve timeliness of reviews	7		37.0
l. quality of responses to authors		23	3.7	
	need to give more detail	9		39.1

(Table 4 continued on next page)

Table 4 *(Continued)*

Frequencies and Percentages for Open-ended Items and Selected Subcategories of Suggested Changes for the *Yearbook*

Item	Selected Subcategories of Suggested Changes	No. of Sugges-tions	Percentage of Total Codable Suggestions	Percentage of Sug-gestions for Item
m. capability of reviewer		20	3.2	
	more careful choosing reviewers	9		45.0

[a]A subcategory of an item is listed if it accounted for at least 20% of the suggestions for the item. Thus, the sum of the frequencies of the subcategories will not, in most cases, be equal to the total number of suggestions for the item itself.

[b]Twenty-six (34.2%) of the 54 suggestions to have fewer reports said there should be fewer but longer reports.

Table 5

Summary Data for Scales

	Scale Created by Averaging Across Items	Mean	*SD*	Number of Responses
Scale for the extent to which respondents agreed with positive statement about:				
Overall quality of the *Yearbook*	4-21[a]	8.08	1.23	366
Quality of the style and format of the *Yearbook*	4–8	8.02	1.47	399
Quality of the content of the *Yearbook*	9–14	8.13	1.47	417
Quality of the review procedures used for the *Yearbook*	15–21	7.71	1.41	137
Scale for the extent to which respondents agreed there should be changes in:				
The *Yearbook* in general	26a–26m, 27, 32–35	5.49	1.30	322
Style and format of the *Yearbook*	26a–26f, 32–34	6.29	1.56	357
Content of the *Yearbook*	26g–26i, 27–30	5.44	1.97	336
Review procedures used for the *Yearbook*	26j–26m, 35	5.68	1.26	260

[a]Scales for respondents who had not answered items 15–21 were obtained by averaging responses to items 4–14.

Opinions about Changes in the Yearbook

Should there be a Yearbook? Responses to item 25 indicated overwhelming belief that there should be a *Yearbook.* Ninety-two percent of the respondents either strongly disagreed or disagreed that the *Yearbook* should be eliminated. Only 2% strongly agreed with the statement.

Should there be changes in the Yearbook? The last four means in Table 5 are for the four scales dealing with the extent to which individuals agreed there should be changes in the *Yearbook.* The means indicated a tendency to moderately disagree or be neutral that changes should be made.

Only two Likert items (other than item 25) on changes for the *Yearbook* elicited even moderately strong reactions from respondents. Members agreed, on the average, that submitted manuscripts should be reviewed with authors' names removed and that there should be a topic index in the *Yearbook* (items 35 and 30, respectively).

There were, however, 621 codable suggested changes received from 255 individuals in response to the open-ended items (36a through 36n). One hundred seven uncodable responses were made by 92 individuals. These responses were most often given to the "other" item (36n) and could not be aggregated or collapsed in any way. Examples of uncodable responses are "have themed sections with introductions" and "the format (organization) within each report should be even more consistent."

While interpreting suggested changes, it is important to keep in mind that comments were highly dispersed among items, so most subcategories contained very small numbers of suggestions. (See Table 4 for numbers of suggestions and subcategory percentages.) Also, individuals had an opportunity to express opinions about specifc changes in some Likert items and therefore may not have felt a need to express even strong opinions in the open-ended section.

The most frequent area for suggested changes was for style and format of the *Yearbook* (53.8% of the codable suggestions). The predominant comments about style and format were that reports should be lengthened and that there should be fewer of them. There was not a clear consensus about which sections of articles should be lengthened.

The second most frequently suggested area for changes was for the content of the *Yearbook* (30.3% of the codable suggestions). The predominant comments were that level of scholarship could be improved and that the contribution articles make to the field could be enhanced. A very small number of comments indicated that reports are too short to make an important contribution, and similarly, a very small number suggested including a broader variety of types of reports.

Relatively few comments were made about the review process (15.9% of the codable suggestions). Overall, among those who made comments, a small number suggested that the review process was not fair. A very small number of suggestions mentioned a need for blind review of articles. Also, a very small number indicated the quality of responses to authors and the capability of reviewers could be improved.

Remaining categories of responses contained very small numbers (less than 10% of the codable suggestions).

Additional Issues

Two additional issues were addressed: Is there a relationship between length of membership in NRC and perceptions of the *Yearbook*'s importance, potential utility, and quality? and Is there a relationship between length of membership in NRC and the extent to which individuals believed that changes should be made in the *Yearbook?*

To address the first issue, a series of analyses of variance and multivariate analyses of variance was done, using length of membership (one to three years, four to nine years, and 10 or more years) as the independent variable and, as dependent variables, items 1, 2, 3a through 3e collectively, and the scale for the extent to which individuals agreed that changes should be made in the *Yearbook,* respectively. Only one significant effect emerged. It was for item 1, where those who had been NRC members for one to three years tended to agree slightly more than members in the 10-year or longer category that the *Yearbook* has the potential to be an important contribution to the field, $F(2, 471) = 3.56, p = .03$. Means for the three subgroups, from fewest to most years, were 9.74, 9.44, and 9.17, and standard deviations were 1.34, 1.79, and 2.18, respectively.

To address the second issue, two analyses of variance were done using length of membership (one to three years, four to nine years, and 10 or more years) as the independent variable and, as the dependent variables, item 25 (reverse scored) and the scale for the extent to which individuals agreed that there should be changes in the *Yearbook.* There were no statistically significant effects.

DISCUSSION

Three sets of conclusions can be made. First, the results suggest individuals tended to agree that the *Yearbook* is an important contribution to the field, and it is potentially useful in a variety of ways, including uses ranging from class handouts to an outlet for research dissemination to a representation of the NRC annual meeting. Also, members were moderately positive about the quality of the *Yearbook* on the whole as well as specifically with regard to its style and format, content, and review procedures.

Second, those who used the *Yearbook* tended to use it mainly as a personal library, next as a resource for research reports, as an outlet for dissemination of research, as a reproduction of the annual NRC meeting, and last for class handouts.

Third, individuals tended to moderately disagree that changes should be made in the *Yearbook.* Only three Likert items on changes for the *Yearbook* evoked even moderately strong opinions: (a) Respondents overwhelmingly agreed that there should be a *Yearbook.* (b) Respondents felt, on the average, that manuscripts submitted to the *Yearbook* should be reviewed with authors' names removed, and (c) that the *Yearbook* should have a topic index.

Although the overall membership appeared to be content with the *Yearbook* on the whole and did not tend to feel sweeping changes should be made, some suggestions for changes were made. Among the most notable suggested changes (from Likert items and open-ended responses) were lengthening reports, reducing the number of reports, including a topic index, and removing authors' names from manuscripts under review.

PROGRAM FOR 1986 NATIONAL READING CONFERENCE
Austin, Texas—December 3-6

1101.1 **Teachers as readers: A study of teacher preparation in reading and literature.** Linda DeGroff and Susan Hynds, Syracuse University

1101.2 **The effects of two types of written responses on student compositions and mastery of course content.** Mary W. Olson, Southwest Texas State University

1102.1 **The roots of metacognition: An extensive historical review.** Maribeth Cassidy Schmitt, Purdue University

1102.2 **Training students in an occupational training program to self-regulate reading comprehension.** R. Timothy Rush and James L. Milburn, University of Wyoming

1103.1 **A descriptive study of the verbal interaction patterns of one reading teacher educator.** Beth Ann Hermann, University of South Carolina

1103.2 **Relationships between preservice teachers' conceptions of reading instruction and their ability to apply conceptions in practice.** Janet Johnson and Gerald G. Duffy, Michigan State University

1104.1 **Directed reading thinking activity and conceptual mapping: Their effects on expository text analysis and recall in a writing task.** Marilyn E. Draheim, University of California-Berkeley

1104.2 **Students' and teachers' perceptions of an innovative reading strategy.** Nancy D. Padak and Gary M. Padak, Kent State University

1105.1 **Dimensions of teaching effectiveness: Implications for reading and writing instructional research.** Linda Anderson, Michigan State University

1105.2 **Translating inservice training in process-centered writing into classroom practice.** Alfred Ciani and Karin L. Dahl, University of Cincinnati

1106.1 **Reading teacher's efficacy: The influence of contextual demands and rewards.** Barb Jean Guzzetti, California State University-Pomona

1106.2 **The congruence of teacher, student, and principal perceptions of classroom teaching activity.** Leonard Breen and Richard P. Williams, University of Oklahoma

1107.1 **Reading comprehension and the learning disabled reader: Generalizations from five years of research (1980-1985).** M. Carrol Tama and David Martinez, Portland State University

1107.2 **Longitudinal case studies of the written language use of two disabled learners.** Patricia Tefft Cousin, Indiana University

1108.1 **Reader processing strategies of low and high ability eighth graders across different levels of text.** Rick J. Bryan and Clyde G. Colwell, Kansas State University

1108.2 **A research study on the discriminating factors predominant in disabled and non-disabled readers.** Mary Monfort, Lisa McQuigg, and Frances Stephens, Central State University

1109.1 **The effects of directed prompts on the written recalls of community college students.** Jennifer L. Stockseth, University of Pittsburgh

1109.2 **The effects of audience-specific prewriting questions on sixth-graders' persuasive letters.** Wayne H. Slater, Sherry C. Scott, and John Guthrie, University of Maryland, and Barbara Kapinus, Maryland State University

1110.1 **Children's miscues through three types of instructional materials.** Michael R. Sampson, East Texas State University, and Marcella Valdez-Hodges, Garland ISD

1110.2 **Curriculum for language development: An interdisciplinary perspective.** Margaret Nardi and Kathleen Hinchman, University of Wyoming

1111.1 **The effect of direct explanation of reading strategies.** Gerald G. Duffy and Laura R. Roehler, Michigan State University

1111.2 **Wait-time during remedial reading questioning segments.** Mary C. Shake, University of Kentucky

1112.1 **Parents' perceptions of factors affecting the reading development of intellectually superior accelerated readers and intellectually superior nonreaders.** Jeanne M. Burns and Martha Collins, Louisiana State University

1112.2 **The functions of language in parent-child bookreading events.** Carolyn P. Panofsky, University of New Mexico, Harry Singer and Catherine A. Letteer, University of California-Riverside

1113.1 **Main idea instructional practices in secondary reading textbooks.** David W. Moore and Bonnie L. Smith, University of Northern Iowa

1113.2 **Qualitative analysis of comprehension instruction in basal readers.** Judythe P. Patberg, Peter Dewitz, and Lois Burke, University of Toledo

1114.1 **Teachers' knowledge about directed reading lessons.** Gerry Shiel and John Lawton Shefelbine, University of Texas-Austin

1114.2 **Classroom teachers' perceptions of basal readers, their use and state-wide applications.** Connie Cloud and Mark Sadoski, Texas A&M University

1115.1 **Cloze and intersentential comprehension: A direct comparison.** Michael C. McKenna and Kent Layton, Wichita State University

1115.2 **Textual sequence, schematic knowledge and cloze procedure.** Jon Jonz and April Ginther, East Texas State University

1116.1 **The nature and function of texts in two basal readers.** Joanne M. Golden, University of Delaware, and Linda Wonderly, Ohio State University

1116.2 **Content analysis of the explicitness of sixth-grade science and social studies textbooks.** Mariam Jean Dreher, University of Maryland

1117.1 **Effects of topic familiarity and generative learning activities on disabled readers' comprehension of expository text structure.** Renee K. Weisberg, Beaver College, and Ernest Balajthy, State University of New York-Geneseo

1117.2 **Teaching informed strategies for learning to LD children.** Mary R. Howell, Theresa R. Rottman, and David R. Cross, Texas Christian University

1118.1 **Enhancing critical comprehension of literary text through writing.** Carolyn Colvin Murphy, University of Nebraska

1118.2 **Some effects of reading and writing on reading and writing persuasion.** Marion Crowhurst, University of British Columbia

1119.1 **Training peer teachers to improve comprehension instruction.** Ruth Justine Kurth, North Texas State University

1120.1 **The influence of written directions on students' summaries.** Victoria Chou Hare, University of Illinois-Chicago

1120.2 **Class size and primary grade reading instruction.** Patrick Shannon, York University

1121.1 **Reading for a multiple-choice test: Headings as schema activators.** Stephen Clark Wilhite, Widener University

1121.2 **The effects of passage length and content on selected reading comprehension test items.** Linda Naomi Hansche and David Mason Roberts, Georgia State University

1122.1 **Emergent literacy: Psychomotor responses to environmental print among children from low and middle income backgrounds.** Sally Lipa and Rebecca Harlin, State University of New York-Geneseo

1123.1 **The influence of home literacy events on the development of story structure knowledge in preschool children.** Joanne L. Ratliff, Louisiana State University

1123.2 **A comparison of nine children's spontaneous questions during story reading: What they wanted to know.** David Byron Yaden, Jr., University of Houston-University Park

1124.1 **Supported oral reading: A year-long intervention study in two inner-city primary grade classrooms.** Laurie Nelson and Darrell Morris, National College of Education

1124.2 **Movement into reading: A longitudinal study of reading development in three kindergarten classrooms.** Darrell Morris and Carol Ivy, National College of Education

1125.1 **Second language reading: A cognitive perspective.** Elizabeth B. Bernhardt, Ohio State University

1125.2 **Training limited-English-proficient students to use cognitive reading strategies.** Yolanda N. Padron, University of Houston-Clear Lake

1201.1 **Relationship of self-efficacy beliefs and outcome expectancy to reading and writing performance.** Roger H. Bruning, Carolyn Colvin Murphy, and Duane Shell, University of Nebraska

1201.2 **Text demands in college classes: An investigation.** Vincent P. Orlando and David C. Caverly, Metropolitan State College, JoAnn Mullen, University of Northern Colorado, and Rona Flippo, Fitchburg State College

1202.1 **Metacomprehension in basal reader instruction: Do teachers promote it?** Maribeth Cassidy Schmitt and James F. Baumann, Purdue University

1202.2 **A longitudinal study of metalinguistic abilities and reading achievement in primary grade children.** Benita A. Blachman and Sharon L. James, Syracuse University

1203.1 **What students know about expository writing.** Judith A. Langer, Stanford University

1203.2 **The relationship between instruction and elementary and special education students' misconceptions about the writing process.** Kathy Fear, Linda Anderson, Carol Sue Englert, and Taffy E. Raphael, Michigan State University

1204.1 **Strategy development in repeated and extended readings: A case study.** R. Kay Moss, Southeastern Louisiana University, and John C. Stansell, Texas A&M University

1204.2 **The effects of retelling practice on comprehension of proficient and less proficient readers.** Barbara A. Kapinus, Maryland State Department of Education, Linda B. Gambrell and Paricia S. Koskinen, University of Maryland

1205.2 **Effects of metacognitive self-monitoring instruction on functional reading ability.** Karen Ortego LaCroix, East Baton Rouge Parish Schools, and Martha D. Collins, Louisiana State University

1206.1 **Fourth-graders' use of story structure elements in reading & writing.** Annette C. Schewe, Winnipeg Child Guidance Clinic, and Victor Froese, University of British Columbia

1206.2 **Poor readers' use of narrative structure; Uncovering systematic individual differences in story comprehension and recall.** Ian Wilkinson, University of Illinois-Champaign/Urbana, John Bain and John Elkins, University of Queensland

1207.1 **Beginning teachers' implementation of strategies for comprehension instruction: From training to practice.** Karri Williams, University of Central Florida

1207.2 **Teachers in reading resource rooms: Theory and practice.** Lynne D. Miller, Amphitheater Junior High-Tucson

1208.1 **The unintended road to ecological invalidity.** Karen Mangus and Victoria Chou Hare, University of Illinois-Chicago

1208.2 **New techniques and statistical methods for assessing the development of reading skills.** Catharine C. Knight, University of Denver, and Diane S. Stupay, Cleveland State University

1209.1 **Problem/solution, text structure and syntax: Fourth and sixth graders' comprehension of social studies texts.** Donald J. Richgels, Northern Illinois University

1209.2 **Children's learning from informative text: The relationship between prior knowledge and text structure.** Nina M. Yochum, University of Michigan

1210.1 **Comprehension of inside view in original stories and their basal reader adaptations.** Cheryl Liebling, BBN Laboratories

1210.2 **Influence of the medium on children's story comprehension.** Susan B. V. Neuman, Education Development Center

1211.1 **Investigating the effectiveness of pre and post graphic organizer instruction on sixth graders' comprehension of science text.** Deborah C. Simmons, Edward J. Kameenui, and Cynthia C. Griffin, Purdue University

1211.2 **The effects of difficult vocabulary and an advance organizer on text comprehension.** Steven A. Stahl and Michael G. Jacobson, Wetern Illinois University

1212.1 **Text elaboration in remedial readers' story sharing.** James Robert King, Texas Woman's University

1212.2 **Developmental and task complexity constraints on children's causal understanding.** Lucy Ann Dahlberg, Governors State University

1213.1 **Depictions of aging and the elderly in primary grade reading instructional materials.** Bruce Arthur Gutknecht, University of North Florida

1213.2 **Promoting voluntary reading: Activities represented in basal reader manuals.** Lesley Mandel Morrow, Rutgers University

1214.1 **An analysis of provisions for dealing with students' prior knowledge in teacher editions of social studies and basal reading texts.** James Flood and Diane Lapp, San Diego State University

1214.2 **The effects of prereading instruction on the comprehension of narrative and expository text.** Janice A. Dole, Michigan State University, Sheila Valencia and Eunice A. Greer, University of Illinois

1215.1 **Inferencing in stories.** Lauren Leslie, Marquette University, and B. Steve Roy, St. Joseph's Indian School

1215.2 **In-process measures of ambiguous text interpretation: A replication study.** William A. Henk, Pennsylvania State University-Harrisburg, and John P. Helfeldt, West Virginia University

1216.1 **Teacher change: A comparison of individual differences as a result of staff development.** Helena Spring, Oswego County BOCES, and Alice Boljonis, SUNY-Oswego

1216.2 **Teaching the writing process: Evaluating teacher change.** Kathleen Hinchman, University of Wyoming, and Alice Boljonis, SUNY-Oswego

1217.1 **The use of concept mapping and knowledge via mapping as an aid to reading comprehension and problem solving.** Marino C. Alvarez and Carole K. Stice, Tennessee State University

1217.2 **Affecting reader's text processing through mapping instruction.** Karen Margolis Samson, Chicago State University

1218.1 **Cue system strategies in good and poor adult readers.** R. Scott Baldwin, University of Miami, and John E. Readence and Jeanne S. Schumm, Louisiana State University

1218.2 **Civic writing: The unexamined component of civic literacy.** Sandra L. Stotsky, Harvard University

1219.1 **Importance assignment: Text type and task demand variables.** Peter Afflerbach, Emory University

1219.2 **The effect of text and task on the inference generation of fifth-grade disabled readers.** Karen Ann Pinter, Sauk Valley College

1220.1 **A comparison of children's integrative processing schemes for reading and listening tasks.** Sandra Thompson Moore, Virginia Tech College of Education

1220.2 **The responses of secondary students to socio-psycholinguistic instruction: An examination of instructional and research paradigms.** Leslie Ann Patterson, Texas A&M University

1221.1 **Validity of the speed of thinking test.** Ronald P. Carver, University of Missouri-Kansas City

1221.2 **Limitations for the application of expert systems methodology in reading.** Victor L. Willson, Texas A&M University

1222.1 **The concept of phonemic awareness: An empirical approach.** Hallie Kay Yopp, University of California-Riverside

1222.2 **Kindergarten spelling: Explaining the improved prediction of first-grade reading achievement.** Lou Ferroli and Timothy Shanahan, University of Illinois-Chicago

1223.1 **What makes a text readable?** Beverly Zakalak, University of Manitoba

1223.2 **The role of phonological and lexical information in word recognition and in spelling.** Priscilla L. Griffith, University of Texas-Austin

1224.1 **Reading comprehension strategies of gifted seventh-graders.** Elizabeth Evelyn Sparks, University of Calgary

1224.2 **An exploration of the relationship between perceived control, value for reading and reading achievement in young readers.** Garland Finchert Niquette and Peter Winograd, University of Kentucky

1225.1 **Young reader's interactions with flashback narrative.** Joan Livingston Prouty, Education Service Center, Region VI

1225.2 **Inferencing ability as an explanation of the comprehension of figurative expression.** David G. O'Brien, Purdue University, and Michael A. Martin, Eastern Michigan University

131.0 **Reading recovery: An early intervention project.**

131.1 **A two year study of students involved in the Ohio Reading Recovery Project.** Gay Su Pinnell, Ohio State University

131.2 **Reading strategy development: Growing through new and familiar materials.** Diane DeFord, Ohio State University

131.3 **A study of teacher/student interactions: Supporting literacy.** Kathy Gnagey Short, Goshen College

132.0 **Findings from research on basal readers and teacher's story-reading from a longitudinal study of reading comprehension development.**

132.1 **Is newer necessarily better or even different? Findings from a systematic investigation of the 1983 and 1986 editions of a basal reader.** Lorraine Crummey, University of Illinois-Champaign/Urbana

132.2 **Children's comprehension of, reactions to and preferences for basal reader stories of varying comprehensibility.** C. Nicholas Hastings, University of Illinois-Champaign/Urbana

132.3 **Teacher's story reading correlates negatively with student achievement in reading: An investigation into this counter-intuitive labyrinth.** Linda A. Meyer, University of Illinois-Champaign/Urbana

133.0 **College Reading: A continuum of instruction.**

133.1 **An investigation into the self-selected study strategies used by college bound secondary students: Implications for the college reading specialist.** Bonnie Higginson, Murray State University

133.2 **The text underlining patterns of college students.** Sherrie L. Nist and Kate Kirby, University of Georgia

133.3 **Coping strategies of successful learning disabled college students: A case study approach.** William G. Brozo and Carol L. Curtis, Northern Illinois University

134.0 **Why we do what we do in the classroom: A framework for examining our beliefs about learning and teaching.** Allan R. Nielsen and Judith Newman, Mt. St. Vincent University

135.0 **Teacher cognition and teacher behavior: The influence of teacher decisions on instruction**

135.1 **Prior knowledge and the comprehension of basal teacher's guides.** Donald J. Leu and Katherine E. Misulis, Syracuse University

135.2 **The translation of belief into practice: Observations of reading instruction.** Charles K. Kinzer, Peabody College of Vanderbilt University

135.3 **Student/teacher interaction during reading instruction: An analysis of verbal behavior.** JoAnn J. Sweetland and Dorothy A. Carrick, Peabody College of Vanderbilt University

136.0 **The acquisition of literacy: A longitudinal study.**

136.1 **Letter names versus phonemes: A little debate.** Ann Mullins Hall, University of Texas-Austin

136.2 **Are the determinants of reading comprehension and writing similar?** Gerry Shiel, University of Texas-Austin

136.3 **The basal reader: Does it leave its mark on reading and writing?** Gary W. Evans, University of Texas-Austin

136.4 **The fate of the poor reader.** Cynthia Ann Farest, University of Texas-Austin

137.0 **Teachers and researchers learn together.**

137.1 **Research and theory as practice: A collaborative study of change.** Diane Stephens, Indiana University

137.2 **Toward a partial theory of teaching style: A microethnography of a secondary teacher working with students having low reading ability.** Deborah R. Dillon, Purdue University

137.3 **How teacher and researcher learn together: Two case studies.** Ruth E. Hubbard and Brenda A. Miller, University of New Hampshire, and Patricia C. McLure, Mast Way School

141.0 **The influence of expository text features on comprehension.**

141.1 **The characteristics of well-designed text.** Marilyn Jewel Chambliss, Stanford University

141.2 **Training teachers to handle big texts.** Robert C. Calfee, Stanford University

141.3 **Using frames to organize expository text.** Bonnie Armbruster, University of Illinois-Champaign/Urbana

141.4 **Expository text features which influence comprehensibility.** Wayne H. Slater, University of Maryland

143.0 **Study strategies and academic achievement.**

143.1 **Learning from school texts: Relationships among reading strategies, text differences and student flexibility.** Judith N. Mitchell, University of Arizona, and Pi A. Irwin, Tucson Unified School District

143.2 **The relationship between students' self-reports of text studying practices and course achievement.** Ann J. Pace and John K. Sherk, Jr., University of Missouri-Kansas City, and Arlie R. Peck, Lincoln Memorial College

143.3 **The relationship between test performance and six study strategy variables.** Michele L. Simpson and Sherrie L. Nist, University of Georgia

143.4 **A systems-oriented description of knowledge growth.** Diane L. Schallert and Barbara J. Lawrence, University of Texas-Austin

145.0 **Congruence of beliefs and practices: Studying preservice, first year and experienced teachers.**

145.1 **How reading education students' instructional beliefs and practices match theoretical models of reading.** Sharon Arthur Moore, University of Northern Iowa

145.2 **Beliefs/Practices congruence of first year teachers as compared with preservice teachers.** David Yellin and Martha Combs, Oklahoma State University

145.3 **Learning to teach Chapter I reading: A case study.** Rosary Lalik, Virginia Polytechnic Institute

146.0 **Emergent (mediated) reading levels: A new construct for placement from a Vygotskian view.**

146.1 **Mediated reading levels: The construct.** William R. Powell, University of Florida

146.2 **An investigation of the zone of proximal development for reading placement.** Lisbeth Dixon, University of West Florida

146.3 **A concurrent validity study of the emergent reading level.** Nile V. Stanley, University of Florida

146.4 **Dynamic versus static testing: Impact on reading placement of reading underachievers.** Sherry E. Kragler, North Texas State University

147.0 **Innovations in assessment: New methods and models.**

147.1 **Michigan educational assessment of reading.** Charles Peters, Oakland Public Schools, and Karen K. Wixson, University of Michigan

147.2 **Strategies to link assessment to instruction: The Illinois Project.** P. David Pearson, University of Illinois-Champaign/Urbana, Timothy Shanahan, University of Illinois-Chicago, and Sheila Valencia, University of Illinois-Champaign/Urbana

151.0 **Assessment, accountability and professional prerogative.** P. David Pearson, University of Illinois-Champaign/Urbana

211.0 **Defining literacy: Testing in Texas . . . and beyond.**

211.1 **Toward redefining what it means to be literate.** Donald H. Graves, University of New Hampshire

211.2 **Testing in Texas: Evidence of the effects of the Texas approach to testing, with a view of how literacy is defined.** Julie Jensen, University of Texas-Austin

212.0 **Comprehending as composing: Theory, development, and application.**

212.1 **A logical validation of a composing model of reading comprehension.** David G. O'Brien, Purdue University

212.2 **A comparison of cognitive processes during reading and writing.** Sarah H. Martin, Louisiana State University

212.3 **An instructional investigation of students' ideas generated during content area writing.** Michael A. Martin, Eastern Michigan University, and Bonnie Carroll Konopak, Louisiana State University

213.0 **Control of cohesion by young readers and writers: Evidence from use of pronouns and determiners in reading and writing.**

213.1 **Readers' miscues on pronouns with varying syntactic, semantic and pragmatic disconfirmation.** David Freeman, Fresno Pacific College

213.2 **Effective and efficient use of pronouns in the writing of third and fourth grade native American pupils.** Suzanne Gespass, University of Arizona

213.3 **How readers' miscues on pronouns and determiners in cohesive texts reflect their linguistic competence.** Kenneth S. Goodman, University of Arizona

214.0 **Instructional Strategies: Reading.**

214.1 **Reciprocal questioning: A strategy for improving learning disabled students' comprehension of instructed and transfer stories.** Naomi Feldman, Northwestern State University of Louisiana

214.2 **The effects of repeated reading on recall of college developmental readers.** S. Corinne Pearce and Lea M. McGee, Louisiana State University

214.3 **Training college students to adjust reading to purpose.** Gary N. Osako, New York University, and Tina Jacobowitz, Montclair State College

215.0 **Teacher researchers document literacy progress—Part I: The effects of supportive reading techniques on special populations.**

215.1 **Evaluating the effects of shared book experiences on the prereading behaviors of low SES four-year-olds.** Gloria Kutasch, Conroe, Texas, ISD

215.2 **Monitoring the effects of assisted reading with predictable books on the reading behavior of severely retarded adolescents.** Gail Sharpe, Brenham State School, and Phil Swicegood, Sam Houston State University

215.3 **Monitoring the effects of assisted reading and writing on four learning-disabled students.** Bessie Johnson, Conroe Texas ISD, and Sheila G. Cohen, Sam Houston State University

215.4 **Monitoring the effects of assisted reading on the reading behavior of moderately retarded students.** Dottie Jones, Redd School

216.0 **Direction in the study of reading as a social event: Conceptual issues.**

216.1 **Reading as cultural activities.** James Heap, Ontario Institute for Studies in Education

216.2 **Making sense of reading in the instructional context.** Judith Green, Ohio State University

216.3 **Reading/literacy as a social event.** David Bloome, University of Michigan

217.0 **Basic Processes: Writing.**

217.1 **Writing in constrained genres: Pushing the limits of writing models.** Gary M. Schumacher, Byron T. Scott, George R. Klare, Frank Cronin, and Ronald J. Foos, Ohio University, and Wendy Schweigert, Plymouth State College

217.2 **Taking control of the text: Transforming through reading and writing.** Cheryl Geisler, Rensselaer Polytechnic Institute

217.3 **The development of competence and awareness in discourse synthesis.** James Robert King, Texas Woman's University, and Nancy Nelson Spivey, Carnegie Mellon University

217.4 **The social orientation of student writing: Problematizing our view of classroom rhetoric.** Louise Wetherbee Phelps and John Edlund, University of Southern California

218.0 **Fifteen things we know for sure about teaching reading with computers.** Michael L. Kamil, University of Illinois-Chicago, Lois G. Dreyer, Columbia University, and Alan E. Farstrup, International Reading Association

221.1 **Emergent literacy: Reading and writing development in early childhood.** William Teale, University of Texas-San Antonio

222.0 **Basal readers: Science or technology for monolingual and bilingual readers?**

222.1 **Basal readers: Science or technology for monolingual readers?** Kenneth S. Goodman, University of Arizona

222.2 **Basal readers: Science or technology for bilingual readers?** Yvonne S. Freeman, University of Arizona

223.0 **Understanding the subcultures of literacy in a sixth grade classroom: A report of a curriculum change project**

223.1 **The evolution of an authoring curriculum in a sixth grade classroom: Process and patterns.** Marjorie Siegel, University of Utah

223.2 **This year there's no work: The students' learning experience.** Becky Reimer, University of Utah

223.3 **The tension between control and support: The teacher's learning experience.** Susan Cook, Granite School District

224.0 **Expanding our view of discourse processing: Intertextuality as a search for multiple connections.**

224.1 **Expanding our notions of discourse processing: The influence of intertextuality upon interactions.** Robert J. Tierney, Ohio State University, and Theresa Rogers, University of Illinois-Champaign/Urbana

224.2 **Literacy learning as an intertextual process.** Deborah Wells Rowe, Vanderbilt University

224.3 **Intertextuality as a process of social negotiation.** Kathy Gnagey Short, Ohio State University

225.0 **Teacher researchers document literacy progress—Part II: The development and use of writing assessment scales.**

225.1 **Teachers experiment to develop a usable writing assessment scale.** Sheila Cohen and Bess Osburn, Sam Houston State University, and Susan Berry, Willis Independent School District

225.2 **The development of a writing assessment scale for young bilingual writers.** Donna Wiseman and Vi Flores, Texas A&M University

225.3 **Chapter I teachers develop writing scales for education purpose.** Gloria McDonnell, Fairfax County Public Schools

225.4 **Involving students in the use of writing instruments.** Mary McChesney, Coy Chrisman, and Elizabeth Campbell, Klein ISD

226.0 **Complex relationships in prior knowledge research: Post hoc insights and future directions.**

226.1 **Prior knowledge: Facilitator or inhibitor of comprehension.** Nancy Marshall, Florida International University

226.2 **Refuting misconceptions: Its effect on middle grade children's comprehension.** Katherine Maria and Evelyn Blustein, College of New Rochelle

226.3 **Hypothesis generation and testing: Prior knowledge and text genre variables.** Peter Afflerbach, Emory University

226.4 **The effects of varying prior knowledge activation modes and text structure on non-science majors' comprehension of physics text.** Donna E. Alvermann, University of Georgia, and Cynthia R. Hynd, Georgia State University

227.0 **Working toward a taxonomy of reading.**

227.1 **Defining taxonomies.** Peter Mosenthal, Syracuse University

227.2 **Classifying three aspects of reading.** John Guthrie, University of Maryland

227.3 **A task analysis of reading.** Edward Fry, Rutgers University

228.0 **Writing apprehension and teacher training.**

228.1 **Writing apprehension: A review of literature.** Greg D. Clark, Texas A&M University

228.2 **Writing apprehension and preservice and inservice teachers.** Donna L. Wiseman, Texas A&M University

228.3 **The effects of a preservice teacher training model designed to reduce writing apprehension.** Sharon Lee, Texas A&M University

230.1 **Ethnography and writing: Through teachers' eyes.** Sondra Perl, Lehman College, City University of New York

241.0 **Examining our assumption about the relationship between teaching and learning.** Kenneth S. Goodman, University of Arizona, and Richard C. Anderson, University fo Illinois-Champaign/Urbana

242.0 **Basal reading programs and their use by teachers.**

242.1 **How do first and second grade basals compare?** Linda A. Meyer, University of Illinois-Champaign/Urbana

242.2 **Two basal reader series and their use in fourth grade classes.** Marilyn W. Sadow, Chicago State University

242.3 **The influence of basal programs on instructional activities.** Rebecca Barr, National College of Education

243.0 **Early book experiences.**

243.2 **Explicit instruction in story structure: Effects on preschoolers' listening comprehension.** JoAnne L. Ratliff and Ray R. Buss, Louisiana State University

243.3 **MILK: Mother-infant literacy knowledge.** Andrea C. Sledge, Lehman College, City University of New York

244.0 **College: Factors affecting college reading.**

244.1 **The relationship of learned helplessness to metacognitive behaviors among college students on academic probation.** Larry Mikulecky and Susan Ruth McIntyre, Indiana University

244.2 **Study skills, academic aptitude and performance of college students.** Harry Norman Blumner, Herbert C. Richards, and Thomas H. Estes, University of Virginia

244.3 **The effects of qualitative differences in prior knowledge on text comprehension.** Maureen E. Byrne, June E. Zack, and Gary N. Osako, New York University

245.0 **Learning to think about the teaching of reading.**

245.1 **The relationship between preservice teacher's conceptions of reading instruction and the content of methods instruction.** Gerald G. Duffy, Laura R. Roehler, and Janet Johnson, Michigan State University

245.2 **Cooperative interaction and the preservice preparation of content area reading teachers.** Mark Conley, Eastern Michigan University

245.3 **Learning to teach reading comprehension: A collaborative approach.** Jerome A. Niles and Rosary V. Lalik, Virginia Polytechnic Institute

245.4 **Understanding the mental structures of pre-service and classroom teachers: Associations between beliefs, the comprehension of basal lessons and lesson-planning decisions.** Donald J. Leu, Jr., and Katherine Misulis, Syracuse University

246.0 **The construction of meaning through teacher-student-text interactions.**

246.1 **Teachers' adjustment of instruction through analysis of how they mediate texts.** Gay Su Pinnell, Ohio State University

246.2 **Teacher-student-text interaction in a sixth grade reading lesson.** Joanne M. Golden, University of Delaware

246.3 **Constructing meaning in eighth grade literature lessons.** Jane L. Davidson, Northern Illinois University, Nancy D. Padak, Kent State University, and Bonnie C. Wilkerson, St. Charles Public Schools

247.0 **Theoretical and pragmatic issues in the analysis of written discourse.**

247.1 **The development of the literate voice.** Beverly E. Cox, Northwestern University, and Margaret Tinzmann, National College of Education

247.2 **Cohesive harmony analysis: Issues of the author's intentions.** Lawrence B. Friedman, North Central Regional Educational Laboratory, and Elizabeth Sulzby, University of Michigan

247.3 **Developmental processes, language functions and the discourse of voices in adolescent written texts.** George Kamberelis and Elizabeth Sulzby, University of Michigan

248.0 **Word recognition: Holistic or letter-by-letter.** S. Jay Samuels, University of Minnesota

251.0 **Perspectives on research: The first grade studies revisited.** David Bloome, University of Michigan, and S. Jay Samuels, University of Minnesota

252.0 **Vocabulary and reading achievement: Language experience approach vs. basal instruction—a debate.**

252.1 **Language experience generated vocabulary vs. basal reader vocabulary at grade one.** Jon Shapiro and Lee Gunderson, University of British Columbia

252.2 **Reading achievement of grade one students involved in language experience programs vs. basal reader programs.** Anthony Carrigan, University of British Columbia

252.3 **Basal reading instruction is superior to LEA in developing vocabulary and reading achievement.** Richard McCallum, University of California-Berkeley

252.4 **Language experience approach is superior to basal instruction in developing vocabulary and reading achievement.** Sandra Murphy, University of California-Berkeley

253.0 **Constructing meaning for college readers through the integration of reading and writing instruction.**

253.1 **Written response to text: Response style preferences in college freshmen readers.** Cynthia Hynd and Nancy Chase, University of Georgia

253.2 **Writing as a means of informing learners about their reading strategies for understanding narrative and expository texts.** Kate Kirby, University of Georgia

253.3 **A validation of the PORPE Strategy: Training college students to use writing as a means of learning in the content areas.** Michele Simpson, University of Georgia, Norman Stahl, Georgia State University, and Dera Weaver, University of Georgia

254.0 **Metacognition and Reading.**

254.1 **The effectiveness of a self-monitoring strategy for training main idea comprehension.** Karen Preul and Peter Dewitz, University of Toledo

254.2 **A comparison of the effects of two vocabulary strategies on vocabulary retention and passage comprehension.** Eileen Margaret Carr, Eastern Michigan University, and Marianne Mazur Stewart, Siena Heights College

254.3 **Two methods of increasing students' self-initiated use of metacognitive skill.** Cathy Diane Collins, Texas Christian University

255.0 **Using discussion in the classroom.**

255.1 **The role of discussion in effective vocabulary instruction.** Steven A. Stahl and Charles H. Clark, Western Illinois University

255.2 **A historical study of discussion as presented in secondary methods texts.** Kathleen H. O'Keefe, University of Georgia

255.3 **Enabling students' reading comprehension through discussion techniques that encourage negotiation of meaning.** Victoria J. Risko and JoAnne Sweetland, Peabody College of Vanderbilt University, and Naomi Feldman, Northwestern Louisiana University

256.0 **Reading, writing and computers.**

256.1 **A cognitive science perspective on computers in reading.** Beth M. Warren, BBN Laboratories

256.2 **The readers' assistant: A microcomputer-based environment for text comprehension.** Ann S. Rosebery, BBN Laboratories

256.3 **Identifying teaching/learning variables in effective word processor use in writing.** Susan B. Neuman and Catherine Cobb Morocco, Education Development Center

256.4 **Writing with word processing: Students' revisions and writing behaviors.** Ruth M. Hansen and Kathleen Stumpf Jongsma, Texas Woman's University

257.0 **An ethnographic assessment of literacy.**

257.1 **History: Personal assessment experiences and assessment background of the school.** Jane Hansen, University of New Hampshire

257.2 **The present: Personal assessment experiences.** Donald Graves, University of New Hampshire

257.3 **The present: Assessment at the school.** Brenda Miller, University of New Hampshire

311.0 **Reform in teacher education: Implications of the Holmes Report.** Norman A. Stahl, Georgia State University, Victoria Risko, Peabody College of Vanderbilt University, Martha Collins, Louisiana State University, and Chet Laine, University of Cincinnati

312.0 **Exploring beneath the surface of children's understanding: Methodological issues in tapping children's inferences.**

312.1 **Tracking students' literary inferences: Reading, talking and reasoning.** Theresa Rogers, University of Illinois-Champaign/Urbana

312.2 **Designing questions that facilitate inference-making during story reading.** Linda G. Fielding, State University of New York-Albany

312.3 **Traditional and novel measures of children's inferences during comprehension of narratives: A comparison.** Ileana Seda, University of Illinois-Champaign/Urbana

313.0 **Student writing processes.**

313.2 **The relationships among coherence, cohesion and quality in children's writing.** Dixie Lee Spiegel and Jill Fitzgerald, University of North Carolina-Chapel Hill

313.3 **Children's in-depth knowledge and writing processes: Of legends on broomsticks and rudderless boats.** Gary M. Schumacher, Jane Gradwohl, Mary Brezin, Ohio University, and Ethel Greenberger Parker, Florida State University

314.0 **Journals: Reflections of process.**

314.1 **Demonstrations and epistemic journeys: The value of personal journals.** Allan R. Neilsen, Mt. St. Vincent University

314.2 **Journals: Mirrors for seeing ourselves as learners and writers.** Judith M. Newman, Mt. St. Vincent University

314.3 **Making connections: Integrating theory, research and practice through journal writing.** Sherry Vaughn, Washington State University

314.4 **Journal writing: Mirrors of comprehension.** Jane H. White, East Texas State University

314.5 **Learner as informant: Becoming aware of reading process.** Karen M. Feathers, East Texas State University

314.6 **On being strategic: Proficient readers as informants.** Jerome C. Harste, Indiana University
315.0 **When is teacher questioning instructional? Converging findings from studies of instructional interaction sequences in basal program-based reading lessons.**
315.1 **Transforming questioning into explanatory behavior: Implications from the research.** Nancy G. Mangano, Kansas State University
315.2 **Creating the means to transfer strategic knowledge about reading: Patterns of more and less effective teacher questioning in extended interaction sequences.** Linda G. Vavrus, University of Nebraska-Lincoln
315.3 **The compromise of transfer: Classroom constraints on interaction and internalization.** James H. Mosenthal, National College of Education
316.0 **Instructional practices in early literacy.**
316.1 **Language development in kindergarten: Current practices.** Donna M. Ogle, National College of Education, and Dorothy S. Strickland, Teachers College, Columbia University
316.2 **Prompting responses to literature: Children's sense of story structure.** Lesley M. Morrow, Rutgers University
316.3 **Functions of children's oral language during reading instruction.** Linda B. Gambrell, University of Maryland
317.0 **Policy and reading research: Implications for reading instruction and assessment.**
317.1 **Improving the climate for reading comprehension instruction.** Peter Winograd, University of Kentucky
317.2 **Minimal competency testing and its consequences.** Irving Balow and Harry Singer, University of California-Riverside
317.3 **Public understanding and instructional validity of reading assessment: Can they be reconciled?** Ramsey Selden, Council of Chief State School Officers
317.4 **Educators and legislative decision-makers: The role of professional organizations in influencing policy and legislation.** Jeannie L. Steele, Blueridge Community College
321.0 **The status of literacy in our society.** Larry Mikulecky, Indiana University
322.0 **The effects of pre-post semantic mapping on intermediate grade students' vocabulary knowledge, reading comprehension, and learning from text.**
322.1 **The need for vocabulary instruction in intermediate grade content areas.** Vienna Moore, University of Minnesota
322.2 **Semantic mapping: A schema approach to vocabulary instruction.** Thomas Gaetz and James Nelson, University of Minnesota
322.3 **The effects of pre-post semantic mapping on vocabulary.** William Book and Carol Huffman, University of Minnesota
322.4 **The effects of pre-post semantic mapping on reading comprehension and learning from text.** Barbara Frye and Adele Greenlee, University of Minnesota
323.0 **Print Awareness.**
323.1 **Young children's attention to graphic detail in functional print.** Lea M. McGee and Richard G. Lomax, Louisiana State University
323.2 **From oral to written language: A longitudinal analysis of preschool children dictating a story.** Clotilde Pontecorvo and Christina Zucchermaglio, Universita di Roma
323.3 **Print awareness in prereaders and subsequent reading achievement.** Mary E. Huba and Susan S. Robinson, Iowa State University, and Susan Kontos, Purdue University
323.4 **A collaborative investigation of the socio-psycholinguistic nature of literacy learning in three- and four-year-old children.** Jean Anne Clyde, Indiana University
325.0 **Imagery and Comprehension.**
325.1 **Creation of an in-text world: Recontextualizing experiences by well-read prereaders.** Victoria L. Purcell-Gates, University of California-Berkeley

325.2 **Relationships between imagery, affect, and structural salience in stories.** Mark Sadoski, Suzanne Kangiser, and Ernest T. Goetz, Texas A&M University

325.3 **The effects of reader and text characteristics on reports of imagery during reading.** Shirley A. Long, Connie Bridge, Peter Winograd, and Lynne Smith, University of Kentucky

326.0 **Developmental differences across ages.**

326.1 **Developmental patterns of minority children.** Margaret M. Griffin, Rose F. Spicola, and Darla S. Shannon, Texas Woman's University

326.2 **Developmental differences in response to a short story.** Richard W. Beach, University of Minnesota

326.3 **Differences in people's schema for writing from kindergarten through graduate school.** Dianne L. Schallert, Joy Lynn Hailey Reed, Edwin L. Young, and Tove Dahl, University of Texas-Austin

326.4 **Reading aloud without comprehension: How frequently does it occur?** Joseph H. Danks, Carl L. Rosen, and Brenda B. Riccio, Kent State University

327.0 **Aspects of evaluation: Taking up what counts**

327.1 **An examination of the context of clinical reading assessment.** Carl Braun, Barbara Rennie, and Christine J. Gordon, University of Calgary

327.2 **Knowing and saying that you know: The language of evaluation in students' awareness of the reading act.** Margaret Hunsberger and George D. Labercane, University of Calgary

327.3 **The impact of state-wide testing on the English curriculum.** John Willinsky and Allen Bobie, University of Calgary

331.0 **Some critical thoughts about critical thinking.** Frank Smith

341.0 **Resolved: That there should be direct instruction in comprehension.** P. David Pearson, University of Illinois-Champaign/Urbana, and Ronald P. Carver, University of Missouri-Kansas City

342.0 **Will new strategies for teaching reading and writing be applied in the content classroom?**

342.1 **Effects of the extended use of previews on students' recall of expository passages.** Maureen Prenn, University of Minnesota

342.2 **Effects of intensive vocabulary instruction on expository writing.** Ann Hill Duin, University of Minnesota

342.3 **Improving disabled readers' summarization skills.** Eileen Carr, Eastern Michigan University, and Donna Ogle, National College of Education

343.0 **Assessment.**

343.1 **Assessing student learning strategies: The development of the learning and study strategies inventory (LASSI).** Claire E. Weinstein, University of Texas-Austin

343.2 **The validity of summary writing as a measure of reading comprehension.** Martha H. Head, Southeastern Louisiana University, John E. Readence and Ray R. Buss, Louisiana State University

343.3 **Developing and evaluating a theoretically-based silent reading comprehension testing technology.** James W. Cunningham and David Allen Koppenhaver, University of North Carolina-Chapel Hill

344.0 **Expanding primary literacy instruction.**

344.1 **Humor and play in the early acquisition of literacy.** James T. Fleming and Peter Johnston, State University of New York-Albany

344.2 **Riddles as facilitators of inferred responses.** Jeraldine K. Otte, Chicago Public Schools, June D. Knafle and Eugene H. Cramer, University of Illinois-Chicago

344.3 **The social and political functions of children's periodicals.** Violet J. Harris, University of Georgia

344.4 **Using writing to establish a social context for the acquisition of literacy in the classroom and the home.** Becky Wendling Kirschner, Michigan State University

345.0 **Teacher theories of language learning: Their process-function and impact on teachers and students.**

345.1 **Teachers' perceptions of the process and functions of theories of language learning.** Sharon Cook Lee, Texas A&M University

345.2 **The impact of teacher theories on student theories and performance.** Karen Joan Ray, Texas A&M University

345.3 **Negotiating a theory change in language instruction.** Leslie Ann Patterson, Conroe High School

346.0 **Understandings of the forms and functions of written language: Insights from children and parents.**

346.1 **Developing notions of the functions of written language among preschool siblings of successful first grade readers.** Lesa A. Kastler, University of Texas-Austin

346.2 **Parent perceptions of a successful literacy environment.** James V. Hoffman and John A. Daly, University of Texas-Austin

346.3 **Developing literacy in young children: A follow-up look.** Nancy L. Roser, University of Texas-Austin

347.0 **Classrooms for authorship.**

347.1 **Exploring the global structure of information books.** Christine C. Pappas, University of Kentucky

347.2 **Contextual variables and the reading/writing process.** Christine J. Gordon and Carl Breul, University of Calgary

347.3 **Text revisions by two young writers following non-directive teacher/student conferences.** Carol Vukelich, University of Delaware

347.4 **The revision process: What components can sixth grade writers control?** Jill Fitzgerald, University of North Carolina-Chapel Hill, and Lynda Markam, Alma College

351.0 **Parts of the world or worlds apart: Qualitative and quantitative approaches to research.** Robert Carey, Rhode Island University, Judith Green, Ohio State University, Michael L. Kamil, University of Illinois-Chicago, and Judith Langer, Stanford University

353.0 **Retrospective miscue analysis.**

353.1 **Theoretical foundations for retrospective miscue analysis.** Yetta Goodman, University of Arizona

353.2 **Applications of retrospective miscue analysis to classroom and clinical settings.** Ann Marek, Nevada State Department of Education

353.3 **Research and computer uses involving retrospective miscue analysis.** John Woodley, University of South Dakota

354.0 **Explicit instruction in reading.**

354.1 **Comprehending texts with and without explicit cueing of graphic aids.** David P. Reinking, David A. Hayes, and John E. McEneany, University of Georgia

354.2 **Text processing strategies: Expectancies are operating, but how important are they?** Deborah P. Birkmire, USA Human Engineering Lab

354.3 **Effects of instruction in use of sentence connectives and text structure on passage recall.** Edith Appell Slaton, Louisiana State University, and Donald J. Richgels, Northern Illinois University

355.0 **Learners teaching learners.**

355.1 **Learners teaching learners: Setting the stage.** Marjorie Siegel, University of Utah

355.2 **Writers teaching writers: Processes of peer teaching in writing instruction.** Karin Dahl, University of Cincinnati

355.3 **Readers teaching readers: Processes of peer teaching in first grade reading instruction.** Jane H. White, East Texas State University

355.4 **Learners teaching learners: Processes of peer teaching across content areas.** Karen Feathers, East Texas State University

356.0 **Teaching vocabulary.**

356.1 **Designing computer-mediated text environments to optimize vocabulary and comprehension performance.** S. Kim MacGregor, Louisiana State University

356.2 **Learning how to deal with long words: Ability-related differences in the acquisition of word-formation rules.** Andrea E. Tyler and William E. Nagy, University of Illinois-Champaign/Urbana

356.3 **Learning relationships: The vocabulary-comprehension connection.** Patricia L. Anders, Candace S. Bos, and Sandra Wilde, University of Arizona

357.0 **Expository reading and writing instruction in upper elementary classrooms.**

357.1 **The effect of text structure instruction in expository text on reading comprehension and summary writing.** Bonnie Betts Armbruster, University of Illinois-Champaign/Urbana

357.2 **Text structure instruction in process writing classrooms: Individual differences in upper elementary students' response to instruction.** Taffy E. Raphael, Becky M. Kirschner, and Carol Sue Englert, Michigan State University

357.3 **Metacognitive knowledge and writing skills of upper elementary students and students with special needs: Extensions of text structure research.** Carol Sue Englert, Linda Anderson, and Taffy E. Raphael, Michigan State University

4101 **Professional development in the elementary school: Contributions to literacy.** Robert Calfee, Stanford University

4102 **The impact of cohesion research on comprehension.** L. John Chapman, The Open University, and Marilyn R. Binkley, Office of Educational Research & Improvement, U.S. Department of Education

4103 **Managing curriculum tasks in classrooms: A retrospective.** Walter Doyle and Kathy Carter, University of Arizona

4104 **Looking for the meaning in children's writing.** Susan Florio-Ruane, Michigan State University

4105 **Are computers shaping a new literacy?** Michael L. Kamil, University of Illinois-Chicago

4106 **Writing across the curriculum.** James L. Kinneavy, University of Texas-Austin

4107 **Reading in two languages: Current and future issues.** Luis Moll, University of Arizona

4108 **Practice sensitive research and research sensitive practice: A report from the Center for the Study of Writing.** Sandra Murphy, University of California-Berkeley

4109 **Policy issues and reading assessment: An update.** Ramsey Selden, Council of Chief State School Officers.

4110 **Schema acquisition for flexibility and transfer.** Rand J. Spiro, University of Illinois-Champaign/Urbana

4111 **The shift from reading readiness to emergent literacy.** Elizabeth Sulzby, University of Michigan

4201 **What works? Does it work?** Richard C. Anderson, University of Illinois-Champaign/Urbana, Allan R. Neilsen, Mt. St. Vincent University, and Linda B. Gambrell, University of Maryland

4202 **Statewide assessments of reading: Are they appropriate?** Robert F. Carey, Rhode Island College, Sheila Valencia, University of Illinois-Champaign/Urbana, and David W. Moore, University of Northern Iowa

4203 **Error and correction in direct instruction.** James F. Baumann, Purdue University, Judith Newman, Mt. St. Vincent University, and Patricia L. Anders, University of Arizona

4204 **Writing and learning.** Arthur Applebee, Stanford University, Donald Graves, University of New Hampshire and Robert J. Tierney, Ohio State University

4205 **The Holmes/Carnegie reports: Implications for reading teacher education.** Irene Athey, Rutgers University, Kenneth S. Goodman, University of Arizona; and Lenore H. Ringler, New York University

AUTHOR INDEX

SUBJECT INDEX